Seth's Broadway Diary:

Inside Scoop on (Almost) Every Broadway Show and Star

Volume 3

By
Seth Rudetsky

Dress Circle Publishing
New York

Dress Circle Publishing
Brisa Trinchero/Roberta Pereira
New York, New York
www.dresscirclepublishing.com

Welcome to Volume 3!

This is a collection of my weekly columns for Playbill.com where I write about the interviews I do every week plus the Broadway stars that I do shows with/make videos with/have game nights with/leave messages for and don't hear back from. It's my third volume (!) and I was going to begin this introduction by writing about what I good time I had editing this particular volume because there were so many amazing Broadway stories I had forgotten about. Then I re-read my intro for volume two and saw that I wrote the exact same thing in that introduction. *Then* I decided to write that there were so many hilarious stories in this volume that I actually laughed out loud numerous times while editing. Well, turns out, I wrote the *exact same thing* the last time. Seriously! I'm going to take it as a good sign and come to the conclusion that this volume is as chock full of inside Broadway stories/hilarious Broadway moments as the last one. Or it could be a sign that I have nothing new to say. Or maybe, as my therapist always says, "It's a little of both."

Here's a quick run-down of some of my favorite parts that are scattered throughout the book:

MOST AMAZING TONY AWARD PLACEMENT
Someone in this book keeps her Tony Award on a shelf with a light shining on it that's attached to a clapper (Clap On, Clap Off). When she wants to cheer herself up, she claps twice and suddenly her Tony Award is fully illuminated! Who?

WORST EXPERIENCE WITH THE TSA
Find out what happened when an alum of the Broadway cast of *Chicago* put a giant butcher knife in his carry-on luggage. #Idiot.

MOST INAPPROPRIATE NAME JOSH GAD CALLED THE CHARACTER OF NABALUNGI
During *BOOK OF MORMON,* Josh was constantly improvising new names he would "mistakenly" call Nabalungi (Nikki M. James). They always began with an N and once, during allergy season, he hilariously called her *Nasonex.* What was the one name the creative team told him to he shouldn't use again??

MOST RECOGNIZABLE VOICE
What actor on The Simpsons is only allowed to do one (1) voice because his/her voice is so distinctive?

BEST PHONE CALL TO ELAINE PAIGE
Right after a black cat crossed Elaine Paige's path, Andrew Lloyd Webber called her and offered a role. What musical did he ask her to join even though it was already in rehearsal?

BEST/WORST OFFER OF A ROLE TO LIN-MANUEL MIRANDA
What happened when Sondheim offered Lin-Manuel Miranda the role of Charley in *Merrily We Roll Along.* Hint; It wound up not being a guarantee that Lin would do the show!

AND *MORE* SONDHEIM
What actor was supposed to have a big 11 o'clock number in a Sondheim musical but, instead, Sondheim wrote a hit song for *another* character, leaving the first actor *sans* song?

WORST AUDIENCE REACTION TO MEGAN MULLALLY
What happened when Megan Mullally had to go on for the role of Rizzo on Broadway...the role usually played by Rosie O'Donnell! Hint: The audience wasn't happy.

MOST SPECIFIC CAISSIE LEVY DRESSING ROOM OBJECT
What did Caissie Levy have in her dressing room at the Lunt-Fontanne theater on Broadway that she used 8 times a week before her show?

BEST REASON FOR NORBERT BUTZ ADDING LEO
Why does Norbert Leo Butz insist on always using his middle name? Hint: S-E-X

STUPIDEST STAGE NAME
What Tony nominated star thought it would be cool to change his name to "Rain Madison"?
Spoiler alert: It wasn't cool.

Yes! All those plus stories about Patti LuPone, Christine Ebersole, Jonathan Groff, Andrea Martin, Matthew Broderick, Audra McDonald, Alice Ripley, Will Swenson, Elaine Stritch, Judy Kuhn, Sutton Foster, Megan Mullally, Michael Cerveris, Stephanie J. Block, Carol Burnett, Michael Urie, Bernadette Peters, Donna Murphy, Jackie Hoffman and *A Chorus Line, Anything Goes, Annie, Next To Normal, In The Heights, Wicked* and so much more!

Wait a minute; Why are you reading this introduction? Dive into the book to find out the answers to the above questions *and* to saturate yourself with Broadway, Broadway and more BROADWAY!

Peace out!

Seth

September 2017, New York City

A *Brief Encounter* with Jonathan Groff
January 3, 2011

Greetings from Provincetown. As Christine Ebersole sang in *Grey Gardens*, it's "Another Winter in a Summer Town". *And seven years later, she started War Paint on Broadway by the same creative team as Grey Gardens. I guess if it ain't broke, don't fix it!* Being here is *much* more relaxing than it was getting here: James and I were supposed to leave on Sunday, but there was an enormous blizzard and all train service to Boston was cancelled. Ditto for Monday. So that night, we trudged through the snow to Studio 54 and saw *Brief Encounter*. We both loved it. There was so much creativity in the direction as well as non-stop music (mainly Noel Coward songs) throughout the whole show performed by the cast who sing amazing harmony and play all of their own instruments. I was a classical piano major at Oberlin Conservatory, and my favorite piece has always been the Rachmaninoff Second Piano Concerto. Turns out, that music is the theme of the show, and the cast performed it as a choral number at pivotal moments. The arrangement was so beautiful and there was something so moving about hearing it sung that I literally began to cry while they were singing it. It's definitely the kind of show I'd see more than once...with a hefty supply of tissues.

Jonathan Groff, pre-London.

Turns out, James and I weren't the only ones seeing it because we were stranded in New York. Sitting in front of us was Jonathan Groff! He was supposed to fly back to London to do *Deathtrap*, but the blizzard canceled his plans as well. I saw him right before the show began and told him we'd chat during intermission. He told me there wasn't an intermission and then, just to sound show-bizzy and make me laugh, he said, "She's ninety minutes." Ew. After the show, we couldn't stop talking about how much we loved it. *If you don't know, Brief Encounter is about a couple that meets and desperately want to have an affair and almost do...but don't. I decided it's play about me and Jonathan Groff. Of course, in his version of the play, it's about a young gay man who meets an older one and keeps him at arms length.*

Tuesday morning dawned, and James and I were determined to get to Provincetown no matter what. Well, *I* was at least. James was more determined to get to Boston and then see if we'd go to P-town that night or the next day. We left at 10 AM to get our 11 AM train to Boston. After walking down our un-shoveled street, we realized we were not going to get a cab to take us to Penn Station, so we hightailed it to the subway. And by "hightailed" I mean "walked incredibly slowly, old man-style, because the sidewalks were covered in slush with a hefty dose of ice as well." I bought James sturdy winter boots for just this reason, but instead he opted to wear the sneakers I got him last year that caused him to fall down some icy stairs and dislocate his shoulder. Yay. I was very supportive of his choice and definitely didn't give him the silent treatment all the way to Penn Station.

We were taking Amtrak to Boston and then Cape Air to Provincetown. Well, our Amtrak train was two hours late! All James wanted was a nice relaxing night so instead of rushing for our plane, he wanted to get a hotel for the night in Boston. But I was determined to get to Ptown! I told James we could always take a cab from Boston to Provincetown if we missed the flight but he was adamant that he did *not* want to take a long, uncomfortable drive all the way to the tip of the Cape. We finally got into Boston's

South Street Station at around 5 and ran for the bus to the airport. Our flight was leaving from terminal C of Logan Airport, and the bus first stopped at terminal A, then terminal B and, naturally, we got off at the next stop. Well, after getting all of our bags and desperately looking for Cape Air, which was nowhere to be found, we were told that we were in terminal B! Why would the bus stop twice in the same terminal!?!?! Is there a terminal B and a half? It was definitely a ton of fun running an entire terminal, carrying all of our bags at 5:45, trying to make a 5:55 flight.

The good news is…we made it! However, *right* before we landed in Provincetown, the wind picked up and suddenly we all saw the lights of Provincetown retreating in the distance. Yes, because of high winds, we were diverted to the nearest airport, Hyannis. Well, I got my wish and made it to the Provincetown by Tuesday night. However, Cape Air got us to Provincetown by generously paying for the cab ride. A lengthy, lengthy cab ride. To the tip of the Cape. The one that James was adamant he didn't want to do and the one I assured him we wouldn't. When he found out we were taking a car, he had the same reaction Carol Channing had when she was told that Barbra would be doing the film version of *Hello, Dolly!* I'm glad that James believes in the sanctity of marriage and is still honoring our engagement.

Anyhoo, we wound up having a great time and the White Wind Inn is beautiful and served a great breakfast every day. I did *Seth's Big Fat Broadway Show* (my deconstructing show) at the Art House, which was so much fun, except for the tech rehearsal when the heat was broken. I literally had to wear my coat *and* scarf the whole time. Fre-zee-zing!

Last week, my sister Nancy and niece Eliana went to see the *Lion King* tour in their hometown of Virginia Beach and loved it! However, for some reason, Nancy assumed the show had all pre-recorded music. She started raging and thinking, "This is Seth's *cause celebre*. I must register my displeasure!" At the curtain call, she saw the cast gesture to the pit and thought, "What nerve! They're gesturing to a person playing a tape recorder. Outrageous!" After the show, she went down the aisle, completely against the traffic of the exiting audience to "confront" the person running the pre-recorded music. Of course, she instead saw an entire orchestra in the pit. Excellent. Really worth having a fit for the entire show. As she was relaying the story to me, I asked, "So you stormed down the aisle past all those people to get to the pit?" and she answered, "Well, I recently had somewhat of a weight gain so it wasn't quite storming. I'd say that I shuffled down the aisle." Speaking of those two (clowns), they're both flying up to New York to see our favorite show, *In the Heights* on its final Sunday. There won't be enough tissues to control our non-stop crying. And, from what Nancy's implied, there won't be enough carbs to control her non-stop eating.

Happy New Year!!!!

Lights Out on Washington Heights
January 10, 2011

In the Heights has closed. *Wow. Remember when In The Heights was the big show Lin-Manuel Miranda wrote? Who knew that six years later he would create a show that surpassed the success of almost any other show on Broadway. Ever!* I was at one of the first workshops and I remember storming up to Kevin McCollum right after and telling him it was going to be "the next *Rent.*" I don't know when I became so cigar-chomping mogul-esque. It was very "Plastics, my boy!" a la "The Graduate." However, it did go on to win the Tony Award for Best musical, so I guess I am a psychic. I was there at the beginning of *In The Heights* and I was there the final day. I feel like Cheryl Freeman when she told Tyler Maynard that she "birthed and buried" *Tommy*. Regardless, I'm so upset that it's no longer on Broadway, but any time I think it didn't last long enough (1,185 performances) I think back to some of favorite musicals like *West Side Story* (732 performances) and *Gypsy* (702 performances) and shut my trap. I will discuss seeing the final matinee later on, but first let me go back to the beginning of the week.

Leaving the gym last week I ran into Chris Fitzgerald *Recently in Waitress!* two days in a row with his youngest son, who is so adorable and tiny. Chris said that his other son is also small. Then he added that he himself is short. He finally decided that if you took both of his sons and stood them one on top of the other on top of his head, they'd be the height of a regular person. I was so excited when he told me that his wife, Jessica, is about to play Erma in the *Anything Goes* revival. This is how long I've known Jessie: I met her in the waiting room of 890 Broadway when she was about to audition for Belle in the original *Beauty And The Beast*. Suffice it to say, she didn't get it. But, lest you judge her for not being up to snuff, just know that one of my other friends was trying out at the same time. And she also didn't get it. And she wasn't even going for one of the leads. My friend who was rejected for the ensemble was ... Audra McDonald! Yes, she got called back, but did not get cast as *any* utensil. I'm sure the first two Tony Awards she subsequently won made up for not being in the original *Beauty and the Beast* cast, and numbers three and four soothed hurt feelings about not being offered the bus and truck tour. *This was before Tony Award five (Porgy and Bess) and six (Lady Day). And before this book goes to print, I'm sure she'll have Tony Award seven for "Best Mention In Seth's Bway Diary". ALSO! Yes, she was rejected from the chorus of Beauty And The Beast, but twenty years later she got to play the opera singing wardrobe in the live action film version. You can't hold her down!*

Speaking of which, I texted Audra late Saturday and asked if she and her daughter Zoe just tried to Skype me. She wrote that they hadn't. I didn't understand because I had gotten a message that Audra and Zoe wanted to talk to me on Skype. I forwarded her the message, and she wrote back "My name isn't Audrey." That's right, ADD style, I saw the essence of the message, but not the whole thing. It actually said, "Audrey, Bill and Zoe Ledbetter want to speak to you on Skype." I had tuned out the Bill and the Ledbetter part and, quite frankly, the "ey" at the end of Audr. P.S. Audra's full message to me was "My name isn't Audrey. Love, Andrea McArdle." Brava!

Speaking of "Brava" and messages, I just got a new phone, which is doing non-stop auto correcting of every text/email I send, and it's driving me cra-za-zy! I wrote to my friend Tim, "Do you want to brave the snow and walk over?" It literally auto-corrected it to "Do you want to *brava* the snow?" He then wrote to me *Wait, are you using "brava" as a catchall word now? It's not even a verb. Or have you used the word "brava" so much that your phone auto-corrected when you typed "brave the snow"? Either option depresses me.* Well said.

James and I saw *The Importance of Being Ernest* on Saturday and lo-o-o-o-oved it. When we saw the revival of *Sunday in the Park With George*, James mentioned that he thought the guy playing the soldier was great. Well, his name is Santino Fontana, and he's now playing the lead in *The Importance of Being Ernest*, and he's perfect in the part. *This was pre-Frozen!* It was so great seeing someone who is not well-known completely win over an audience by inhabiting a character and being completely charming and funny. And, P.S., I totally thought he was British. Brava on the accent! (Brave on the accent?) *Then* I found out I've been listening to him on my *Fantasticks* recording because he also played Matt in the recent 2006 revival. You're not allowed to be an incredible actor in classic plays *and* have a great voice, too.

This week at my SiriusXM show, I interviewed Olga Merediz, Arielle Jacobs and Chris Jackson from *In the Heights*. *Of course, now it's Chris Jackson from Hamilton* As usual, I asked about on-stage mishaps and turns out, recently Chris forgot to come on for his final scene with Nina's father, Rick Negron. The scene is just the two of them, so Rick "solved" the problem by having the conversation on his cell phone. "What's that you say? You left your uniform and keys inside the dispatch office?" I'm sure that was very satisfying to the audience. I'm not saying that's why the show closed, but you do the math.

Varla Jean Merman!

Speaking of my 13-year-old niece, you know that both she *and* my aging sister Nancy have a crush on Chris. I took a picture of him holding a sign that said, "Hi, Eliana" and sent it to her. She wrote back how excited she was and that she was going to hang it on her locker at school. Nancy then wrote me: "Picture is amazing! Please tell Chris, though, that I spell my name 'N-A-N-C-Y' and not the old fashioned way of 'E-L-I-A-N-A.' Other than that, I simply love it and it's going on *my* locker also!!!" She's still got it. And by "it" I mean a delusional cougar-like crush.

Well, I saw the final matinee of *In the Heights*, and it was wonderful. There are so many brilliant and satisfying and pure-theatre moments in that show. I was in tears for so much of it. *Now that Hamilton is such a hit, I beg someone to revive In the Heights. It's like when "The Firm" became a bestseller, they reissued John Grisham's first book A Time To Kill. Please reissue In The Heights!* Afterwards, I met up backstage with my friends in the show and saw Priscilla Lopez collecting the photos that were hung up inside the dispatch booth for the entire run of the show. They were shots of her, Rick Negron and all the different girls who played Nina. Sad face. As the character of Sonny says, this is the end of an era. Then I saw Andrea Burns who gave a hilarious and amazing-sounding performance but spent the whole show in crazy pain because she was doing it all with a broken toe! She had broken it a while ago executing some of the rigorous Andy Blankenbuehler choreograph. Actually, she actually broke it on her night off, walking casually around her apartment. Did she then switch her footwear to flats to let it heal? Of course not. She refused to sacrifice glamour and has been doing the show, eight times a week, in Daniela's signature crazy high heels. And by "Daniela's signature" crazy high heels," I also mean Andrea's signature. When I went to her baby shower six years ago, I remember being horrified/impressed that she showed up with a nine months pregnant upper half sassing her lower half in full-out high heels. You can take the girl out of Miami, etc....

I ended the week on a delicious note: I got into the "Bullseye" in Entertainment Weekly. If you don't know what the bullseye is, it's on the last page of the magazine and it's headlined as "a look at the pop culture news that was right on target this week and the events that missed the mark." Of course, I was nervous I'd be in the "miss the mark" section... perhaps based on the jazz dance I did to "I Am What I Am" in high school for a cable TV program, but thankfully I was right near the center!

Seth-tions & Answers
January 17, 2011

I'm going to Springfield, OH, this weekend to play for Betty Buckley on Friday night and then do *Seth's Big Fat Broadway Show* on Saturday night. I've been doing a lot of interviews (to promote the shows), which have been fun, *but* I've found that I'm answering a lot of the same questions. Plus, I get emails at my website that also seem to ask the same questions often. So, I thought I'd do a column dedicated to the questions I get asked in order to form a clearinghouse where I can direct people when they haul out "Where did you grow up?"

1. Childhood: I was born in Jamaica. Not tropical Jamaica. The Jamaica with the 718 area code. Queens. I moved to Long Island when I was four. Got the *hell* out of Long Island when I was 17.

2. First Broadway show: My parents took me to see *Hair* right before it closed when I was four. I don't remember much except my mom's hands being over my eyes during the nude scene. That hand position was hauled out many times in the future due to the fact that my parents never hired a babysitter on movie nights, they just took me along. So, my eyes were shaded many times during those great 1970's children's films: "Death Wish," "Taxi Driver" and "One Flew Over the Cuckoo's Nest." For real!

3. First Broadway obsession: The show that I first became obsessed with was *The Pajama Game*. I saw the revival when I was seven years old and listened to the cast album over and over again. Listen to "Hurry Up/Racing With The Clock", it's Broadway gold!

4. First professional performing job: *Oliver!* at the Northstage Dinner Theater. I was one of the workhouse orphans who sang "Food Glorious Food," which was appropriate since that's what I focused on in my free time. Suffice it to say, that was the period in which my jeans said "husky" but my behind said "fat." The whole *Oliver!* experience gave me a complete idea of professional theatre. I had the thrill of working with a real celebrity (Shani Wallis, who played Nancy in the film version), I learned what it was like to do eight shows a week (amazing!), and I learned how to perform even while devastated. We previewed for a week and right before opening night, the director/choreographer decided he didn't want an uneven amount of kids in "Be Back Soon," and I was unceremoniously cut from the number. I was *devastated* and called my parents after rehearsal while crying hysterically… but I went on that night and did the show. I learned the lesson that in the theatre, the show comes first and people's feelings come second. Perhaps it would have been an easier lesson to learn at 15 years old instead of 12, but I got through it. And what lessened the blow was I was the only kid with a delicious solo in "Who Will Buy?" Of course, the mortifying part was my character's name was "The Milkmaid" but we changed it to "The Milkboy."

5. College: I went to the Oberlin College Conservatory of Music and majored in piano performance. Classical piano performance. To this day, I don't know what I was thinking. I think I was so shocked that I got into the conservatory that I felt I had no choice but to go. Plus, I visited the campus after I was accepted and developed a *huge* crush on a sophomore. P.S. We never dated. P.P.S. Still not 100 percent over it.

6. First music director job: Surflight Summer Theater on Long Beach Island in New Jersey while I was in college. We did a different show every week for 12 weeks. Surflight was a great learning experience for me. Because we had *such* limited rehearsal time, I was able to figure out *exactly* what I needed to do to teach an entire show incredibly fast. My first big job out of college was playing in the band for *Singin' in* *the Rain* at the Darien Dinner Theater. I was there for around three weeks in December and then my mother "forbid" me from playing New Year's Eve because she didn't want me in a car "on an expressway with those drunken lunatics." The conductor told me not to worry about missing the show. He got the boyfriend of the girl who played Lena Lamont to sit next to my keyboard so it looked like there was a full band that night (PS why didn't he tell me to get a sub?). The producer found out about the scam, and the conductor was fired. Oh, I'm sorry, *I* was fired even though *he* perpetuated the whole hoax! Yes, still angry! *It happened in 1988, I wrote this column in 2011 and today I am, indeed, still angry!*

7. How did I get into comedy? People had often told me I should try stand-up comedy. My friend Jack Plotnick moved to LA, started doing stand-up and told me I had to do it. I went to "The Stars of Tomorrow" contest at The Duplex and did a three-minute set, which consisted of a true story of me being startled by a horrifically large water bug in my bathroom, at 2 AM in the morning...

It was right after I stepped out of the shower, so I put my underwear on and then chased it through my apartment with a sneaker. It ran into the hallway of my building, and I followed closely ...and my apartment door closed behind me and *locked*. Yes, I had to walk on the streets of Brooklyn wearing only underwear and *a* sneaker. And, because it was the 80s, a gold chain. I told this story and immediately made it into the semi-finals of the contest. I went back the next week and B-O-M-B-E-D. The audience was severely not amused. I've never seen that much staring except watching Barbra Streisand react to her tribute at the Kennedy Center Honors. I was mortified but knew the only way I'd learn how to be good was to go back each week. I kept going (it was every Friday at midnight) and eventually made it back into the semi-finals, and then the finals...and then I won the Grand Prize! The prize was money which I spent on jeans with a waist size I look back on fondly. As well as an opportunity to do my own show at the Duplex which I have not yet performed. The contest was in 1996.

8. How did I start doing my deconstructing show? I began doing stand-up by telling real stories that happened to me, but then I began adding music clips like Patti LuPone's Evita versus Madonna's. I was asked by BC/EFA to do a piece in the 2004 *Gypsy of the Year* contest, and I performed a bit about Barbra Streisand's crazy changing of consonants and combined it with the mind-boggling version of "Don't Rain On My Parade" as sung by Bea Arthur. Rosie O'Donnell was in the audience and told me I should do a whole show of just "that" (later to be known as deconstructing) and she would produce it. I then put together a whole show of "that" and called it *Deconstructing Broadway* now called *Seth's Big Fat Broadway Show.* I'm still waiting for her to produce it. Anybody? Apparently, nobody.

9. The most annoying question: What do I think about *Spider-Man? Can you tell I wrote this a while back?* Why are people so interested in this show? Is it because people have gotten injured? People are *always* being injured in Broadway shows. Why the sudden interest now? What about raked stages? That means the stage is tilted (to make the back of the stage more visible to the audience), and it's injured many more people than *Spiderman*. I just interviewed Chris Jackson, and when he played Simba in *The Lion King*, he had three knee surgeries. In his 20's! I was doing an *Easter Bonnet Competition* rehearsal on the stage of *Miss Saigon*, which had a six-foot rake and the assistant choreographer was just *walking* across and ripped his Achilles tendon! One of my friends in *Women on the Verge of a Nervous Breakdown* got adult onset asthma because of the smoke used in the show. I feel if people are going to be concerned about injuries in shows, be concerned with *all* Broadway shows, not just the one making headlines now.

On Sunday, my niece, my sister, her husband and I all went to see Mandy Gonzales in *Wicked* where she's playing Elphaba. She was fabulous and after the show, she told us that she saw the last performance of *In the Heights*. Turns out, it was the first time she had ever seen the show! I can't imagine how overwhelming it was to be at the show after not doing it for a year, see all the brilliant staging for the first time, see so many people still in it that she had done the show with *and* to know it was the final performance.

All right, I'm exhausted from going through my history and must now reward myself with low-calorie chocolate chip cookies. *I have no idea what brand of cookie I'm referring to, but now I'm dying to have one. Anyone know!?!?* Delish... peace out!

Why, Oh, Why Ohio?
January 24, 2011

I spent my college years in Ohio where it was freezing. My first winter there had lows of 20 degrees below zero…. and that was *before* the wind chill factor! My point in bringing up Ohio is that I am back again in that freezing state. What was/am I thinking? I'm playing Betty Buckley's *Broadway By Request* and doing my own show as well. The trip here was a headache: I was supposed to fly out Friday morning, tech Betty's show and then play it Friday night. Well, Thursday at around noon I get a call from the airline telling me that my Friday flight had been cancelled! That's right, because New York expected a little snow in the A.M., they decided to do a pre-emptive canceling. The next flight on Friday wouldn't get me in until that afternoon and what if that was cancelled or delayed? Betty called and begged me to come out Thursday. I got booked on a 4:40 flight but when I got to the gate at 3:30, they announced that my 4:40 flight was being postponed to 6:07. P.S. why such a specific time? Why not 6:10? Are they trying to show how accurate they are about when planes leave? If so, why not leave at the original 4:40 time! Anyhoo, I resigned myself to waiting until 6:07 but then at around 4:30 they suddenly announced we were going to leave at 5 PM. Yay! That euphoria lasted only a few minutes because they then announced that the flight was no longer delayed…it was simply cancelled. Yowtch!

Sonja, from the Springfield Arts Center, got me a reservation on the 9:30 flight to Columbus. So I "only" had to wait at LaGuardia airport for a total of six hours. I landed at around midnight and got to my hotel at 1:30 AM…just in time to welcome in the coldest day of the year so far in Columbus.

Chris Moore, the executive director of the Springfield Arts Council, came backstage and showed me amazing programs from *Sweet Charity* and *West Side Story* from his college years at the Cincinnati Conservatory of Music. What I loved is that it featured Linda Wonneberger on the cover as Charity. Linda is Laura Benanti's mother! *P.S. Now they do an act together. AND Laura Benanti is a mother herself!* And, in the *West Side Story* program there's a picture of Bernardo played by Marty Vidnovic…Laura's biological father! Chris (who played Baby John) told me that both he and Linda (who played Anybodys) injured their arms during *West Side Story* and performed the show with their arms in slings. He recently re-connected with her on Facebook and she told him her arm is *still* crooked. It paid off for Chris, however, because that arm injury kept him out of Vietnam. So, maybe one day, the cast of *Spider-Man* will say, "It was worth it."

Back to the *West Side Story* program; it also featured the great opera star Kathleen Battle as Maria! Oh, I'm sorry, she's actually listed as "Kathy" Battle and her role is "ensemble." Remember that fact, all of you young people who are devastated when you don't get a lead role in a school show. You, too, can grow up to be a world-class opera singer and win three Grammy awards…and scandalously be fired from the Metropolitan Opera for diva-like behavior. And, P.S., to be fired from the Met for being *too* much of a diva is a major achievement. It's like being fired from "The Real Housewives" for being too skinny.

I've recently become obsessed with the bruhaha surrounding the book "Battle Hymn of the Tiger Mother." It was written by a Chinese mother who raised her American children with no play dates, sleepovers, school plays, etc., and instead, made them devote hours to piano and violin practice every day, as well as ridiculously high academic achievement. First, I saw a review of the book on Emily Skinner's Facebook wall so I posted all the details on my ex's wall (he's first-generation Chinese). His reaction was hilarious. He simply wrote "…And?" He then wrote "Everyone knows an A is really an A minus if an A plus was available." Anyhoo, my fascination with the saga wrapped up when I was signing autographs after the show in Ohio. An adorable six-year-old Asian girl approached me with her Mom who told me that her daughter listens to my show every day. I then asked the girl if she was an actress and she said "No." And by "she" I mean "her Mom." I mentioned the book and her Mom said that she's *nothing* like that mother. She then immediately followed it with the open-minded, "I've told my daughter if she wants to be an actress, she can." And then followed it with "Just so long as she has something to fall back on." She then ended with the warm "I told her she can go to Columbia in New York... as long as she majors in engineering." Phew. I'm glad she's nothing like the mother in the book. It's totally appropriate to tell your six-year-old what major they're "allowed" to have when they go to their Ivy League University in 12 years. And I'm out.

I just got asked to do a benefit with Audra MacDonald for the Desert AIDS Project in Palm Desert, CA. She recently texted me and here is the transcript:

AUDRA: When do we do that benefit in Pasadena?
SETH: A.) It's Palm Desert. B.) It's March 12th.
AUDRA: Stop yelling.
SETH: That was a mezzo forte.
AUDRA: Yes, but high mix.

Obviously Audra and I went to Juilliard and Oberlin, respectively. That back-and-forth joking would have brought down the house at a conservatory function...and gotten us labeled as nerds anywhere else.

Peace out!

Andrea Martin, Stephanie J. Block and "Friending" *Chicago* Fans
January 31, 2011

Greetings from Toronto, Canada. And by "Toronto" I mean "Belleville." I tour with Andrea Martin and we're constantly hitting towns in Canada that are well-known if you're from North of the border, but not if you are only familiar with West 42nd to West 96th street. Belleville, Hunstville, Sudbury…you might as well say Brooklyn. I know nothing of it. Speaking of obscure towns, Andrea and I were lamenting the food choices in non-New York towns. She was taking her son to various colleges in the Midwest and had the following conversation in a restaurant:

ANDREA: Can I have an egg white omelet?
WAITER: (Staring)
NDREA: An egg white omelet.
WAITER: (Same facial expression)
ANDREA: (Finally) Do you make omelets with egg whites?
WAITER: (Still staring….ten years later).

So many times I've gone out of town and had this conversation in a Chinese restaurant:

ME: Can I have brown rice?
WAITER: Fried rice?
E: No, brown rice.
WAITER: You mean *fried* rice.

Hendrick Riik, who is working with Andrea on the show, told us that, on a drive through Alabama, he stopped in a tiny diner and had this conversation:

HENDRICK: Can I have a cup of tea?
WAITRESS: A glass of iced tea?
HENDRICK: No, a cup of tea.
WAITRESS: So, iced tea in a cup?
HENDRICK: No. *Hot* tea.
WAITRESS: (Mulling). Hot, huh… Well, I guess we could take it outta the fridge, pour it in a cup and then heat it in the microwave.

Hendrick now lives in Canada.

Any to the hoo, this week I had the fabulous beltress Stephanie J. Block on my SiriusXM "Live On Broadway" show because she is one of the featured singers on songwriter Scott Alan's newest CD. I interviewed Scott as well and he said that he funded his first CD himself by working three jobs; Starbucks, waitering and bartending. He wound up raising $25,000 from those jobs! Wait a minute; how come I spent years writing on "The Rosie O'Donnell Show" and I have nothing in my bank account? Answer: Non-stop cab rides and relentless ordering of Chinese food.

Regardless, Scott's first CD became a cult favorite and now he's on his third! I asked Stephanie how she got involved and she told me that she was at a concert and muttered out loud that she loved one of the songs that had just been sung. Scott was sitting next to her and overheard the muttering. He tapped her and told her that he wrote it! (P.S. this could have been a devastating story if she had muttered something else.) Scott told her that he'd love it if she sang one of his songs at a concert. They met in a rehearsal studio, he played her all of his songs but none felt like the perfect choice for Stephanie. Scott was mortified because he didn't have any songs left. Except for one that he had played for his friends and they had deemed "awful." He knew he shouldn't play it for her but in a moment of weakness, he admitted that he had one more song. She asked to hear it and, terrified, he played it for her. She wound up *loving* it and asked if she could sing it in an upcoming concert. Scott remembers that night and how nervous he was because the song that everyone told him to "never play in public" was getting its first public performance. Stephanie sang it and, turns out, it became one of his big hits! And it's a great lesson for artists everywhere to remember: People have different opinions. I know a very famous comedian who "just doesn't get" TV's "Seinfeld." Something may be considered a great work of art, but there are *always* people who don't like it. It's so hard to accept! My friend Kristine Zbornik had a great line in her show where she told the audience she's spent years waiting for "global acknowledgment of my talent." Hilarious and on the nose. I think most creative types have a secret desire to create something that is universally embraced. It has yet to happen. Although the opposite has. And it's called Mariah Carey's "Glitter."

My friend Colleen Ballinger is doing her character, Miranda Sings, at the Matchbox Theater in Red Deer, Canada, where I did *Rhapsody in Seth* last October. Matt Grue, who runs the theatre, wrote out the dialogue he heard in the theatre when two women, on their way to the Miranda show, saw my poster. This is what he sent:

WOMAN 1: *Rhapsody in Seth*. Did we see that?
WOMAN 2: Sure. It was with that guy from the radio. SAM RABINSKY.
WOMAN 1: Right. Sam Rabinsky.
WOMAN 2: He's married to Patti LuPone.
WOMAN 1: What?
WOMAN 2: I read it in the New York Times.
WOMAN 1: But that whole show was about him growing up gay in New York.
WOMAN 2: That was the *character* he was playing. "Seth."
WOMAN 1: Oh. Obviously. The title.
WOMAN 2: Right. (*Silence*)
WOMAN 1: So what's THIS show about? Miranda sings?
WOMAN 2: I think it's about a clown who learns to sing.
WOMAN 1: Sounds interesting.

I'm obsessed!

Of course, Miranda Sings is now crazily super famous, has millions of followers on youtube and her own TV show. And I have this book.

It reminds me of the famous dialogue supposedly heard before a performance of *Cats* in the 1980s right after Betty Buckley won the Tony Award:

WOMAN 1: I'm very excited to see this show. It stars Betsy Buckles.
WOMAN 2: Ooh! She was wonderful in that TV show..."Enough is Enough."

And now, I'm back in NYC. I co-hosted an event on the Broadway stage of *Chicago* and gave away a prize based on a trivia contest. I got two Super Fans who were both extremely excited, and told them they had to go back and forth, each saying a name of an actress who's played Velma Kelly. Whoever can't think of one is the loser. Well, even though they were both obviously knowledgeable about the show, it ended pretty quickly.

ME: Start naming Velma Kellys.
FAN 1: Chita Rivera.
FAN 2: Bebe Neuwirth.
FAN 1: Ashlee Simpson. (*Gasp* from the audience.)

I informed him that he lost because Ashlee played Roxie, not Velma. I followed that statement by seriously intoning "And we *never* speak of it." He was a great sport and said that he panicked because he was so excited.

Peace out!

Jan Brady Superstar!
February 7, 2011

Oftentimes on my SiriusXM radio show I give a special shout-out to children who are listening; I tell them that when I was their age, I was like them...obsessed about celebrities. I would fantasize about Fonzie coming over to my house or about hanging out with Patti LuPone. Then I tell them that I grew up and not only got to meet most of the celebs I loved while I was a child, but I also got to accompany them while they sang the songs I listened to relentlessly in my youth! I've played for Betty Buckley as she sang "He Plays the Violin," Patti LuPone singing "Anything Goes," Howard McGillin doing "A Man Could Go Quite Mad," Andrea McArdle belting "Tomorrow," Melba Moore sassing "I Got Love" and many more. I want kids to know that they can go from being a fan to one day being (some sort of version of) a peer. It's my way of counteracting what I think a lot of children are told, which is summed up by Cassie's line in "Hello Twelve...": *Listen to your mother, those stage and movie people got there...because they're special.*

Well, yet again I got to meet and hang out with one of childhood faves: Eve Plumb! Yes, *the* Jan Brady and I chatted it up at my SiriusXM "Live on Broadway" show. I met her last year at *Broadway Backwards* and she told me that she wanted to do a play in New York. Cut to one year later, she's doing *Miss Abigail's Guide to Dating, Mating and Marriage*! Brava Secret-ing it, Oprah-style. Of course, I immediately bypassed "The Brady Bunch" and instead asked her about the "Brady Bunch Variety Hour." If you do not know, there was an hour-long series in 1977 that featured the Brady Bunch singing and dancing. To pop/rock/disco songs. In Spandex pants suits. Suffice it to say, it was cancelled after nine episodes. Even in the '70s it was too much for us to bear and, quite frankly, at that time the country was using a pretty low bar. Anyhoo, if you have any knowledge of the show, you're aware that the whole Brady Bunch family did it... except Jan. The producers had the bright idea that if they got another girl with blonde hair, no one would notice. Apparently, they had just seen the film "The Stepford Wives" and thought the country would fall for the ruse. For those of us obsessed with that show, the rumor had always been that Eve couldn't do the TV show because she was filming "Dawn: Portrait of a Teenage Runaway." Well, I finally got to ask Eve where she was during those nine delicious episodes and, turns out, "Dawn" was not the reason! She told me that her father knew of Sid and Marty Krofft's oeuvre (they were the producers) and he told Eve that if she did the Brady Bunch Variety Hour, it would be a low point in her career. That's right, she turned it down because her father knew it was going to clank! Was he a psychic? A mystic? Why would he think a full hour of the Brady Bunch dancing and singing hits like "Shake Your Booty" (featuring Alice in a bedazzled pants suit) and "When You Wish Upon a Star" as a disco song would be a misstep? The good news is it allowed me to create and entire show dedicated to deconstructing the "highlights" from each episode. So many years later that show is finally paying off...for me.

Eve ended the interview with a performance of "When You're Good To Mama" and I decided she needs to be in a musical ASAP! We've already had Greg in *Romance Romance*, Marcia in *Grease* and Carol in a string of musicals during the Golden Age. Bring Jan to Broadway! P.S. *Two years later she wound up starring off-broadway in my husband's play "Unbroken Circle". She was fantastic!*

I also interviewed Billy Stritch and Jim Caruso who run *Cast Party* at Birdland every Monday night. Jim is the host and Billy is the music director/pianist. *Cast Party* is basically an open mic where everyone from Broadway stars to amateurs get up and sing. They've had a slew of amazing people there, including multiple appearances by Liza. I asked Billy and Jim how they hooked up with Liza. Turns out, in the early '90s, Billy was playing at a piano bar in the Village. Liza came in and he decided *not* to play "New York,

New York" or one of her signature hits. Instead, he played a theme to one of Vincente Minnelli's films. Liza was so impressed that she wound up promising him she'd come to his show at a club called Eighty-Eights. Billy called his good friend Jim (whom he knew from their home state of Texas) and told him Liza was coming to his show. Jim said there was no way she was showing up...but, of course, that didn't stop him from coming to the show just to make sure. Lo and behold, Liza *did* show up, Jim chatted her up in the audience and they all became friends. And eventually collaborators. Billy has music-directed for her many times and Jim was one of her fabulous sidemen in her last Broadway venture. And all because she wandered into Billy's piano bar. Hmm...let me think of something similar that happened to me when I worked at a piano bar in the Village. Well, once on my day off, someone got so drunk that they peed on the floor. So...yeah. *This happened at Rose's Turn, the piano bar where I played for many years. My brilliant talented friend Kristine Zbornik was performing. And the brilliant synergy between song and lack of bladder control is that while the guy was peeing, Kristine was singing "Cry Me A River". Perfect!*

I asked Jim to tell me one of his many showbiz stories, and he and Billy started cackling over a classic Lisa Kirk tale I had never heard. She was the original Lois in *Kiss Me, Kate* and I was obsessed with her "Tom, Dick or Harry" when I was a kid. P.S. Not only did I listen to that on a record (remember records?), but it was literally a 78. When did I grow up? During the '40s? Anyhoo, Lisa Kirk lived in a big apartment building and Billy and Jim heard that she always wanted people to recognize her. She'd be on an elevator and wait the whole time for a fan to be star-struck and if no one gave her a second glance, she would make herself known by talking to herself. And using her name. How? Well, she'd wait a respectable amount of time and finally she'd let out little laugh like she was remembering something silly she had just done, then follow it with "Oh, silly me. Silly me...*Lisa Kirk*." I'm obsessed with how pointed and specific it is. Some people say, "So, I said to myself, 'Self'..." but she spoke to herself with her first *and* last name.

Speaking of needy celebs, *I* had a great time in Sioux City last weekend. A wonderful gay couple who teach at Morningside College hosted me and told me they've been together for 23 years! Iowa is one of the few states that allows gay marriage and they got married last year. Sadly, the Republicans gained power in the last election and are using it to try to take away marriage rights. What does anyone gain out of nullifying their relationship? I find it so sad and mean-spirited. Regardless, my master class went great and I got a delicious standing O at *Deconstructing Broadway*. Because it wasn't cold enough in Iowa (minus 4!), this week I'm in New Market, Ontario, with Andrea Martin. *And*, by the by, Andrea's show won Best Theatrical Event in the Broadway World Toronto Awards. And, not to brag, my show *Deconstructing Broadway*, placed. And in a very specific place. My show was not just a runner-up, but it was actually *second* runner-up. And not just second runner-up, it tied with two other shows. I haven't seen that much qualifying since my friend auditioned for *La Cage Aux Folles* and was told she was third choice... to be the understudy. Yowtch! *OMG, I'm racking my brain trying to remember who told me that and I can't! If anyone knows, please email me because I think it's hilarious! And going back to Kristine Zbornik and a story that relates, one time she auditioned for a show and when she found out how little they paid, she told them she couldn't take the job. She thanked them and left. The next day they called her to say that she hadn't been cast. That's right, they wanted her to know, regardless of whether she wanted the job or not, she was not up to snuff. Hilarious...and devastating.*

Peace to the out!

Flubbing Lines, Remembering Oberlin
February 14, 2011

On Thursday, I flew up to Toronto to do Andrea Martin's show and I shared my flight with Peter Flynn, who's directing Andrea's show. We were talking about "riders", which are what celebs send out with their shows telling the theatre what provisions they want. Peter and his wife Andrea Burns are obsessed with Faye Dunaway's rider during the tour of *Master Class*. It supposedly demanded a pound (!) of Canadian bacon be prepared after every show, for Ms. Dunaway's consumption. A pound? Was she on Atkins at the time? Peter and Andrea play a game with their theatre friends where they ask "What's *your* pound of bacon?" meaning, "What would you love to have, when you're on tour, that's outlandish but would be fabulous?" Peter said he'd love to demand a flight home after every show so he can always sleep in his own bed. Delicious.

The one thing Andrea Martin *should* have in her rider after Thursday's performance is a teleprompter. She's never had a problem with lyrics before, but suddenly during her opening number, she got to the bridge and blanked. Instead of asking me for the lyric (I'm playing the piano onstage) she decided that any noise is better than no noise and just started singing the word "Aaaaaaaaaaaaah" on a weird low note. Relentlessly. She held it, took a breath and then started again. Over and over again. Added to that was a crazy walk in a low crouch which looked like a chicken in a deep plié. I have no idea what the audience was thinking but I knew I had to put a stop to it. But how? She wasn't asking me for the lyrics. Finally, I just yelled out the words for her. Unfortunately, she was in the middle of a never-ending "Ah" so she didn't hear it. So instead of her starting the bridge, the audience got to watch the awkward moment of her turning to me and asking "What?" I repeated the lyric and she *finally* started the bridge. Peter, Andrea and I were obsessed and couldn't stop re-hashing the whole thing in the car ride home. P.S. Peter and Andrea have an adorable son named Hudson. Hudson is super-talented and, even though both Peter and Andrea have dark hair, his is blond and curly. Peter said that periodically Brooks Ashmanskas will look at Hudson, then at Peter and say, "I have only one word about the father of Hudson: Norbert Leo Butz."

Speaking of forgetting words, Peter told me about doing a Lyrics & Lyricists concert at the 92nd Street Y that was hosted by a certain older grand dame of the theater. In the year-long series, every host would sing a song after the first act break and the Grand Dame told the director she'd be singing "I Could Have Danced All Night." He told her that Christine Andreas would be singing it in Act Two. Instead of thinking of another song, she told him that people would love to hear it twice. Really? Anyhoo, Peter said that the opening lyrics were a major challenge for her every night. It was essentially: "Bed, Bed, there's nothing like a bed. It's time to sleep but I will not be there. Sleep, Bed, it's bed and sleeping both, etc...." But then she'd perfectly launch into "I could have danced all night...". The cast would all listen in their dressing rooms through the backstage speakers and, every night, they'd hear the crazy lyrics and then the correct ones when the chorus began.

Until, the final performance.

The intro played and, out of the blue, she sang, "Bed, Bed... I couldn't go to bed. My head's too light to try to set it down." Perfect! Karen Mason ran into Peter's dressing and yelled, "She's got it! Let's go watch her do the rest of the song." They ran to the wings to as the Grand Dame correctly sang "Sleep, Sleep, I couldn't go to sleep. Not for all the jewels in the crown." Hooray! Peter and Karen grinned at each other with the subtext of "She got through it and now it'll be smooth sailing."

Then the Grand Dame began the main section with a firm: "I could have slept all night..." And cut.

This week I interviewed composer/lyricist Lance Horne, who has a new CD out. He told me he was a composition major at Juilliard and I immediately asked him how headache-y his pieces were in college. Why? Well, when I went to Oberlin Conservatory, my freshman-year roommate was a composition major and one of his "pieces" was a colored mobile. Seriously. If you performed his piece, you'd know what notes to play depending on which way the wind blew the mobile. For instance, if the wind blew the mobile so you saw blue, you played a C, red meant a D sharp etc. Suffice it say, I needed a pair of earplugs from age 17 to 18. Lance said he never wrote such obscure pieces in Juilliard. As a matter of fact, his taste was quite different; his freshman year, he got musicians, dancers and actors together and they put on a Sondheim revue. Sondheim? In a classical music school? I wasn't surprised with what happened next: he was promptly called to the dean's office. Juilliard is like Oberlin in that there is not much respect given to musical theatre. And that's being polite.

When I was at Oberlin the only musical theater there was being done by students *and* we weren't even allowed to use the theater. We had a full cast and full orchestra performing in a room at the student union. Literally a room. Well, you say, Oberlin is a state school, they didn't have much money. Actually, it's a private school and we were paying a ton of money in tuition! Argh! But even with those obstacles, it's the alma mater of amazing musical theatre alums like Will Chase, Judy Kuhn and John Kander. And P.S. I still *loved* going to Oberlin. It was a community of bright, artistic people who believed in social justice. I just read that Rick Sperling, who directed the production of *Runaways* that I music-directed at Oberlin back in '86, started a great theatre program for kids in Detroit called Mosaic Youth Theatre. What I love is that the discipline kids are taught to use while performing theatre pays off in other aspects of their lives. According to their website, even though Mosaic students are disproportionately minority and from low-income families, 95 percent of Mosaic's Youth Ensemble members graduate from high school and go on to college. Which, P.S., is dramatically above the national average for young people from similar backgrounds. Brava!

I also interviewed Brent Barrett who is playing Billy Flynn in *Chicago*. I asked Brent how thrilling it was to perform the *Grand Hotel* number on the Tony Awards and he said it was more nerve-wracking than thrilling. Turns out, the stage where the Tony Awards were that year was super-slippery and he and Michael Jeter had no idea if they were going to go sprawling across the stage. And furthermore, the number featured Michael Jeter's character getting more and more drunk as he hung onto the bar and brilliantly flopped his body around. In the Broadway show, the bar was attached to something sturdy on either side of the stage. During the Tony Awards, the bar was held up by two actors! So, Brent and Michael Jeter had to pretend like they were leaning against the bar, but in reality they could only place half their weight against it! Yikes! And yet, the performance is fantastic! YouTube is ASAP! And while you're there, watch my deconstruction of David Carroll's big song "Love Can't Happen". I'll never forget sitting in the balcony with my friend Eric Woodall (who's now a big casting director) and hearing that last note live. It's one of my favorite memories of Broadway.

Speaking of Broadway, my friend Jennifer Simard just started rehearsals for the musical *Sister Act* and posted how much she loved her fellow nuns. *She's now a Tony Nominee for playing the nun in my show Disaster!* Her status was: "I've always wanted a sister...now I have 18 of them. And they are kind and loving. Thank you, Sisters." Of course, it took two bitter crones like Jen Cody and me to immediately comment on her sunny disposition: I posted, "Get back to me during 10 out of 12's" (meaning horrible tech rehearsal week) and Jen Cody wrote, "Ahhhh...the first weeks of rehearsals...cut to— ." I love how Jen didn't state *what* it cuts to, she just implied something horrible.

17

On the home front, I went to go see *Wicked* with my sister Nancy and niece Eliana. Nancy made me laugh during intermission by turning to Eliana and asking, "What are you doing? Are you mourning the wicked? After you were specifically told not to?"

And on that note, peace out!

Poolside With Marissa Jaret Winokur in L.A.
February 21, 2011

Hello from Sunny Los Angeles! Although, for the last two days it's been cold and rainy Los Angeles. Literally arrived for the two days out of the year when it rains. And, because there was a massive inch of rain spread out over a 12-hour period, the streets flooded. Let's be honest — Los Angeles is a wimp. Regardless, now it's sunny and beautiful and all I want to do is move here.

While I was in New York, I filmed a new "Obsessed" Playbill video with Varla Jean Merman. Varla's real name is Jeffrey Roberson, and he told me a crazy story that happened to him recently in L.A. He was there on tour with his show, *The Loose Chanteuse*, which is hilarious. Anyhoo, he gets sponsored in part by Fleet Enemas (seriously) and does a hilarious number called "The Fleet's In." He also gives out enemas to the audience, so there was a ton of them in the trunk of his L.A. car. And his back seat was crammed with all of his drag costumes. One morning, he drove to the grocery store for some food but the parking lot was full so he drove home. As soon as he pulled up to his house, four (!) policemen surrounded his car and forced him to get out with his hands up.

SCARY POLICEMAN: Where were you just now?

JEFF: The grocery store...

SCARY POLICEMAN (checking back seat): There are no groceries in the car! You're coming with us!

JEFF: But —

They put him in a police car and wouldn't tell him why he was being held. Then they searched his car and found numerous large women's outfits...and boxes of enemas.

SCARY POLICEMAN: Why do you have all these enemas?

JEFF: Well, I do a show...and there's a medical segment...

That was it! They pulled him out of the cop car and handcuffed him. Then another car pulled up and the cops shined a light on Jeffery's face. Jeff realized that there must have been a witness in the other car who was looking at him and telling the police whether or not he was whomever they were looking for. Finally, they let Jeff go. Apparently, there had been an armed robbery in the neighborhood and Jeff fit the description. Cra-za-zy. Jeff's manager Mark Cortale begged Jeff *not* to tell the story in his show that night. Of course, Jeff thought it was hilarious and defiantly told it in the middle of the show. The audience was laughing up a storm...for a while. Then Jeff began to realize that the story simply got depressing.... and there was no actual punch line. And...fade out. The energy of the show was completely lost and Jeff saw Mark in the audience, staring smugly.

When we got to L.A., James, Juli and I took the Warner Brothers studio tour. It's really great. Unlike Universal, which is pretty much a giant ride, you get to walk around the Warner Brothers soundstages and sets. The tour guide drove us a little crazy because she wouldn't stop busting us for "being gullible." It was literally, "Over here is what you *think* is a house...but it's not. It's fake, but you believe it's real because you're gullible. Then you'll see actors walk to the back of the house, but the whole house is really just a front. And yet, you *think* there's a back because you're gullible. Then you'll see an actor go to the second floor, but it's actually a staircase to nowhere! You all think there's a second floor because you're so gullible."

I finally yelled out, "I never thought there was a second floor!" Which isn't true, I've always completely fallen for every film illusion, but I couldn't take the accusations anymore.

On the way out of the tour, we ran into Ana Gasteyer, on the Warner Brothers lot, who was with her husband, Charlie. We were laughing about celebrity tweeting. She read one from a famous actress lauding another famous actress who just joined her Broadway show. Ana knew the lauding was fake because the new actress wasn't actually good in the role. The tweet read "It's official; *New Actress* is fabulous in her role!" Ana wanted to tweet back "It's official; You aren't threatened by her."

My former landlord, Marissa Jaret Winokur (photo credit: Rob Johnston).

Zev has one of these. Amazing!

Marissa Jaret Winokur invited us to stay with her in L.A. and we're loving it...ish. The actual bed for me and James is actually an enormous couch that forces my back to do Cirque Du Soleil contortions while I'm sleeping. The best part is her two-and-a-half-year-old son, Zev, who is adorable. He and Juli are now best friends. *My* best friend Jack Plotnick came to visit and, of course, we immediately snooped in Marissa's bedroom. We were so excited to see her Tony Award lying around. Then we looked closer and saw it wasn't a Tony, it was an Emmy. What the — ? *Then* we picked it up and saw it wasn't even for Marissa...it belonged to Adrian Zmed! I confronted Marissa when she got home (blaming the snooping on Jack) and she revealed that she stored some boxes for Adrian when his house flooded. They're still friends from the 1990s *Grease* national tour. However, she hasn't yet returned the Emmy. *And* she used it for her own hilarity. She took a picture of Zev holding the Emmy and then blew it up to the size of a door. Then, after her good friend Matt Morrison lost the Emmy Award this year, she literally drove to his house and put the picture on his front door with the caption: *You lost? Ouch. Even*

My favorite Marissa story involves the original workshop of *Hairspray* where she was Tracy, and Jennifer Lewis was Motor Mouth. Jennifer is the height of sass and every time she would see Marissa, she'd point and joke: "Marissa! You will *never* be as famous as Miss Jennifer Lewis! You will *never* have as much money as Miss Jennifer Lewis! You will *never* be as black as Miss Jennifer Lewis." The words always came so fast and furious that Marissa would be stymied and never have a comeback. Cut to, a few years after *Hairspray* opened, many of the original cast went to see the first high school production. They all took an enormous limo and Marissa got dressed up and brought a giant handbag. As soon as she sat down on the spacious back seat Jennifer started her signature "You will *never* be as rich as Miss Jennifer Lewis! You will *never* have as much soul as Miss Jennifer Lewis..." Marissa cut her off by reaching into her handbag and saying, "And, Miss Jennifer Lewis, you will *never* have one of these!" — and she pulled out her Tony Award! *Silence*. Then Jennifer looked at Marissa with admiration and said, "You have shut up Miss Jennifer Lewis!"

Right now, I'm lounging next to the pool while Marissa, her husband Judah, Juli and Zev frolic in the hot tub. I'm the uptight New Yorker, sitting at the side of the pool, fully clothed and "freezing." I don't really fit in L.A., but this week there was a great feature about me in the L.A. Times. They asked me what my influences were and one of the shows I mentioned was *Hair*, which was the first show I ever saw when I was a toddler.

All right, I have to get ready. I'm playing Betty Buckley's amazing show tonight, *Broadway By Request,* at a benefit for Reprise.

Happy Birthday to Me...and Bernadette and Tommy and Bill and Kelly
February 28, 2011

As the leading lady in *I'm Getting My Act Together and Taking It On The Road* sang, "This is the day I was born..." That's right, it's my birthday! It's also the birthday of William Finn, Kelly Bishop, Bernadette Peters and Tommy Tune!

Speaking of Tony Awards, I wrote in my last diary entry about how I spent a few days staying at Marissa Jaret Winokur's house in Los Angeles. We were, naturally, discussing her Tony Award and she told me she used to have it displayed on a shelf and her brother had hooked up two lights that shined on it. The lights were connected to a Clapper (as in "Clap on...clap off") and Marissa said any time she wanted to cheer herself up, she would just clap twice and suddenly her Tony was fully illuminated. Brava!

I was thinking about birthdays from my past and the first one that had a Broadway theme was in 1980, when my sister Beth took me to brunch and then a matinee of *Sweeney Todd*. What a great present! And speaking of seeing *Sweeney Todd* at a young age, I just had an article in the L.A. Times where I talked about how, in my day, there were no "kids shows" on Broadway, there were just shows. Well, last week after I played the Betty Buckley concert at Reprise, a nice guy introduced himself to me and told me that he recently brought his young daughter to New York City and, because of my article, decided to get her hooked on Broadway by taking her to see regular Broadway shows and not just "kid shows." Thank you! I'm sure his seven-year-old enjoyed *Agnes of God*. (Had to go back to the '80s to think of a show that even *I* think is inappropriate).

I always enjoy working on my birthday. One time I was playing piano for *Grease* understudy rehearsal on Broadway. I didn't mind going into work because rehearsal for that show was fun. Plus, there always something I could gossip about later. A.K.A. when Maureen McCormick joined the show as Rizzo we were all mortified when someone on the creative team said, "Marcia! Enter from stage left." Followed by the uncomfortable correction of "I mean, *Maureen*."

Speaking of being busted, I was with Jack Plotnick at an improv show in LA last week and we had to run out before the show ended to pick up Juli. I grabbed his coat quickly and fled before we'd be seen by the actors onstage. A few days later, Jack got a call from someone in the audience whom we were sitting near and who Jack happened to know. Turns out, when I grabbed Jack's coat I was actually grabbing someone else's coat! *And* the gentleman informed Jack, in rather stern words that the coat had the keys to his Mercedes in the pocket. And the guy had to get the car towed... and it cost him $250! I only heard Jack's side of the conversation and it sounded like this, "I'm so sorry! (Pause.) Yes, of course you can get the keys back right away! I'll be home tonight and you can come by anytime. (Pause.) Mm-hm. Yes. What's your address?" I'm sure the part of the conversation I didn't hear was, "You expect me to come by *your* house for the keys *you* had the nerve to take!?!?! Drop them off at my place ASAP." Anyhoo, it all worked out. A.K.A. I left for New York the next day.

I interviewed Varla Jean Merman (real name: Jeff Roberson) at my SiriusXM "Live On Broadway" show and I asked him about playing Mary Sunshine in *Chicago*. He did the show on Broadway as well as on the road. He said at one point there was an actress in the show who was, in his words, "*extremely* broad and over-the-top. (pause) Even by my standards." There's one moment where the actress is supposed to be shocked and she would add 90 seconds of heavy breathing and ooh-ing and ah-ing. His imitation of it sounded *crazy*. One night, he was backstage, and he wanted someone else to bear witness. He called our mutual friend, Kristine Zbornik but her machine came on. So, instead of leaving a message, he just held the phone up to the speaker backstage. He recorded all the crazy sounds coming out of the actress and then he promptly hung up. He didn't speak to Kristine for a few weeks and finally he called her and asked if she got his message. When he described what it was she was furious. Turns out, she thought that one of her elderly relatives had called her... and had a stroke! Seriously. She wound up calling them all to see if they needed help and they didn't know what she was talking about.

I guess the good news was her relatives were all healthy?

A Walk with Andy and Zeth
March 7, 2011

I've had a birthday party pretty much every year since I can remember. When I was a kid on Long Island, I had the requisite bowling parties every year. And, P.S., we actually bowled. What the H is with the bumpers at bowling alleys now for kids? Have you seen them? It's literally two walls that come up and block the ball from going in the gutter! How will anyone ever learn how to bowl if they don't fear humiliation that comes from getting non-stop gutter balls? Are kids not allowed to fail at anything these days? I trace it all back to "Family Feud," where every answer, no matter how completely moronic, gets a rousing "Good Answer! Good answer!" from the team that's playing. When did that supportive catch phrase completely lose its meaning? Why attach an adjective to it at all since it's inaccurate anyway? Why not just chant the noun by itself; "_____ answer! ____answer"!

Anyhoo, when I got to high school, I put my b-day parties on hold since I've found that it's hard to find kids to come to your party when you're terrified of most of them. Then in college, my parties resumed, and I've pretty much had one every year of my adult life. Cut to this year; I started asking people to come to a party that would be held on the Saturday after my birthday, and almost every single person was not going to be in New York for the weekend! Didn't they get my "save the date" email that I never sent? I guess that's what I get for inviting people to a party five days before an event. I finally sent a cancellation email saying, "I haven't seen this many people leave town at one time since the final scene in *Fiddler on the Roof*."

Instead of the party, I had a mini-rehearsal with Audra McDonald because I'm playing for her next weekend in Palm Desert at a fundraiser for Desert AIDS (www.DesertAIDS.com). She decided to sing the great song, "Some Days" by Steve Marzullo, which I've played for her before so our "rehearsal" was just us chatting in my apartment. Then James, Juli, Audra's daughter Zoe and I hooked up with Andrea Burns and her son Hudson, and we saw "Rangoo." The movie was thoroughly enjoyable. The animation is amazing, plus there were some hilarious throw-away lines. At one point, the lizard voiced by Johnny Depp is asked his name, and he goes into a long diatribe about all the different names he has. He literally mentions his CB handle *and* says that he's one of the few men who has a maiden name. Hi-larious!

Audra and I were talking about her role on "Private Practice" and, turns out, some people don't realize it's a role. She said that she'll often meet fans of the show who will berate her for her behavior. She posted a little reminder on her Twitter that when people meet her, they're meeting Audra, not Dr. Naomi Bennett. Recently, some woman at a gas station yelled at her, "How could you kiss him like that?!" I laughed at the woman's lack of reality...but followed it by asking Audra why she made Coalhouse come to New Rochelle so many times before she came down from the attic? Why such a prima donna? Still waiting for a satisfactory response.

Last Sunday I ran into my good friend Dev Janki (who directed and choreographed one of my favorite shows, *Zanna Don't)*. While we were chatting, an older woman walked by, said something to Dev, he said a friendly "Hi" but then he looked at me with an embarrassed face. I asked him what I missed and he explained that he's been taking yoga from for years but for some reason, she thinks his name is Andy. It's been so long that, at this point, he's stopped correcting her. He was mortified because he thought I watched him give a huge smile and wave back to her when she greeted him with "Hi, Andy!" The only event in my life I can relate this to is when composer Michael John LaChiusa used to think my name was *Zeth* and I never corrected him. He finally realized he was wrong but it never bothered me that much because at least three of the letters were correct. But how did "Dev" become "Andy"? It's not even the correct amount of syllables.

The week began in New York where I interviewed Ben Vereen for my SiriusXM "Live On Broadway" show. He relayed to me an old piece of theatre lore: once there was a big snowstorm in New York and only *one* person showed up to see a certain show. Backstage, the lead actor made a big speech to the cast saying, even an audience of one deserved a good show and even more so on that night because he actually got himself to the theatre. After the performance, the actor broke the fourth wall and thanked the man for coming. He then asked him how far he traveled to be in the audience. "Traveled?" the man replied. "I work here! I'm just waiting for you guys to finish so I can clean up." It sounds like a made-up story, but I recall many a freezing night at the Sullivan Street Playhouse where I was playing piano for *The Fantasticks* and the cast onstage (6) outnumbered the audience.

Ben sang "Magic To Do" and he still sounds great. I had a flashback to *The Ritz*, where I sang part of that song. I had to wear a unitard and after the show one of my famous actor friends met me backstage and asked how they padded the unitard so it looked like I had a fat gut. There was an awkward silence and I then quietly replied that I didn't use any padding. I informed her, in actuality, it was my own fat. Then she backpedaled with "What? You don't have any fat on you!" as she poked me to prove it. However, her ruse was to completely avoid my fat stomach area and poke my ribs...the one area where fat cannot gather on any torso. I guess I fell for it because I'm still using tons of half and half in my coffee. Peace out!

In the Desert With Dionne, Diahann and Audra
March 14, 2011

Right now I'm at LAX, heading home. I was here to play in a benefit for Desert AIDS Project, which is a wonderful organization that's been around for 30 years. During the event, they told everyone that when they first started working with AIDS patients, there was no real treatment and a long-time survivor meant 18 months. Nowadays, they have clients who were infected years ago, but are still going strong. Desert AIDS has built amazing medical facilities and housing units for clients, and provides educational outreach, HIV testing, legal assistance and much more. They also deliver food to low-income clients and one of the deliverymen is… my Dad! He lives in Palm Desert and has been volunteering at the food bank for years. And, P.S., he's about to turn 80 next week. He's still got it!

My Dad!

My friend Jack Plotnick drove me from L.A. to Palm Springs and we met my Dad and his wife, Gloria, for brunch. Jack was asking my father about being in the Korean War and I found out a story I didn't know. Turns out, he was stationed in Germany when the war ended but still had a few weeks left in the army. He was thrilled when he found out that he was approved for a month's leave before his final discharge. He was able to use the army plane for free and flew immediately to Paris. He was all set for a delicious month of museum-going, wine-drinking and dame-dating. His first afternoon there, he was sitting in an outdoor café, drinking espresso. Suddenly, two army men came up and told him he had to come back to the base. He had no idea what he had done but he had no choice but to go with them. When he got back, he found out the "good" news; a few weeks before, he had told his mother that even though the war had ended, he couldn't get an early leave. Well, she made tons of phone calls and finally convinced the army to let him end his service early. Yay? He got to curtail his 30 days in Paris to leave Europe immediately — for Brooklyn. That was 55 years ago. Still devastated.

The Desert AIDS event began with a fancy dinner on the night before and it was star-studded. Jack and I showed up at the restaurant and when we walked to the entrance, I saw a group of smokers. I'm always passive/aggressive when I pass by a group of people with cigarettes, so as I walked in, I glared and loudly intoned, "C'mon Jack. Let's walk quickly past all of this smoke!" Of course, as soon as I got indoors, Jack said that the smoker nearest to my hostile comment was Dionne Warwick. Yowtch! Well…shouldn't she have been able to psychically predict that I'd be rude? (Psychic Friends Network? Anyone?)

Anyhoo, once we got inside the restaurant we were seated at the same table as Joan Collins and George Hamilton! I've never felt less glamorous. My next star-spotting refers back to what I did before I got to Palm Springs; At SiriusXM, I interviewed Anne Garefino who is one of the producers of *The Book of Mormon*. She's been with "South Park" since it began on television, but she's always loved theatre so this is a dream come true for her. I asked her about one of the shocking moments in the show, in which a bunch of people spend a whole song cursing God. She told me that the song has gotten a great response because the audience seems to understand where it's coming from. It's sung by a group of people who truly feel that God has deserted them and they're simply singing their feelings. The reality is, many people have that feeling at some point in their lives and this song is giving voice to it. She feels that theatre has always been able to go much further than film or TV and has always paved the way for breaking taboos. Ann mentioned shows like *Next to Normal* and *La Cage Aux Folles*, which were ground-breaking, and I brought up *No Strings* which was on Broadway in the early '60s and had an interracial relationship as the main love story. The leading man was Richard Kiley and the leading lady was Diahann Carroll. Cut to one week later: I go backstage at Desert AIDS, walk into Audra McDonald's dressing room and see that she's sharing it with...Diahann Carroll! Turns out, *I* should be on the Psychic Friends Network! I asked Diahann how scandalous *No Strings* was. She said that even though it was on Broadway and Civil Rights were still being fought for around the country (interracial marriage wasn't legal in all of the U.S. until 1967!), it didn't cause that much of a stir on Broadway because the story wasn't focused on the fact that it was an interracial relationship — it was about an American woman with a European man. Yet again, theater is ahead of the rest of the country in terms of acceptance. I loved talking to Audra and Diahann while they were looking into their dressing room mirror, so I took a photo of them. They tried to hold very serious diva expressions, but I told them to "work it" and they immediately broke up and I got a great shot of them laughing.

Ann-Margret is a big supporter of Desert AIDS and before she went on, she was introduced to Audra backstage. Audra expected a polite "hello," but the first thing Ann-Margret said to her was, "So, will Naomi get back together with Sam?" Turns out, even Kim McAfee watches "Private Practice"!

The event was black tie and I had to haul out the tux I had bought when I played for Audra for the Leading Ladies event at Carnegie Hall...in 1998! Suffice it to say, I'm not quite the same weight. I took it to a tailor and instead of telling me she needed to let it out an inch or two she told me she was going to simply let the entire waist out as much as possible. Sadly, it was still unbearably snug. Of course, I didn't start getting dressed until 15 minutes before the event and I suddenly realized that my tuxedo shirt needed buttons and cufflinks and I had neither! Jack let me borrow his shirt which was crazily small on me and therefore wouldn't completely close in the middle. We literally had to safety pin it. He then had to wear his tux jacket with a black shirt (!) he had worn the night before and not washed. Also, I couldn't find my shoes before I left NYC so I had to bring James' shoes, which were too big. *To this day I've been begging for a pregnancy patch on men's pants.*

Audra and I were talking about our dogs and she told me that her new doggie sleeps at the foot of the bed and snores up a storm. The laundry basket in the bedroom is on Audra's side of the bed and in the morning she'll look toward the bottom of the bed and notice that her dog is covered in socks and random bras. Even though Audra doesn't remember because she's only half awake, she obviously gets woken up in the middle of the night by the snoring, reaches over the side of the bed and flings various underthings to quiet that mutt! It's either that, or her dog is a drag queen. Speaking of dogs, I was chatting with my sister, Nancy, who told me that everybody seems to have one in Virginia Beach (where she lives). She always forgets how much of a dog culture she's in and is constantly misunderstanding things. For instance, someone posted on Facebook that they almost "lost their baby" and Nancy was devastated thinking there was a pregnancy mishap, but it turned out that the woman's dog almost got off its leash. Nancy is now trying to remember that most things pertain to dogs in her part of the state and she told me about a conversation she recently had with a friend. When you read it, make sure you do it sing-song style, a la Alexi Darling in *Rent*. "Nancy!" the woman trilled. "Our family's about to get a new addition!" The last word was sustained with vibrato. "Details!" Nancy sang back.

"Terry is moving in!" The woman continued, with the same melody.

"That's a-dorable!" Nancy sing-song'd.

Then *silence*.

Finally, the woman glared and said, "Uh...I guess it's 'adorable' that my 17-year-old stepson is moving in with us." Wait...*not* a dog? Nancy thought quickly and said, "Well, it's adorable because of all that youthful energy!" Huh? First of all, her cover-up makes no sense. But more importantly, Nancy asked me, "Why would the woman add vibrato to the word 'addition' if it wasn't about a dog?" Valid point. Every professor in music conservatory teaches: Dog = vibrato, stepson = straight tone.

On my flight out to L.A., I got to be in First Class! It was delicious! It had a fabulous meal, direct TV, enormous seats and non-stop coffee. Then, at the very end, I smelled something yummy. That's right, they brought out the signature, First Class warm cookie! I was thrilled beyond belief. Finally, a First Class that meets my expectations. As I was served the cookie, I asked the flight attendant for some milk because, while I like cookies, my favorite snack in the world is cookies and milk. She looked at me and stated, "Sorry, sir. We don't serve milk." *What?* Unbelievable. I've said it before and I'll say it again: "My personal shopper is the worst!" *That is a callback to an article from the parody newspaper The Onion where there's an editorial from a very uptight looking rich woman who is lamenting how horrible her personal shopper is. I quote it all the time whenever I realize I'm not appreciating something luxurious.*

Mormon's Boys, _Priscilla_'s Passion
March 21, 2011

I spent last weekend in Palm Springs, got back Sunday evening, and on Monday morning I had a ticket to fly to New Orleans on an 8 AM flight. The night before, James and I went to sleep at 11 (old lady-style). I set my alarm for 6:15 so I could eat, walk the dog and get to the airport by 7 AM. Well, the next thing I know I was waking up to the sound of James' voice saying, "Seth! It's 10 after 7!" That's right. I woke up ten minutes _after_ I wanted to actually be at the airport. Because it was so outrageously late, I didn't even jump up and start rushing around. I just rolled my eyes and said, "Well, I missed the plane." James told me that I might as well try to make it so I got up and went to my suitcase. Not to grab it and run for a cab, but to actually pack it. That's right, my suitcase wasn't even packed. I finally got everything inside and left the apartment. Right when I got to my corner, a cab sped by. Oh, well, I'll get the next one. And, then — no cab for the next five minutes. I hauled it over to 72nd Street and hailed one…going up Central Park West. That's right, we didn't even go up Amsterdam where the lights stay green the whole time, we went up Central Park West and had a red light every three blocks. James texted me asking where I was and, at 7:44, I was still in a cab. I finally got to the airport and, typical-style, couldn't find my gate number. I figured it out and went over to the security line. A nice lady let me go to the front, but at the x-ray machine there were three people in front of me. I waited a while and the nice lady walked over and told me to cut them. I got through, grabbed my stuff and ran to my gate area. There weren't any passengers around and all the doors leading to jetways were closed so I couldn't even figure out which one was mine. An employee asked me where I was going and when I said New Orleans, he opened the door to the jetway and let me on! That's right…I made the flight! _And_ there were two girls in back of me running on, so I wasn't even the last one to make it! I still don't quite understand how I did it. Was I able to stop time? _That's_ what I wasted my superpowers for? An 8 AM flight? When I could have just waited for the noon flight? Hmph. I haven't seen superpowers wasted like that since… insert tired/unfunny _Spider-Man_ joke here.

Anyhoo, New Orleans was beautiful and I spent that night watching a benefit screening of "Varla Jean and the Mushroomheads," the feature film I did with Varla (Jeff Roberson). _It just became available on DVD and Jacques Lamarre, the co-writer, posted on Facebook "Now available on DVD. Right when no one uses DVDs anymore." Exactly!_

This week I finally saw _The Book Of Mormon_ and, not surprisingly, it's fantastic. So funny, tuneful, smart, well-performed and, despite its salty language (salty meaning shockingly foul), it has plenty of heart. It's one of those shows I could see numerous times, and hopefully, I will! _I wound up seeing it two more times …including once in L.A. with Gavin Creel who was amazing!_ I got to interview a few of the stars of the show on SiriusXM and asked Andrew Rannells (_way before "Girls" and Falsettos on Broadway_), who plays the clean-cut missionary Elder Price, what his audition was like. He told me that after he auditioned in New York, he was asked to fly out to L.A. to read with Josh Gad, who was already cast. I am always fascinated by the awkward social protocol of seeing people you're competing against in the waiting area, and I asked him what that was like. He told me that right before he went in, he saw a well-known TV star go in. Andrew heard him sing and do the scene — that's the "fun" part about auditioning in rickety-rackety audition studios; the walls are made out of balsa wood — and he couldn't help but notice that it didn't go too well. On the way out, the TV star looked at Andrew and said, "Man…singing is _hard_." What a general, yet specific, comment.

I also asked Josh Gad _(before he guest starred on my Audible.com book "My Awesome/Awful_

Popularity Plan" and then stole the film "Frozen" as Olaf) who plays the hapless Elder Cunningham what his big role was in high school and turns out, unlike me — who played the cameo role of the Rabbi in his high school production of *Fiddler on the Rood* — Josh scored a coup and got the role of Tevye. *As a sophomore!* He told me that after that triumph, his head swelled and when he was cast as Charlemagne in his junior-year production of *Pippin*, he pulled a Julie Andrews and turned down the Tony nomination (a.k.a. role). It made no sense to me. Charlemagne is a great part for him and I asked what part he had wanted instead. No answer. Pippin? Fastrada? *Silence*. The next year, he realized the errors of his ways and accepted the supporting role of Nicely Nicely in his senior-year musical, *Guys and Dolls*. As for *Book of Mormon*, he was offered the role because Bobby Lopez (who co-wrote this score, as well as *Avenue Q*) saw him in the film "Twenty One." At that time, Josh was in *Spelling Bee* on Broadway, so Bobby called the music director, Vadim Feichtner, and asked if he had any kind of recording of Josh singing. Vadim sent over a recording from the BC/EFA fundraiser CD "Carols for a Cure," Bobby listened and thought Josh had a fantastic voice. He therefore asked Josh to do the first workshop but soon noticed that Josh's voice sounded different than what he had heard. Turns out, the song Bobby had listened to on the CD was a group number and the voice he thought was "fantastic" actually belonged to Barrett Foa! Regardless, Josh has a great voice and kept getting asked to do each subsequent workshop and now he brings down the house with his brilliant performance. And it worked out for Barrett, too who's doing great on the TV show, "NCIS: L.A." And Barrett's blond and blue-eyed so he's basically set for life.

Now, I'm preparing to go to a commercial audition. The commercial features a funny guy and an older lady who is known in the script simply as "Nag." Naturally, my agent got me an audition along with... *my mother*. Life imitates art? Are we the new Shirley Jones/David Cassidy but without Mr. Kincaid? Speaking of my mom, I took her to see *Priscilla Queen of the Desert* because I knew she'd love it, which she did. If you recall, I was asked to audition for that show. Not for the young hottie played by Nick Adams, nor the cute bisexual dad played by Will Swenson. No, I went in for the aging transsexual played by Tony Sheldon who mentions in his bio that he's been in the business for *40 years*. That's apparently my age range now. I recall that the audition was actually amazing, but me and the other guys auditioning were stressing about having to sing the word "We" in the song "We Belong." It's on a horrible E vowel and the song was in a key that placed the word on a note that falls right on a normal person's break. They were insisting at the audition that we sing it in that key and I assumed that was because it's an amazing solo in the show, where the singer has to nail the high note. Well, I saw the Wednesday matinee and, turns out, it's a *group number*, sung in harmony and there's no way to tell who's actually hitting the A flat! Why did I have to a.) stress about it; b.) give myself pre-vocal damage trying to hit it; and c.) make them endure hearing me hit an A flat with an emphasis on the word "flat"?

Regardless, after the show, I was texting with Will Swenson who is so loveable as the dad and I wrote, "Stop having a good body. It's shame-inducing." He texted back: "Shut it. I have to stand next to Nick Adams all day. Talk about shame." Hmm...I guess the word "shame" uses a sliding scale.

Happy Spring...stay warm and dry!

Popping Into *Anything Goes* and *Wonderland*
March 28, 2011

So tired. I'm on the 7 AM flight to Phoenix to go play for Betty Buckley in Scottsdale, AZ! It's so early! The last time I remember having to do things at 7 AM was when I took "driver's ed" in high school. The good news, I got my license! The bad news, I basically haven't driven since. It reminds me of the comic who talked about getting a year's membership at a gym: "I went every day the first week, every other day the second week and then never again for the rest of the year."

In terms of Broadway, my mom and I saw the Wednesday matinee of *Anything Goes* and loved it. I'm obsessed with "Arrested Development" so I got an extra kick out of seeing Jessica Walter (who played Lucille Bluth on TV) as Evangeline. Plus, at the end she sang part of a song and I was shocked to hear she has a great voice. It's always weird when you know a celeb solely as a straight actor and you suddenly hear that they have a good singing voice. Those of you who grew up watching "The Andy Griffith Show," I dare you to listen to *Destry Rides Again*. Turns out, Andy Griffith has a full, sassy vibrato! Who knew?

Anyhoo, Sutton Foster has the nerve to be a full triple threat —she's great at all three. As I mentioned, I was at the show with my mother, who never fails to live up to her reputation as befuddled with a dash of hostility; halfway through Act One, Joel Grey was in the middle of his fourth scene when my mom leaned over to me and whispered, "Joel Grey is wonderful." Actually, *no*. That's what a normal person would have done. Instead, she leaned over and angrily whispered, "Isn't that the Joel Grey part? *Why* isn't he on today?" I didn't know what to do besides hiss, "That *is* Joel Grey!" and then I had to let her spend five minutes registering shock while I went back to watching the show. She pulled another typical moment a few weeks ago when she randomly said, with annoyance in her voice: "So! I guess you've already seen *Kiss of the Spider Woman* without me!" Huh? Yes, I played keyboard for that show in the mid-'90s but I had no idea why she was referencing it. Was it being revived and she knew before I did? No, I finally realized she was trying to make me guilty for not taking her to enough Broadway shows and had meant to say, "I guess you've already seen *Spider-Man*." You literally need a Berlitz course to understand what she means. On a related note, I had the commercial audition with my mother I had mentioned last week. The two different roles were an "Albert Brooks type" and a "Nag." We both went in together and it was a little mortifying to stand before the camera and slate our name. "Seth Rudetsky." *Pause*. "Sally Rudetsky." Of course, when I first got to the waiting area with the sign-in sheet and the script, I saw that my mother wasn't reviewing her lines for the audition. Instead, she was holding court with a casting director intern and telling a story that happened to her in the '50s. Why go over lines for an audition happening in ten minutes when you can instead tell someone about an anti-Semitic event that happened to you 60 years ago? Anyhoo, the audition actually went well, but suffice it to say they're filming it today in Los Angeles and my mother and I are firmly ensconced in New York.

This was a week of seeing *lots* of stuff. Juli was on a school break but was being babysat by her grandmother, so James and I could go out at night. Monday night I saw the hilarious Jackie Hoffman in her Joe's Pub show, *Jackie 5-0*. I sat with my manager, Mark Cortale, and Jeff Roberson (who plays Varla Jean Merman) and we all loved it. Jackie is currently playing Grandma in *The Addams Family* and told us that during the first few months of a Broadway show, the audiences are all savvy theatre insiders... and then come tourists. She lamented that *The Addams Family* managed to skip the insiders and go right to tourists. She then added, "I'm in the only musical on Broadway that doesn't appeal to gay people!" Her act also has a hilarious section about people from her old Long Island neighborhood who don't really understand what she does and always make her feel horrible. (Note, in the following, when you read the word "second," make sure you elongate it as much as possible and make it incredibly nasal and Long Island-sounding.) "Jackie! I saw you on TV last night...I think. You were on for like a *se-cond*. I think it was you, but who knows, because it was like a *se-cond*. Your mother told me to watch but I don't know why because you were on for like a *se-cond*." The audience on Monday night was lucky enough to catch her right after her most recent TV devastation. She told us that she just booked a great role on "The Good Wife" and they offered her a great salary. She then informed us that night, right before she came onstage, she found out that *The Addams Family* won't let her take off a show to film it! The filming date happens to be right during a publicity event when they're claiming it's "Grandma's Birthday." "So, I have to miss a great role on TV so I can take a photo backstage with some theatre party ladies." I told James and he said, "I wanna see that photo!"

Speaking of Grandma, Jackie mentioned that she's the only character in the show who doesn't have a song. "Lurch has a song and he doesn't even speak!" During previews a year ago, she took matters into her own hands and actually wrote a song for her character (which she sang for us) and asked if it could be put in. She then gave us some "advice": "If you want to ingratiate yourself to a creative team working on a new show, make sure you write a song for yourself and give it to them." Ouch. *Addams Family* opened months ago but she told us that she's still "waiting to hear" if the song is going in.

The next night, James and I caught the Transport's Group revival of *Hello Again*. We're lucky we didn't catch anything else, if you get my drift. The partially clothed actors are *very close* to you throughout the show. The good news is, there's no audience participation but, boy, there almost was. When I see a show, I'm hoping to love it, not actually make love. Regardless, it was a great production. The sound balance in the room was great (it's performed in an enormous downtown loft) and the thrilling part is, *there are no mics*! I've said it before and I'll say it again: Seeing an Off-Broadway show is sometimes so much more theatrical than seeing a Broadway show. How amazing to hear acoustic instruments and be that close to a group of great actors as we hear their voices simply as they sound when they come out of their mouths. Delicious! Listening to the music was also very nostalgic for me because I was the assistant music director on the workshop at Lincoln Center back in 1993! So many memories! Donna Murphy (who always wore a rehearsal skirt...I was obsessed) played Leocadia and I remember her talking about her upcoming auditioning for *Passion*. Who knew that she'd win her first Tony from that? Also, one of the guys in the cast was doing his own show, and I remember getting an invite from him that was an unclear Xerox of himself in a crazy wig. It listed the performance location in a club downtown. Club? Downtown? *So* not my style. Cut to: It was John Cameron Mitchell developing *Hedwig*! To this day I'm devastated I didn't go.

James and I also went to see *Wonderland* and, holy nodes, the singers in that show are *amazing*. Let me sum it up by saying that I went backstage to laud everyone and when I got to Kate Shindle I complimented her on the amazing last note she sings at the top of Act Two. Her response was, "it's just an E." Nuff said.

Peace out and stay warm!!

Celebrating Terrence McNally
April 4, 2011

Yay. It's spring and it snowed last week. What is up with that? Is it too much to ask for the weather to simply follow a schedule? Does the weather also have ADD like I do? Anyhoo, this week I saw more Broadway because everything is opening at once and I'm frantically trying to keep up like Lucy in the chocolate factory. On Wednesday, I took my mom to see *Catch Me If You Can*. Not surprisingly, I'm totally obsessed with Norbert Leo Butz's voice. If you haven't seen my deconstruction of his vibrato and amazing hard R's, please watch it on YouTube ASAP. Also, it was great to see Rachelle Rak in a perfect role as a Playboy bunny. If you don't remember, she was the one featured in the documentary "Every Little Step" — she was the frontrunner for the role of Sheila in the *Chorus Line* revival. At the final call back, she was told to simply do what she did at the last audition. The advice wasn't really helpful because the audition had been months before and she didn't remember what she had done. It put her into a panic and she lost the role. I mean, "spoiler alert". Regardless, now she's triumphing and looks amazing!

My Mom and got to the theater early and she pulled her usual panic based on nothing. We were standing in the lobby before the show and she immediately tensed because she heard the noise that signals the show is about to begin. What she actually heard was the beeping sound a truck makes when it backs up. Why would the new Broadway signal for starting a show be a slow "beep...beep...beep" issued *from the street*?

Monday night I went to a great fundraiser for Juilliard's The Acting Company, saluting Terrence McNally. There were so many great performances. Emily Skinner, who starred in *The Full Monty (and is now starring in Hal Prince's Prince of Broadway)* told a great story before she sang. She was doing *Full Monty* when 9/11 happened and all Broadway shows were cancelled. A few days later they resumed and she (and I) remember there was a feeling from some people on Broadway of "why are we doing something so shallow when there are deep things in the world to be dealt with?" Cut to, a few performances later, Emily came out of the stage door and was suddenly enveloped in a bear hug from behind. She reminded us that when a friend does that, it's a good feeling, when a stranger does, it's terrifying. Nonetheless, the stranger let her go and informed her that he was an NYC firefighter. He told her that seeing the show that night made him feel something for the first time since 9/11. Emily was, of course, incredibly moved and after she left she waited at the end of the block and watched. Sure enough, he did that to *every* person exiting the stage door! Musicians, actors, hair, wardrobe etc.

John Glover did the phone monologue from *The Lisbon Traviata* and was hilarious. If you don't know it, the monologue is spoken by an opera fanatic who is desperate for a bootleg recording of Maria Callas' *Traviata* from Lisbon. He's on the phone with a young guy who doesn't quite remember whether he saw it or not and John Glover is mind-boggled at how casual the guy is. First he says, "Believe me, if you saw it, you'd remember it," but it soon becomes clear that the guy may have seen it and hardly remembers it. It essentially ends with John Glover telling him that Maria Callas died because people didn't fully appreciate how brilliant she was. He then yells "Murderer!" and hangs up. So funny! P.S. John Glover trying to jar the memory of this younger person reminded me of two things; First, growing up obsessed with musical theatre and having no one with my knowledge/passion/obsession to share it with. This was before online message boards. When I was nine, I was walking around constantly asking adults if they'd heard of *Chicago* and they'd always nod yes and then start singing the Judy Garland song, "Chicago, Chicago." NO! Infuriating! Had no one heard of the Fosse show besides me and Chita Rivera? Secondly, I was once on SiriusXM, interviewing a pretty famous female Broadway producer. I mentioned the

Dreamgirls concert I put up for the Actors Fund. She nodded vaguely and said, "Hmm...I think I saw it." I was flummoxed! She literally didn't remember? It starred Audra McDonald, Heather Headley and Lillias White and was the first big theatrical event after 9/11! It literally took place ten days later! Everyone who was there that night (onstage and in the audience) told me that the experience was so emotionally cathartic for them and all she gives me is a "Hmmm...I think I saw it"? Unbelievable! I'm still in a rage. The interview didn't quite end with me yelling "Murderer!" but only because of my fear of copyright infringement.

Also at the McNally tribute, *Ragtime*'s original stars Marin Mazzie and Brian Stokes Mitchell performed their signature song "Back to Before" as well as "Wheels Of A Dream". Both said *Ragtime* was their most fulfilling theatrical experience. I'm so lucky I got to play piano in the pit orchestra as the sub for Steve Marzullo, the original pianist. It was so moving to me to hear them sing again, *and* see Stephen Flaherty, the composer himself, playing for them! John Doyle directed the evening and asked Tom Kirdahy (Terrence's husband...they were married in DC), "Who would really surprise Terrence and mean the most to him to have onstage?" Well, up came Dr. Valeria Rusch, who operated on Terrence when he had cancer. She was so well-spoken and warm. And funny! She began by saying, "I'm Terrence's cancer surgeon. *Cancer* surgeon. Not plastic." Brava on the opening joke! The most moving part for me was when Angela Lansbury (who hosted) introduced Terrence at the end. She thanked him for bringing her back to Broadway (she starred in *Deuce* a few years ago after more than 20 years away from Broadway). And when she thanked him, she started crying. P.S. I quickly went from being moved to jealous because Angela has the nerve to be in her 80s and be in better shape than me! How dare she be a size four? I'm out.

At my SiriusXM radio show, I interviewed "The Midtown Men," who originally toured as the original "Jersey Boys" until a lawsuit put the kibosh on that. Christian Hoff, who won the Tony Award for playing Tommy DeVito, was in the original cast of *Tommy*, which was in one of those tight Tony Award races, similar to what happened with *Avenue Q* vs. *Wicked*...all the way back to *Music Man* vs. *West Side Story*. What's nice to know is that even though the shows were competing, the casts got along. As a matter of fact, Christian said that he and some cast members had a break in the middle of their show that directly coincided with Chita Rivera's break during *Spider Woman* so the *Tommy* cast would spend their break hanging out with Chita in her dressing room! My question is, if they were in different theatres, how did they know their breaks were at the same time? Did Christian and his friends look across the street and see Chita through the window of her dressing room, sitting on her divan? Did they go to the stage doorman and ask if she was available for a playdate? Speaking of *Spider Woman*, I used to work as a keyboard sub on that show as well. I was subbing for Jeff Saver, who also conducted and is an all-around great guy. He just moved back to New York after spending a few years out of town. He moved away so his wife could get treatment for colon cancer, from which she eventually died. He wants me to spread the word that *women need colonoscopies*! Get one early, ladies! When his wife was diagnosed, she was 40 years old and had *no* family history. He told me that by the time you feel something, it's too late and if they had caught a polyp early on, it would have been easy to treat. So, ladies...get thee to a colonoscopy. ASAP!

This week, I fly to Winnipeg (!) to play for Andrea Martin on a TV comedy special and then I play for Betty Buckley in New York for two shows. Go to YouTube for my latest Playbill Obsessed! video where Tituss Burgess sings "Meadowlark," which was originally recorded by Patti LuPone. Tituss has the nerve to take it only *one* step down from Patti's key! Watch, listen and have prednisone on hand. *Of course, this was before Tituss was nominated twice for an Emmy Award for starring in Unbreakable Kimmy Schmidt. Amazing actor, amazing singer.*

Tonight, April 4, I'm going to a benefit for the Point Foundation which helps fund LGBT young people who are pursuing academia. It's star-studded! Kelly Ripa, Andy Cohen, Ellen Barkin, Rob Thomas, etc., plus Montego Glover (*before playing one of the Schuyler sisters in Hamilton*) is singing. And, I'm playing for Kerry Butler, who's performing the 11 o'clock number from *Catch Me If You Can*, which brought down the house on the day I saw it. *If you haven't heard it, get thee to Youtube and look for "Fly, Fly Away". So gorgeous.*

Misidentifying Mark Consuelos
April 11, 2011

Greetings from...Brooklyn. That's right, usually I'm writing from some far away locale, but this weekend I'm playing for Betty Buckley in exotic Brooklyn and Queens. The good news is, tickets sales are great. The bad news is, driving here took as long as a plane ride to Chicago. Speaking of which, that's where I had to change planes this week on the way back from Winnipeg, Canada. I went there to play for Andrea Martin who was hosting a TV variety show for the Winnipeg Comedy Festival. She was, of course, hilarious. She talked about being Armenian (her family's last name was originally Popasian). She explained that all Armenian last names end in "i-a-n" and that the Kardashians are also Armenian. She then said, "Kim isn't the only Armenian with a sex tape. I also have a sex tape coming out." She nodded proudly. "It's an audio tape."

Andrea looks so amazing. She's the only woman I know who looks like she's wearing Spanx but isn't. Speaking of great bodies, I just interviewed Emily Skinner on my SiriusXM show. She is now essentially a size zero and had the nerve to tell me it's simply from doing *Billy Elliot*. Really? *I* did a Broadway show and I didn't shrink my dress size. I busted her and said she sounds like those models who say, "Why am I so skinny? Chasing around my toddler." She then told me that she also does cardio. Hmph. *I* do cardio...-ish. I made her re-tell one of my favorite stories; her first job on Broadway was being in the ensemble of *Jekyll and Hyde* and understudying Linda Eder. During previews, Linda lost her voice and the powers-that-be told Emily she was on. Not only had she never rehearsed anything (none of the blocking or crazy fight scenes), but the stage was constantly covered in fog! Equity said it was too dangerous and wouldn't let her go on, so Linda Eder had to do the show. But she really had lost her voice. So, whenever Linda got to a song, Emily stood backstage with a microphone and sang it and Linda stood onstage and lip-synched it! Pre-dating Ashlee Simpson by a decade. Brava! *Is that reference too old? Google Ashlee Simpson and SNL then return to the book.*

More on the inspiring Point Foundation event I mentioned. One of the "scholars" (as they're called) who had received funding was Maggie Keenan-Bolger, sister of Celia and Andrew and fellow Oberlin College graduate. There were many celebs at the event but I, of course, never recognize *anyone*. I've said this so many times, but I'll say it again; I have major trouble differentiating faces yet people always think I'm being rude for not knowing who they are. It's not my fault! An example of my crazy facial-spotting issue is that for the first year of "Friends," I thought Matt LeBlanc and Matthew Perry looked like twins. Literally couldn't tell them apart. At the beginning of the event, I was looking for Kelly Ripa and her husband Mark Consuelos because I had worked with them in 1998 on an "All My Children" production number (to the tune of "Oklahoma") for "The Rosie O'Donnell Show." I saw Mark on the red carpet and he was super friendly and knew who I was. I reminded him we met when he sang "Oklahoma" for me. He kept denying it and I kept reminding him of the lyrics. Finally, after a lot of back and forth featuring me actually singing some of the song, I found out it *wasn't* Mark Consuelos. It actually was the head of the Point Foundation, Jorge Valencia. Apparently, the only similarity is they're both Hispanic. Great. So now I look like a racist. And, FYI, I pointed at him before I walked over and said, "Is that Mark Consuelos" to someone who works there and he said, "Yes!" He then claimed he thought I was pointing further down the red carpet to where Mark was. And, to continue my facial non-recognition, I was there to co-host the auction and throughout it, I kept seeing a lovely woman raising her hand to bid. I thought, "Boy, she's pretty." I later found out the "pretty lady" I saw was super-model Iman. Let it be known; I don't recognize people! Off my back.

Speaking of the auction, at the last minute I added an item: a chance to co-host on my radio show. I was nervous I'd only get a $10 bid from James, but I raised them a delicious $6,000. I still got it! The whole evening honored Bravo's Andy Cohen and Margarethe Cammermeyer. Andy was adorable and brought his mother as his date, taking a page out of my Oedipal diary. If you don't know Margarethe's story, here's the brief version: she was a nurse in Vietnam and eventually became Chief Nurse of the Washington State National Guard. In 1989, during an interview for Top Secret clearance, she mentioned that she was a lesbian. She was immediately fired from the military despite her exemplary military and civilian professional record. She filed a suit which challenged the existing ban on homosexuals in the military and requested her reinstatement. After 25 months of being in and out of court, the judge ruled it unconstitutional and based on prejudice and she was reinstated. The tribute to Margarethe was fantastic. Neil Meron and Craig Zadan talked about making the film "Serving in Silence" and then they brought up Glenn Close, who had run over right after filming "Damages." As Glenn talked about what an honor it was to play Margarethe, she became so moved she started crying. Then Margarethe came up and, turns out, even though she looks stern in photos, she's a great and very funny speaker. She talked about getting a call from Barwood, Barbra Streisand's production company in the early '90s who asked her to fly out and meet with them about making the TV movie. Since she was in the middle of the actual lawsuit, she felt she had to ask her lawyer. "I called my lawyer and she told me that because of the upcoming trial I could *not* fly to Malibu to meet with Barbra Streisand..."*Pause.* "...without my lawyer." Hilarious.

This week I'm actually staying in New York and then next week I'm off to sunny Florida to do my show at The Kravis Center and The Broward Center. And, harkening back to the Andy Cohen school of apron strings, I'm bringing my mother along. Peace out!

My Great Big Disastrous New Musical; Plus a Passover *Gypsy*
April 18, 2011

This is where I first talk about Disaster!! Well, the big news is, I'm finally putting up a show I've been wanting to write for almost 20 years! Only Make Believe is a great charity that I do benefits for every year and they asked me to do one in May. I decided to use it as an opportunity that would force me to write what I've been talking about since the days when I was playing for *Forever Plaid* (1993!). Drew Geraci and I have always been obsessed with 1970s disaster movies like "The Poseidon Adventure," "Towering Inferno," "Earthquake," "Airport '77," etc. So, along with my hilarious friend Jack Plotnick, we're writing *1970s Disaster Movie Musical. That was the original name til it was shortened a few months later at the advice of a big Bway producer.* It features all the disasters from those 70s disaster movies. And the score is *all* amazing 1970s songs. I'm basing this whole experiment on Charles Busch, who was offered a performance date for a show and was then forced to write *Vampire Lesbians of Sodom* so he'd have something to perform. We picked the date and then we wrote the script. So far, it's pretty hilarious. There's a nun, an aging couple, a disaster expert, a diabetic 11-year-old boy and many more characters based on all those '70s classics. Dena Hammerstein, who runs Only Make Believe, has a son who owns the hip, downtown club called The Box. Though I'm not cool enough to gain admission to it on a normal night, he is graciously allowing us to use it for the show which is perfect because the performance area sort of looks like the inside of a luxury cruise ship!

The good news, weather-wise, is that it's warm...ish. We finally started working on our garden in the backyard. We put down new soil, tilled it, put bamboo up on the backyard walls, secured fencing so the dogs don't eat the plants and laid down white gravel to brighten everything up. Now, go back and read the last two sentences and substitute "James" for "we." My job was watching him do it.

This week I'm headed to Florida! I'm in West Palm Beach and Ft. Lauderdale, which apparently are very close to each other. First, I will hit the Broward Center and then I perform for two nights at the Kravis Center. I'm bringing my mom with me on the trip. Her obsession on airplanes lately is getting into the First Class bathroom. "Why shouldn't I be allowed in? I'm almost 80!" First of all, what does age have to do with it? Next time, buy a first class ticket. And secondly, does she think the First Class bathroom is extra special with a full bath and bidet? It's the same 2-by-3 box as the one at the back of the plane. She's the Rosa Parks of Continental Airlines, without the valid cause.

Speaking of my mom, this week I'm going out to Long Island for the seder and I'm prepared for all the old chestnuts we haul out during the Haggadah reading. Every time we get to the name "Nahor" I say, "Who you calling Na-whore?" My sister's friend Mike added a quip that I'm keeping. When he read the section that begins with, "Verily I am a man of 90," he added, "...though I look 60." Brava on biblical Match.com.

Speaking of Passover, last week I got to play Moses in *Everything's Coming Up Moses* which is a telling of the Passover story through the story and songs of *Gypsy*. Rachel Shukert wrote it all and it's really brilliant. I did it last year and it's easy to know who the real *Gypsy* fans are by how they react to certain lines. The first line they all loved was right at the very beginning. Aaron tells me to stop making the Hebrew slaves think they're going to escape one day. I say, "You just don't get it. Anyone who stays in Egypt is dead!" That was followed by the first knowing laugh. I continued with, "If I die, it won't be from slaving, it'll be from fighting to get up and get out!" Then I sang:

Some Hebrews can get a thrill
hauling stones up a sandy hill.
That's perfect for some Hebrews
who don't know they're alive!

Some Hebrews can thrive and bloom
Digging pits for some Pharaoh's tomb.
That's peachy for some Hebrews
For four centuries or five!

Later on I go into:

I had a dream!
A wonderful dream, Aaron.
All about God in a bush that was burning,
That's all it took for the wheels to start turning...

Then, I bring it home with:

Goodbye! To Desert Sinai!
Good riddance to all the rocks that I had to carry,
All the bricks that I had to cart,
All the mummies I had to bury,
Hey, Red Sea! Get ready to part!

Matt Cavenaugh was Pharaoh but I don't think Pharaoh looked like Matt does in jeans. Hubba hubba. He got a big laugh in the stripper number which was re-done to be about three Jews touting the value of a career. Just like you could tell who the true *Gypsy* fans were from certain laughs, you could tell who the Super Jews were from other laughs. His first lyric was, "You can sing Aleinu, 'til they shout Dayenu!" and it brought down the Shul (AKA 92 Street Y). Bob Morris, who writes for the New York Times and wrote and starred in *Assisted Loving*, played God. At the very end, when all the Jews have left for the Promised Land, but Moses is on Mt. Nebo, I tell him my dream. "An enormous billboard with a picture of your face and mine. Well, actually, just of mine. Yours was hidden." He's supposed to say, "Naturally." But in rehearsal he wanted to add, "And it'll *stay* hidden 'til I get the chin done," but he opted out. My favorite line was right after that. "The Billboard said, 'Holy Moses...and his almighty God. Next year...in Jerusalem." L'chaim!

This week, I saw *The People in the Picture* at the Roundabout's Studio 54. There was added poignancy for me because I went to high school with Leora Brayer (who was part of the theatre gang) and her 9-year-old daughter is making her Broadway debut in the show! *And* Leora was sitting right in front of me watching the matinee when I was there. I felt very proud...and old. During intermission I ran into Iris Rainer Dart, who wrote the script and lyrics (as well as the novel and film "Beaches"). The show is about Holocaust survivors and she told me that *both* little girls in the show are grandchildren of survivors. Amazing. In the show, Donna Murphy has to go back and forth from playing an old lady to very young woman. I saw her backstage and told her that she's doing the Jewish *Color Purple*. (Remember how LaChanze was 14 and then 80). I ran into Chip Zien, who's part of the comedy duo in the show, and, for some reason, we started talking about *Little Shop of Horrors*. He told me that he worked with Howard

Ashman on *Real Life Funnies* (based on the Village Voice comic strip by Stan Mack). Chip and Howard had a falling out and one day he got a call saying that if he apologized to Howard, he would be cast as the lead in a new musical. Chip went to the audition, apologized and waited for the offer. Soon, his good friend Lee Wilkof called him from L.A. and asked what he knew about *Little Shop of Horrors* because they wanted him to audition. Chip said, "Well, I don't know how to tell you this, but I think I have the role already." Lee told him that they had offered to fly him in for the audition so he thought he might as well go. Cut to: Lee got the part! I guess the moral is, don't apologize 'til you get something in writing. Chip gave me the follow-up which is he went to see the show in previews, didn't like it and was thankful he was saved from doing a show that was going to be a flop. I guess he only considers show that run for 2,210 performances a hit. (It ran for 2,209.)

The follow-up to the follow-up is that now Chip has a weekend house in Connecticut. He and his wife swim for exercise and recently, while they were swimming, they saw a canoe coming towards them. His wife kept saying, "I think it's going to hit us" and the canoe kept getting closer. Finally, it came right up to them, and hit Chip on the head! Chip came up from the water and glared at the guy in the canoe... and it was Alan Menken! Chip was like, "What is going on?" Alan said, "I just got this and I don't know how to steer it." Oy! Too many unathletic Jews in one lake. P.S. I guess, now, Alan is the one who has to apologize at the next audition.

O.K., everyone, next week I'll have plenty of material about Florida, the elderly, Jewish people and all of the above wrapped into one — my mother!

My New Radio Show
April 25, 2011

It's finally time to call me the Jewish Oprah. That's right... I'm getting my own talk show! Yes, it's not on TV; yes, it's not every weekday like hers; yes, my listeners will probably be one-tenth of one percent of her viewers; and, yes, my Emmy count is far less than hers at this point (zero vs. many). But, nonetheless, I'm super-excited. I've always wanted to have a talk show on SiriusXM that wasn't just about Broadway. I pitched my idea to the head of the talk channels and he told me I could do a pilot. I was assigned a great producer, booked my guests and we recorded the show in December. And on Sunday May 7, I go on the air! The show is going to run every Sunday from 5-6 PM on Sirius Starz. *And now the show also runs on the Entertainment Weekly channel and the Broadway channel!* Starz is where all the sassy talk shows are; as in Rosie O'Donnell and Barbara Walters *P.S. both of their talk shows are now gone. I am the sole survivor. Along with everyone else who's still on the channel.*

Right now, I'm in sunny West Palm Beach, Florida, looking out my hotel window at the view; tons of cars on the highway. Beautiful? I actually don't mind the totally depressing visage because I'm spending the whole day writing. I'm almost finished with Act Two of my *Disaster* musical (a.k.a. I'm up to the tap dance where a main character dies). Of course, we're having a read-through on Monday and I'm still not done. Why has nothing changed since I took AP English? I still do all of my writing the day before something is due. At least now I don't have a hostile 75-year-old teacher who hates me (Mrs. Jaffe). One time, in the middle of class, she wagged her finger and admitted, "They warned me not to put you in the class!" I, of course, remained blank-faced and said, "Well, now you've learned your lesson." Then she became outraged and let loose with what she deemed her worst insult, sputtering, "Why don't you get out and....and *play your music*!" Yet again, I didn't change my facial expression and asked, "*That* was your best comeback?" Suffice it to say, I didn't ask her to sign my yearbook.

I've been in Florida doing my deconstructing show and so far it's been great. The shows have sold really well and the audiences have been super-responsive. My mother, however, is traveling with me and sharing my hotel room. Here's the "fun" about being with her; when I got back from tech rehearsal, she told me that she complained to the housecleaning staff because the soap in the bathroom was unwrapped *and* wet. I told her that, shockingly, *I* had used the soap! How did she not know that? Did she think she was traveling alone? It reminds me of the time she, not surprisingly, complained to the housecleaning staff because it was noon and they still hadn't cleaned the room. She later realized that she was in California and hadn't re-set her watch, so it was actually just 9 AM when she started her complaint. Yay! Disliked across the country.

Speaking of dislike, we flew Spirit Airlines here. As they say in text language, OMG! WTF! We decided just to take carry-on bags for the trip because it's so much quicker when you get off the flight. When we were getting on, they told us we had to pay for our bags. I explained that they were the standard small carry-on's that would fit in the space above the seat. (I fly almost every week and always take a small bag with me.) Turns out, on Spirit Air, you have to pay $30 to put your bag above your seat! And because I didn't pay when I bought my ticket, I was charged another $15, so it was *$90* for our carry-on bags!!!

Then we got on the flight and the food cart came around. We had eaten so we didn't need to buy food, so my mom just ordered a coffee. Turns out, they charge $2! "But," the flight attendant added, "refills are free." Why wouldn't they be free? The coffee should be free, too! I didn't want coffee so I asked for just a cup of water. "We have bottled water for $3." I didn't want that much, so I just asked for a little cup. *No cups of water.* Yay! Just as Mrs. Jaffe said about the decision to put me in her class: "Never again!"

On Wednesday, I interviewed the lovely Laura Benanti, who is so crazily funny. I was so excited that she got a TV pilot playing the first Playboy bunny. I thought for sure it would highlight her amazing comic chops. Turns out, it's a drama. And not even that new hybrid type of TV show, where it's neither a drama *nor* a comedy, but is oddly considered a comedy because there are so few sitcoms on the air these days. No, it's literally a drama. Someone please write Laura a hilarious role; *Women on the Verge* didn't last long enough and the Chris Durang show she did Off-Broadway was a limited run. Speaking of *Women on the Verge*, the CD has just come out. Laura sings a song that goes incredibly fast and has a *ton* of lyrics. She told me that backstage she would always joke and sing the lyric about how she feels like she swallowed a rock. But she would change the word "rock" to something that rhymed and was, shall we say, raunchier. Cut to: she was onstage and when she got to that lyric she started saying her joke word, but then quickly realized, so it came out "Feel like I swallowed a crock." A crock of what? Country Crock butter? One of the things I love about Laura is that she's so good at making fun of annoying singers. I remember the voice majors at school who wore the musical note scarves tied tightly around their throats (in the spring) and always had hot tea firmly in hand at all times. I asked Laura how she knows everything that self-indulgent singers do and she said because that was pretty much her in high school. We did a Playbill Obsessed video highlighting everything we hate/love about sopranos. Watch on YouTube ASAP!

This week James and I saw *War Horse*, and it was incredibly creative. It's mind-boggling that the horse is such an obvious puppet and has a face that doesn't even move, yet it's able to convey so much emotion. And with a very minimal set, the show made me see what war is really like — more than I ever have before. It's really a testament to the magic of theatre. However, I'm so obsessed with animals that it was difficult for me to watch the show because I kept imagining what I would feel like if I were separated from my dog. I've essentially become like those people who only want to see shows that make them happy. Yay wearing blinders to reality!

This week I'm so excited to see the *Easter Bonnet Competition* which is Monday and Tuesday afternoons. Go to BCEFA.org for tickets for what is always one of the most amazing shows in New York. *This happens every year and in the fall is the Gypsy of the Year competition. It is one of the most incredible shows you will see on Broadway every year. Get tickets whenever you can.* OK, since I'm on a plane back to NYC, I'm going to put my tray into an upright and locked position and take a nap. Peace out!

I Won an IRNE!
May 2, 2011

I won! First of all, let me say that for weeks I had "The Teddy Awards" written on my iPhone calendar. I could not remember what the H it was. Was I hosting? Nominated? I did a search of all of my emails and couldn't find any mention of it. I Googled it and saw that is was a gay/lesbian award…in Berlin. Was I nominated for my piano playing on the German tour of *A Chorus Line* in the early '90s? Why did I write down "The Teddy Awards"? *Finally*, I realized that I was referring to the Independent Reviewers of New England Award, for which I was nominated. I had thought it was so hilarious that the acronym was the "IRNE" and therefore basically unpronounceable. I finally found out it's pronounced "Ernie" but I had put it on my calendar as the Teddy Awards because it reminded me of the awards ceremony that Mary Tyler Moore was always going to on her show. Remember? One year, she doesn't hear the name of the winner and Rhoda tells her she won *but she didn't*? And she goes up to the stage? Hilarious and devastating. Anyhoo, I wanted to travel to Boston for the ceremony but I had a read-through of my new *Disaster* musical on Monday and couldn't make it up there in time. I sent a speech to read in case I won and, turns out, I did! *Deconstructing Broadway* won "Best Visiting Show" for when I did it at SpeakEasy Stage Company. I wish I had seen my speech read, but this is what I made the representative from SpeakEasy read:

"Hi, everyone. It's Seth writing on my laptop because, unfortunately, I had to be in New York tonight. Let me first say 'Yay! I'm so excited I won. If that 'yay' seemed a little low energy it's because the person reading it didn't convey the energy I wanted to express. Perhaps he or she is tired after a long day. Let me also say thank you so much for voting for my show. If that 'thank you' seemed a little disingenuous, yet again it's because the person reading it wasn't able to convey my gratitude and perhaps he or she has difficulty in his or her own life saying 'thank you.' Finally, let me give a big thank you to Speakeasy for bringing me up to Boston and if any of you missed my show, I'm happy to say I'll be doing it all summer long at the Art House in Provincetown. Hopefully, the reader of this speech conveyed my internal desperation for an audience and my annoying penchant for self-promotion. Peace out!"

Now, on to the next piece of business: Attention theatre audiences — stop applauding at the end of scenes! I can't take it. I went to see *The Normal Heart*, which was phenomenal in so many different aspects — which I will relate — but first, let me address my initial comment. There were so many incredible scenes that ended with me riveted and wanting to bask in the various emotions that were stirred, but instead, because there was a blackout, some idiot in the audience felt "When there's a blackout, we must applaud." No, we mustn't! It was so infuriating. There was electricity in the audience that no one wanted to break, but then the idiot, or idiots would start their crazy clapping and the rest of the audience felt the peer pressure and joined in. Stop! Have some sense of theatricality! That's right, I've had it. *I'm editing this in Provincetown and that literally just happened in the boot camp class! The instructor said something positive and some idjit felt the need to start applause. Only a few people joined in so it wound up being extremely awkward. Only applaud when absolutely necessary. Make it mean something!*

Now, back to the show. It was so fantastic for many reasons. First of all, the history lessons were fascinating. The fact that no one knew what AIDS was at first, yet people kept dying. I remember talking to Dick Scanlan, who wrote the book/lyrics to *Thoroughly Modern Millie*, and he told me how scared everyone was in the early '80s when they were trying to figure out what the disease was and how people caught it. He remembered one theory about people getting it at discos when their sweat flew onto someone else. In *The Normal Heart* it makes it so clear how the mayor refused to address the

43

disease as more and more people literally died *in the city of which he was the mayor*! How President Reagan, the so-called "Great Communicator," didn't even mention the word AIDS until 20,849 people had *died* in the country that he was the president of. It's so shameful, I'm mortified writing about it. The play is by Larry Kramer and it describes how he founded, and was ultimately kicked out of, the Gay Men's Health Crisis. Joe Mantello is fantastic playing the play's version of Larry. The character, Ned Weeks, is so angry and bombastic (basically the reason why he was kicked out of GMHC) yet Joe is able to play so many layers of him. After I lauded Joe in an email , he wrote me back that he had seen the original production back at the Public Theater and it stayed with him ever since. "That's why I'm up there on that stage every night," he wrote me. I have to say the whole cast was so good, I wish there was a Best Ensemble Tony Award. Ellen Barkin portrays the doctor based on Dr. Linda Laubenstein who, at one point, was seeing more AIDS patients than anyone in the world and she developed the chemotherapy combinations that are still used to this day. There's a scene in the play that gave me one of those theatrical experiences I'll always remember: the doctor is addressing the National Institute of Health, the leaders of which have decided to deny ample funding to AIDS research despite the thousands of deaths that had happened already. There's mention of the horrific fact that within two weeks of the Tylenol poisoning case (where *seven* people died) *$10 million* was spent. Ellen Barkin lashes out at them in such a brilliantly scathing yet devastating way that I had the same reaction I had when I went to the ER with a finger infection. In 2003, I was doing *Rhapsody in Seth*, where I had to play *Rhapsody in Blue*, and I had this infection on my finger that was getting worse and worse. I finally couldn't sleep and went to the Roosevelt Hospital ER. The doctor told me she would take care of it but the anesthesia would hurt, so I could just skip it and get right to the lancing. When she cut it, it hurt *so much* but I was so happy to have it over that I was crying *and* laughing at the same time. Ellen Barkin's diatribe against the National Institute of Health was so scathing yet oddly hilarious that when she yelled her last line I sat in the blackout literally crying and laughing just like I did in the ER. *The Normal Heart* makes you realize how much impact theatre can have and how incredibly important it is for everyone to have access to it. What a difference it would make if everyone could see the struggle those early AIDS pioneers faced and how bravely they overcame the incredible obstacles put in front of them not only by the government by their own gay community. Go see it ASAP! *It's no longer on Broadway but they wound up filming it for HBO so, as I just said, see it ASAP!*

Speaking of AIDS organizations, I went to see the *Easter Bonnet Competition*. So many great moments, but of course one of my favorites was Jen Cody and Don Richard as their *Urinetown* characters dishing Broadway. They came out in hazmat suits and Officer Lockstock said, "Well, Little Sally, after a long absence, we have been asked back by BC/EFA to head their new disaster response team. We are here to help prevent any disasters before they hit Broadway." Jen responded, "Too late." Then, I loved the fact that Jen is married to Hunter Foster yet has no shame dishing him. At one point, Officer Lockstock offers a way to protect audiences by asking if they should find "a large, empty space where people can find shelter." She asks, "How about *Million Dollar Quartet* at around 8 PM?" Hunter literally stars in that show! Brava future marriage counseling.

I love my latest *Obsessed* video because I did it with my old friend, Traci Lyn Thomas, and we re-hashed stories from the last 20 years, including her *Les Miz* audition where she tried to end Cosette's song on a Mariah Carey whistle tone. Horrifying. Yet *she got cast*!

P.S. I got sassed by a Tony and Emmy Award winner on Twitter. I posted: "35 min on stair climber! I want to look 1970's skinny for my Disaster Movie Musical. 23 days to go." I got mostly laudatory comments and then Andrea Martin posted: "Someone might want to commit to more than 35 minutes, if you get my drift. But good for you." *P.S. To this day, Andrea and I are constantly complaining to* each other about our own weight and obsessing about dieting. As Andrea often says to me, 'I'd kill for diarrhea'.

Speaking of *Disaster!!!*, I had lots of the actors over at my apartment to read the script for the first time. My co-writer is Jack Plotnick and he was "at" the read-thru on Skype. It was so modern-age. The only mind-boggling part was when we all saw the computer moving around on his end and we finally realized he was taking us with him...to go pee. Wow. Tip o' the hat to *Urinetown*? I'm just glad he didn't double book the read-thru and a colonoscopy. Regardless, the script got so many laughs. Now we just have to finish it. Ouch. Nonetheless, I'm very excited about the show! Now...peace out!

The Tenth Anniversary of *The Producers*
May 9, 2011

So much is going on! Let me start from the top of the week. On Sunday night, I went out to the George Street Playhouse to do their yearly fundraiser. Tyler Maynard and I sang "Two Nobodies in New York" from *[title of show]*, which was so much fun to haul out again. What was *not* fun is that Tyler has been working out and looks amazing where I resembled Tawny Jo. Who's Tawny Jo you ask? Well, the first show I did in NYC was *Pageant*, which was a beauty pageant with the contestants played by men in drag and the audience voting on who won. It's truly one of the funniest shows I've ever seen and I was SO happy to be a part of it. At one point, Miss West Coast is voted Miss Congeniality, which the host says is bestowed on "the one contestant the other girls would most like to be friends with...if they only had the time." Right after that award, the finals begin. The host calls the names of the finalists: Miss Industrial Northeast, Miss Great Plains, Miss Deep South, Miss Texas and finally Miss Bible Belt. It always brought the house down when the audience realized that poor Miss West Coast is the *only* contestant who doesn't make it to the finals. After all the finalists are called forward, she stands by herself in the background as the curtain sl-o-o-o-owly closes in front of her. At the last minute, she plaintively holds out her "Miss Congeniality" medallion...and the curtain completely shuts with her in that pose. Hilarious. Then, at the end, the winner of last year's pageant (played by the actor playing Miss West Coast) comes back to crown whomever the new winner is. Her name is Tawny Jo and, the joke is, she's gained around 100 pounds since last year's pageant. So, I felt like Tawny Jo next to Tyler. P.S. I haven't gained 100 pounds (maybe 5...rounded down from 10) but singing next to someone who now wears a size zero gave me a healthy dose of body shame.

Right after I made my appearance as Orca, I hightailed it back to the city to go to *The Producers* tenth anniversary party. Ten years! Yowtch! I remember when I first got that gig. I was walking home with Paul Castree after going out to brunch for my birthday. Phil Reno (who was the associate conductor) asked me if I could assist on the show. Patrick Brady, the conductor, told him it was his compensation to me because in 1997 Patrick was conducting *Triumph of Love* and, when he had to leave to do *Fosse*, he asked me to take over as pianist-conductor. I started working on the score so I could take over at the beginning of January when all of a sudden, the show got its closing notice. Wah wah. Well, I thought, I'll just stay at Grease where I'm assistant music director. Then *Grease* got its closing notice! Not cool! *But*, before I was out of a job, I got an offer to be a comedy writer on the "The Rosie O'Donnell Show," so it worked out deliciously. When Phil Reno called me for *The Producers*, though, I was l-o-w on money so it was great timing. The show got great reviews in its Chicago tryout but of course nobody could predict what a massive hit it would become. I remember Mel Brooks saying during previews, 'Yes, we got great reviews out-of-town, but who knows what the New York ones will be." Well, they were incredible! For those of you too young to remember that triumph — it was *The Book of Mormon* of its day. And for those of you way too old, it was the *Tobacco Road* of its day. *And now I can say it was the Dear Evan Hansen of its day!* I remember going to 42nd Street Studios to watch them do run-throughs. Thrilling. And I remember Nathan Lane asking me one day during a break if I knew Jim Borstelmann. Of course, yenta-style I said, "Why? Does somebody have a crush on him?" No. It was because they decided to add one more male swing to the Broadway company and Jim was making the bold move of leaving his steady job in *Chicago* to do it. What's crazy about Broadway is that Jim did the entire run of *The Producers* and *Young Frankenstein* and is now in *The Addams Family* and... *Chicago* is still going strong! *And as I edit this, it's still hauling 8 shows a week!* What was really different for me about *The Producers* is that I usually came into the pits of Broadway shows once they were running so I was used to hearing the songs played with an orchestra. When I joined, they hadn't yet made a cast album so I only know how the songs sounded with rehearsal piano. *Then* I got to sit in the pit and hear how Larry Blank and Doug Besterman orchestrated it. I wish I could describe how exciting that was for me. For instance, I had only known the introduction of the song "Opening Night" as a vamp played in my right and left hand. Suddenly, I was in the pit and the right hand part I knew was being played by muted brass/woodwinds and the left was played by the string section. So cool!!!!

Last Sunday, as soon as I walked into the party I saw Matthew Broderick texting and I decided to give him what James always busts me with: "Be present!" I sassed as I walked by. It was super crowded and Eric Gunhus (who was the original blond Nazi who sang "Springtime for Hitler") put together a great treat for us: video footage of the show. There was something very magical about watching "Springtime for Hitler" with the people who performed it while Susan Stroman was sitting to the left of me. When it got to the final part of the number where the ensemble is doing a formation that is reflected in the mirrors on the ceiling and literally looks like a swastika, everyone broke into applause. Then Eric showed a photo montage of the courtroom scene and played the audio from the night that Mel Brooks himself went on as the judge. He was hilarious. At one point, we watched the character of Leo reappears with his new wife, Ulla. He gives back all the money that was stolen and says, "Here's all the money. Minus two tickets for Brazil and one large tub of cocoa butter." Mel muttered, "That never got a laugh." Which was a hilarious inside bust because it really was a funny line and it literally never got a laugh. Then Nathan and Matthew sang the beautiful song "'Til Him" and after all the applause died down, the Judge declared, "Whoever wrote that song is a genius!" Brava.

This week was the debut of my new talk show on SiriusXM Stars called *Seth Speaks*. It went SO well. I interviewed Louise Owen who was recently featured on "60 Minutes" because she has "superior autobiographical memory" meaning she can remember any day of her life; the day of the week, the weather, the main events that happened that day, etc. Speaking of *The Producers*, she was a violinist in that pit, although I know we met at some time before that. I didn't recall exactly when but, naturally, she did. She told me "I first saw you perform on January 9th, 1997, at Caroline's but we met when you were hosting a comedy show downtown on April 26th in 1997." I asked what day of the week that was and she immediately told me Thursday and Saturday. Yikes!

I also had the hilarious Ana Gasteyer from "SNL" and we talked about when she played Celine Dion on the show and then actually appeared in one of Celine Dion's concerts. She was hilarious describing how she had to wear what Celine was wearing that night — a "ladies tuxedo with an extended cummerbund." It was the year of the "Titanic" song and Ana told us that she walked out onto the stage at Madison Square Garden and launched into it. Then Celine "surprised" her onstage and the audience went crazy. On "SNL," Ana would play Celine as an incredible narcissist and would constantly repeat, in her French Canadian accent, "I 'ave the best voice...in the *world*!" Celine, though, didn't understand what the joke was and actually thought people laughed because Ana didn't sing well! Which is crazy because Ana sings great. Celine gave her the run-down of how the scene in her concert would work and said, "Ana! It will be 'ilarious because you will come out singing and everyone will laugh because you sound *so 'orrible*!" Ana is doing her own show and I'm obsessed with the title: *Elegant Songs from a Handsome Lady*. Brava!

On Saturday night, James and I went to Birdland and saw *Boom*, featuring sisters Liz Callaway and Ann Hampton Callaway singing amazing Alex Rybeck arrangements of 1960s and '70s classics. I cannot *wait* for the CD so I can deconstruct it. *I got the CD and my deconstruction of Ann's "Blowing In The Wind" is on my Youtube channel. I love it!* Not surprisingly, Liz was so funny. First she outed Ann for being the older sister by saying, "I was at Ann's apartment and saw a really interesting article in her

AARP magazine." Ann then busted Liz for recently becoming old enough for AARP and Liz countered with, "Yes, but I just started getting the magazine. I'm glad I know where to go to get *lots* of back issues." They sound so great together and James and I are obsessed with Liz's voice because it always has this sweet young girl quality, which is something Lillias White has as well. Ann was *brilliant* on "You've Lost That Loving Feeling," which is not even a song I particularly like. At first she literally sounded like a smoky bass, but was then belting crazy high notes, singing soprano *and* doing incredibly fluid riffs. After the show I praised her and she told me that because she's classically trained, she literally thinks of her voice as an orchestra, i.e. the low strings, the high brass, the mellow clarinets etc. O.K. I can also "think of my voice" that way but I can't actually create it! P.S. Speaking of belting, the reason I was there is because Steve Marzullo, my music director for *Disaster!* told me that Liz is belting higher than ever before in the show. He knows I love belting so, of course, that led me to immediately get tickets through Jim Caruso, even though it was officially sold out. Liz did belt but I didn't think it was any higher than I've heard her before. After the show, Liz proudly 'fessed up that she used Steve as a tool to get me there and told him to lie and tell me she was belting F's. Well, quite frankly, it worked! Even though I love seeing theatre where people are playing characters, there was something very special about being at an evening that was all about music. So many musicians were in the audience, loving it. Jeff Saver, my friend who's played and conducted tons of Broadway shows brought his two daughters and sitting in the

front row was lyricist (and great singer) Lynn Ahrens, who told me she didn't know where to look onstage because the singing *and* the band were both so amazing. Jeff texted me after: "Wasn't that some sort of wonderful? I'm so joyful tonight!" I concur! You must order their CD. The show was amazing!!!

My "crew": Lin, Andrea and Peter.

I'm in Canada this weekend with Andrea Martin's show *and* we had rehearsal this week with director Peter Flynn because adding an amazing rap for her Edith Prickley character written by Lin-Manuel Miranda. *Yes, he wrote rap for "In The Heights", "Hamilton"....and Andrea Martin!* And speaking of hip hop, peace out!

Disaster by Skype, My Celebrity Party and Stritch Meets Walsh
May 16, 2011

I'm writing this on Andrea Martin's deck that looks out onto the beautiful Toronto River. P.S. I have no idea if there is indeed a "Toronto River" but I'm in Toronto and there's water in front of me, ergo Toronto River. Anyhoo, having this lovely Toronto view is the great part. The sad part is that I agreed to do this gig before I knew I'd be in rehearsals for my *1970's Disaster Movie Musical* (that happens on May 23rd !) so I'm devastated that I have to miss two days of rehearsals. BUT, apparently this is 2011 and there are many means of communication. That's right, I finally got Skype on my Mac and watched rehearsal from Toronto. It was amazing! It was literally like I was there; I was able to give ideas, change or add lines, and watch how the show is progressing. The only annoying thing was, even though I was "at" rehearsal, I was really just a face on a computer, sitting on a desk. Whenever I wanted to pipe up with a comment, it involved a lot of arm waving, yelling and continuous pointing to my own face until someone noticed me. I had so much fun watching the scene where George Dvorsky is trapped in a room on the ship and seawater starts to flood in. I don't want to ruin the plot, but suffice it to say things don't turn out so well. Especially after two sharks appear.

I started the week with a benefit for the Upper West Side JCC, with a cast that included Tituss Burgess *way before "Unbreakable Kimmy Schmidt" and his two Emmy nominations!,* Andrea Burns, Andrea McArdle and Ana Gasteyer. When I interviewed Ana last on *Seth Speaks* (my new radio show), she told me that even though she starred in *Wicked* for more than a year, she's forgotten most of the show. She said it extended not only to the various songs she sang, but to the actual plot. Basically, she pretty much only remembers there's a green witch at some point in the show. After that, blank. I loved her (what I thought was) exaggeration. Cut to: we did a sound check for the JCC event and ran "The Wizard and I." I then discovered she wasn't telling me one of those exaggerated talk show stories. She literally had forgotten large parts of the lyrics...and the actual melody! I think it must be from doing sketches on "SNL." You cram them for one week and then put them out of your head. Luckily, before the performance, we had time to review (and print out the lyrics!) and she wound up bringing down ye olde house. I had rehearsed my *Disaster!* musical all day and was so unprepared for the show that night. There was so much last minute rehearsing printing of music, trying to find an outfit etc. I filmed it all and you can watch it online! *Maybe it was a mistake to post a video of how unprofessional I was. Guess who was never hired back by the JCC?* Afterwards, Ana and Andrea joined me at Citrus (on 75th Street) for dinner and the conversation turned to getting busted for dishing someone. Ana has a good friend (whose name you'd know from TV) who was auditioning for a film. Well, sometimes when you go in for films, the casting person has photos of the people starring in the film outside the audition room. So, the famous friend walked in, pointed to a photo of one of the big stars and entertained the room by saying, "Look at this one! She wasn't exactly hit with the funny stick, was she?" Meaning, she's decidedly not funny. One of the women behind the desk looked up and simply said, "I'm her mother." Yowtch! And *then* the famous friend got cast in the movie. Excellent. I'm sure it was not at all awkward on the set.

Tuesday I recorded my second *Seth Speaks* show and it was so fun. I had Patrick Wilson as my celeb guest. I can't take the gorgeousness. I first met him in 1997 when he played the role of Chopin in *Harmony* by Barry Manilow and Bruce Sussman, and, 14 years later, he actually looks better. Also on the show, I played the game "Celebrity" with Ana Gasteyer because I had once invited her to my birthday party which was going to be a game night... specifically Celebrity (where one player has a hatful of celeb names and gives clues so the other player can guess). So I called and invited her to my Celebrity Birthday Party and she said yes, but sounded miffed on the phone. Finally, we spoke a few days later and I found out the reason for her weirdness on the phone: she thought that having a Celebrity Birthday Party meant I was only inviting celebrities! What the — ? Like, I was having my birthday party so I could make it into Walter Winchell's column??

Anyhoo, I played Celebrity with Ana on my first radio show and she only guessed five names in the one minute allotted. But then Patrick and I played…. and he got 11 names! We still got it! I then made him re-tell my favorite *Full Monty* story which begins when they were on Broadway doing the final strip from the show and at one point, the guys realized the light cues were off. They didn't know if the cues were ahead or behind, but they knew they were off. Suddenly, they all realized the cues were ahead. This was a nightmare because the song normally ended with all the guys getting *totally* nude and a big light from behind would blind the audience. This was immediately followed by the curtain call. That night, the guys realized that the blinding light would come one cue early and then, when they became totally nude, the lights would be the curtain-call cue. In other words, the nude scene would have the *brightest lights of the night*! They all accepted they had to finish the number, and right before a mortified Patrick took it all off, he happened to lock eyes with someone in the audience…a ten-year-old girl. He said that when the final moment came, she looked horrified and he ran the gamut from trying to convey sympathy with his eyes Norma Desmond-style, to complete annoyance that the girl had been brought to the show in the first place.

This week I'm interviewing one of my comedy idols: Martin Short. I cannot tell you how excited I am!

Good ol' "Elaine Stritch."

I also interviewed Barbara Walsh who is so funny and talented. I asked her about playing Joanne in the revival of *Company*. During the run, she met Elaine Stritch at a fancy lunch. Elaine took one look at her and said in her signature growl, "You're too young for the part." Barbara was confused because she was actually *older* than Elaine was when she played it. The lunch itself was actually an interview with the both of them for a magazine. And by "interview" Barbara explained that Elaine did all the talking. At the end of the lunch Elaine told her, "I'm gonna come see the show, but I won't tell you when because I don't want you to be nervous knowing I'm in the audience." Cut to: Elaine showed up one night and was her version of non-descript by sitting in the fifth row wearing a *white* suit with a *white* cap. If a lighthouse could get a ticket to a Broadway show, then Elaine was that lighthouse. The nice part is that backstage after the show Barbara heard, "Where's Barbara? Where's Barbara?" Elaine found her, held her face in her hands and told her how wonderful she was. Someone then asked for a photo of the two of them, and suddenly Barbara was confused because she didn't hear any joke being told. Why was she thinking a joke was told? Because at the moment the picture was taken, Elaine threw her head back in laughter. That's right. Apparently, Elaine likes to take all photos with her signature *At Liberty* head-thrown-back, mouth-agape pose.

Last week, I posted on my Facebook that I couldn't get my iPhone to work with my computer. Everyone had advice for me and suddenly I had a message from Alison Fraser. Turns out, the guy who runs her website, Kristopher Monroe, was over at her place and kept seeing people posting *wrong* advice under my profile! He couldn't take it anymore, so he asked her to message me that he would look at my computer if I wanted. The delicious part is that he lives *around the corner* from me. I dropped off my computer and got it back the next morning, completely sassed out! *Everything* was updated, cleaned and sassified. I literally thought I was going to have to buy a new computer because so many things were clanky, but now it's like I have a brand new model. Essentially, my computer pulled a Hollywood star routine: it went away for "rest and relaxation" and came back looking completely different. Kris also does computer training for show biz folks so I commandeered him into showing me things like transferring my old phone contacts into my new iPhone. That's right, for months my response to almost every text I've gotten is "Who is this?" Yay! Now I know it's my boyfriend and not my mother when I receive a text saying, "See you tonight, sexy." And on that inappropriate note, let me wrap it up by saying that this week I'm seeing the opening night of *Lucky Guy* starring Leslie Jordan and Varla Jean Merman. Peace out!

A *Disaster* in the Making, Plus a Few Minutes With Jiminy Glick
May 23, 2011

What a week! First of all, tonight is the very first performance of *Disaster*, the '70's disaster-movie musical I wrote with my friends Jack Plotnick with additional material by Drew Geraci. Tomorrow, I'm off to Boston to do an expanded version of my "Brady Bunch Variety Hour" deconstruction show called *That 70's Deconstruction Show* which features not just the Brady Bunch singing (-ish) and (sort of) dancing to 70s pop and disco hits, but also other 70s Variety Shows that perhaps should be forgotten.
Sunday night I saw Susie Mosher's amazing one-woman-show *The Great Daisy Theory* and, wow, was it good! I'm obsessed with the section where she shows a montage of all the small film and TV roles she played when she lived in L.A. She accompanies the montage by singing "Eye of the Tiger" and ends it by singing "And he's watchin' us all in the eye..." and it segues to her saying the word "I-i-i-i-I" and then the full sentence, "I-i-i-i-I made $30,000!" Pause. "In ten years." Devastating poverty level living. I went to see it with Jack Plotnick who had just flown in from London where he was filming a Best Buy commercial. When he got the audition, he was doing a movie in L.A. and the London people asked him to film himself dancing down the street for his commercial audition. He kept his film costume on and got his friend to film him. He was dancing to "Stayin' Alive" but after he filmed, he changed it to the song that the commercial was going to use and it weirdly matched up perfectly. He sent in the tape and booked the job. He just put his audition tape up on youtube. It's so much fun!

Last Tuesday, I recorded my new talk show *Seth Speaks*, and had my comedy idol, Martin Short, as the guest star. There's always this idiot theory amongst certain comics that women aren't funny which is so strange to me because my favorite comics growing up were mainly women; Lucy, Carol Burnett, Andrea Martin, Gilda Radner and Catherine O'Hara. And there were very few guys I really worshipped, but Martin was one of them. Anyway, I was so thrilled to talk to him and he was, of course, brilliantly funny. I literally wanted to spend hours with him asking him about every character. I asked him to do Jiminy Glick for me and he told me that the voice was based on a man who lived in his neighborhood who would promise to "(in high voice) Take ya to the movies (low voice) if ya stay off my lawn all year."

He mentioned that he's 61 and I asked him why he looked so young and he said he never got any work done, "Because no one ever looks at that person and says, 'Ooh, there goes that 38-year-old,' they say, 'There goes that 61-year-old who looks like a burn victim.'"

He's from Canada and was in that amazing before-they-were-stars production of *Godspell* with Andrea Martin, Gilda Radner, Eugene Levy, Victor Garber and, as music director Paul Shaffer. Marty had just come from doing "Letterman" and was meeting Paul Shaffer for dinner after my show. Paul came with him to SiriusXM and was sitting in the audio booth and Marty brought him into the studio after the interview. I was telling the audience how Paul had written the amazing song "It's Raining Men" years before for Donna Summer but she didn't want to sing it because she was a Christian and there were too many "Hallelujahs," etc. The next thing I know, Paul is sitting at the piano and starts playing "It's Raining Men" and I start singing it...in the original key. It was a crazy combination of belting, head voice and vocal damage. Then Marty told us that there's going to be a *Godspell* reunion in NYC featuring everyone cast from the last 40 years. That lead to a rousing version of "God Save the People" featuring Paul and Marty...and me on the last note. This whole thing was videotaped so go to Youtube and look up Martin Short, Seth Rudetsky and Paul Shaffer! So much fun!

The bad part about the week is that I had started to feel sick last Monday night and it got worse. On Friday, I showed up to rehearsal and literally had to lie down with my eyes closed. I felt like I had to go to sleep no matter what *and* the liquid in my head was giving me crazy vertigo. I felt *so* sick that I was terrified I wouldn't be able to do my *Disaster* show. P.S. Everyone was obsessed with the fact that I was lying down completely, with my eyes closed, yet I was still giving notes on the show. Nothing stops my controlling ways! I actually had to leave rehearsal (!) and saw the allergist to the stars, Barry Kohn, who prescribed me tons of stuff and I was able to be at rehearsal the next day, good as new! Yay Barry, Claritin, Z-pac, Flonase and steroids!

And Yay Varla Jean Merman. I went to the opening night of *Lucky Guy* which stars Varla Jean (real name Jeffrey Roberson) and Leslie Jordan. First of all, Jenn Colella does so much great comedy in the show and hits crazy belted high notes. *And now she's a Tony nominee for Come From Away!* And Varla pulls *every* comedy trick out of the book. The audience *loved* all of her hilarious bits and, even though I hate to read reviews, I was thrilled that the New York Times compared Varla and Leslie to Carol Burnett and Harvey Korman. What a coup!

All right, I've spent the whole week obsessing about *Disaster!*, changing lines and piping up during rehearsal with comedy bits and now I have to actually learn my part. The show is about to happen! Peace out 'til next week!

My *Disaster!* Sings
May 31, 2011

Hello from Logan Airport. I'm in Boston after doing my *The '70s Deconstruction Show* which is basically my "Brady Bunch Variety Hour" show with some other variety shows thrown in for shock value. I must say, the SpeakEasy Stage audience up here is amazing! I had heard Boston audiences can be hard, but the people that show up for my shows are so responsive. Essentially, if they had been in Boston in the early '70s, *Prettybelle* would have been a smash. Now I'm flying up to Canada to do two shows with Andrea Martin. I'm obsessed with the new Edith Prickley rap that Lin-Manuel Miranda wrote. Fave part? "I'm Prickley and I'm loud! I'm Prickley and I'm proud! I'm wearing leopard print so you can pick me in a crowd!"

May 23 was the first performance ever of *Disaster!* If you don't know, for around 15 years I've been wanting to write a jukebox musical based on 1970s disaster movies. My friend Drew Geraci and I were doing *Forever Plaid* back in the '90s, and we wanted the show to be called *Blackout '77*. The show was going to be about the big New York City blackout that happened during that summer. We would talk about it but always faded out when it came to writing it. Then Dena Hammerstein and Pam Pariseau, who run the not-for-profit Only Make Believe, asked me to do a benefit. They helm a great organization that brings theatre to hospitalized kids, and I work with them every year on their big gala benefit. They told me that their donors are big fans of mine and would love to see me do a show. Well, I decided to strike! I picked a date and knew that would force me to write the show. It began as a musical about the 1977 blackout into a show but I suddenly thought it would more fun if it featured every disaster-movie disaster: earthquake, tidal wave, fire, rats, killer fish, etc. Dena Hammerstein's son owns The Box and donated it for the night so we could do our show. I am thoroughly un-hip and I wasn't quite familiar with what The Box is famous for. Let's just say, they have very "unique" acts. My friend went to a show there and told me that he saw a reverse striptease. Meaning? A woman came out totally nude and got dressed using clothes she had on her person. What's that, you ask? Where did she get her clothes from if she was completely nude? Think it through. That's correct.

Me and Jack in DISASTER! costume!

Also, while we were rehearsing, some of the ladies went to the toilet downstairs. Suddenly, they started posting a slew of pictures taken of each of them in the stall. Why? Because the toilet had stirrups on either side of it...with a mirror angled down from the ceiling. I guess if you're going to "do it," you might as well watch it. And I'm out. Regardless, the club is so cool-looking inside and was perfect for our show. Literally like a luxurious cruise ship. We tech'd it all day on Monday and suddenly it was 7 PM. The place was filled with supporters of Only Make Believe, and from the get-go they were completely on board. They got *all* of the jokes, and because they all knew me from the previous benefits, I got full entrance applause. I felt like Angela Lansbury coming out at the beginning of "It's Today." The most moving part for me was watching Will Reynolds sing "Alone Again, Naturally." I love that song so much, and when I started thinking of '70s songs for the show, I was obsessed with getting that song in. after I started writing it, I was in Palm Springs, and driving around with Jack Plotnick. We kept brainstorming how to make the song work. We were blasting it on his CD player in the car and after listening again and again, we *finally* came up with an idea that we thought would make the song make sense in the show. On the night of the show, I was watching from the back as Will started singing and I got tears in my eyes because I remembered us struggling to get the song into the show and suddenly it was happening in front of me. So exciting! *And we wound up losing the rights to that song and had to replace it on Broadway! Thankfully, the replacement was one of the biggest highlights of the show! It was Adam Pascal singing "(I Can't Live! If Living is) Without You!" and he ended it on a high B. Listen to the cast album to hear it!* One problem we had during the tech was getting a good look for Michael Longoria. He played ten-year-old twins, Ben and Lisa. As Ben, he just wore a baseball cap, but for Lisa they gave him a baseball cap with braids the color of his hair. The problem was the braids were far back in the cap and the color of the hair was so dark that they didn't really change his face enough to make us able to differentiate him as Lisa. Thankfully, Lauren Kennedy (who plays his sexy mom in the show) is new-school (AKA when she wants to grow her hair longer, she simply attaches extensions). She had a *ton* of extra extensions that she wasn't planning on using and, right before the show, Michael had long plaits of Lauren-colored hair attached to his baseball cap. And...ten-year-old girl!

The cast was so great and I filmed a little bit of rehearsal for my Playbill.com Obsessed! series. In the second act, Ben (played by Michael) passes out because he's diabetic and Lisa (played by Michael) has to carry him to get his insulin. In the show, Michael carried a dummy dressed exactly like Ben. The video is on Youtube and he sounds amazing! *We realized when it moved Off-Broadway that we had to use a child to make it more real and 13-year-old Clark Oliver got the part and was amazing!*

In the Secret Garden photo frame

While I was rehearsing *Disaster!*, Juli was rehearsing *The Secret Garden: Spring Version*. It was a 70-minute edition put on by The Broadway Workshop that will soon be available for schools to do. Marc Tuminelli directed it amazingly. I couldn't believe the focus of those kids! Everyone in the ensemble had to stay onstage throughout the *entire* show and sit on chairs that were lined up on the perimeter of the stage. But they weren't allowed to sit like I do (legs splayed, upper body hunched), they had to sit at the edge of their seats, hands clasped in their laps and back completely straight. For the whole show! Hmm...how do I get Juli to do that at home? The kids were also fully costumed, mic'd and either had their hair done up 1800s style, or they were wigged. They also had cool giant set pieces (see photo). Where was The Broadway Workshop when I was a kid? Why was I forced to hole up for hours in my den choreographing a solo version of "Magic To Do" that never got performed? Go to www.The BroadwayWorkshop.com for info on their next workshop/class.

On Saturday night, James and I went to see "Bridesmaids" starring Kristen Wiig. First of all, I thought it was so incredibly funny. I was laughing with crazy heaving noises. Secondly, on the way out we ran into Gavin Creel, who *also* loved it. He got a super short haircut and looks great. We were talking about goals and I know that he usually gets what he sets his sights on. I remember he told me that when he was in college, he dreamed of originating a role in a brand new Sondheim show that wasn't a revival *and* getting his own song. Cut to: just a few years after college he debuted an original part and song in Sondheim's *Bounce*! As Oprah says, "Secret!!!!"

Speaking of funny women from "SNL," I *loved* "Bossypants," the comic memoir by Tina Fey. I was reading it on a plane and I know the guy next to me thought I was crazy. Why? Because every minute I was laughing full volume, and he never turned and asked "Wow! What are you reading?" or, "Must be a funny book." He literally just stared straight ahead as I broke into loud guffaws. He was employing my patented technique of "If I don't acknowledge the craziness next to me, I can't be sucked into it." Here is one of my favorite sections. Tina Fey writes about the rules of doing a magazine cover shoot. This is the part where she discusses what to do when they ask you what kind of music you want to have played throughout the shoot.

She writes, "Remember that whatever you choose will be blasted through the loft and heard by an entire crew of people who are all so cool that the Board of Ed. officially closed. Just murmur 'Hip-hop,' or make up the name of a hipster-sounding band and then act superior when they've never heard of it. 'Do you guys have any Asphalt of Pinking? [*disappointed*] Really? [*shrug*] Whatever you want then.' Sometimes they ask if you want to hook up your iPod for background music. Do not do this. It's a trap. They'll put it on shuffle, and no matter how much Beastie Boys or Velvet Underground you have on there, the following four tracks will play in a row: 'We'd Like to Thank You, Herbert Hoover' (from *Annie*), 'Hold On' by Wilson Phillips, 'That's What Friends Are For' and "We'd Like to Thank You, Herbert Hoover.'"

She is so funny! Speaking of *Annie* (and Gavin), not only am I going to be doing my own show three days a week in Provincetown at The Art House, but I'm also heading a Broadway series there. I booked some of my favorite performers to come up and do their show with me playing. The line-up is: Jackie Hoffman, Charles Busch, Ana Gasteyer, Marilyn Maye, Adam Pascal, Andrea McArdle and Gavin Creel. Yowza! *Wow! Thanks to my producer Mark Cortale who still produces them, Provincetown Broadway series has been running all these years and now I also do it in Ft. Lauderdale, Los Angeles, New Orleans, San Francisco and London!*

Peace out!

Brian Bedford, Nicole Parker, Those *Mormon* Kids
June 7, 2011

Maggie outside the Tony Awards

Welcome to June! We are getting so close to Tony Award time and, quite literally, the Tony Awards are so close to me. "Meaning what," you ask? Well, this year they're being held at the Beacon Theater which is down the block from my apartment! I literally walk my dog, Maggie, past where the red carpet will be. P.S. If Maggie had access to that red carpet it would soon have a lovely yellow tinge. That's right, there's nothing she loves more that peeing on any object on the street: plastic bags, scraps of fabric and, perhaps soon, right near the nicely polished shoes of a Tony nominee. I decided to go to YouTube to see if they had the opening I wrote way back in 1998 and they did! Back then, I was working on "The Rosie O'Donnell Show" and when Rosie was asked to come back as the Tony Awards host and she asked me to write a song highlighting three divas. I remember she mentioned one "diva" who didn't belt above a B flat and I quickly put the kibosh on that idea. Instead, I picked my three of my faves and luckily she agreed: Patti LuPone (singing "Don't Cry For Me, Argentina"), Jennifer Holliday (singing "And I Am Telling You") and Betty Buckley (singing "Mem'ry"). The revival of *Chicago* had opened two years before and Rosie was obsessed with it so I picked "Roxie" as the song to parody. I wrote one of my fave lyrics for Rosie which also re-claimed one of Rosie's bad educational experiences. Here are the opening lyrics (sung to the tune of "Roxie"):

The thing that actors all adore is simply the…Tony

But there's one thing that I want more than winning a …Tony

I wanna be a Diva, I wish there was some way I could learn.

I try to sing like Patti LuPone but I sound like Rhoda Morgenstern.

A.) I love that I used Rhoda's full name…so awkward! And B.) That line was influenced by the story Rosie tells about her early college theatre experience. After she read a scene in her theatre class, her professor commented, "Ms. O'Donnell, the role of Rhoda Morgenstern has already been cast." Ouch. Cut to, many years later, it was used to get a laugh while hosting the Tony Awards. Delicious revenge served cold. All the ladies sounded so great on their songs and one of my favorite moments is Patti LuPone's enthusiastic but bizarre ad lib near the end when she shouts "Go, Tony!" Is the Tony Award a person? Is she sassing someone named Tony? I still don't know. Watch and see if you can figure it out! What was so fun for me was experiencing my first time seeing the Tony Awards from the audience and having it be the time I wrote the opening number! So amazing!

Speaking of Tony Awards, I had *all* four Tony-nominated *Book of Mormon* actors at my SiriusXM "Live on Broadway" show: Andrew Rannells, Rory O'Malley, Josh Gad and Nikki M. James. They're all really funny and so excited about their show being such a hit. By the way, I feel so old-school because I keep calling it *The Mormon Musical* which is what it was called before people officially knew the name. It reminds me of right when I got out of college and *Jerome Robbins' Broadway* was running but I always called it *The Robbins Project* because that's what people called it when it first began rehearsals. As a matter of fact, I still think of "The Triad" as "Paulsons" which is what it was called when *Forbidden Broadway* was there in the '80s. In other words, I live in the past and I'm unyielding. Anyhoo, Rory told us that his role was literally ensemble but throughout the various readings and workshops he'd get more and more lines thrown his way. It wasn't considered a principal role 'til the Broadway contracts were signed. He told us that his mom was the first person he called when he found out he got a Tony nomination. Even though it was before 9 AM, she was already at work. When he told her he got a Tony nomination, the first thing she said, in a Midwest twang, was "Are you sure???" He confirmed that it had been announced on TV. Then she responded, nervously, "Well, somebody ought to double check!" She'll see proof soon enough because he's taking her to the Tony Awards!

In the show, Nikki's character name is Nabalungi. In rehearsal, Josh would joke as his character by calling her by any other name that began with an N... and now it's a permanent part of the show. But nothing is actually set. He changes it all the time. He calls her Noxema, Nutrigena and lately he said he's made the name more season-appropriate because he's added Nasonex. He also gave a shout-out to fellow Broadway lovers when recently he called her *Next to Normal*. Hilarious. The creators usually let him go wherever he wants. Although, one night they ixnayed one of his name choices from being used again when, instead of calling her Nabalungi or a variant beginning with N, he called her "Sharon." Too far.

I asked the four actors if they were going to do a big group number on the Tony Awards, or a medley that featured their greatest hits, but turns out they're doing "I Believe," which is Andrew's big 11-o'clock number. I asked if that song was completely a solo and Nikki said, "Yes. We're all really happy about that." Brava on keeping the subtext sub. Brava to Andrew, though!!

On Friday I saw *Lysistrata Jones*, based on *The Lysistrata* which was written centuries ago. I think the title is so funny. It's based on the fact that the opera *Carmen* was turned into a contemporary musical by changing the name to *Carmen Jones*. I love the implied theory that any classic from yesteryear can become contemporary by simply adding "Jones" to the leading person's last name. Hilarious. The title role was played by Patti Murin who was great. Really funny, sassy dancing and *great* high notes *And she's now starring in Frozen!* As a matter of fact, Jack Cummings III who runs The Transport Group, told me I *had* to come because I'd be obsessed with the belting. Everyone knows that high notes are the carrot to dangle in front of my face to ensure my presence. The cast was so talented and they all did Dan Knechtges' choreography so well. I was super impressed that so many people nowadays are such triple threats. I used to love looking at cast lists from the 1950s: there was a "singing chorus" and a "dancing chorus." Nowadays, they've been combined *and* they're called "the ensemble." But, my questions is, what happened to the dismissive comment people used to rattle off about a certain type of guy: "He's just a chorus boy". Do they now say, "He's just an ensemble boy"? It doesn't really sound insulting. Just blandly factual.

On June 6, my schedule included going to Birdland to see *Show Some Beauty* which is a concert featuring the songs of Steve Marzullo. Steve wrote "Some Days," that great song that Audra McDonald recorded and performs all over the place. I played it for her at a marriage equality rally, the rFamily Vacation in Club Med Mexico *and*, tying back to my first paragraph, on "The Rosie O'Donnell Show."

The Birdland show celebrated Steve's first CD. Ann Harada, Michael Winther, Rachel Ulanet, Judy Blazer, Sally Wilfert, Stephanie Card, Andrea Burns, Ric Ryder, Terry Klausner and Heidi Blickenstaff sang. Get it on iTunes!

The hilarious Nicole Parker was my guest on my Playbill Obsessed video. I first saw her do her Ellen DeGeneres imitation on "MadTV" and I asked her to incorporate it into her Broadway career. What follows is what would happen if Ellen played Elphaba. Translation: 10 percent singing and 90 percent chatter.

On my new SiriusXM talk show, *Seth Speaks*, I had Tony Award nominee Brian Bedford. He's so fantastic in *The Importance of Being Ernest*, but do you know where he's *not* fantastic? Playing the game "Celebrity." I play every week with my guest, and, after I explained the game to him, we put on the timer so he'd have a minute to guess as many celebrity names as he could. I pulled the first name out from the hat of names the audience had filled out before the show and said, "She's blonde, she starred in *Wicked,*, she's really short..." *Silence*. I continued, "Um...she won the Emmy for 'Pushing Daisies.'" *Staring*. Finally I got a response from him which was simply, "What?" "What" what? Could he not hear a certain word I said? A phrase? Was he actually questioning the whole concept of the game? I think the answer is yes to all of the above. I haven't seen that many layers of subtext in one word since he, as Lady Bracknell, intoned "Found????" You people who saw the show know what I mean. I decided to break down her name into syllables. "OK. On December 25th one says 'Merry' what?" *Silence*. "Um...what's the word after 'Merry'...?" *Silence* followed by an eyebrow raised to the audience. Well, by that point a full minute had gone by. *Buzzer*. I haven't seen a game played like that since Martin Short, who only guessed five names in 60 seconds. Of course, when I confronted Marty about being terrible at "Celebrity" he countered with, "Well next time put some actual famous people in the hat." Ouch. And accurate.

Peace out til next week!

The Tonys, Ana Gasteyer and Judy Gold
June 13, 2011

Happy post-Tony Awards! I spent last night doing a live play-by-play of the CBS broadcast for SiriusXM with Julie James. Also, my friend Jack Plotnick joined me which was so fun. We both loved hearing Sutton's speech because she gave an emotional shout-out to her dresser, Julian, whom Jack and I both worked with when we first met! The first big show Jack and I both did in New York was *Pageant* back in the early '90s and Julian was one of the dressers!

This year the Tonys were at the Beacon Theatre and I was constantly walking by the theatre since it's so near my apartment. When I walked Maggie on Sunday, I had to take a picture of her near the red carpet because I knew it would be the closest she'd get to an awards show. I still feel guilty for curtailing her performing career. Years ago, Bebe Neuwirth was about to film "Tadpole," and she called me because she had to film a scene in Central Park with a dog. She thought Maggie was perfect because she's so sweet and pretty. I went into my full Mama Rose mode and was preparing to put Maggie on a modified Atkins diet so the blogs wouldn't comment on the ten pounds the camera adds, but then Bebe began to describe the scene: "I'll be walking Maggie and let her off the leash. She'll sit with me near a bench and then we'll walk off together." I knew I had to say what the reality would be: "Um, actually Bebe, what will happen is….she'll pull you like crazy while she's on the leash, and then when you let her off, she'll run off chasing a squirrel." *Silence*. And thus ended Maggie's film career.

This week on my SiriusXM talk show I interviewed Ana Gasteyer. We discussed her stint in *Wicked* and I asked her if she enjoyed doing the same show, night after night. Turns out, she loves it. She said that doing "Saturday Night Live" is so fast and panic-filled. Essentially, your goal is simply to "not fail." If you don't completely bomb in a sketch, then it's considered a triumph. Doing a long run is so enjoyable to her because there're *so* many chances to perfect specific moments. Of course, she said, it also leads to obsessive behavior and perfectionism. Ana told us that even though people think "Defying Gravity" is the hard song to sing, the part of the show that Elphabas dread is the last note of "The Wizard and I." It's on a C, which a lot of women find not quite high or low enough to sing well, *plus* it's Elphaba's first number so there's pressure to impress the audience, *plus* the staging involves dealing with two suitcases. When I'm belting I don't want to have worry about my carry-on luggage! Ana's show is call *Elegant Songs From a Handsome Woman* and the title is based on her obsession with that term. First of all, she told me that when she was a teen, someone asked her teacher what a "handsome woman" was. There was a pause and then the teacher answered, "Barbra Streisand is a handsome woman." Then, recently, her mom proudly told her, "Ana…you're developing into quite a handsome woman." She was horrified her mother would use that term with her and even more mortified that she also used the gerund "developing." It's like a sentence from a Judy Blume book, but instead of being about Sally J. Friedman it features a woman in her 40s.

I also interviewed the stunning Broadway couple Matt Cavenaugh (*West Side Story* and Off-Broadway's *Death Takes a Holiday*) and Jenny Powers (*Grease* and Off-Broadway's *Happiness*). I asked if they met on Gorgeous.com but Matt told me they met because they both had teeny roles in *The Secret Garden* concert Jamie McGonnigal put together a few years ago. After rehearsal one day, Matt asked Jenny out for coffee and she said yes. *After* the date she told him she already had a boyfriend. I asked her why that reveal took so long and she claimed she didn't want to presume anything when he first asked her out. I glared. Jenny said it took *nine months* for her to break off her relationship and finally start dating Matt, which then led to their marriage. *And* to their CD! *And now they have a child! In other words, there's three stunning people now living in their house.*

I also interviewed Judy Gold on SiriusXM and she was so much fun. Even though I know Judy from when she was a produer on "The Rosie O'Donnell Show" and I was a comedy writer, I don't know much about her early life. She told me that she went to college as a piano major (!), and Rutgers is where she started her comedy career. Her dorm did Secret Santa (where people secretly buy each other presents during December) and before you got your present, you had to do a dare. One day her Secret Santa wrote that she had to do a ten-minute stand-up act making fun of people in her dorm. There was a lounge on her floor where she did her "act" and Judy said that the feeling she got from everyone laughing made her realize that comedy is what she wanted to do more than anything else. She started going into to New York and doing open mics where she'd see "up and comers" like Ray Romano and Jerry Seinfeld. I asked her what some of her jokes were and she remembers she'd say "People don't know it, but I'm a major coke fiend. Yeah, this is my coke spoon" and then she'd reach into the back of her pants and pull out a giant ladle she'd stolen from the cafeteria. So stupid but funny! She has two children; her then-partner Sharon gave birth to her first one. Back in the late '90s, when Madonna came on "The Rosie O'Donnell Show," she was holding a baby during the interview. Rosie then told the audience that even though it looked like Madonna was holding her new baby, Lourdes, she was actually holding Henry, Judy Gold's new baby. Cut to: Judy Gold's mother's phone ringing off the hook with "*Judith has a baby*?! " Judy wasn't out as a lesbian yet so her mother started telling people, "Well, Judith's roommate had a baby. And...Judith decided to adopt it." Judy's obsessed with that stretch of reality. Who adopts their roommate's baby? Judy then continues her mother's logic by saying, "You know, her roommate always picks up the mail whenever Judith is out of town, so Judith felt she should return the favor by adopting her child." A few years later, Judy got pregnant and she claims this is how her mother told her friends about it: (*Said very slowly*) "Judith was walking down the street, (*speeding up*) there was a hypodermic needle flying around, it had some sperm on it, it stuck Judith in her privates, (*slowly and proudly*) and now she's pregnant!" Look for me and Judy on my Playbill "Obsessed" series on youtube where she not only tells a hilarious story about her mother, but she plays an actual answering machine message!

L'chaim and peace out!

Post-Tony Reflections, and *Now. Here. This.*
June 20, 2011

My summer traveling officially begins this week. Starting Thursday I'll be in Provincetown at The Art House doing *Deconstructing Broadway* which I'm now calling *Seth's Big Fat Broadway*. It sounds new, but it's really just the exact same show with a different title. Like "Buffy" and "Charmed." This weekend begins my *Broadway At The Art House* series with my first guest, Jackie Hoffman. I went to *The Addams Family*'s theatre to rehearse with her, and her stuff is, as usual, hilarious. She has a song that anyone who rides the subway will identify with. The main part goes

Stop making out in front of me
You're both gonna make me hurl
Stop making out in front of me
You trash skank boy and girl

As for the recent Tony Awards, brava for having such a Broadway-themed show, instead of a "Broadway isn't important, so let's bring on the vaguely-related pop/movie stars and let them awkwardly perform" show. Neil Patrick Harris is a great host. I was trying to describe why he's funny, and Christine Pedi said that he's so good at being charmingly wry and sarcastic. That made me remember when I was in an elevator with him and his partner David Burtka (*now married!*), and we were talking about kids. The subject of in-vitro fertilization came up. I laughed and said it was *so* crazily expensive and who had thousands of dollars to spend on it?? Neil softly responded/sang: "I do." His honesty was refreshing, hilarious...and devastating. *And now they have two children!*

As for the Tony wins, I was so happy for everyone, especially for Sutton Foster whom I've known since we did *Grease* together back in the mid 90s. As many of you must know, she was cast as the understudy in *Thoroughly Modern Millie* and was then given the lead role. I love the story about when she heard she was taking over the role of Millie. It was the day of the first out-of-town preview and she was on the phone with her then-boyfriend. She got a call waiting and clicked over to the other line to hear Michael Mayer, the director, tell her that she was going to play the lead role instead of her chorus part. She wanted to get all the details, so she immediately clicked to the other line and told her boyfriend she would call him back. It sounds normal, but her boyfriend was totally traumatized waiting for her to call him back because when Sutton found out she had the role she, naturally, started weeping. In other words, all her boyfriend heard during that phone call was Sutton first saying, "Hold on a minute..." ...*silence*...then hysterical sobbing cries as she sputtered, "I'll call you later," *click*. He was imagining her comforting a dying relative in a hospital, when all the while she was actually getting a costume fitting and stretching her Achilles tendon for the big second-act tap number. P.S. Speaking of hospitals, I just saw *Now. Here. This.* at the Vineyard Theatre. It's a new show by the people who brought you *[title of show]*. There are so many parts I loved, but I laughed so hard during one part of the section about Hunter Bell and Heidi Blickenstaff's sick grandmothers. It's a moving scene about dealing with the death of a grandparent, but at one point they talk about their respective grandmothers being in bed but unresponsive. Hunter doesn't know whether or not his grandmother can hear what's going on around her and says something like, "We want to know whether she can hear us, but Grandmother isn't telling." They then immediately comment on how that phrase would be an amazing title for a horror movie. Susan intones scarily, "Is she... or isn't she? *Grandmother isn't telling*." Hilarious...*and* terrifying.

Back to the Tony Awards. I was also excited for Norbert Leo Butz, who did such a great job with that tour-de-force song from *Catch Me If You Can*. By the way, usually a person adds a middle name when they join Equity because there's another person with that same name. Not surprisingly, there was not another Norbert Butz when he joined, *but* he added the Leo because there *is* another Norbert Butz...his father. And Norbert felt the need to differentiate. They both went by the name Norbert Butz for years until the time Norbert's girlfriend sent him a letter and his father opened it. And by "letter," I mean "explicit letter." And by "opened it" I mean read some and then needed heart medication. And, thus the "Leo" was permanently added.

I was excited for my friend Stephen Oremus, who won the Tony for orchestration and is yet *again* involved with the hottest show on Broadway. If you recall, back in 2004, he was the music director for *Avenue Q* and *Wicked*. That's like living in the 1970s and getting to date Paul Newman *and* Robert Redford. What's hilarious to me is that he and Julia Murney still call me "Asssss." Why? It all started because *years ago*, literally in 2000, I was walking by Cosi on Broadway and 76th. Julia was sitting at an outside table with my friend Gordon Greenberg. Gordon introduced me to her and told me she was an amazing belter (something I later found out to be true). After we chatted for a while, I left and Julia claims I looked at her and slowly said, "Bye, asssssss." She was miffed...and obsessed. She immediately told her good friend Stephen Oremus and that's become my permanent nickname all of these years. Of course, what actually happened is I have notoriously bad diction and I make up nicknames for people based on parts of words. I thought Julia was sassy, so I actually said, "Bye, Sass...", but she refuses to give up the nickname I never asked for. And, to this day, whenever I run into to either one of them, I accept their "asssss."

My friend Jack Plotnick was visiting me and we took Juli to the playground. Never again. It was like being the ugly girl forced to stand with Pamela Anderson at a straight man's convention. Those playground kids were all *over* Jack because they recognized him from "Sharpay's Fabulous Adventure." If you don't know, it's the newest of the "High School Musical" franchise films, and it wound up being the highest-rated Disney movie on the channel. He and Alec Mapa play opposite each other and apparently, according to the 8-10 years olds in the playground, Jack's performance is groundbreaking. They didn't just love him in that movie, they also recognized him from the slew of other kids TV he's done: "Good Luck, Charlie," "Wizards of Waverly Place" and the Trix bunny commercial. I was shocked and mortified that not *one* of those children saw me in *The Ritz*. Hmph. I never missed a performance!

Sunday was Father's Day so James, Juli and went bowling. Here's a lesson for parents: You know those bowling bumpers for kids I wrote about before? It's essentially a wall that comes up and prevents a ball from ever going in the gutter. In my day, we just bowled. Well, Juli asked (and by "asked" I mean "begged") to use the bumpers and we told her she had to try to bowl without them. We said if she went three turns without getting any pins, she could use the bumpers. She complained but tried it without the bumpers, and by the third game she got a spare *and* a strike! She literally beat James! She wanted the easy way and we made her try. On a side note, that do-it-yourself/pioneer attitude I espoused lasted until we got out of Chelsea Piers and I realized we'd have to walk a few blocks to the subway. Who has that kind of energy? Taxi!

On that note, peace out and come visit Provincetown!

Remembering Alice Playten, and Playing P-Town
June 27, 2011

Let me start my column by mourning the loss of Alice Playten. She passed away suddenly last Saturday, and I was so shocked and saddened. I first heard her when I was playing in the pit of *Seussical* and she was playing the Mayor's wife. I loved her old-school style of singing. I then realized I had heard her numerous times while listening to the *Hello, Dolly!* and *Oliver!* cast albums because she was the original Ermengarde and Bet. We then worked together on a workshop of Michael John LaChiusa's *R Shomon*, and when Kelly Bishop had to leave my Actors Fund concert of *Funny Girl* due to a family emergency, Alice stepped in with a few days' notice. She was *such* a great stage comedienne. I also got to interview her a few times about being part of those great Golden Age shows. Such stories! When she replaced Baby Louise in the original run of *Gypsy* (!) she was introduced by the stage manager to Ethel Merman who immediately asked him, "Does she know about the joke?" Ethel was insistent that Alice set up her joke well; Baby Louise has to clearly say, "Mama. Why do I have five fathers?," so Mama Rose can quickly answer, "Because you're lucky!" Alice then told me she went back to Broadway years later to see one of the numerous Broadway revivals of *Gypsy,* and the Baby Louise asked, barely audibly, "Mam, why I ha fi fath?" and the Mama Rose slowly intoned, "Because...you're *lucky*." Alice told me, "Apparently, *neither* of them knew about the joke." Excellent bust! She got a Tony nomination for her part as the lovably evil girl named Kafritz (from *Henry, Sweet Henry*), and I've obsessed about her performance on "The Ed Sullivan Show" many times. Go to youtube and see for yourself. You *must* look at the face she makes when she sees the paltry amount in her hand that the audience has donated. Brilliant!

Well, last week I started my summer run in Provincetown! And I continued my lifetime run of making mistakes that lead to incredible stress. On Thursday, I caught a cab before 7 AM so I could get to JFK at least 45 minutes before my 8:38 flight. As I was waiting on the security line, I checked my boarding pass and the time. My watch said 7:38, and my boarding pass said 7:38. Huh? I kept checking back and forth. Boarding pass: 7:38. Watch: 7:38. My mind couldn't wrap itself around what it was seeing. Finally, I went online and checked my itinerary. Yes. The *time* was 7:38 and my *flight* was at 7:38, not 8:38. Yay. Thankfully, JetBlue let me on the next flight to Boston for no extra charge (!) and then I hopped on a Cape Air flight to Provincetown with no more problems. James and Juli, however, took Amtrak because Juli had to go to her last day of school. They got to Boston at 5 PM and it was a.) freezing, and b.) pouring rain. It was doubly devastating because James was a.) wearing shorts, and b.) not carrying an umbrella. They took the ferry to Provincetown and were warned that they would have rough seas all the way there and "not to be shy and to ask for a barf bag whenever necessary." They were also told that the best way not to be seasick was to sit on the top, open deck which was a wonderful place to sit while wearing the aforementioned shorts and carrying no umbrella. They arrived in Provincetown crankier than Barbra Streisand when Carol Channing won the Tony Award over her for *Funny Girl*. Or Carol Channing when she read the *Hello, Dolly!* film breakdown in Backstage and saw "Dolly Levi: CAST (Barbra Streisand)." Despite all the crankiness, we had a great time and my first weekend was super fun.

Jackie Hoffman's show (part of my Broadway Series at the Art House) sold out and was hi-larious! She told us that she had done a show written by David Sedaris where she played a very patrician, rich woman. Her line was supposed to be "How long will this trip take? We have children in the car." One day in rehearsal, just for fun, she changed it to, "How long will this trip take? We have Jews in the car." David *loved* it kept it in the show. It always got a laugh, but one day after the show, a Jewish woman approached Jackie after the show and asked in a loud, New York-accented voice, "I don't get that joke you did. What did that mean? What did it mean when you said, 'We have Jews in the car'?" Jackie calmly explained that her character wanted the car trip to be short. "But why? Why would she want the trip to be short?" the woman aggressively asked. Jackie finally said, "Well, I guess having Jews in a car for a long period of time could get annoying." Jackie claimed the woman repeated in a stronger New York accent, "But why? Why??? Why would it be annoying? Why?? I don't get what could be annoying about Jews in a car for a long period of ti-i-i-i-i-i-i-ime!"

On my *Seth Speaks* radio show I got to interview Joyce DeWitt. Right now, she's starring in *Miss Abigail's Guide to Dating, Mating and Marriage*, but of course I had to ask her about "Three's Company." Turns out, she was called in to audition for the role of Fonzie's girlfriend in a spin-off of "Happy Days." She knew she looked nothing like the tall, leggy chicks waiting in the hall but she decided to audition anyway. She walked in to the audition room and there were a ton of people there. Because it was a "Happy Days" spin-off, and the show was such a hit, all of the bigwigs were there to watch auditions. The casting director took one look at the makeshift outfit she had on (she claimed she was "fat" that day and couldn't fit into any of her regular clothes) and called her by her first name. Right after she read, the casting director changed his tune and said, "Ms. DeWitt, please wait for a moment." That's right, suddenly she had a last name and her first name was "Ms." They called later that day and offered to pay her a lot of money to keep her on hold until a sitcom came along she was right for. Of course, she wound up getting the role of Janet Wood on "Three's Company" and loved doing it. I asked her about the hilarious Don Knotts and she said he was quite the ladies man. Who knew he was a playa? She remembered that it was impossible for anyone to keep a straight face during the first costume run-through of each episode if they had to open the door to Mr. Furley because it would be the first time they'd see one of his "swinging" outfits. P.S. I just Googled him and his character is on one of TV's Top Ten Worst Dressed list! Brava?

This week, my nieces Eliana and Rachel Sarah visited, and I put them in my Playbill Obsessed! video. It features them pulling Broadway star names out of a hat, and John Tartaglia has to imitate their voices while singing "On My Own." Watch it on Youtube!

Last Wednesday, I had a reunion with my high school theatre friends. Eric Ronis, who was so funny when he played the old actor in *The Fantasticks* (I was Mortimer), brought his young son. I saw him at my radio show and came to say hello but his son just buried his face in Eric's chest. I said, "Oh...he's shy." Eric smiled and said, "No... he just hates you." The truth will set you free?

O.K., Southerners, tomorrow I perform in Columbus, GA! So peace out, y'all!

Marsha Mason and My Malted Milk Balls
July 5, 2011

Happy Independence Day! I hope everyone had a great barbeque while blasting *1776* (not the movie version, I beg you). P.S. *1776* suffers from preconceived notions. Everyone thinks it's going to be a boring history lesson with somber, important songs thrown in. And cut. It's actually a *great* script and a fantastic score. It's so amazing that the show has any dramatic tension whatsoever considering the big question is "Will Congress sign the Declaration of Independence?" And yet, librettist Peter Stone was able to keep that question alive up until the very end. I once saw him speak, and he said that when he was writing the show, people thought the idea of a musical about the Continental Congress sounded horribly boring. As a matter of fact, he claimed that when people would ask what he was writing they would fall asleep between the "17" and the "76." Hilarious. If you refuse to listen to the score on principle, at least watch my deconstruction of "He Plays The Violin" on Youtube where 21-year-old Betty Buckley hits one of the first belted D's on Broadway!

This week began with me seeing Ana Gasteyer do her act. It was *so good*. First of all, she sounded amazing. She was singing songs that were so much fun *and* she added so many additional high notes. And I mean crazy high notes. What I loved is that she didn't seem to have any anxiety or deep preparation about hitting them. She would just sing whatever she wanted without worrying about how high it was. It sounded amazing. *Plus*, her patter was hilarious. In the middle of the show, she brought out the book she claimed she was reading: Barbra Streisand's "My Passion For Decorating." She pointed out so many crazy things in the book. On one page, there's a picture of a boat floating on a pond on Barbra's estate. In the book, Barbra writes how she made sure that the koi in the pond are only black and white. Barbra claims it's because "I'm obsessed with color." Ana comments, "First of all, black and white aren't colors…" Then Ana talked about how many of us collect things — dolls, stamps etc. Well, instead of storing them in a basement like most of us do when we've moved on, Ana tells us about the section in the book where Barbra reveals that she's turned her enormous basement into an underground mall with fake stores. Ana said, "That's right. This way, she and James Brolin can spend a lazy Sunday strolling through their mall hand in hand, pretending to buy back the sh*t they already own." *Barbra and her underground mall became the basis of Jonathan Tollin's hit play "Buyer and Cellar" with Michael Urie.*

On Tuesday, I flew down to Columbus, GA, to do *Deconstructing Broadway*. It's a small city that's two hours from Atlanta. Well, the city may be small, but I was performing in the Parthenon. I walked out onstage and felt like I was in the Hal Prince *Show Boat* revival from the '90s. (Remember? More than 50 people in the cast? And the length of the show was equal to the size of the cast multiplied by 1,000 minutes?). Anyhoo, it was thrilling to do the show in such a big space, and the Georgia audience was fantastic. It was really wonderful to be in a place where the people could just drive to Atlanta for their arts, but instead they choose to keep it alive in their own city. Back in NYC, I interviewed Mary Faber, Chris Hanke and Rob Bartlett from *How To Succeed….* for my SiriusXM talk show. Chris recounted the time he was playing Mark in *Rent* on Broadway and being thrown for a loop because he hit foot while jumping up onto the table to sing "La Vie Boheme." He wound up forgetting the early lyrics of the song and told us that once you forget a lyric in that song, it's impossible to come back in on any of them because it's a patter song and when you're lost, you're lost. So, instead of singing, he did a monologue taunting Benny (sample line: "That's right! We're in your restaurant!") while he did a dance retrospective of the last 30 years, including such signature hits as the "Roger Rabbit" and "The Swim." He took that platitude "Dance as if no one is watching" too far. People actually *were* watching. And the only one pleased was his mother who happened to be in the audience that day and told him the show was "wonderful." He thought her comment was suspect but then remembered that before the show, she had imbibed some delicious drinks at lunch and had then taken what he called "two mysterious Advil." And I'm out.

I also had Marsha Mason on the show. James and I just rented "The Goodbye Girl" and it was shocking to us because the neighborhood where the apartment Marsha Mason lives in is so broken down and scary. Turns out, it's 78th and Amsterdam which is now super fancy schamncy! Who knew it was terrifying in 1977? Marsha looks *amazing* and was in New York, visiting from her home in New Mexico. She said that one day, years ago, while living in Los Angeles, Shirley MacLaine called her (just like one of my typical days) and told Marsha that they both needed to move to New Mexico. They're good friends and Shirley said she was going to scout around and find somewhere nice. Shirley flew down and called back a few days saying she'd found a perfect spot for Marsha to build a house and Shirley was going to take "the mountain in back." So, Shirley still lives on that mountain and Marsha lives in the valley. Marsha said that every Thanksgiving, Shirley comes down from the mountain for a big meal that Marsha cooks. She also said it's scary to watch because the mountain is a little treacherous and Shirley comes down the mountain in a golf cart. If any of this story makes sense to you, get back to me!

I was fascinated by the fact that Richard Dreyfus won the Oscar for Best Actor for "The Goodbye Girl." I think it's the only time an actor got respect from the Academy for doing a comedy. Marsha pointed out that it was also the year that the Best Picture Oscar went to the comedy *Annie Hall*. Why just that year? Did Groucho Marx vote 200 times? Marsha herself has been nominated four times (!) but said that the whole thing has changed. Back then, she just wore a "nice dress," but now it's so elaborate and there's pressure all the time and nominees have to use designers and stylists. Luckily I did not have to worry about it then, nor have I had any opportunity to worry about it now.

When Marsha moved to New York, she made money doing all sorts of odd jobs, but I was obsessed with the fact that at one point she was a go-go dancer! She would dance on a bar but finally decided to quit when a guy was looking up her dress and asking her to dance with her legs wider. Yowtch! In "The Goodbye Girl," she plays a Broadway dancer and I told her I was so impressed with the fact that they film her doing jazz combinations using full body shots. It's not "Black Swan"-style where the face is completely shrouded in make-up and there are constant cut-aways and close-ups of feet, shoulders and wrists. I couldn't believe what a natural dancer Marsha was and how she keeps up with the other dancers. She then revealed that six weeks before filming began she worked on the few jazz combinations she had to perform …and the other dancers in the scenes learned them on the day they filmed. Oh.

Speaking of "The Goodbye Girl," Marsha and I took a picture recreating the moment where she has on her signature cranky face as Richard Dreyfus goes into her bathroom, sees her undergarments drying and says rhythmically, "I don't like the panties hanging in the shower!"

Right now I'm sitting at a lovely spot in Provincetown that faces the water. I wasn't feeling so lovely when I got here because I realized that I left my key to the place where I'm staying back in New York. I tracked down the guy who has a key and we decided, because he didn't have another copy, that I would keep my door unlocked the whole time I was up here. Then, my food addiction backfired. I spent the whole first day obsessing about the malted milk balls they sell at the fudge place, and, by 11:45 PM, I couldn't resist any longer. I fled my place and bought a bagful of chocolate, dark chocolate and peanut butter malted milk balls. I got back to my place and discovered that, somehow, my door had locked when I left on my obsessive sugar quest. It was now midnight and the guy who had my key was gone.

I'm not proud of what followed. Suffice it to say, it involved me slicing into the screen with a random coin, removing said screen and then awkwardly hauling my ever-growing body through the slim window opening while *still eating the malted milk balls*. I refused to stop for even one minute. You'd think I had hit rock bottom, but the next night I was back at the fudge store again with a fistful of dollars. If the whole thing was caught on film, it would be part of my opening montage for "Semi-Celebrity Rehab." But since it's not, I'll be hitting the candy again tonight. Peace out!

The Inspirational Charles Busch (By Way of Judy Garland)
July 11, 2011

I'm on a JetBlue flight to West Palm Beach to start my week at Club Med. This is the second time R Family Vacations has been at a Club Med and I'm hoping that this one is as much fun as last year's — but with less weight gain. I was looking back and noticed that there has been a constant supply of adult ADD (left my key in NYC, showed up for a 7:38 AM flight at 7:38), and this will be no exception. Last Monday, when I was in Provincetown, I scheduled my cab to pick me up at 7:15 AM to catch an 8:15 flight to Boston and then to New York. I first woke up at 6:15 AM and decided to get more sleep. The next time I woke up was 8:15. That's right, I woke up at the exact time my plane was about to depart. Unfortunately, I wasn't sleeping at the Provincetown airport, so I couldn't just roll out of bed and onto the plane. I called the Cape Air counter at the Provincetown Airport, which has a very mom-and-pop feel. As a matter of fact, when I told the lady on the phone that I was scheduled for the 8:15 flight and had overslept, I didn't receive a corporate, impersonal response. Instead she asked, "Is this Seth?" Either she had recently seen my name on the passenger list, or she'd been reading my Playbill columns. Regardless, I got on the next Cape Air flight and was able to easily change my JetBlue one as well! Why take Ritalin when it only costs $45 to change a flight?

Besides doing my own show in Provincetown, I've been heading a Broadway Series at the Art House, and last week I got to do a show with Charles Busch. He had so many amazing stories about his career. He told us that in the mid-'90s he was hired to write a film for Disney. They give you a time period and/or idea and you write a treatment. First, they asked him to write something about witches. He wrote a treatment about a young witch going to witch school (this was before "Harry Potter"). After they read it, they told him to "be Charles Busch." He responded, "I *am* Charles Busch. If this were a play, I'd be playing the young witch." They still rejected it. Next, they asked him to write something that took place in ancient Egyptian times. He wrote about a young princess like Cleopatra, who had a Scarab (beetle) that spoke to her. The Disney people called him and said it was cute but they wanted him to lose the beetle. Charles told them that the beetle was adorable and a big part of the story. They told him, in no uncertain terms, "beetles don't talk." He immediately said, "Hold, please. I'm getting a call. There's a teapot on my other line." He then told us that he essentially lost the job because of his need to make a sassy quip. He later found out that in the world of Disney, a beetle can talk to a dragonfly, or a teapot can talk to a plate, but you can't mix worlds. Who knew? Besides Angela Lansbury?

He talked about a show he did where one of the actors stormed off and quit right before it opened. No one on the creative staff knew what to do, so Charles took it upon himself to try to convince the actor to come back. Charles found the actor 30 minutes later, sitting on the stoop to his building. Charles told us that he hauled out every platitude he could think of — "the show must go on," "you must be professional no matter what," etc. — and suddenly Charles remembered that the actor had recently come out as bisexual. That meant, Charles thought, that the actor had probably not seen the entire Judy Garland oeuvre. In other words, while he may have seen "The Wizard of Oz" and "A Star Is Born," there was no way he had yet seen Judy Garland's final film, "I Could Go On Singing." Charles claims that only if he was "full-tilt gay" would he have seen it. So, Charles thought back to a dramatic moment in the film, and hauled out a pivotal line: He looked at the actor and earnestly told him, "I don't care who you disappoint…but I don't want you to disappoint *yourself*." Charles admitted to us that he never quite understood what that line meant, but in the films, it did the trick. Well, life imitates art, because suddenly the actor looked like a light had been turned on inside his head as he mulled it over and said, "You're right. I can't disappoint myself!" Rehearsals immediately resumed and the only lasting problem is Charles' fear that the actor will one day see "I Could Go On Singing" and realize that he played a modern-day Judy Garland.

On Facebook, I posted a promo for *Seth Speaks* and Jen Cody responded with the question, "Has there ever been a moment where Seth hasn't spoken?" Rude. And honest. This week on the show, I had Kathie Lee Gifford. She recounted her time in Los Angeles when she was called in to audition for a new TV show. Unfortunately for her, she was sick that day. And even more stressful, the audition was to play a new angel on "Charlie's Angels." Still, she got herself dolled up and all "f'pitz'd," as my mother would say, and showed up for the audition. However, before she even walked in to do the scene, she was told by the receptionist, "This audition isn't for you. We're looking for beautiful women." Ouch! Kathie Lee left, but on her way out turned back and told her, "Well, if you ever need a voice for a cartoon, give me a call." The old "over the shoulder sassy comment" doesn't always pay off, but it gave her the confidence to know she wouldn't be broken by the business. My fave Kathie Lee story is about her time playing Carol Burnett's part for the matinees of *Putting It Together* on Broadway. One of her songs was "Could I Leave You?," but because of her particular religious beliefs, she didn't want to say "wait a Goddamned minute!" So, Sondheim told her to change it to "Wait a bloody minute!" Kathie Lee tried it, but felt it didn't ring true to the character and emotion of the moment. Especially because she's not British. She suggested to Sondheim that she might make the same sort of impact if she instead said, "Wait a f***ing minute!" Sondheim loved it and it went into the show. And Kathie Lee told me that one of her favorite moments of the experience was seeing the faces of the women who were coming to the show — only knowing her as sweet, perky Kathie Lee — and then letting the F word fly. Delicious.

This week's, Playbill "Obsessed!" video, which you can see on Youtube is with adorable Kerry Butler from *Catch Me If You Can and later on Disaster!*. She and I performed in a kid's nightclub when we were young and, in the video, we re-create the opening number from the early '80s...which I just realized is 30 years ago! It's essentially our version of *Follies*. And, unlike the current revival, it's apparent we're not transferring to Broadway. Enjoy...and peace out!

Alec Mapa and Gavin Creel in Florida, When It Sizzles
July 18, 2011

I'm back from Florida.. It is *hot* in Florida! Last year, R Family did Club Med in Ixtapa, Mexico, which was hot but James and I realized that none of the restaurants needed air conditioning. They kept the doors open and had fans overhead and it was always deliciously comfortable. Not in Florida. There was major air-conditioning needed everywhere — and it still wasn't enough. We realized that Club Med in Ixtapa had the beach next to it, for delightful ocean breezes. There was a body of water next to the one in Florida but I suspected it was man-made. The water was just right for breeding an army of mosquitoes. How many bites on my back, you ask? Juli counted. Let's just say it could be the sequel to "13." Three years later. That's right, 16! Yay?

Everyone had a great time, though. The first big show featured Marya Grandy who is a fantastic singer and musician. She also has amazing and bizarre comebacks. I sassed her about something and she commented back: "Seth, out of all the things you've said to me, that was the most recent." *She recently sang at the Chicago "Concert For America"! Watch her on youtube. So good!*

The comic for the week was Alec Mapa, who is hy-sterical! I interviewed him for *Seth Speaks* (which I recorded from Club Med) and asked him about being the original understudy for *M. Butterfly*. He said that while he was doing the show, he lived in a dicey neighborhood in Brooklyn. One day some tough chick sitting on a stoop mentioned that she saw photos of the cast and he wasn't in them. He explained that he was the understudy and would only go on if the star got sick or injured. She looked at him and asked, "You want me to do something about that?" Wow. Change the name of the show to *T. Harding*? *For you young people, google tennis and Harding.*

The next night, I played for Gavin Creel's act. First, he brought up his collaborator, Robbie Roth, to play guitar and I joined in for the second half. At one point, Gavin started telling parents in the audience to be worried if their kids visited the Club Med bar (where they serve non-alcoholic drinks) because there's a pool table. The parents didn't know what he was talking about... until he then launched into a fantastic version of "Trouble." It was so funny, especially when he replaced River City with the awkward name of the Florida town where the Club Med was located. "Well, ya got trouble, my friend, right here, I say, trouble right here in Port Saint Lucy." Ow! I literally played the piano with one hand so I could hold the other one over my ear.

The extra thing added to this R Family Vacation was a theater camp. We divided the groups into ages: under 8, 8-10, 11-17 and adults. The youngest kids learned "So Long, Farewell," the next group learned "Do Re Mi," the older kids learned "Supercalifragilistixexpalidocious" and the adults learned "All That Jazz." Let me say that the adults were more focused than most Broadway rehearsals I've been in. Everyone was getting to live out their dream of being a Broadway dancer. Dan LuBuono, who has been in *Chicago* on Broadway more than 4,000 times (!) put the number together, and created an "It Gets Better" video with various R Family guests and their kids. So good!

Alec Mapa said that there should be a video called "It Doesn't Get Better," aimed at parents of young children, and featuring experienced (and exhausted) parents of teenagers. Juli is 11. Great. *Now Juli is a late teen and, holy cow, was he right.*

Gavin Creel led the kids doing "Supercali..." and was an amazing teacher. R Family Vacations is mainly for children being raised by gay and lesbian parents. Juli put her own R Family spin on the song. You know

71

the lyric that goes "Because I was afraid to speak when I was just a lad, my father gave my nose a tweak and told me I was bad"? Juli had everyone change it to, "Because I was afraid to speak when I was just a lad. My father*s* gave my nose a tweak and told me I was bad." Brava on the specificity. During the actual performance, Gavin called the kids onstage to do the number. Unfortunately, he apparently wasn't 100 percent clear. The number began with all the kids in place, ready to do their choreography. As Gavin was singing, he did a little turn, and when he faced the kids, he noticed there was a kid from a totally different group standing onstage. By the way, when this kid came onstage, he didn't realize he was in the wrong number. Instead, he literally stood center stage, ready to perform. I don't know *what* he was ready to perform, but he was prepped for something. Gavin stopped singing in the middle of a phrase, started laughing and gently led him off the stage, saying, "this is your time to *watch* a song."

The most amazing thing about R Family Vacations are the people and they didn't disappoint. If you don't know, it's run by Gregg Kaminsky and Kelli Carpenter and it's for gay parents and their kids...and the people who love them. There were so many phenomenal families there. One Mom told us how she's adopted five kids, all of whom have special needs. One boy, who's now a teen, was five when she got him. He's autistic and, back then, couldn't speak *at all*. Cut to, not only does he speak now, but he was in "Supercalifragilisticexpialidocious"!... and nailed *all* the lyrics and choreography!

Michael Lee Scott, who is the creative director of R Family, regaled us with stories all week. We were talking about signature sayings that couples have between themselves and he told me that his boyfriend, who's a great dancer, was once called at the last minute to do a music video. His boyfriend showed up and all the dancers were putting the finishing touches on the dance. The choreographer approached him and went into a long-winded, earnest discussion about the meaning of the dance, using phrases like "dreams lost and re-found" and "destiny unfolded," and summing up the dance by saying that, although the story involves love being destroyed, it eventually comes back...even stronger and with, perhaps, more dignity. Michael Lee's boyfriend blandly smiled and said, "Whatever, baby, just show me the steps." Amazing. Now, whenever one of them is babbling, the other one says, "Whatever, baby, just show me the steps."

When we got back to NYC, James and I went to see "Super 8" and, due to my constant muttering/commenting/critiquing/huffing/puffing etc throughout, James told me that I "suck the joy" out of seeing films. Hmph. The sad part is, I didn't mutter half as much as I wanted to. I go crazy when something has a plot hole and I *must* make my feelings known. I won't write the many issues that I had, but let me ask this to those who saw the film: If the heavyset kid wants *no one* to even *speak* about the train crash, why is he getting the film developed to put into his movie? Won't it then be seen by many people? So...no one may speak of it, but it's fine to be in a film, viewed by many? Excellent.

Well, I hope I haven't sucked the joy out of this. Whether I have or not, peace out!

The Music and the Broken Mirror
July 25, 2011

I am writing this from Provincetown on the day that I am finally not covered in sweat.

Yes, the Cape, which is known for staying cool no matter what happens on the rest of the East Coast, had a heat wave. My friend, who has lived here for years, said he's never experienced anything like it. The fun part is, this was the weekend I decided to take my mom with me. And, she's 79.

If you don't know, P-town prides itself on never being hot, so much of the housing doesn't have A/C. Cut to, my mother was completely red-faced from the heat when we were walking around Provincetown, and I was so dying from my house having no air circulation that I wound up buying an emergency air conditioner. But before it got installed, I decided to take the teeny, tiny fan that was provided in my house and plug it into her room. I moved the dresser to get to a plug, and the mirror which I thought was attached to the dresser, wasn't. Yes, it completely fell forward...on my mother's head. It was fun for us to spend the end of the heat wave at Urgent Care while her reflexes were tested and she was asked if she was nauseous or dizzy. Thankfully, she didn't require a CATscan. And now she has a new story to add to her roster of things I've done wrong (including the time I made a left turn as a teenager and "looked over his shoulder by *completely* turning his body around!").

My Mom in Ptown!

The last time my mother stayed for a long time in Provincetown was in the late 50's when she was pregnant with my oldest sister. She and my dad had a place near the water, and even though my mom was pregnant, she did most of the housework. My dad enjoyed himself by lying outside, strumming on his guitar. My mom couldn't understand why the neighbors seemed to ignore her and yet were friendly to him. She finally found out that they thought he was gay...and she was the maid! And that sums up my childhood.

Before I got up here, I did my talk show, *Seth Speaks,* for SiriusXM. Brooke Shields came by, and even though it was post-matinee so she was in some *Addams Family* Morticia make-up, she looked stunning. She told us that show is going great. The audience has such a strong reaction to seeing the iconic Morticia Addams played by Brooke, who also has such iconic status in America. We actually met up the day before the show at our mutual massage therapist, Greg Miele. My knee is killing me constantly because apparently you're supposed to stretch at some point if you work out six days a week. Oh. And Brooke's body is always aching because she was to wear a corset-like thing and during her tango number keep her upper half still while sassing her bottom half. Anyhoo, we both recovered from our massage (which is the kind where no massage cream is used...essentially just pain inflicted on top of your already existing pain), and she was delightful in her interview. We reminisced about doing *Grease* on Broadway, and I reminded her that I played her audition for Rizzo. Turns out, she told me that it wasn't supposed to be an audition! She was told to come to the theatre for a meet and greet with the artistic team. Cut to, she was put onstage at the Eugene O'Neill Theatre, I was at the piano, and she was suddenly asked to sing "There Are Worse Things I Could Do." I guess that's a meet and greet...and/or a terrifying Broadway audition. Well, she obviously got the part, did it for a few months, and the next thing I knew was she was starring on "Suddenly Susan" and I was playing a put-in rehearsal for Linda Blair. I asked her for details about a backstage mishap that I remembered; she told us that after "Look At Me, I'm Sandra Dee," Sandy would fight her and, during the scuffle, Brooke's earrings would get pulled off. Her ears would get a little scraped up and get infected, so she asked her dresser to sterilize her earrings to minimize the damage. Cut to, she went to take a swig of water before a scene and by accident she swigged the cup that just had the earrings. In other words, she drank a big gulp of hydrogen peroxide! It burned her throat, but she *still* finished Act One. Besides the pain, she was terrified the whole time she was onstage that she was going to die from ingesting it (this is before Doctors.com). Near the end of the act the stage manager, who had researched, whispered to her from offstage, "Don't worry! We checked. You're not going to die." I guess that's comforting. She had to take off the second act and the next show. She remembered that when she came back, the hallway was filled with "hilarious" signs like, "The Cleanest Insides on Broadway."

We also talked about doing *Gypsy of the Year*. Back in November of 1995, we did a sketch/song where I played Fran Weissler, and Jessica Stone played Barry. Paul Castree and I wrote the lyrics, and the number was about looking for a new Rizzo after Rosie O'Donnell. Here's a smattering...sung to the tune of "You're The One That I Want":

Fran and Barry: *We got bills! They're multiplying.*
And we nee-e-e-e-ed...to find a Rizzo.
Employee: *I'm suggesting...Bonnie Franklin.*
All: *It's mortifying! (echo: mortifying, mortifying, mortifying...)*
When we finally brought Brooke onstage and decided to cast her, cash fell from the sky as we all sang... "You're the one that I want! (You are the one I want) Ooh, ooh, ooh...*money*!"

I also had Jeffrey Sewell on *Seth Speaks*. He made a video of himself on youtube singing "So Much Better" that was sent to me by numerous Broadway folks because his singing and acting is amazing. He told me that he made the video just for fun and went to sleep. When he woke up the next day, he expected the views to be in the teens, but he was shocked to see he had 300 views. Then, not much later, it was over 1,000, and now he has an agent and has started auditioning for Broadway shows. *I just checked Facebook and thought it was so fun how he looks so much older. Then I looked in the mirror and conversely it's decidedly NOT fun.*

Adam Pascal was my guest at my Broadway Series at The Art House and sounded fantastic. He began as a personal trainer, and I told him that his bod looked amazing when he played Radames in *Aida*. He revealed that because the show was physically easy for him, he started to put on weight. His costume was an open shirt that had a cummerbund-like fabric that went around his middle, and by the end of the run and his 15-pound weight gain, he told me the cummerbund swelled out in a manner I'm familiar with. Maybe "Radames" is Egyptian for "slightly pregnant man."

Tonight I'm playing and hosting the New York Civil Liberties Union benefit at NYU's Skirball Center. There are so many performers, and off the top of my head I know Gavin Creel, Nellie McKay, John Tartaglia, Daphne Rubin-Vega, Andrew Rannells and Nikki Rene Daniels are going to be there. *And*, if you love high belting that's incredibly inappropriate, watch my latest *Obsessed* video where Kate *Shindle (now president of Equity!*) adds high A flats to a slew of songs. Earplugs not included. Peace out!

Adam Pascal's Secret Stage Name and Andrea McArdle's *Annie* 'Do
August 1, 2011

I'm in Provincetown yet again, but this time I'm spending seven days here! It's "Family Week" which means that there are special events planned for parents and kids and it's sponsored by Family Equality Council, which is an amazing lobbying group for gay parents (www.FamilyEquality.org).

I got back to NYC last Monday from P-town and hightailed it to the Skirball Center at NYU to tech the New York Civil Liberties Union benefit. The show went great! Moises Kaufman, who directed and wrote *Gross Indecency: The Three Trials of Oscar Wilde* and *3 Variations*, started off the evening and spoke about growing up in South America where he was gay and Jewish in a country that was macho and Catholic. When he came out to his father as a boy, his father's solution was to place him in martial arts class. Although at first apprehensive, Moises said, he wound up enjoying it based on the outfit and the after-class group showering. Werk!

I hosted and played piano for most of the acts, and one of my favorites was John Tartaglia, who performed with Rod, the gay puppet in *Avenue Q*. Since the NYCLU was part of getting marriage equality passed in New York state, a lot of the acts had to do with marriage. So, when Rod came out, he held out his puppet hand that had a ring on it and said, "Yeah, it's real, b*tches!" Rod talked about finally getting married to Ricky (the puppet he meets at the end of *Avenue Q*), and then launched into "Can't Help Lovin' That Man." Near the end, he went into "bring-it-home" tempo and he pulled out a full feather boa. Not John...Rod!

Carly Rose Sonenclar, who starred in *Wonderland*, and hit it big with "America's Got Talent" showed off her amazing voice with "I Am What I Am," and I cannot wait to see the video for two reasons. First, because Carly is only 12 but has an incredibly mature and beautifully musical voice. Secondly, because of the ending of the song. Gavin Creel was backstage and thought that Carly had modulated without telling me. He then thought that I was brilliant and kept changing keys to figure out what key she was in. Well, yes... I was switching keys a lot, but it's not because I'm brilliant, it's because I'm an idiot. Carly and I decided that she'd add a modulation for the last verse of the song, and adult ADD-style, I didn't write in the new chords because I was *positive* I could do it during the performance. Yes, I can transpose on sight, but unfortunately, I forgot in the actual moment if we were modulating up a half or a whole step. So I kept frantically switching keys *while she kept singing*! Thankfully, her voice sounded phenomenal and she got the most extended applause of anyone in the show. Unfortunately, she now has a "hilarious" story with video proof she can use on various talk shows when she gets famous. Hopefully, my last name will prove too difficult for her to pronounce.

More Adam Pascal stories I forgot to write about from last week. We were talking about "One Song Glory" from *Rent*. If you've ever seen it, you know that the Roger character sings most of it sitting down and only stands up when he sings the long "Glo-o-o-o-ry." What ingenious blocking, you'd think. Roger is homebound, afraid to move emotionally and physically, and can only feel the impetus to actually get up when he sings what he truly wants..."glory." Actually... the real reason for the blocking is because Adam couldn't remember the lyrics for the song so they were written out and placed in front of him! The only part he felt secure with was "Glo-o-o-o-ory." Immediately after he would sing that, he'd skedaddle back to look at the lyrics for the last verse. And that became the blocking used on Broadway and every national tour — and it was up to the actor to find the subtext. Adam's subtext was: "What're my lyrics?" Speaking of lyrics, when we did the Actors Fund *Chess* concert in 2003 (he was the American and Josh Groban was the Russian), we had the singers hold their lyrics because they didn't have a lot of rehearsal.

The London version that was filmed for PBS gives the illusion that everyone was off-book. Turns out, they had their lyrics streaming on teleprompter! Delicious! Or as they say in Britain about anything whatsover, "brilliant"!

Adam talked about his initial *Rent* audition, which came about because Idina Menzel (who lived around the block from him when they were growing up) told him that they were looking for an actor with a real rock voice. Since he was pursuing a rock career at that time, he went in. He was *outraged* that he was asked to come back a third time and, at first, refused to go (!). How dare they not decide after two auditions! P.S. That set the stage for the future of *Rent* auditions where I had friends go back ten times. And still not get it. Anyhoo, he finally went back in and Michael Greif, the director, had one concern: the fact that Adam sometimes kept his eyes closed when he sang. He asked Adam to sing his Mimi love song directly into the eyes of Daphne Rubin-Vega. Actually, no. She was not at his audition So they used who was available; yes, he was asked to sing the love song directly into the eyes of the casting director, Bernie Telsey. Let's just say, Daphne and Bernie have never been up for the same roles. Adam realized they needed to know if he could act. And he did it! Cut to: Broadway, Tony nomination, film version, national tour, triumphant return to Broadway. And, 15 years later, he still looks the same. *And then I got to do Disaster! with him on Broadway and he was amazing to work with. And so incredibly consistent!*

My fave story of the evening was told only because I happened to ask a random question. I knew he had been a rocker, and I jokingly asked if he ever had some stupid rock name like "Axl" or "Flash." Instead of laughing and saying no, he paused and said, "Well...at this point, I think only my wife knows." *Knows what?* I demanded. Turns out, while he was in the band, he decided he wanted to be more like Bono or Sting and he showed up one day at band rehearsal and told everyone that from now on, his name was no longer Adam, it was...*Rain.* Finally, he decided to add a new last name. Yes, he soon wanted to be called "Rain Madison". His bandmates were mortified and would often be at a bar and ask, "You wanna beer, Adam?" There'd be an awkward pause, then, with very little conviction..."I mean, *Rain.*" He also revealed that there are some girls out there he dated who only know him as his fake name! I'm very thankful he went back to his birth name and we didn't have to hear, "And the 1996 nominees for Best Actor in a musical are Nathan Lane, Savion Glover, Lou Diamond Phillips...and *Rain.*"

This weekend I had Andrea McArdle who sounded fabulous as usual. Usually, at the end of each Broadway Series, we've gotten a standing ovation, but this time we got a standing ovation when Andrea first walked onstage! Mark Collins, who was running spotlight, told her that he's never seen anyone get a standing O for just walking out, and Andrea said, "It actually just means I'm old." Not true, but sassy comeback.

I showed the video of her singing "Tomorrow" on the Tony Awards and she asked us to notice how much she flips her head. She said it was because she was a natural brunette with long hair so the *Annie* people got her hair dyed red and gave her a sassy haircut/dye job at Vidal Sassoon every few weeks that cost a few hundred dollars. She described her hairstyle as a "Dorothy Hamill/Toni Tennille modified wedge". While she was playing Annie, she wanted the audience to see how nice it layered, so she got used to constantly flipping it up and back. Go to youtube and take a gander.

And finally, the hilarious and high-belting Nancy Opel was my Playbill Video "Obsessed!" guest this week, telling of her mishap when she went on for Patti LuPone in *Evita*. It involves Mandy Patinkin, a large bunch of onstage cables and her uterus. Watch it, and peace out!

Cruising the Mediterranean
August 8, 2011

Yawn! I'm on an R Family cruise to Greece and there is a seven-hour time difference between here and the good ol' U.S. of A. I posted on my Facebook wall that I was so exhausted from the time difference that I had to have a "lie down" in the middle of the afternoon like an old British dowager. Apparently it's not cool to complain about being on a luxurious cruise in the Mediterranean, because right underneath my post someone commented: "My personal shopper is the *worst*!" Brava callback to The Onion and a previous column of mine. But seriously, my personal shopper *is* the worst.

I am so tired! I left Provincetown on the 10:30 AM ferry with James and Juli in tow. We got into Boston at noon and took a water taxi to the airport. And by "to the airport," we discovered that the water taxi actually takes you to an area *near* the airport where you then take an additional shuttle. It reminds me of when I was in college and would tell people I was from New York. What I meant was: I was from a place where you could take a shuttle to New York (Long Island). Anyhoo, we checked into our flight and hung out at Logan Airport in the swanky Lufthansa waiting room, for rich passengers. Why were we allowed in there? Well, it all began a week ago. James and I planned to treat this working vacation as a romantic getaway for us. Cut to: we found out that the childcare we arranged for Juli fell through so we decided to take her along. Thankfully, James had enough miles to get Juli a plane ticket, but all that was left, for *both* ways, was first class. Mind you, not business class — literally first class. James and I wanted to sit together since that would be the only romantic part of the trip, so we stayed in coach the whole time. I'm not gonna say we felt like losers compared to her, but suffice it to say that James was in a middle seat. We were essentially starring in our own version of "Upstairs, Downstairs" because the plane was an old-school 747, so the first class was literally up the stairs. Of course, when James left his seat and started up the stairs to see Juli, he got the panicked "Sir, Sir, SIR!" from the flight attendant. He hauled out the ol' facing-forward/not-looking-back routine and hightailed it to Juli's seat.

Juli (and a jealous James) in First Class

Luckily, first class was 30 percent full and the seat next to her was empty. James sat and talked with her for a little bit and then the first class flight attendant told him, "You're not supposed to sit up here." Not at all humiliating. Juli told us later that once dinner was over, she was given slippers and pajamas (!) and when we asked her where she put them on, she told us she changed in the bathroom. We couldn't understand how the bathroom had enough room until she informed us that the first class bathroom has a window. 'Nuff said. While she was in her chair that became a full bed, I had a little bit of a different time trying to sleep in coach because there was a movie above our heads playing endlessly. In other words, the whole time my eyes were closed, I saw non-stop bright light through my lids. Plus, there were children sitting directly in back of us who thought the movie was a laugh riot. And, they had obviously seen it before, because I heard a continuous "Here comes a really funny part. This part is really funny. This part. It's funny. See, this part." Ah…I'm finally falling asleep… "*THIS part*."

Anyhoo, we landed in Frankfurt at 5:30 AM and waited at the airport for our connecting flight to Venice. The last time I was in Frankfurt was the early '90s when I was the pianist for *A Chorus Line*. The cast was all dancers so that meant one thing: non-stop smoking. What made it even more European was that the rehearsal rooms had no windows. Yay? Back then, our fabulous director was Mitzi Hamilton who was the basis for the character Val. Pam Blair got the part originally, but Mitzi took over the role on Broadway and at one point was playing Sheila in one of the tours. And speaking of smoking, one night she had a phlegm attack during "Hello Twelve..." By the time she cleared her throat, she ran out of music. It was the part where she's supposed to sing, "Darling...I can tell you now. Your father went through life with an open fly." But, according to onstage witnesses, it sounded like this: "Darling (*clears throat*)...I can tell- (*clears throat*)...Your father-(*clears throat*)....(realizes she's out of music, rolls her eyes, mutters) *f- - - it*." Hilarious.

Anyhoo, now James, Juli and I are onboard and today we made our first stop: Corfu. My sister Nancy says it sounds like I'm saying tofu right after I had my wisdom teeth removed. It's one of the Ionian islands that's part of Greece and it's also where Prince Phillip was born. We went to a small family-run business that was the first soap-making factory in Greece and is now the last one around! They make it all in the back of their store with just olive oil and palm kernel oil. James and Juli loaded up on them but I demurred because I only like Body Shop-style soap...AKA it has to smell like it's been soaked in a vat full of raspberry juice. Delicious.

Michael Lee Scott from R Family is again on board and, as I mentioned from our Mexico trip, he always has a hilarious story to share. He told me that a while ago he went to a party and ran into a guy he knew from his midtown neighborhood. Now, for this story to have the full effect, you have to know that the guy was much older than Michael Lee and though Michael Lee thought he was nice, he found him *very* unattractive. The guy mentioned that he and his partner had been together for ten years and, because the guy had a 1970s vibe, Michael Lee was making conversation and asked if they had an open relationship. It was just a passing comment meant to fill dead air. Well, after Michael Lee asked, the guy's face turned very apologetic. Michael Lee didn't know what was going on until the guy said, "An open relationship? No, we don't. I'm *so sorry*!" Michael Lee suddenly realized the guy thought Michael Lee had asked the question because he was interested in taking advantage of said open relationship!!!! Michael Lee didn't know how to tell him he was totally *not*, on any level, interested without appearing rude, so instead he had to spend ten minutes listening to guy keep saying with a pitying look "I'm so sorry. I feel really, really bad." Yay. It's fun to be rejected by someone you're not even interested in.

Last week, I interviewed Mo Rocca on my SiriusXM talk show, *Seth Speaks*. Turns out, even though Mo is known for his hilarious commentary on "The Daily Show" and "Foodography," he grew up obsessed with Broadway. He told me and my audience that he spent many obsessive weeks when he was a teenager memorizing the role of Che in *Evita*. Why, you ask? Well, even though he was savvy enough to have the album, he didn't really know anything about how Broadway worked and he worried what would happen if Mandy Patinkin ever got sick. Therefore, he wanted to make sure he knew the all of the lyrics, word-for-word in case he they called him (?) and he had to go on (???). I asked him how he thought it would happen. Mandy would get sick and they would somehow know to contact him? A teenager not even living in New York? How would the *Evita* creative staff be aware of the fact that he was ready to go on? With their psychic powers? As much as I wanted to laugh, I remembered being 12 years old and working night and day to memorize the role of the little boy in *A Thousand Clowns*. Because I had the role, you ask? No. Because my picture and resume had been submitted to the casting director, and I figured that after numerous call-backs, if it came down to a choice between me and another kid, they would go with the child who had it memorized. Cut to: Not only was I only able to memorize around two pages, I never actually got an audition. Wonderful!

Mo told us that he was also obsessed with *Cats* when it came out and wrote *everyone* in the cast a fan letter. He remembers getting a cover of Time magazine and cutting it up so it was just a border and then putting Betty Buckley's face in the middle. After all of those fan letters, he finally got to speak to a member of the cast...-ish. He found a New York City phone book and looked up everyone's phone number and called them (!), but when he called the number for Cynthia Onrubia, it was actually her Mom's apartment. He began by telling her what a big fan he was of the show and that he wanted to know how Cynthia got to be where she was in her career. Turns out, they wound up having a long conversation on the phone! Brava Mrs. Onrubia!

OK, I'm about to do my *Deconstructing Broadway* show for the cruise guests, so I need to prepare. And by "prepare," I mean hit one of the many food options onboard. So, let me end by saying "*Ciao*," which roughly translates to mean "I'm on my way to becoming morbidly obese."

It's Greek to Me — Literally
August 16, 2011

Marco! *Polo*. No, I'm not in a swimming pool playing that incredibly frustrating game, I'm actually in Marco Polo Airport! It's the big Venice airport and I'm on my way back home. I've spent a little more than a week in Europe, and boy is my wallet tired. First, let me write about the R Family cruise where we stopped in all different places in Greece. James is gung-ho to do anything and loves exploring and experiencing the city as a native does. After one of my many "I *guess* this place is nice" comments, James finally looked at me and said, "You're not actually interested in seeing things. All you want is a lounge chair, a book and a latte." I couldn't even deny it. It was like he saw into my soul, and inside is a lazy a**. It reminded me of when I was doing *A Chorus Line* in Paris years ago and I called my mom to tell her I was bored. "How can you be bored in Paris?!?" she shrieked over the transatlantic connection. But apparently I found a way. After James spelled it out, I had a flashback to when I was Juli's age and my ideal vacation was solidified; One elementary school summer, my parents took me to Montauk to stay at a hotel called The Royal Atlantic, which is right on the beach. The clearest/happiest memory I have is of me sitting on the deck, drinking a diet black cherry soda (pre-coffee addiction) and reading Stephen King's "Carrie." My tastes haven't changed. P.S. Why "Carrie," you ask? Because I had just finished John Saul's "Suffer the Children." If the book was terrifying, I had a copy.

Back to Greece. The entertainment staff for this cruise was super small, since R Family hadn't chartered the whole ship. So, the performers were me, Michael Lee Scott, James and Anne Steele...who's also the girlfriend of the co-founder of R Family, Kelli Carpenter Now they're married! Essentially, we could all fit in the palm of my hand. For the first show, I thought it would be fun if we made it like a piano bar with requests made in advance. So, before "sail away" (as they call it in the cruise business), we sent an email asking the guest for songs they wanted to hear and why. We got fun requests with some sweet reasons attached to them. One Australian couple had just gotten married and decided to take their honeymoon on the cruise because, months before, they had met Anne Steele at Don't Tell Mama and she told them about the cruise. They wanted to hear one of Anne Steele's signature songs, "Gravity," and if you've never seen her sing it, take a gander!

I did a little chat before each song with the passenger who requested it, and at one point I went over to the two dads who asked for "Good Morning, Baltimore." I told the audience that they sent an email telling us that *Hairspray* is their son's favorite show. At that moment, I called over their young son who was in the back of the room. I stood next to him with my microphone asked him, "What's your favorite show?" With no hesitation, he replied "*Shrek*." It's always fun to be mortified by a ten-year-old.

Before the devastating walk down the mountain which made Anne (center) "hate her life"!

That night I did *Deconstructing Broadway* and, thankfully, it was a hit. As a matter of fact, since R Family is always trying to recruit new passengers, Anne Steele saw a gay couple on the cruise who didn't know anything about us. She invited them to the show so they could see what our entertainment is like. They were both major travelers, and even though one of the men was only in his 40s, he had been on 50 (!) cruises. After my performance, he told Anne it was the *first* show he's seen on a cruise that he hasn't walked out on! As I've always said, if I can make just one person not walk out, then my job as a performer is done.

The next day we stopped in Santorini, the city whose name constantly reminds me of "Project Runway" designer Santino. The area is a lot of islands that were formed by an enormous volcanic explosion. People also think that perhaps the ancient city of Atlantis was lost there during another explosion. The city is at the top of an enormous cliff that you can walk up to or take a cable car. I was so hot waiting for the cable car that I bought a hat which either makes me look mysterious/sexy or nerdy/tip o' the hat to my grandfather. Regardless, all of the guests met at a great restaurant on the very top called Argo's. Delish...for adults. But not for ten-year-olds. After course-after-course of hummus, calamari and olives, we decided Juli should actually *eat* something so we left to get some food on the cruise. We bid everyone adieu, took the cable car down and were on the boat in 20 minutes. We had briefly considered walking down the mountain/cliff but decided to take the cable car because it was faster. Little did we know how lucky we were. We found out the next day that by the time all the cruise guests left the restaurant, the cable cars had crazily long lines because every cruise passenger in Santorini decided to go back to the boat at the same time. The R Family people were nervous that they'd miss the cruise if they waited for the cable car so they all walked down the mountain. First of all, imagine people walking down a steep mountain while wearing completely inappropriate shoes. Next, add in the factor that there are donkeys that use the trail all day long. And there are no donkey pooper-scooper laws in Santorini. So, from what we were told, it was non-stop passengers awkwardly trying to walk in sandals and completely wiping out every two minutes. That's right: you were either walking directly in donkey dung or you were falling in it. And speaking of which, the donkeys themselves were constantly pushing their way through the crowds of people as they ran up or down the mountain. Anne, who always has a smile on her face, told us that after 15 minutes of tripping constantly — and encountering donkeys and dung — she literally started chanting, "I hate my life." I haven't hauled that out since I was 14!

The next day we went to Mykonos, and we noticed that women in Greece are not like Americans, i.e., they have no shame about their bodies aging. James, Juli and I saw what looked like a casting call for Madame Armfeldt, all in skimpy bikinis! They were showing more skin than I do at the beach, and let me just say that the casting call also specified the Madame Armfeldts could be any size. That's right...I've finally seen a size 16 string bikini. Anne told us that she spent a whole summer there working in a piano bar. They gave her housing, a good salary and all she had to do was sing a few hours a night. She would wake up late and spend the whole day on the beach, then go a belt a few tunes. Delicious! She informed us that most women on Greek beaches rarely wear tops. Va-va-voom. It's so common that stores sell full and half bikinis. You can just buy the bottom half if you want. I actually want a three-piece for myself.

We were finally at the end of the week and James, Michael Lee and Anne starred in a little show I put together especially for the cruise. I knew what songs James and Anne were going to sing, and I *loosely* linked them all together with a story I wrote. Of course, adult ADD-style, I wrote it the night before, but thankfully it went over great. I decided to make it Greek-themed, so Michael Lee played the brother of Aphrodite, named Aphro-sassy. His Greek God power was putting people in relationships that are wrong for them. Anne played JodieFosterus, who Aphro-sassy puts in a relationship with Homer's brother, Ho*mo* (played by James). The story barely made sense, but it worked and everyone's favorite line was about JodieFosterus. Michael Lee as the narrator intoned: "JodieFosterus was stuck. Stuck in her bad relationship and stuck in a dead-end day job at a hummus factory and a night job carving those little washing stones for the shower. That's right, she had days of hummus and nights of pumice." By the end of the show, Anne was paired off with Kelli and James was paired off with me. P.S. I played the brother of Persephone: Per*Seth*one. Juli came up with that joke, which shows the level of humor I was going for.

After the cruise, we went to Venice for two days and I loved it. That city is gorgeous! Literally, wherever you look, it's stunning. There are no cars, so you can walk in the street, plus there's coffee everywhere and you are constantly near a beautiful canal. Our only issue was, they don't give extra food to Americans who are used to overeating. First example, we went out to lunch and Juli ordered old school

With rare sugar and cheese in Italy.

spaghetti. The waitress sprinkled some parmesan cheese on it, and when Juli asked for a little more, the waitress told us in no uncertain terms that she'd have to charge us. I first thought that perhaps there was a cheese shortage in Italy, but cut to: a little later, we went to an outdoor café. James got a bottle of water, but asked if he could use a few sugar packets that were sitting out (he knew I'd want some later because I always over-sugar my coffee). When James went to take the packets, the woman shook her head with a decisive "no." Cheese *and* sugar shortage? Finally, today at Marco Polo Airport I got some gnocchi at a little food place. The woman serving the food put some tomato sauce on the gnocchi and I asked for a little more. The good news is she did give it to me. But I haven't seen that much reluctance to do something since Mary Tyler Moore flung that food into her shopping cart during the opening credits of "The Mary Tyler Moore Show."

Ciao!

When Christine Ebersole Met Richard Burton
August 22, 2011

Me, Christine and Mark pre-show!

Hello from Provincetown. I'm back after jet-setting through Europe. This weekend Christine Ebersole joined my series at the Art House and she was fantastic. We tried to format the show with a smattering of everything from her career, so we started with her first big musical role, Ado Annie. She did the late '70s revival of *Oklahoma!* with Christine Andreas, Marty Vidnovic, Harry Groener and Laurence Guittard. When she was at the very end of her run, she was asked to audition to play Guinevere in a big tour because the production had fired the leading lady. Old school-style, she auditioned at a Broadway theatre and while she was reading the scene with the reader, she heard a mellifluous voice from the back of the house say, "I'd like to read it with her." Cut to: Richard Burton came onstage wearing what she described as a powder-blue cashmere sweater. Christine told us that she tried to appear like a confident actress and continued reading the scene calmly, but inside she was screaming, "AH!!!!! It's Richard Burton!" She got the gig and then found out she only had *five days* to learn the part! The show tech'd on Monday-Wednesday, so she knew she'd only get one run-through with Richard Burton on Thursday night before opening (in front of an audience of 3,500 people). Right before the final run-through, Richard Burton came to her dressing room and said, "Oh, Christine, the stage lights are killing my eyes. I'm sure you won't mind... I'm going to skip the run-through. "

That's right. She didn't get to play the role opposite him until opening night. *And* she didn't get to wear her costumes until opening because they weren't made yet. During the afternoon run, right before opening, the orchestra played her intro to "The Simple Joys of Maidenhood," and when it came time for her to sing...*silence*. She couldn't remember anything. At All. They swooped her away sent her to a "dark room" where they told her to sit and think of nothing. Christine said that her brain had had it and couldn't deal with any more information coming into it. Finally, opening night arrived. Before each scene, they would quickly dress her in the wings and, because she had no sense of the continuity of the show, they told her what scene she was about to do. At first, everything went smoothly because she forced herself to stay in the moment. But there was one section where she was onstage and didn't have lines for a while. Suddenly a voice in her head laughed maniacally and whispered in her ear, "You have *no idea* what your next line is!" Panic. She then had *another* voice in her head say, "Just be here now," and the two battled it out. Finally, the moment came for her to speak, and even though she didn't know what the line was going to be, it magically came out of her mouth. I'm sweating writing about it. My question is: Do people in other fields go through that kind of terror? Does a brain surgeon have a dinner party and tell a "hilarious" story about how he couldn't remember which cortex to operate on, but thankfully — right when the scalpel went down — he severed the correct artery? Does it get as many laughs?

I met Christine during the first reading presentation of *Thoroughly Modern Millie*. She played Muzzie, the role played by Carol Channing in the film. Amanda Naughton played Millie. The role of Mrs. Meers, played by Bea Lillie in the film, was played by...Edward Hibbert! It's always fun to find out who played roles in early readings of musicals. When *Wicked* had early presentations, the role of Boq was played by Gavin Creel! Kristin Chenoweth as Glinda would point to him and say, "Do you see that unusually tall munchkin?" The first reading of *Aida* had Audra McDonald in the title role, and the early versions of *Parade* starred Matthew Broderick! When Christine was doing *Millie* she was still living in California. Thankfully, she moved back to NYC and returned to Broadway (and two Tony Awards). Once she hit 40, she said that her LA agent "stopped making outgoing phone calls"; she knew that Broadway would be better for a woman of her age. Apparently, she claims there's a theory that the older you get, the further East you should move. She then waved to the audience and said, "See you in Hong Kong." P.S. She didn't move to New York City proper, she moved to Maplewood, NJ. As she always quotes, "From *Holly*wood...to *Maple*wood. (Pause.) What a difference a leaf makes."

On my trip home last week from Europe, James, Juli and I were in line to show our passports at the Frankfurt airport. That area of the airport is always very strict and has signs everywhere saying "no cell phone use." Juli had an empty bottle and wanted to throw it out, but James thought she shouldn't leave the line. I didn't want her to have to carry it, so I asked one of the security people if she could throw it out. He looked at me strangely, but nodded. Juli left the line, threw it out and came back. He then approached me and told me, in not great English, that I had to sign. Huh? Was I signing a permission slip retroactively to let Juli out of line? Was I signing to admit I had broken the rules? I then realized...he was asking me for an autograph! What the — ? I looked at him and asked if he was serious. He pointed at me and said, "Broad-way." Hmm...succinct but correct. I asked how he knew who I was, and he said, "From the internet." How cool is that? I'm assuming he's seen my *Deconstruction* videos. And/or my old desperate dating profile from Jdate.

The great Marilyn Maye performed in P-town last week and the response was amazing. People continually kept coming up and telling me that they wept during her show. *She's now been singing there every summer since and people are still obsessed*. One of her friends knows that I love Barbra so he told me this story: On the final week of the last Barbra tour, there was a party for the orchestra that had been traveling with her. The musicians were informed that if they wanted a photo with Barbra, the party would be the time to get one. One of the trumpeters decided to get a photo with her and was sent to a room to do it. When he walked in, Barbra wasn't there. Strange. Suddenly he noticed...a green screen. FYI, that's what they use in horror films so they can film scenes without the special effect and

With the Hi-larious Miss Richfield 1981

then put them in later. Apparently, Barbra was a special effect and would be put in later! I haven't gotten verification for the story but if it's true, it's hilarious!

Provincetown always has tons of shows playing and I took Juli to see Miss Richfield, 1981 who is playing at the Crown and Anchor. Miss Richfield, 1981 refers to "her" title and to the year she was crowned in Minnesota. The show was hilarious. The highlight is when she calls up two people from the audience for a spelling bee. It's really just an excuse for her to be politically incorrect. Each word the contestants must spell has a category assigned to it. The first category is "Jewish." The word was "Christmas" and the sentence Miss Richfield used to demonstrate it was: "Little Rachel Rabinowitz received eight highly discounted gifts during Chanukkah, the Jewish *Christmas*."

L'chaim!

Pointless in P-Town, Plus Yeardley Smith Speaks!
August 29, 2011

I am writing this pre-hurricane. It's 10:30 Saturday night and the rain has begun but not much else. Here's the lead-up to this moment. When I heard the hurricane was coming, I wanted to cancel my shows in Provincetown and be with James and Juli and the dogs in New York. I knew I'd be incredibly stressed being separated from them. But that would involve not only ixnaying my three performances in Provincetown but also cancelling Gavin Creel's two shows. I called him and asked whether or not we should cancel and he said whatever I decided was fine. His attitude is as easygoing as his voice. I had a restless night but finally decided I would fly there. The next day, I left my apartment at 10 AM for my 11:50 AM flight. Unfortunately, I didn't check my flight status and when I got to the airport, I found out we were delayed until 2:45! Gavin wasn't due to fly til the next day so I was by myself at JFK for a bunch of hours, checking weather.com. My flight was to Boston, where I would then take a Cape Air flight to Provincetown. I postponed my Cape Air flight and then found out my Boston flight was even more delayed. I postponed my Cape Air flight again. Finally, we took off at 5 (!) and I got to Boston at 5:41. My connecting flight was at 5:44. Luckily, Cape Air is very Mom and Pop so my manager was able to call them to tell them I was running crazily late and they told him they'd try to hold the plane for me. I ran like a lunatic to the gate, but the flight had *just* left. Literally, I felt like crying. I then booked a 7 PM flight which would get me to P-town at 7:30, the same time that my show is supposed to start. I called my manager and asked him, since the P-town airport is so close to the Art House, if they would hold the curtain for me, David Merrick-style. P.S. Do you remember the ad I'm talking about? When *42 Street* was in its dwindling years, *Phantom of the Opera* was the biggest show on Broadway. People would line up outside the Majestic Theatre and wait for *Phantom* ticket cancellations. David Merrick knew that there were plenty of people who wouldn't be able to get into P*hantom* every night and they wouldn't know til around 8PM and by then it would be too late to see another show. Well, because *42nd Street* was playing directly across the street, he decided to start *42 Street* at 8:15 to nab all the disappointed people who couldn't get into *Phantom*. I remember there was an ad campaign that featured a big photo of him pulling back an ornate curtain. Underneath, it read, "David Merrick is holding the curtain for YOU!" It was inventive/creepy.

Anyhoo, my manager put the kibosh on the David Merrick held curtain because he was nervous my plane would be late and the audience would be held indefinitely. He told me to cancel the show for that night. That was all it took for my mother to start a texting rampage. She wrote and told me that I already cancelled one show and it was a sign that I should come back to New York. She hauled out her theory that if there are constant obstacles being put before you, you should take it as a message. I never buy that because it can be applied in any way to anything. In the old days, I'd dial someone on the phone and I would decide that if I got a busy signal (I said it was the old days), it was a sign that I shouldn't be calling them. Of course, looking back, I realize that the theory was completely appropriate because I'd only apply it to people I was completely romantically obsessed with who had zero interest me. I remember finally getting through to one of them, who I nervously asked out. His response was a repeated "You're too kind." AKA "no."

Regardless, I got so anxiety-ridden thinking about leaving the family/dogs in New York and then thinking about being stuck in Provincetown that I called my manager and Gavin Creel and we all decided to ixnay the weekend of shows. I went to the JetBlue counter and got the next flight out. So, all in all, I left my apartment at 10 AM and got back at 11 PM.

Before all of this happened, I did my *Seth Speaks* for SiriusXM Stars. My main guest was Yeardley Smith who is best known as Lisa Simpson on "The Simpsons." I am so obsessed with her and that show, but managed to speak of other things as well. First of all, her first name. It was her dad's middle name and it's pronounced like "Yard-ley." The spelling is Irish and she's been annoyed about the irrelevant E for years. I suggested that she pull a Barbra and have it legally removed, and she said that my suggestion is 25 years too late. She was wearing an amazing pair of shoes and, turns out, it's from her own line! They're called "Marchez Vous" and she designs them all. Unfortunately, none for men. On "The Simpsons", she's the only cast member who only does one voice. The creative staff thinks her voice is way too distinctive to do another character on the show. As a matter of fact, she's not even allowed to be a voice in a crowd scene! She did some background voices in earlier episodes and people immediately wondered why Lisa Simpson was in the crowd. P.S. What she really said was, "I'm not even allowed to do *walla walla*" which I eventually figured out was a term for background voices. I was very proud of my language deduction.

She also told me that the cast records episodes every Monday...all together! I was so shocked. I thought that they all record them from various locales around the globe, but she said that it's always been that way from the beginning. She thinks it may be because none of the creators had ever done an animated series before so they just assumed the actors had to be in the same room. Yeardley said that by being together, it also gives the actors opportunities to ad lib lines which can make it into the episode. (She said that Dan Castellaneta and Hank Azaria were brilliant at ad libs). The most fun part of the interview for me was seeing Juli be completely star-struck. She's met some pretty famous people but she was literally mouth agape/grinning throughout the whole interview. Afterwards, Yeardley recorded her a message that Juli plays obsessively.

The shocking part of the radio show happened in the middle when I got an unexpected guest: Alice Cooper! He was doing an interview in another studio and asked if I was there. Apparently, he listens to my show every day. What the — ? I immediately asked him what was up with the name and he said he wanted a name that would "piss off" the parents of America. He said that "Alice Cooper" sounds like the kindly old lady down the block... who has bodies buried under her porch. Since he's constantly photographed with snakes, I asked him for a snake story and he told us that he put one of his snakes, either Eva Marie Snake or Boa Derek, in the bathtub for the night. When Alice came back the next morning, the snake was gone. He knew the snake couldn't open the door or sneak underneath it. Where was it? The medicine cabinet? Finally, he realized...it went down the toilet! It was missing for days and finally turned up...in Charley Pride's toilet! I decided to forego the explanation of how it was found.

Well, now it's after the hurricane and I guess my mom was right and I *was* supposed to come back to New York because before the hurricane, we found out that the part of Long Island where my sister and mother live had to be evacuated. They've now moved in with us. So, mother, sister, partner, kid, lab/hound, lab/terrier and my sister's two shih tzus. One apartment. That was the reason I had to be in New York. To share in the "fun". Tune in next week to hear how much fun it was. *"Good" news: They had to stay again the following year during Superstorm Sandy.*

Varla Jean Merman in P-Town, Or, The Fleet's In
September 6, 2011

It was my last week going back and forth to Provincetown, and what is a week of travel for me without a headache-y airport experience? Here goes: I left my apartment at around 10:15 to make my 11:50 flight. No bags to check and I already had my boarding pass. The cab took me all the way uptown to cross the bridge into Queens…and it was closed. Oy! My driver decided to go downtown to the midtown tunnel (which is really far from where we were). When we finally got on the FDR drive to head down, we looked to the left…and the bridge was open. There was traffic going both ways on it. We don't know if there was a secret entrance or a detour, but he felt we had to go downtown to be safe. When we finally got to JFK, I still had to wait on the security line. I was having a panic attack but finally got through the x-ray, looked up at the monitors to see what gate the plane was at and right next to the gate number, it didn't say "boarding." It said CLOSED. I knew that it wasn't yet 11:50, so I ran like a lunatic to the gate and made it there at 11:43…*and got on the plane*! So relieved! I could not believe I was able to get on the plane minutes before departure, and I knew everyone's eyes were on me as I walked down the aisle. Then, as I sat down and finally stopped my panting, all the passenger's eyes shifted…to two other people boarding *after* me! How dare they trump my drama!

Anyhoo, it's finally September and I'm about to be on the road again. And by "road," I mean "sea." I leave on Thursday for the Playbill cruise, so the next time I write this column, I'll have my signature jet lag and weight gain. But until then, here's the update from my last week in Provincetown.

Andrea Martin was the final celeb from the Broadway Series at the Art House and on Friday night, I took her to see Varla Jean Merman's hilarious show. Varla is played by Jeff Roberson, and he usually performs in P-town for the whole summer, but he was planning on spending June and July Off-Broadway starring with Leslie Jordan in *Lucky Guy*. If you don't know, even though Varla and Leslie got amazing reviews, the show closed ten days after opening. In his Provincetown show, he tells the audience that he was starring in an Off-Broadway show, but it abruptly closed after opening. He quickly says, "Not my fault!," but then thoughtfully admits, "…well, I guess, partially." In his show, he sings "Children Will Listen" as he shows a montage of possible children's books he can write (instead of "Curious George," there's a cover photo of "Bi-curious George"), and he intros the song with a knowing, wise face: "Be careful around children, because they're like sponges. (Pause.) Full of bacteria." I also love that every time Varla mentions someone like Rihanna or Lady Gaga, she'll give a knowing nod and call them a "colleague."

In order for me to enjoy my delicious Provincetown food binges, I started pushing my workouts here by taking boot camp-style classes. The annoying thing is that Jeff takes the classes with me and he's like one of those ex-smokers who suddenly can't stand to be around smoke. He used to weigh another 100 pounds, and now that he's lost the weight, he's in incredible shape and is continually pushing himself…and people who don't want to be pushed. The instructor gave us a slew of exercises to do and Jeff made the suggestion that we take a "break" between sets…by doing a run! That's not called taking a break! It's actually the opposite. And speaking of weight/food/etc., Andrea Martin was casually walking through town the other morning and a woman came up to her, desperately. Here's the dialogue:

WOMAN: Are you from around here?
ANDREA: Not really, but can I help you with anything?
WOMAN: Do you know a place where I can get a hot dog?
ANDREA: Uh…not really. What about a bagel or some eggs.
WOMAN: (Adamant) No! A hot dog. I just need something to tide me over.

Andrea saw me minutes later and was obsessed with the conversation. First of all, a hot dog? It was 10:20 in the morning. Second of all, tide her over until *what*? *P.S. We quote this exchange to this day!*

Andrea's shows were both sold out and it was a great way to end the series. Standing ovations as well. Not for my show, FYI. But for her show. I'm so "happy" for her. She's coming on the Playbill Cruise, too and she's bringing one of her best friends, Debra Monk. They will either have an amazing time. Or it will be the ruination of their friendship.

In preparation for my European cruise, I cashed in my Groupon for teeth whitening. The whole experience is crazy. You sit in a chair and they put a thing in your mouth that makes you have your teeth permanently exposed. Then the technician paints a layer or some kind of bleach on your chompers and shines an ultraviolet light directly on them. She did warn me repeatedly not to look at the light so, of course, I spent the whole time wanting to look at it and/or obsessing that I *did* look at it by accident and permanently ruining my cornea. After around an hour, the whole thing was finally done. Then the dentist came in and asked me what kind of stuff I ingested that could stain teeth. I said that I don't smoke and I hate wine. And that I mainly drink ice coffee with a straw. I knew that if you used a straw, the staining coffee mainly bypassed your teeth. I was then about to leave when he told me that I had to take extra care 'til the whitening fully took hold. Huh? First, he told me not to drink coffee for two days. I reiterated that I drank through a straw and he still told me to stop for two days. What? I'm supposed to go through a Yom Kippur caffeine withdrawal just for whiter teeth? I flat out told him to forget it. I don't think any other patient had ever reacted that way because he looked taken aback. Then he said not to eat anything with any soy sauce. What? All I eat is Chinese food. I just glared. Suffice it to say, I decided to try to avoid the staining foods for two days but lasted a little less than that. Within 40 minutes, I was eating frozen yogurt and the flavor I chose was "Red Velvet". What is my problem? James was horrified when he saw and told me to stop. I learned my lesson. Avoid James. Twenty minutes later, I was hiding in the kitchen eating two chocolate chip cookies. Conclusion: my teeth were white for as long as the run of *Lucky Guy*.

Happy Labor Day and Back-to-School week!

Travel Is So Broadening
September 12, 2011

Like the song from the '70s, I ask, "Where do I begin?" First of all, my computer karma. Every year I do a benefit for the charity Only Make Believe and last year the founder got me an iPad as a thank-you gift. Much more functional than the traditional bouquet, and yet I can get on the internet using a bouquet of flowers easier than I can with the iPad. That is to say, I don't quite know how it works. All right, all right, I'm exaggerating...ish. Regardless, it comes with a built in Nook so I decided that for my upcoming European cruise, instead of carrying around a lot of heavy trashy novels, I would download them (with some help getting on the internet). The day before I left, my iPad stopped working. Completely. So now I'm being forced to read books the old-fashioned way. Ugh! It's so tiring to lift *each* page and turn it.

Regardless, that was just part of my computer karma. What also began happening a few weeks ago is that the shift button on my Mac decided to not recognize certain letters. You may think that capitals aren't so important if you happen to be doing your thesis on e.e. cummings but they are important when you make (some) part of your income as a writer. What keys wouldn't do a capital, you ask? How about "I" for starters. That's right! The one word I'm obsessed with! I decided I couldn't spare my computer overnight to let the Mac store fix it (Why?) so I adjusted instead. My left shift key was the temperamental one, so I forced myself to get used to using the one on the right. Did you even know there was a shift key on the right? P.S. I just left London, and using the right shift key is as bizarre, weird and uncalled for as their insistence on driving on the wrong side of the road.

So, to continue my karma, I brought my broken shift key laptop with me since I'd learned to deal with it, but once I got to Europe, it added a new twist: *Both* my shift keys stopped working...as well as my return button! I'd call it my "enter button" but I don't have the energy for the requisite sassy double entendre that should follow. My point is, when you don't have a return button, you can't do *anything*! I type in the name of a website and it literally just stays in the toolbar. Nothing. I hit return and there's less reaction than when Nicole Kidman registers intense surprise. P.S. I had so many ways to go with that joke and I picked the easiest. P.P.S. Speaking of jokes, Varla Jean Merman's P-town show is themed around her writing a novel, and at one point she sings a lyric imploring someone to Kindle her Nook. Brava bizarre double meaning! Back to my computer: Thankfully, James happened to be carrying an extra keyboard (!) and it's plugged into my Mac at this moment. Hence I, can capitalize everything. Take that, E. E. Cummings!

Before I write about my European excursion, let me describe the myriad of interviews I conducted before I left. Because I'm gone for two weeks, I doubled up on *Seth Speaks*, my SiriusXM talk show. I always give the details of when it airs because I'm constantly running into my "biggest fans," who literally know nothing about my new talk show. *This just happened recently. I ran into super-fans and when I mentioned the "Concert For America" that was happening in their hometown, they stared blankly. Not only not knowing it was going to be where they lived, but having never heard of the concert. The concert James and I have been doing every month since January 2017!*

Anyhoo, two weeks ago I got a great "get." Isn't that what real journalists call it when they snag someone hot? Or was that just in the film "Anchorman." Either way, I got to interview Meredith Vieira! I asked why she had left "The Today Show," and she mentioned the old chestnut of wanting to spend more time with her family which I was a tad skeptical of until she told me that her wake-up time was 2:30 in the morning. I calculated that in order to get eight hours of sleep, she'd have to be in bed by 6:30 PM! I then amended her "I want to spend more time with my family" sentence to "I want to be awake with my family for at least 30 minutes a day." After a little prodding, she revealed that when she was younger, she wanted to be an actress! Perhaps there's still a chance, I ventured? I don't want to say I see a tour of *Legends* in her future starring herself and Barbara Walters, but I am slightly psychic. Actually, speaking of Barbara Walters, Meredith said that the first people who tried out for "The View" were herself, Star Jones and Debbie Matenopoulos. They auditioned lots of other people but it was the three ladies who went in first that got the gig. I guess it pays to be first. However, Betty Buckley's theory is that you should *always* try to be the "last girl" on the last day because it worked for her when she did *1776* and *Promises, Promises*. I guess both theories can work. Unfortunately, I'm usually the middle girl on the fourth day.

I also interviewed the hilarious Kristine Zbornik, who's just back from the *9 to 5* tour, for which she played the secretary obsessed with Mr. Hart. We were reminiscing about our days working in piano bars and she recalled the horrifying/hilarious day when she was singing a torch song and a man at the bar watched her intently. Unfortunately, as he was watching her, he was also drunkenly urinating! She noticed a puddle forming on the floor near where she was singing and ironically realized she was singing "Cry Me A River." After she finished (and he did, as well), he dropped $40 bucks on the floor and left. I nervously asked her if she took the cash, and she looked at me like I was crazy. She told me, "I picked it up, washed it off and gave it to my cab driver on the way home." La vie boheme!

O.K. Let me now share the beginning of my European foray. James and I decided to take Juli with us because we didn't want to leave her for such a long period of time, but because it's the beginning of the school year, we needed a tutor — so James' mother is with us as well. As opposed to my usual last-minute entrance to the New York metropolitan airports, the four of us actually got to Newark with plenty of time to spare and therefore decided to get something to eat. We actually went to a sit-down place at the airport and ordered. We were patiently waiting for our food when James casually looked at his watch. Yowtch! Yes, we had plenty of time to spare when we first got to the airport, but that was spent checking in, getting our luggage weighed, going through security, etc. When we realized how crazily late it was, we panicked-ly asked for our food to-go and ran to the gate. I will simply say that I wasn't the last passenger to board...James was.

On the flight to London I tried to get a little sleep but suddenly heard James' mother making a comment into her microphone. My eyes flew open and I was surprised to see she wasn't wearing a microphone — she just sounded like it. Not since Merman. Regardless, none of us really had any sleep when we landed at 6:30 AM London time. We assumed we'd get to our hotel by 8 AM and be able to sleep 'til our pre-arranged 12:30 lunch date at Parliament. Turns out, there's such a thing as "customs." We waited for a crazily long length of time. How do the Brits stand it? Now I know why it was no issue when the original version of *Les Miz* was 3 hours and 20 minutes. After we were finished at Heathrow, we were told that taking a cab to our hotel would include bad traffic and that we should take the "tube" instead. Cut to: the four of us lugging crazily heavy luggage all over the underground and the "speedy" tube still taking so long that we didn't get to our hotel til 10 AM! In conclusion, I was able to sleep from 11 to noon. *One hour*! And then I had to get dressed nicely for Parliament. I knew we wouldn't go to sleep til that night and I was devastated to know we'd pretty much be without sleep for 48 hours. James tried to mollify me by saying it would only be for 36 hours. *That's only marginally better!*! I will write about our private tour of Parliament next week, but let me say that it was amazing. And that night James and I went to see *Road Show* starring David Bedella who won the Olivier for playing Satan in *Jerry Springer* and, more importantly, dated me when he used to live in NYC. I had a whole plan laid out where I'd pit current boyfriend against ex, but I was too exhausted to carry it out. David was fantastic in the show (playing the Michael Cerveris tole) and he not only sounded great but he did some amazing tap dancing. David also just filmed a sitcom pilot for British television that's all about putting up a big musical! He plays the mean choreographer. A perfect role for me if the show becomes a hit and transfers to America and they want to have an American cast. Wait. He is American. I'm out of a job before I even get it? Not cool. *P.S. What happened to that show? We had "Smash" here in the US and I was indeed cast on it. For one (1) episode with four (4) lines. Yay?*

Well, by the time *Road Show* was over we were exhausted but stayed awake to have dinner with David and his co-star Michael Jibson. Afterwards, we stumbled back to our hotel and went to sleep. Everyone had assured us that if we stayed up it would cure our jetlag because we'd be forcing ourselves to get on British time. Unfortunately, Juli took a nap during the day and therefore woke up bright and early... at 2 AM. Since she didn't have a job to go to like Meredith Vieira she instead decided to wake up James' mother every half hour. Juli then took her charm to our room at 6 AM and I did my signature rolling over while James took her to breakfast. For the rest of the day, all irritation shifted to Juli. Throughout this trip, there's always been one of us four whom the other three are mad. I was so mind-bogglingly cranky at Heathrow I had to tweet that my behavior proves James and I should never be on "The Amazing Race." I was then corrected by another tweet that couples hating each other is precisely the kind of behavior "The Amazing Race" is looking for. Touche.

All right, I'm about to go out to a delicious European dinner so I must bid you adieu, but stay tuned next week for more of my overseas adventure. And my new dating profile which I may be soon be forced to post on Match.com ASAP.

Pip Pip, London! Ciao, Italy!
September 19, 2011

I am looking out at a pitch dark sky. It's 11 PM and we're sailing somewhere off the coast of Italy. I guess there must be no moon in the sky because I haven't seen anything this dark since "Rosie Live." (FYI, I was a writer on that show and didn't notice the lighting was dark, but that's what everyone told me after we aired). Anyhoo, I'm writing this week's column on my terrace on the deck of the Seven Seas Mariner, which is the ship being used for the inaugural Playbill Cruise. Before I get into that, let me tell about the end of my London trip. I emailed Caissie Levy (pronounced "Leave-ee" who played Sheila in *Hair* on Broadway and on the West End *And is now playing Elsa in Frozen!* and she hooked me up with tickets to see *Ghost*. One of the co-composers is Dave Stewart from the Eurythmics (I love their music).

Caissie Levy and I as showgirls (for some reason).

The special effects were super cool and I could *not* figure out how the leading man walked *through* a door. Brava modern-day Doug Henning! Caissie sounded amazing as usual but I got a total anxiety attack because her first note in the show is a high D! I told her afterwards that it's so mean to start a show on such a crazy high note and she completely agreed. Sweet dreams are *not* made of this. She's taking off two weeks to go to Florida to get married and then she finishes up in London during the winter. I asked her if she was coming with the show to New York and I got the Broadway shrug/smile which usually means "I can't talk until the negotiations are over." *She did come to NYC with the show! And, P.S., James and I recently ran into Caissie and her husband on 72nd street. Holy cow, is he cute! I'm not saying I flirted non-stop but I'm sure Caissie wanted me to Lev-y her husband alone.*

When we all first got to London (during the crazy sleep-deprived day), my friend John Reid set us up a private tour of Parliament led by one his good friends. Margaret McDonough is not only in the House of Lords but she's also a Baroness. Turns out, that title doesn't necessarily mean you're married to a Baron, it can be bestowed upon you by the head of your government party. I kept wanting to launch into "Liaisons" so I could sing that part that went "...and when things got rather touchy... deeded me a Duchy." Anyhoo, she's such a cool person; she was Tony Blair's campaign manager twice, and she later helped with Obama's campaign. Even though she's obviously incredibly busy, she spent so much time with us and took us all over Parliament. One of the cool things she showed us was where you're supposed to store your sword (!) when you enter. And speaking of swords, she mentioned that in the old days during voting time, things would get so heated that members on opposite sides of the vote would kill each other! After a while, there was a line made on the floor that you had to stand behind. It was far enough away from the other side that a sword wouldn't reach. Everyone has to stand behind it and that's where the expression "toe the line" comes from. Who knew? Or, tip o' the hat to the Brits: "'Oo knew?" She also showed us the bag where you're supposed to put your written vote, hence the expression "It's in the bag." So much history! Essentially, every expression started in England. I was a little mortified to be an American. What expressions have we come up with? Just "Dude, where's my car?"

And now, my signature travel karma. To say this one was a doozy is an understatement. Our flight to Rome was at 7 AM so the front desk told us that we should be picked up at 5 AM. He told us that if we were going to Rome, we'd definitely be at Terminal 3. We ordered the cab and went to bed. The first thing that happened was I called Elizabeth and Juli's room at 4:45 to make sure they were up. They didn't answer but James told me not to worry. We went to get them at 5...and they were still asleep. We had all forgotten that their room phone *never worked*! Since we hadn't asked to get it fixed, their wake-up call never came. Nonetheless, they hopped to it and we were on our way very quickly. The trip to Heathrow took around an hour and as we were pulling up, James wanted to make sure we were being dropped off at the right terminal. Yes, the front desk guy said it's always Terminal 3 to Rome, but James asked me to use my phone to go online and check our tickets. I looked and it said Terminal N. What the H was N? I thought maybe it meant not assigned. We asked the cab driver and he said it was probably Terminal 3. I checked again. N. Did that mean North? Not available? Then the cab driver murmured that there *is* a terminal N....at Gatwick Airport. That's right, folks, we went to the *wrong airport*. How far away was Gatwick? One hour. When did our plane leave? One hour. Every story about traveling to England always mentions Heathrow! Who knew London has its own Newark airport!?! James completely blamed himself because he arranged the tickets, but I knew I couldn't bust him because this is the kind of thing I pull every week. We got our bags and headed right into the Heathrow British Airways counter. I explained the situation and the ticket man checked all of the outgoing flights: sold out. I was momentarily devastated, but the next thing I knew, he made some phone calls and we all had tickets for the 7:05 flight. *And* I was in Business class! Brava Brits!

By the way, I did skip over our visit to Buckingham Palace because there's not much to the story except that it was beautiful and that as we passed through the music room, James' mother whispered to me, in full Texas accent, "Look at those plants. They're so tacky!" The guard then immediately walked over and said to her with a British smile, "Those plants were brought in recently." Yay. Her "whispering" was heard by a palace official. The whole whispered comment being overheard event reminded me of years ago when I was at a restaurant with my sister. Nancy looked at the modern art paintings on the wall and said, "I don't know why anybody would want crazy-looking paint splatterings on a wall." One minute later, the owner of the restaurant appeared, and instead of saying, "I heard you dishing the paintings on the wall," she said, "I understand you're interested in hearing about the art my daughter painted." Ah! What an amazing passive/aggressive bust on hearing Nancy's comment! Nancy was then forced to go along with the obvious lie and listen to a ten-minute explanation on the technique used to make each one while nodding with an interested smile. Brilliant!

When we got to Rome, we checked into the Excelsior, an amazing five-star hotel that Playbill got for us. Andrea Martin and Debra Monk were already checked in and we all went out to dinner. Andrea's sister runs the travel channel in Canada and Andrea decided to document her trip to make some webisodes entitled "Andrea and Deb Go To Europe." Andrea told us at dinner that her filming only lasted for half a day. She and Deb went to the zoo together and as soon as Andrea began filming, Deb waved the camera away angrily. They then didn't speak for an hour. Then reconciled. Crazy. We all went out to dinner and while we were ordering, the waitress suddenly looked at Deb, pointed and said "The Devil's Advocate!" in Italian. That was a movie Deb had been in and the waitress recognized her. More and more waitstaff began coming over and smiling. I then piped up, pointed to Andrea and asked, "Don't you all recognize her?" That was met by a bevy of miffed expressions. Andrea then spent a frantic six minutes trying to translate "My Big Fat Greek Wedding" into Italian. It ended with vague nodding from a smattering of waitresses as they slowly walked away. I'm still working on translating "*Legally Blonde*: The Search for the Next Elle Woods."

OK, I'm finishing this up while looking out my balcony window at Mt. Etna, an active volcano. Yay? Tonight I do *Deconstructing Broadway* and then Christine Ebersole does her show. As they say in the travel-postcard business: Having a wonderful time! Wish you were here!

Playbill Cruise With Christine Ebersole, Brian Stokes Mitchell, Andrea Martin and Debra Monk
September 26, 2011

Hello from Lufthansa flight 463. I'm on my way back from the inaugural Playbill Cruise and it was a brava! We boarded the ship on Tuesday and the delicious part about the Regent line is that every room has a balcony. Speaking of delish, I did non-stop eating but somehow Andrea Martin wound up losing four pounds. How does she know she lost? From obsessively weighing herself every day. Unfortunately, it took an incredible effort from her to actually see how much weight she lost because she can't see well without her glasses and, naturally, she took them off when she weighed herself because she didn't want the added poundage. Seriously. She would stand on the scale and completely contort her upper body down to the ground to get her eyes as close as possible to the scale readout. Not since Cirque du Soleil.

Four leaning towers.

A word about the Playbill Cruise. The ship itself held around 700 passengers and around 130 of them were Playbill passengers. So, everybody on the boat saw the main shows that the Playbill performers put on, and then there were special shows and events just for the Playbill passengers. Therefore, Andrea was nervous about doing her show because it was the first time she had an audience that just happened to show up. Every time we've done this show before, people have come because they're fans or, as Andrea said, someone they know forced them to come. Because it was such a general audience, she was nervous that her show wouldn't work. I, of course, fixed her with my signature Bea Arthur blank-faced stare every time she mentioned that she was nervous because I knew her show would be amazing whether or not the audience was familiar with her *ouevre*. Nonetheless, she still was nervous and cut to: not only an entire audience crazily laughing and applauding non-stop throughout the show, but two standing ovations at the end. *And* the cruise director, Lorraine, told us she has never seen a show on a cruise get a standing ovation. Speaking of Lorraine, every day she made a video that played in our rooms and she was always in a great mood with a big, big, *big* smile on her face. Andrea used her to get some new Edith Prickley material. She came out as Edith at the end of the show told everyone that she was the new cruise director. "That's right. Lorraine didn't make it back to the boat in time after Pisa. But don't worry. She's right behind us, swimming as fast as she can. *Smiling* all the way."

The next show was Debra Monk's chatterbox. I interviewed her for an hour and she sang three songs, including "Everybody's Girl" which she did in Kander and Ebb's *Steel Pier*. P.S. When she first came to New York, her name was Deborah Monk but her agent made her change it. Why? Because he said Deborah was wa-a-a-a-ay to long to fit on a marquee. She immediately changed it to Debra. She told us it took only 36 years for it to actually get on a marquee.

Before she moved to New York, she got her master's degree. Why? Because her college professor told her she'd want one in order to teach since she'd probably never work. Yay? She got her degree and moved to NYC where she worked as a waitress for a couple of years. She and Cass Morgan became friends and decided to help each other out. Since Cass is such a great musician, she helped Debra with singing and since Deb had so many years of theatre school, she helped her with acting. They decided to write some songs about waitressing and, one night in a benefit, they were teamed up with some guys who were writing about working in a gas station. It was a you-just-got-your-chocolate-in-my-peanut-butter moment — AKA a perfect combination — and that was the beginning of *Pump Boys and Dinettes*. The show started at the West Side Arts Theater and, after fantastic reviews, moved to Broadway where it was Tony-nominated as Best Musical! One year later, the show closed, and, in a testament to how hard the business is, after writing and starring in a Tony-nominated musical, Debra *still* didn't have an agent. Since then, she's worked non-stop, and after I interviewed her, even her close friend Andrea Martin was shocked by how many amazing projects Debra's been involved in. I had forgotten I saw her in the Off-Broadway play Woody Allen wrote (one of the acts in *Death Defying Acts*). She kindly reminded me of her very first line in the show: "What's the difference between sushi and p---y?" Pause. "Rice."

The next show on the cruise was the amazing Christine Ebersole. She began with songs that she's done throughout her Broadway career and from her various shows at the Cinegrill and Café Carlyle. Then I got up and we did a Chatterbox/performance section all about *Grey Gardens*. She told us about the people who bought the house from Little Edie after all those years of misuse. Christine said that Little Edie sales pitch was looking around the dilapidated mansion and telling them with a casual air, "All it needs is a coat of paint!" Christine added, "...and then the piano fell through the floor." She sang "Another Winter in a Summer Town," "Will You" and "Around the World." Not only did she sound fantastic and completely transform into the character, but what I was most impressed with was the fact that, yet again, the audience didn't necessarily know her, but whenever there was a pause in the music, there was absolutely silence in the house. They were riveted.

The final big show featured Brian Stokes Mitchell. But it almost didn't happen. I'm obsessed with this story because it's so twilight zone. Stokes had to do some concerts in Cincinnati so he was scheduled to join the cruise in Corfu, Greece. He first flew to Athens and then got on his flight to Corfu. He had been traveling for many hours and took a delicious nap on the plane. When he landed, he went to baggage but didn't see his bags anywhere. He couldn't find any info on which baggage carousel had his luggage so he asked someone for help. The man asked where his flight came and stokes said, "Athens." The man looked at him and said, "You're in Athens." Stokes thought there must have been a language barrier so he repeated in a clearer voice, "My flight came *from* Athens." The man then repeated, "You're *in* Athens." Stokes backed away and went to a woman who looked more official. He repeated his signature, "I just flew in from Athens," and she repeated the now oft-repeated statement, "You're *in* Athens." Stokes didn't know if he was out of his mind or if he was still asleep on the plane. Then he thought that maybe he slept so deeply that he never got off when it landed in Corfu and the plane then made its return trip to Athens. Finally, he gave his flight number and found out what happened: when the flight got to Corfu, it started to circle because of bad weather. Finally, it was forced to go back to Athens! Stokes didn't wake up until the plane landed and missed all the information about the flights diversion. But, the cruise was about to leave Corfu and now there was no way to catch it. Playbill president and publisher Phil Birsh and Judy Perl from Judy Perl Travel arranged for him to fly to Dubrovnik (natch!) and then have a driver take him to Cotor, our next stop. He got on the boat in the afternoon, and despite non-stop traveling, sounded amazing in his show. His voice is *so* solid. And, I had forgotten how riffy and jazzy he can be. Recently, he's been playing old-school leading men roles and singing legit, but on the cruise, he hauled out two *Porgy and Bess* songs and sassed them out. Speaking of which, Norm Lewis was originally scheduled to do the cruise (with Audra McDonald) but they both had to cancel when they got *Porgy and Bess*. Norm was overjoyed because he said it was the first time Stokes has ever replaced *him*!

Speaking of Corfu, Deb Monk, Andrea Martin, Christine Ebersole and her husband and my family went on an excursion together. The tour guide on our bus was torturous to my ear. First of all, she had no inflection to her voice. No words in a sentence had any emphasis. Most annoyingly, though, she linked every two to three words with "uh…" So, it sounded like (flat tone in a thick Greek accent) "Corfu is full of uuuuuuuh many stories that uuuuuuuuh are part myth and uuuuuuuh part fact and uuuuuuuh." I thought I was the only one having a breakdown, but then suddenly Christine turned around, looked at us and went "Uuuuuuuh." We were all like, "I know!!!" We could not stop obsessing. Then the tour guide coughed softly a few times and there was silence. I looked at Andrea and whispered, "She died?" Andrea then launged into an amazing imitation where she flatly spoke a few words with a Greek accent, went "uuuuuuh," coughed quietly and then closed her eyes as her head dropped to the side. It was so

In Venice, on a gondola, on Juli's birthday.

hilarious because it all had the same low energy. Andrea said, "She died as boringly as she spoke." Doing these excursions was like traveling with my 7th grade class, maturity-wise. Andrea also came with us to the Leaning Tower of Pisa. It was built to be the tallest bell tower in Italy. When we got there, though, we noticed it wasn't as tall as we expected. Andrea was disappointed and said it was like when you read a Match.com ad that says *Handsome, writer/director, brown hair/hazel eyes, 6'3'* and he shows up and is 4'2."

On our last night, we were docked in Venice. It also happened to be Juli's birthday. We spent the day shopping at Juli's favorite Venice mask store and that night Phil Birsh took us all out to dinner at a stunning/delicious restaurant. Fantastic! Before dinner we took a real Venice gondola ride. We were told that the gondola could only fit three people, but we wound up getting one for six so Juli, James' mom, James, Deb Monk, Andrea Martin and I all got to be together. It was so crazily beautiful. I keep thinking how cool it is that when Juli gets older she can say, "When I turned 11, I spent my birthday in Venice."

Now, I'm going to finish my book, as the unfunny refrigerator magnet says, but I actually mean: "My diet starts tomorrow!"

Audra & Norm and the Beauty of *Porgy and Bess*
October 3, 2011

Ah! Delicious Fall weather. We lit our first fire this weekend in the fireplace. And by "fire" I mean Duraflame fake log that essentially gives off no heat but looks pretty and is crazily expensive. Anyhoo, this week began with my signature vertigo that I get every six months. Kristin Chenoweth gets it, too, but she has a Tony and Emmy to keep her company while the room is spinning. I only have a Bistro and a Playbill Leading Man Award. Regardless, the vertigo may have been brought on by taking an eight-hour international flight and only drinking one half cup of water. It was probably exacerbated by my then doing an intense cardio workout to try to lose all the weight I gained during my two week European trip (in one trip to the gym). Thankfully, I was functional on Sunday during the Broadway Flea Market but felt myself fading throughout the day. The good news is, not only did I sell tons of stuff from my booth, but BC/EFA auctioned off a chance to co-host with me on SiriusXM and it went for $4,000! Then I went home and pretty much couldn't function. I got it together enough to do *Seth Speaks* and had Sharon Wheatley as one of my guests. Sharon is an actress I've known for years and she wrote a great book a few years ago called "Til the Fat Girl Sings." It's about her childhood — growing up overweight yet wanting to perform. She was told repeatedly that she was too big to ever "make it," yet she's now done four Broadway shows! One of the people who told her it wouldn't happen was her father who not only told her she had to be thin to be an actress but, for some reason, kept telling her she had to look like Geena Davis. To this day, Sharon has no idea why Geena was the go-to body he kept referencing. After her book came out, it was optioned by Rosie O'Donnell to become a TV series. Sharon now realizes she should have known it would perhaps not work out because the day the contracts were signed was also the day that Rosie and Elizabeth Hasselback had their famous split-screen argument on *The View*, which led to Rosie leaving the show. Regardless, the book is now an ebook as well, and Sharon has started writing a blog about being a mother of two while pursuing theatre. She essentially wants to be the Broadway version of Erma Bombeck. Each column ends with a cliffhanger, so be prepared to be frustrated until the next installment. *Not only does the column have a fabulous twist halfway through where she winds up leaving her marriage and marrying a woman (!) it also details how fabulous it is to be one of the stars of a hit Broadway show…Come From Away!*

My main guest on *Seth Speaks* was West End star Elaine Paige. I wish I had a million more hours with her because her career has been amazing. She *originated* the roles of Evita, Grizabella and Florence in *Chess*! As many people know, the original Grizabella was Judi Dench, who had to leave the show right before previews because she injured herself. And saved us from hearing what probably would have sounded like a monologue version of "Mem'ry." At that point, Elaine had finished Evita and didn't know what her next gig would be. She told me that she was driving home, listening to the radio and the deejay played a short instrumental version of "Memory" that Andrew Lloyd Webber had sent to the station. Elaine thought the melody was incredibly beautiful and since the deejay promised a longer version was coming up, she hightailed it to her house to record it. As she approached her front door, a black cat suddenly appeared! She was excited because she had been told by her mother that a black cat crossing your path is *good* luck. (Remember: In Britain, people drive on the opposite side of the road. They also think Blood Pudding tastes good. Everything is reversed.) She took the cat into her house and taped the song off of the radio. That night, she went to bed listening to the song over and over again on her Walkman. P.S. I still call my Ipod a Walkman. P.P.S. And I call my Walkman a Victrola. Anyhoo, the next day she got a call from Andrew Lloyd Webber, who asked her if she'd step into the show at the last minute. He explained that it wasn't a very big part, just a feature, but it had a great song. She tentatively/excitedly asked, "Is the song 'Mem'ry'?" Of course, when he told her it was she immediately said yes. Elaine remembers showing up at rehearsal and the dancers asking her in hushed tones, "What are you doing here? We're playing *dancing cats*. This show is going to bomb!" Cut to: one of the longest-running shows ever.

In the late '80s, she went to see Patti LuPone in *Anything Goes* and really wanted to play the role on the West End. She didn't know how to guarantee it until she decided she'd produce it herself! Brava! She also discovered John Barrowman and gave him the role of Billy after Howard McGillin left.

She talked about playing Carlotta in *Follies* on Broadway and told me that at one performance, all the lights went completely out in the middle of her big number, "I'm Still Here." Since she's old-school, she kept going and when she got to the big final notes, the lights literally came up on the word "He-e-e-e-re!" Brava timing!

At the beginning of the week, I saw a show at the Triad called *Awesomer and Awesomer* and it was so great! Phoebe Kreutz writes folk-joke songs (a genre I never heard of but when you hear the music, you'll understand the name) and Alan Muraoka helped take her solo songs and turn them into an evening of various solos, duets and group numbers. Alan's direction was amazing and each number was so well-staged and acted.

On Thursday, James and Juli and I hiked it up to Boston to see *Porgy and Bess*. I've known Audra McDonald and Norm Lewis for 20 years, and I was *so* excited to see them play title roles in a musical. James asked me if they'd ever done a show opposite each other and I told him *absolutely not*. It was definitely the first time. Then I remembered that they both starred in The Actors Fund production of *Dreamgirls* that I put together and conducted. In 2001. Pass the gingko biloba?

Both Audra and Norm were fantastic. I don't know the show very well, except for the medley I sang in High School Chorus. Yes, my school was 99 percent Jewish and, yes, we sang the grammatically incorrect "Bess, You *Is* My Woman Now." Regardless, the music is so beautiful and all the singing in the show is unbelievable. Every person sounds amazing, including David Alan Grier who is perfect as Sportin' Life. Josh Henry (the Tony-nominated star of *The Scottsboro Boys who then starred in Violet, Hamilton and is doing Carousel opposite Jessie Mueller*) gets many chances to show off his gorgeous voice and his crazily blinding smile. I was mortified that I recently had my teeth whitened and mine look like pieces of coal next to his. As for Audra, first of all, she comes on looking stunning and then immediately pulls a Caissie Levy. What do I mean by that? Remember how I said that Caissie's first note in *Ghost* is crazily high? Well, Audra walks on, looks beautiful and then within ten seconds has to hit a high B! She can't pull the ol' Ethel Merman warm up. (Apparently when Ethel Merman was asked if she warms up before a show, she responded, "What do you think the first number's for?"). Norm was also fabulous and moving as Porgy but I got a complete anxiety attack watching him walk around with his legs so twisted. He said that he does non-stop stretching backstage so he doesn't injure himself. I'm so happy he finally has a show where he can show off the voice I've been obsessed with since the late '80s when we did *Joseph*…. He ends Act Two singing such a beautiful phrase that I immediately started crying when he hit the last note. I can't take it! The two of them have amazing chemistry and it's the kind of show I could see over and over again on Broadway.

After the show, we all went out and I wanted to take a pic but Audra had post-show wig hair with a crazy do-rag on top. I told her that we would all wear one in solidarity. Norm refused, but his out of control white beard adds its own crazy.

Afterwards, I immediately asked for fun onstage mishap stories. Audra said that recently her garters snapped in the opening scene and her sassy panties fell down her legs! She knew she had to get them off because the scene ends with Porgy beckoning to her as she slowly crosses the stage. It would have been too hilarious for her to make the long, slow walk across the stage with her panties around her ankles (!), so while the scene was happening, she got them off. But then she didn't know what to do with them! Finally, she decided to throw them offstage quickly. Unfortunately, she threw it right into the male quick-change area. So, as the ensemble men were putting on their next costume, they were suddenly and angrily accosted by a pair of flying panties. If I had a dime for every time that's happened to me...

Peace out!

Audra McDonald Gets "Foreword" and Bonnie Franklin Tied Up
October 10, 2011

Spring cleaning! And by "spring" I mean "fall." This week we re-signed our lease, and the landlord had our downstairs painted. Instead of boring white, James and I wanted some fun colors. Unfortunately, we have terrible taste. Andrea Martin has an amazing eye, and her New York apartment and Toronto house are both beautifully decorated. So, I texted her and asked for some advice about what colors we should choose. She, of course, suggested that we get various samples and paint each one on the wall to pick which one looks best. I considered that idea...for many, many days. Suddenly, I was at the Janovic Plaza and the painter was standing in my apartment, impatiently waiting to begin. Andrea suggested various tasteful, muted colors. James and I took her suggestion under advisement... and picked out blue and yellow instead. I thought perhaps Andrea would see the colors we chose and give me a major thumbs up. Instead, the text I received from her said: "Easter Egg time." I was a nervous wreck to see what it would look like, but now that it's painted it looks great. As well as being a very realistic facsimile of living inside an Easter egg basket.

Besides the painting, this week was also exciting because my novel, "Broadway Nights," has been re-published by a new publisher. Vantage Press re-released the book, and my editor, Joe Pittman, asked me to write a sassy new intro. He also suggested I ask one of my friends to write a new foreword. Since the book is about Broadway, he wanted one of my Broadway friends. I decided to ask Audra McDonald, even though I knew she's always super busy. She said yes right away and then I didn't hear anything from her for weeks. The day it was due, I wrote to her, and she sent me back a document with the comment "This is probably bad." It was very Kelly Clarkson on "American Idol." Every time Kelly would sound amazing, she'd pretend to be shocked that the judges lauded her. Or she'd belt a crazy F and then haul out the ol' "I have laryngitis."

Anyway, Audra's version of a bad foreword is *so* great. It's super-sweet and yet hilariously slightly hostile. Here's a section of it:

It's July of 2010 and I am at a lovely resort in Ixtapa Mexico performing for wonderful LGBT families and friends as a part of R family vacations entertainment. I am in the middle of singing "I Could Have Danced All Night" when the Entertainment coordinator/Music Director/ pianist decided to modulate an already high song even higher forcing me to sing a note (d-flat) I had not yet ever sung in public. I hit the note, finished the song... and flipped him off. (YouTube it). Flashback 17 years to Paul Recital Hall at the Juilliard School of music...I am performing in my senior recital singing "Can't Help Lovin' That Man" as an encore. I get to the end of the bridge headed to the final "A" section when the pianist/ new friend/ music director (of the sassy part of my classical recital) decides to modulate to a new key forcing me to belt a note I had not yet ever belted in the hallowed halls of Juilliard. I belted the note, finished the song, and flipped him off. (You can't YouTube it as I own the only copy of the video and doubt that I will ever upload it.) The pianist at each of these 2 events in my musical life (and hundreds more in the 21 years I have known him) was Seth Rudetsky. In his own funny, audacious, skilled (transposing on-site mid-performance, folks!) and annoying way he pushed me out of my comfort zone in to new uncharted territory and was the first to greet me with applause and "Brava's" on the other side. He made me better. He makes everything he is a part of better. He does all of this because of his deep and passionate love of musical theater and every aspect that it encompasses. There is no one I know who is more obsessed with, knowledgeable about or more dedicated to musical theater than Seth Rudetsky. It is quite literally in his blood. It's not enough that he has already established himself as an incredible pianist (with serious classical chops), accompanist, vocal coach, stand-up comedian, comedy writer, producer and musical director. It's so much more than that. He's carved out a unique niche in the world of musical theater for himself. He has made the world of musical theater a better, richer, and much funnier place. If there were a Student Body President of Musical Theater then Broadway Seth Rudetsky would be it.

How sweet is that? Besides the flipping me off part...twice.

This week I also did a great *Seth Speaks* with the star from one of my fave 1970's sitcoms, Bonnie Franklin *who sadly passed away around a year later*. I, of course, first asked her about *Applause*, which is the Broadway show that put her on the map. She played a chorus gypsy named Bonnie ('natch) who sings the title song and I immediately asked her if Lauren Bacall is a nachtmare to work with. First off, Bonnie called her "Betty," which is her real name, and then she said that Betty got along great with her leading man, Len Cariou, and when she gets along great with her leading man, she's happy. Bonnie added a lot of subtext when she said that Len and Betty "got along," and I got the message. Bonnie said that "Applause" was the only song that didn't change from the first out-of-town try-out 'til the opening on Broadway. Everything else in the show kept changing, including casting a new Eve Harrington (the fabulous Penny Fuller). And "Applause" always brought down the house. In terms of Betty being a kind leading lady, Bonnie said that if it had been a Merman show, Bonnie would have been fired (because La Merm didn't like other ladies in her shows getting big applause), but Betty had no qualms about "Applause" stopping the show. Although, speaking of someone else named Betty but spelled B-e-t-t-e, years later Bonnie ran into Bette Davis in LA and asked her if she'd seen *Applause*. Turns out, Bette had seen it, and she *hated* it! She said that the theme of the story is about aging, yet Lauren Bacall always looked stunning throughout the whole show. Maybe so, but she made up for it by taking every song down the octave.

Go to Youtube and watch Bonnie do her big number on the Tony Awards. Side note: the waiter with the mustache is Sammy Williams, who went on to win a Tony Award as Paul in *A Chorus Line*; one of the other waiters is Nick Dante, whom the role of Paul is based on (and who co-wrote the book of *A Chorus Line*), *and* the woman talking at the beginning is Mitzi Hamilton, whom the role of Val is based on!

I asked Bonnie about other musicals she'd done, and she said that one of her favorite roles was Peter Pan. She told us why she thinks women love playing the role—because it's a very sexual experience. Huh? How is it sexual? She's dressed like a boy for the whole show! Turns out, Bonnie said that the harness is tied tightly to your body and every time you fly...there's fabulous "stimulation" involved. I didn't need any more details and filed it away under "Why Mary Martin is always smiling in *Peter Pan* photos."

Bonnie was nominated for a Tony Award for *Applause* and then went to LA to meet with the Mary Tyler Moore people and Norman Lear. She and Norman hit it off and, after their meeting, he brought her in to read. After several call-backs and a final audition for the network executives, she got the lead in "One Day At A Time." Just kidding. She met with him once...and was then offered the lead. Bonnie said it was a different time back then, and you didn't have to first get past the casting director before you got to the director/producer.

Turns out, "One Day At A Time" was based on the real-life mother of Meredith Baxter-Birney. Since the character whom Ann Romano was based on only had one child, that's how they did the pilot of the show, which didn't work. They then went back and changed things, including adding another kid ...and the show ran for ten years! When Mackenzie Phillips was first cast, Bonnie thought she was wrong for her daughter because she was too old. Bonnie was only 31 when the show began, and Mackenzie was

15! But then Bonnie saw that they both had prominent mouths and decided she looked like she could be her daughter so the age thing didn't matter.

This weekend, I hightail it to Ithaca to do *Rhapsody in Seth*. I gots ta go and finish memorizing. It's just me onstage talking non-top for an hour and a half. AKA, my dream come true!

Texts, Tweets and Michael Urie's Secret to Booking a Job
October 17, 2011

Hello from backstage at the Hangar Theatre in Ithaca, NY. I'm about to do *Rhapsody in Seth*, the play I wrote about my childhood, which I did at the Actors Playhouse back in 2003. It was directed by Peter Flynn, and now he runs the Hangar Theatre, so he asked me to come up here and put it up again. The nice part is, I was given a large dressing room backstage. The odd part? It's literally the ladies dressing room — and they left the men's dressing room vacant. Passive/aggressive. Anyhoo, it's very weird to do a show again that you haven't done in a while. I started rehearsing it last Monday and I had to have 40 percent of the lines literally fed to me. Not just the first few words of the lines, the whole line. Then, the next day I ran it again, and I suddenly knew almost all of it by heart. It's as if the words were behind a door in my head, and even though I needed help opening it, once I did, they all just came out. I wonder if that's the case for every show I've ever done. Are they all in my head somewhere? If so, does that mean that the horrific Broadway revue I did in summer camp entitled *Broadway Rainbow* is lurking in my cranium? Is *that* why I keep having vertigo attacks? Speaking of which, I finally went to an ear, nose and throat doctor because I wanted to know why the H I keep getting random vertigo attacks every six months. She checked me out (including a hearing test) and finally told me that I have "Benign Positional Vertigo." Yay! A diagnosis! She said it can be brought on by various things like airplane trips (just took a ten-hour trip from Europe) and, here's the kicker, sodium. Devastating. Why? Because James has been telling me for *years* that I can't keep ordering in Chinese food every night of the week because the sodium is terrible for me. I couldn't believe I had to tell him he was right. The doctor told me I could look up more info online about "Benign Positional Vertigo" and the more I read about (i.e. nothing definite brings it on, nothing definite stops it, it lasts for indefinite periods of time), I finally realized I have what used to be referred to in Victorian times as "the vapors." Maybe *now* I can finally be cast in a Merchant/Ivory film.

While I was at the Hangar, my friend Ana Gasteyer was doing a big benefit in L.A. for the Motion Picture and Television Fund with Kerry Butler, Matt Morrison, Angela Lansbury and more. We were texting back and forth about how great it was to have Broadway singers in Los Angeles and how audiences today across the world are so used to the horrid sound of auto-tuning. She agreed and texted: "My biggest beef! As well as one that has brought me full circle back to becoming the modern day version of my mother." This referred to the fact that her mother only likes classical music and, when Ana was a kid, wouldn't allow her to belt. I got one more text from Ana describing her morph into her mother: "It's true! At a certain point last night, I think people were avoiding me just to get away from my incessant remarks about 'how rich the live orchestra sounds.'"

Speaking of films, I interviewed Michael Urie for *Seth Speaks* this week. He just produced a film called "Thank You For Judging," which is about to be featured at the Austin Film Festival. It's all about Texas high school forensics competitions. Forensics includes things like the debate team and extemporaneous speaking, but there are also theatre competitions. There are categories like "humorous interpretation" and "dramatic interpretation," or, as we in the business call them, "H.I." and "D.I." Michael said that he saw that amazing documentary about the National Spelling Bee ("Spellbound") and knew that a docu about forensics would have the same dramatic highs and lows. I must agree because I, myself, was a fierce competitor in high school in the field of humorous interpretation. I did various monologues from *Feiffer's People* and made it to the state level where I was ranked first (!) in *all* the preliminary rounds. Then, in the semi-finals, I wound up having certain judges who didn't appreciate my comedic sass. Just so you know, the judges are actually teachers from other schools, some public and some private. As in Catholic schools. I'm not saying that perhaps I wasn't fully up to snuff during the semi-finals, but let's please acknowledge that a slew of *nuns* aren't known for their amazing senses of humor. The top eight made it to the finals and I missed making it by one (1) point. Yes, I was ranked ninth, one away from being in the finals. Of course, it hardly had any effect on me and I let it go right away. Just like I'm sure Priscilla Lopez is at peace with her experience at The High School of Performing Arts.

When Michael Urie was in a Texas community college, he visited NYC. His teacher recommended that he try out for Juilliard and he got in! While he was on that first trip to NYC, he saw tons of shows. One of them was *Ragtime*, and afterwards there was a talkback with various members of the cast. The little girl in the show had a very frank talk with the college students about what it was like doing eight shows a week and various other "I'm-a-Broadway-vet-in-the-body-of-a-ten-year-old"-type things. Michael completely remembers her no-nonsense show biz talk. Later on, he realized it was…Lea Michele! Even back then she had seen it, done it, been it, lived it. Brava!

Michael also told us that he was doing a movie recently and was asked to audition for the upcoming production of *The Cherry Orchard*. Since he was filming, he didn't have a lot of time to prepare the audition scenes and was about to cancel the audition. Finally, though, he decided to go anyway and wing it, since he knew the director (he was at Juilliard when Michael was a student). Cut to: the director didn't even want him to read the scenes. He just had Michael do really fun acting exercises as the character…like, "as you enter the stage, you notice your shoes squeak." Michael had a great time and got a call back for the following week. A day later, he was filming his movie in an underground locale where his cell phone didn't work. When he finally got reception, he had tons of messages from his agent. Turns out, the call-back was not in a week, it was *that day*! Michael hoped he could come in another day, but Dianne Wiest (who is slated to star in it) was only available that day. Since he was deep in the heart of Brooklyn and there was no way he could make it to the callback, he decided to just let it go. Cut to: the director called him and offered him the gig! Michael said that the moral is to work with people you know. Is it? Could it actually be: don't prepare for an audition? Turn off your cell phone for long periods of time? Skip callbacks and hope for the best? Or is it literally pure happenstance? It reminds me of the article in the Onion where a 114-year-old woman is continually asked the secret of her longevity and she angrily keeps saying it's simply chance. So hilarious.

Speaking of hilarious, I must go back to Ana Gasteyer to say that she has one of my favorite twitter accounts, @AnaGasteyer. The tweet this week I'm obsessed with all began when I made this video highlighting Idina Menzel in *Wicked* and *Wild Party*. At one point, I talk about how Brian d'Arcy James sings "…when we met, you were less than a dirty whore!" I love his vibrato on the last note. Watch! So, first one of my followers, Joe Halpin tweeted: "It's okay to call someone 'less than a dirty whore', just so long as you add a vibrato to whore. #StuffSethRudetskytaughtme." Then, BD Wong wrote: "I think 'whore' has to be up a fifth, like Joanne Worley. No?" I, of course, replied that *everything* should be up a fifth. Then Brian d'Arcy James wrote that he'd have to have the song *down* a fifth before he could sing it *up* a fifth. Finally, Ana tweeted my favorite tweet: "Drop the R in Whore, make it a dipthong, and KEY CHANGE mid-vowel. Always works. Yes, spin the end." I'm so obsessed with babbling that makes no sense, yet the capitals to show assuredness.

Tonight, I'm headed to the Laurie Beechman room to see the fabulous Carole Demas do her act. Carole was the original Sandy in *Grease* on Broadway, and I spent many mornings in the 1970s watching her on TV because she and Paula Janis were the hosts of TV's "The Magic Garden." If you don't remember, take a gander on youtube for her video doing "Summer Nights" and on the Magic Garden. Peace out!

Cable Is a Harsh Mistress, Plus Betty Buckley and Ilene Kristen
October 24, 2011

Greetings from Soy, a delish little coffee place in the Village where James loves to come and write. *Ugh.* *Which closed recently.* I decided to join him so I'd have a nice place to write my column and because I love soy lattes. I was excited to be at a place where I could just order a latte and *not* have to qualify that it's soy. When I got there, I walked up to the counter and ordered an iced latte with a smug smile. The woman behind the counter then asked me what kind of milk I wanted. What the — ?!? It's literally called *Soy*! What a misleading moniker. It reminds of a scene in the hilarious film "Girls Will Be Girls": Varla Jean Merman is doing a commercial for "Bizzy Gal Dinners," which are TV dinners you can serve right away because they don't have to be heated up. The commercial says they've been treated with "nutridation" which makes the food molecules feel hot in your mouth. After the commercial, there's a streaming list of side effects and qualifications, one of which is "not intended for human consumption." Hilarious!

This week I interviewed Betty Buckley on *Seth Speaks*. Betty's performing at Feinstein's in her show called *Ah-men,* where she sings Broadway songs made famous by men. *Now a fabulous album.* I asked her about playing Abby Bradford on "Eight is Enough" and she told us that the reason she had been brought in is because Brandon Tartikoff (who was working with Fred Silverman at ABC) saw the film "Carrie" and thought the character she played (Miss Collins the gym teacher) would be right as Abby Bradford. Speaking of Miss Collins, I asked Betty what it was like doing (Spoiler alert!) the big death scene in "Carrie". To refresh your memory, while Carrie is wreaking havoc on the prom guests, an enormous basketball backboard breaks off and slams into Miss Collins. Betty said that it was rigged so it would stop ri-i-i-i-ight before hitting her, but they had never actually tested it. So, in the film when she covers her head and looks completely terrified as the backboard flies towards her, she's not acting. Who needs sense memory when your actual life is being threatened?

Last year, James, Juli and I moved back to the Upper West Side, James and I decided we had had it with paying tons of money for cable TV and decided to stick it to "the man" by not having cable installed in our new place. We proudly had nothing to watch for a few weeks. *So, yeah…* We then decided that Tivo wasn't quite the same thing as cable, so we wouldn't feel guilty if we had *that* installed. Suddenly, we were able to watch Hulu Plus and stream movies from Netflix. Ah. Delish. Then we heard that the new season of "Project Runway" began and we discovered we couldn't watch it on Hulu Plus or Tivo without cable TV. We bravely soldiered on because we were *making a point*! I called my friend Paul Castree, who lives down the street, and begged him to let us watch it with him but he wasn't home at the time so we *missed the first episode*. That was it. We immediately had cable installed. Yes, we gave in. But, we didn't go back to where we started. No, this time it's much worse. Now, we're paying for Hulu Plus, Tivo *and* HBO and Showtime, which we never even had before. That's right, we stuck to our values for less than a year and although it feels terrible to have no backbone, now we don't have to wrack our brains every night, trying to make conversation. We can finally sit again in awkward silence watching TV.

On Monday, I ran into Ilene Kristen while I was sitting with Andrea Brown (my former jazz dance teacher from Broadway Dance Center). Ilene is probably best known from her long running roles in "Ryan's Hope" and "One Life to Live," but she was also the original Patty Simcox in *Grease*. Ilene told us that she was also in *Henry, Sweet Henry*…when she was 15! Before it came to Broadway, it toured out of town and I didn't understand how she went without her parents. She told us that her mom said, "You've been to sleep-away camp. It'll be fine." Not since we didn't have to wear seat belts or bike helmets. #TheOldDays #HorrificLackOfSafety. I asked Ilene to tell me about Michael Bennett and her response was exactly like Priscilla Lopez's when asked the same question. They both said he was a genius and they also both brought up the fact that he wasn't necessarily attractive, yet all of their fellow females were *in love* with him. Go to youtube and watch the clip of *Henry, Sweet Henry* starring the late, great Alice Playten. Ilene is in the red coat in the front row when they start the dance step that always got applause. P.S. She's right next to Pia Zadora.

We were all at the West Bank Cafe (because downstairs is the Laurie Beechman Theater) and Andrea and I had just seen Carole Demas' act called *Summer Nights*. Why that title? Because Carole was the first Sandy in *Grease* on Broadway. She did the song with Matthew Hydzik as Danny, and her sidekick from "The Magic Garden" (Paula Janis) and Ilene Kristen as back-up girls. First of all, even though *Grease* was 40 years ago (!), Carole looks amazing. It's cra-za-zy. Secondly she sounded great. Such a pretty, girlish tone still! And she sang so much! What stamina! At one point in the act, she talked about *The Baker's Wife*. If you don't know, that's a musical by Stephen Schwartz that was major trouble for the cast and creative team and never actually made it to Broadway. There were lots of firings, including the original director and the original leading lady — Carole! She had played the title role, Genevieve, and got to debut "Meadowlark," or as producer David Merrick called it, "That damned bird song." On Monday, she sang the entire song and I'm so glad she did because it was such a different rendition than I've heard before. There's a lyric about the blind meadowlark gaining her sight. Normally, I've never really taken in the fact that the lyric repeats ("...and her singing moved him so he came and brought her the gift of sight. He gave her sight!"). Carole added such wonder and joy to the repeated lyric "he gave her *sight*" that I'm now completely obsessed with her version of the song. Brava!

Peace out!!!

Obsessed With the *Evita* Album
October 31, 2011

I've had it! I've always been obsessed with weather and natural disasters, and not only did I *not* feel any earthquake this summer, but the one time New York gets snow in October, I'm in Pittsburgh. Not cool, man. Not cool. Any to the hoo, I spent the weekend at City Theatre and did five performances of *Deconstructing Broadway*. I was sold out (except the Saturday matinee....synagogue?) and the audiences were great.

Before we got lost...

I began my week doing a family outing with James, Juli, Tim Pinckney (from The Actors Fund), his partner Eddie Carlo and Andrea Burns, Peter Flynn and their son Hudson. We decided to go to a corn maze, which is pretty much what it sounds like. Once we were in, it was essentially James and Peter trying to find a way out while the rest of us followed in the background singing selections from our favorite Broadway show albums from yesteryear. I don't know how we got to this particular one, but at one point, we were all doing Juan Peron's bizarre *sprechtstime* section from the top of *Evita*, Act Two — "Argentinos, Aregentinos! We are all shirtless now..."

Speaking of Hudson and Andrea, this summer Andrea played Rosie in *Bye Bye Birdie* at the St. Louis Muny. Hudson came with her and because Andrea would be rehearsing all day and Hudson needed something to do, the director said Hudson could be in one of the town crowd scenes. During rehearsal, he asked Hudson to come forward and do a little dance to fill a few bars of music. Of course, since Hudson has seen *In the Heights* a ton of times, he immediately launched into some funky hip-hop steps. The kibosh was put on that and instead they taught him the twist. Even though it was one little scene, Andrea was so relieved he had something to do in the show. Cut to: The show opens and what was the review headline? "Andrea Burns Nails It?" No.

"A Worthy Successor to Chita?" No.

It was "7-year-old Steals the Muny Spotlight." Seriously. Not since "All About Eve" and/or "Mildred Pierce."

This week I saw *Judy Gold: My Life as a Sitcom*, Judy Gold's Off-Broadway show at the DR2 Theatre on West 15th Street. Throughout it, I was made aware of the scientific question, "How can Judy and I both have the same mother?" Mind-boggling. Judy talks about how her mother went into a full depression when David Berkowitz was found out to be Son of Sam. "How could a young Jewish man do such things? I don't understand," muttered her mother, walking around in a daze. Then, Judy recalls that a few days later her mother haughtily sat down at dinner. She looked at everyone with an *I-told-you-so* triumphant stare and announced her newfound knowledge with undisguised glee: "*Adopted*!"

This week on *Seth Speaks* I got to meet someone I talk about very often in my comedy show....*Fake Jan*! For those of you who don't know, after "The Brady Bunch" was cancelled, producers Sid and Marty Krofft ("H.R. Pufnstuf") decided to bring them back to television for an hour of them singing and dancing...even though very few of them could do either, let alone both. One of the things that was crazy about that show is that it wasn't a variety show starring the actual actors, it starred The Bradys. So, Mike Brady was an architect who *also* happened to be starring in his own variety show and poor Alice was starring in a network variety show but, for some reason, was forced to keep her job as a maid. Anyhoo, back to Jan. All of the original actors playing the family returned, except Jan. As I mentioned in a previous column, the father of the original Jan (Eve Plumb) knew Sid and Marty Krofft's *oeuvre*, and he effectively told Eve that she couldn't do it because it would be *the* worst show on television. So, the Kroffts decided they wouldn't do something like pretend that Jan was in boarding school (although that probably would have pleased Marcia), so they decided to hire another girl: Geri Reischl. They assumed that since she had blonde hair, no one would know the difference. What the — ? This isn't Stepford! Of course we knew, and thus came the nickname "Fake Jan." And in case you think I'm the only one who called her that, go to Geri's website; www. FakeJan.com. And now Geri has her own CD called "Fake Jan Sings"! Brava! And, just to show you how bizarre my life is, right after I met Geri, I went to a reading of *Unbroken Circle* a play written by James starring...Eve Plumb! That's right! Within an hour, I went from Fake to real Jan. Next week, I'm hanging with Dick York *and* Sergeant.

Allen and I recreating our opening Oliver! pose: Holding our bowls as the curtain rose for "Food Glorious, Food"!

When I was in Pittsburgh I reconnected with an old friend of mine named Allen Hahn. Allen is now a lighting designer, but we met when we were both tweens in *Oliver!* at the Northstage Dinner Theater. It starred Shani Wallis, who played Nancy in the movie. Doing that show was an amazing time for me. I not only got to a miss a week of horrible, horrible school for rehearsal, but after that I got to leave early every Wednesday for the matinee. Delish! I'm not saying I was obsessed with that experience and talked about it non-stop for the next five years, but suffice it to say that my nickname on the bus was "Ollie." Allen was one of the other orphans, and we recently reconnected on Facebook. It was amazing seeing him again because he was such a vital part of my childhood. Not only because we shared the *Oliver!* experience but because he came to my Bar Mitzvah and bought me two albums: the soundtrack of the film "All That Jazz" and the record that hooked me into a deep obsession to this day — *Evita*. I still remember sitting down on my couch in the den, getting out the *included lyrics* (!) and listening to it for the first time. Cut to 30 years later, singing it in a corn maze with Andrea Burns.

What goes around comes around. Peace out!

Be a Clown… in First Class
November 7, 2011

Hello from delicious First Class!

I so love getting my Elite status because I've been getting fabulous upgrades. Last Sunday night, I flew home from Pittsburgh, and then Monday morning I had to take a 6:45 AM flight to West Palm Beach. I found out Sunday night that I was getting an upgrade, and the only thing that got me up the next morning was looking forward to shoveling delicious first-class food into my gullet. Mmmm. I was flying down to Florida because the Kravis Center asked me to promote the upcoming Broadway musicals that are coming to their theatre over the next year. So, I prepared a special deconstruction show featuring *The Addams Family, Les Miz, La Cage Aux Folles, Come Fly Away* and *Hair*. For *Hair* I told everyone how it was the first Broadway show I saw (at age four) and how James and I took Juli to see it when she was eight (she loved it). I then played a medley of the phenomenal high belting that the character of Dionne has to do. Dionne was originally the brilliant Melba Moore, so I told the story of when she was first offered the show. Galt MacDermot (the composer) heard her in a studio session and wanted her to be in his new Broadway company (*Hair* had opened Off-Broadway and was about to transfer). He approached her after her session and asked her, very excitedly, "How would you like to do *Hair* on Broadway?" She glared and responded, "I didn't go to four years of music school to do nobody's hair on Broadway!" Sass!

I also found a way to promote *my* upcoming April show at the Kravis (and coming to the Broward Center as well). I'm doing *Seth's Big Fat 70's Show* where I deconstruct 70's variety shows as well as myself, so for *La Cage Aux Folles* I talked about how amazing Jerry Herman's music is and how nothing could ever sully it. Except…I then proceeded to show the video of Florence Henderson singing "The Best Of Times" during a live variety show, with a full body shot of her tripping onstage. Anybody tripping is usually hilarious, but it was made more so when she told me what really happened during a Chatterbox. Siegfried and Roy had performed right before her and one of their tigers *peed on the stage*! When she stepped into that puddle, she went a-skidding. Since I didn't want to only dish other people, I also showed the old video of me jazz dancing to that Jerry Herman classic, "I Am What I Am." There are so many things to deconstruct about that video but just imagine a 17-year-old me in purple plastic jazz pants, black leg warmers and *white* Capezio jazz shoes. Why not black Capezios, you ask? Because white draws the eye and makes for a better line. Next question. *The video is now on youtube! Look for my hour-long OBSESSED episode on the Youtube Playbill channel!*

P.S. I was just handed something by the flight attendant, and it reminds me of a classic story from my family. Many years ago, my Aunt Phyllis went to a nice Japanese restaurant and was excited to get some kind of free appetizer. She wasn't really listening and thought she heard someone call it *Ha tau*. Even though she didn't know exactly what it was, she decided to be open-minded and eat it without asking for details. Unfortunately, her bravery backfired because what she was served was not for consumption. That's right, she nodded kindly to the waitress, brought the item to her lips and eagerly bit into a *hot towel*.

Anyhoo, after my Kravis presentation the audience told me how excited they were for the various musicals and, hopefully, they bought tickets for all of them. Speaking of musicals, I've played *A Chorus Line* a few times, and last week in Pittsburgh I ran into one of my former Maggies. Sharon Schaller (nee Connelly) and I did it at Candlewood Playhouse back in 1993. We laughed our heads off remembering how she got in trouble because she wore an orange shade of lipstick. The director/choreographer was outraged and told her during an angry note session, "Maggie isn't a *clown*!" For the rest of the run, we kept riffing on that idea and would improv Maggie showing up in full circus regalia to show off her clowning skills. First, we'd demonstrate her trying to do the opening choreography with crazy extra large clown shoes on, (incredibly awkward), then we decided that when she's not dancing, Maggie is perched on a unicycle. So, whenever the dancers are standing in the famous line, she's in the signature Maggie pose, but she has to constantly keep pedaling the unicycle front and back so she can keep from falling off. Then, at the end of the show, when Maggie doesn't get the gig and has to exit with the other dancers, we see that amazing moment of the rejected dancers leave the stage in total silence...except for the squeakity-squawkity of her unicycle being ridden offstage.

This week on *Seth Speaks* I interviewed one of my favorite comics, Sarah Silverman. Last year, the Actors Fund was going to do another one-night concert of *Funny Girl* like we did on Broadway in 2003. It was going to have the same format as that concert (a different woman playing Fanny for each number), and I wanted Sarah to sing "You Are Woman." I knew my friend Jack Plotnick was friends with her, and I asked him to ask her if I could have her email. She wrote back right away and, turns out, listens to my show on SiriusXM every day! She said yes to doing *Funny Girl* but then the whole concert had to be cancelled (more on that in my one-day memoirs). Regardless, we kept in touch, and I knew she was coming to town so I asked her to guest on my show. She just did a big fundraiser in Texas for the NAACP and the title was a bust on Rick Perry's hunting lodge; it was literally called *Live From N*****head*. Brava! She grew up in New Hampshire and did theatre throughout her childhood, including playing *my* dream role, Annie. There was an alternate girl playing the role as well, but Sarah was the main one. However, when the publicity photos were taken, Sarah made the bizarre decision that the biggest, widest smile was the best smile to give. Suffice it to say, when the publicity photos were printed in the newspaper, they featured the *other* girl. When questioned why she wasn't in the paper, the publicist for the show showed Sarah the photo of herself with her crazy open-mouthed smile and simply said, "Look."

Despite her LA address, Sarah is a major Broadway lover and, when she was young, had always wanted to play Eponine in *Les Miz*. Off the cuff, I decided to give her a chance to do her dream role and played the intro to "On My Own." She sang it all! Then we did "I Don't Need Anything But You" (I was Daddy Warbucks and she did the signature Annie harmony, with some hilarious asides), and we closed the show with an angry version of "Aldonza." I was so impressed that she knew so many lyrics! Look for the video on Youtube! Then peace out!

Saving Cats (Not the Musical), Plus Craig Bierko
November 14, 2011

It finally happened. Juli has been begging for years to get a cat, but we already have two dogs and didn't think they would want a cat in their midst — except as a delicious dinner. Cut to: Juli's grandmother lives next door to a farm in Washington Heights (really!) and suddenly has a mouse infestation. We read that cats give off a smell that make mice wanna take a hike so we told Juli she could have a cat at her grandmother's apartment. I was out of town, so they all went without me to New York Animal Care and Control. That's a shelter where the animals are held for a few days and then euthanized. P.S. I hate that term because it's actually a euphemism; euthanizing an animal is supposed to happen when it's in too much pain to stay alive. These animals are killed because no one wants to adopt them. It's devastating. So many animals are young and healthy, but are given up because of financial problems or a landlord suddenly not allowing animals. One woman had to give up her dog for some reason and spent a half hour in the waiting room hugging him. James said it was heartbreaking. After hanging out in the cat room, Juli found a gray cat she really wanted. However, a young boy who was behind her in line also wanted the gray cat. There was a black cat that Juli liked as well and the shelter woman told her that because black cats are rarely adopted because they're considered bad luck they. Seriously? Are we all in a live action *The Crucible*? James told Juli that if she adopted the black cat she'd be doing a mitzvah because she'd be saving the lives of both cats. While I was silently in a rage that James, who grew up going to a Unitarian Church in Texas, thinks he can use the word "mitzvah," I nonetheless appreciated his point and gave Juli a brava for adopting the little black cat now known as Princess Penelope Panther. In conclusion, please be like Bernadette Peters and adopt some animals. Even if you're not 100 percent interested, go to www.petfinder.com. It's so fun to look at all the different cute animals!

And speaking of cats, I was hanging out with Andrea Martin and we were talking about career low points. She remembered going in to audition for the voice of a cat for a pet food commercial. When she got there, she saw the role actually specified "Senior Cat." Devastating. Regardless, Andrea read the commercial with her version of an old cat voice. Halfway through her audition, they cut her off and told her that the old cat voice was not necessary and that her regular voice was perfect for a senior cat. And thus, the low point got lower.

At the Hangar Theater in Ithaca this past weekend was Tim Pinckney, whose play *Ever So Humble* was a big hit there this summer. Tim also works at the Actors Fund where he produces their big concerts. He was talking about the upcoming concert of *The Visit* starring Chita Rivera and John Cullum. Chita told him, "I haven't worked with John since 1492." I laughed when he told me because I thought she was joking about how old they are. Turns out, there was a flop musical called *1492*. Who knew? And speaking of dates, we somehow segued the conversation to be about Gregg Edelman, and Andrea seriously asked, "Wasn't he in *1774*?" *1774*? We were all obsessed with the fact that she could get that title wrong. Doesn't every American know that date? Is *1774* a little-known musical about the fascinating two years before *1776*?

My guest on *Seth Speaks* was Craig Bierko, who is starring in *Standing On Ceremony* alongside a ton of great actors. He talked about how nervous he was to do the recent concert of *Company* because it would only be a two-week rehearsal period. But then he thought about his high school choir teacher, Mr. Trautwein. Mr. Trautwein was very influential to Craig, especially his expression, "We Go On" (pre-dating Tim Gunn's "Make It Work"). Craig decided to do *Company* as a tribute to Mr. Trautwein, who had recently died. After the concert, he made sure to go up to Stephen Sondheim and tell him why he did the concert and Sondheim said, "We all have a Mr. Trautwein in our lives." Craig knew Mr. Trautwein would have loved the fact that Sondheim actually spoke his name. But, following that touching story, Craig and I were laughing about his role in the show. He played Peter, a part no one necessarily knows right away (he's the character married to Susan and they're getting divorced). To prove that it wasn't a well-known role, Craig would tell people that he was doing *Company* and then make up the name of the character he was playing (usually "Glen"). They would vaguely smile and nod. Then he would correct himself and say he was actually playing Peter. Literally same reaction.

I, of course, had to mention the big career choice he made back in the '90s. He was offered the role of Chandler on "Friends" and turned it down. He was offered two different sitcoms at the same time and decided to go with the other one. What's interesting is that Matthew Perry is one of his close friends, and when Craig auditioned for Chandler, he was actually doing a Matthew Perry imitation! We also talked about Craig's online talk show called "Bathing With Bierko." He hates the fake intimacy of talk shows and also doesn't understand why every talk show host has a desk. He doesn't understand why it's so universally accepted. He asked, "What in their line of work necessitates them having a desk? What do they need it for?" Thankfully, I sit behind a piano during *Seth Speaks*. We ended my segment by playing "Celebrity," which I always do with my guests. But before we began, Craig told me that he hates games. I still forced him to play and his answers were all passive/aggressive and hilarious. The first person I had to describe was Nancy Grace. I said, "She's on CNN! She's blonde! She's hostile!" He responded, "Kristin Chenoweth"? And I'm out.

Remember how I mentioned that I had Sarah Silverman and I wrote about how she knew the lyrics to tons of Broadway songs? Turns out, the video made of her singing all those songs with me got onto The Huffington Post, The New York Times online and Perez Hilton! Still got it!

In Praise of Stephanie J. Block, Kissing Chris Meloni, Meeting R.L. Stine
November 21, 2011

Stephanie J. Block is crazily talented. And brave. James and I went to see the Sunday matinee of *Anything Goes* and she was faboo. If you don't know, Sutton Foster has taken off a few weeks to film a new TV pilot ("Bunheads") *of which I wound up being on the final episode! I'm not saying I got the show cancelled, but...* and Stephanie has taken over the role of Reno Sweeney. Stephanie had gone in for an audition a while ago when they were looking for a replacement for the far future. Kathleen Marshall knew she could act/belt it, but wanted to know if she could dance it. She taught Stephanie some sections from the show and then gave her the thumbs up. Stephanie heard from her agent and assumed they were going to offer her something for 2012 or '13. Instead, they asked if she could learn the show in a *week*. What the — ? She was in the middle of doing a reading of a new musical with Sting (natch) *and* she had a solo concert to do in the Midwest. They worked around her schedule and she began sporadic rehearsals. All in all, she had 23 hours of actual rehearsal and then took over. The title song in *Anything Goes* in this revival is so freaking long, and yet I was amazed she was not at all winded for the last section of singing. And when she slid up to the belted D at the end of it, I literally started crying because it was so good. Brava!!!

On to SiriusXM radio. This week I had R.L. Stine on *Seth Speaks*, and for those of you without kids, R.L. Stine is the author of the "Goosebumps" series. First of all, you may wonder how I know him. Well, I do a comedy bit in my *Deconstructing Broadway* show where I talk about my precious, precious subscription to Dynamite magazine I had back in the late '70s. For those of you pretending to be under 30, Dynamite was a magazine you could order through Scholastic. It was like People magazine for kids. They had stories on all the hottest stars of the day; JJ Walker, Lee Majors, Melissa Gilbert, Beth Howland etc. When I was 11, I had a pen pal from Dynamite named Debbie who lived in Downingtown, PA. After she wrote me, I had a typical thought for an 11-year-old boy: "Why should I write her back a plain ol' letter, when instead I can make her a 45-minute tape of myself playing the piano and singing!" In my comedy act, I play the tape, which included my audition song ("Tomorrow") and it becomes obvious to the audience why my childhood was not filled with theatrical roles. Anyhoo, after I did my bit at the New York Civil Liberties Union benefit, R.L. Stine and his wife, Jane, approached me and they proudly told me that Jane created Dynamite! It was so cool to meet her and then R.L. told me that he created Bananas. Ouch. Bananas was the magazine you were supposed to graduate to after you turned 14, but I refused to relinquish my Dynamite subscription, even after my body's maturation. As a matter of fact, my friend Anne visited me while we were well into high school and she saw a copy of Dynamite sitting out with a telltale address label on it. She confronted me and I told her it was a *way* old issue. Meanwhile, the cover completely gave me away because it had something like "The Current Cast of 'Friends.'" I was mortified.

Regardless, I invited R.L. (he goes by Bob) to my radio show. Before the whole "Goosebumps" series, he was a writer of jokebooks and went by the name "Jovial Bob Stine." His publisher took him to lunch one day and said, "I think you could write a really scary book for kids." Bob agreed but thought "Jovial Bob Stine" wasn't that scary of a name so he decided to change it for the new series. Also, he said that everyone in publishing knew boys "didn't read." Obviously, that's an exaggeration (I read "Carrie" in sixth grade...still terrified) but it was what the book world believed. So, in order to appeal to girls, he decided to take a name that could possibly be a woman's name. He decided to use his initials because of the female author of "The Outsiders," S.E. Hinton. I guess B.D. Wong was already taken so he settled on R.L. Stine. I asked him how he writes and he said he comes up with the title first. Then he figures out what the story can be about, based on that title. And then he figures out the ending so he knows how he'll trick the reader. He started being a writer of scary books with the "Fear Street" series for teens and then decided to write a series for younger kids. Thus, "Goosebumps" was born. And also, from what I've read, a mind-boggling bank account was born. For three years in the 1990s he was *the* best-selling author in America! Not just children's-book author, but any type of book. He told me that at one point, he was selling four million books *per month*! Speaking of which, that's the amount of copies of any of my books I'm aiming to sell. And thanks for doing your part by buying this one!

Last week began with a big Broadway benefit at the Shubert Theater for Only Make Believe (OnlyMakeBelieve.org). That's the organization founded by Dena Hammerstein that brings theatre to chronically ill children in hospitals. Or as they say in Europe, "in hospital." Brad Oscar has done a lot of the events and his partner (soon-to-be husband) Diego Prieto was so moved by the video showing what the actors do in the hospital, he joined the Only Make Believe acting troupe and now performs in all of the New York City hospitals! Brava! Before the event, I tweeted that I was excited for the benefit and hoping for a make-out session with cute, cute, cute Chris Meloni (who was making an appearance). I was completely joking and knew he wouldn't be making out with anybody. Well, before I went on, I saw him stage left with Grandma, the Big Apple Circus clown who was slated to perform. If you don't know, Grandma is played by a guy and looks like a middle aged lady. Well, I heard Chris, un-prompted, say, "It would be really funny if we went onstage together and *I kissed you*! He told Grandma that he would dip her and kiss her first, then they should pause, and then Grandma should dip Chris and kiss him. Then they proceeded to practice the bit *in front of me*! I felt like Eponine when she's forced to watch Marius and Cosette make out. And *she* at least won a Tony.

On Sunday, I did a fundraiser at the home of Douglas Carter Beane and his partner Lewis Flinn for Music For Autism. It's often difficult for families with autistic kids to go to musicals or concerts because they feel that the kids' behavior can be too distracting to the other audience members or because they can't afford the ticket price. Music For Autism provides fully-funded concerts where the artist is paid and admission is free! It allows families and those with autism to enjoy music and not worry that their behavior is going to ruin it for everyone else. It's a great idea and letters were read from parents with autistic kids where they talked about how much the kids loved the concerts and what a difference it made for their families. Doug (who wrote *Xanadu*) asked his former star, Kerry Butler, to sing. And she asked me to play. The apartment was crammed with people, so Doug suggested that Kerry stand on the coffee table in order for people to see her better. He then told everybody that it's the same coffee table his very young children would stand on when they would do their own version of *Xanadu*...and both his daughter *and* son would fight over who got to play Kerry's part. I completely identify.

I ran into Jack Cummings III who directs all the time for The Transport Group. He is *so* funny in real life. I wrote on my Facebook that I was looking for a web designer and people were posting suggestions. Well, before [title of show] became successful, Jeff Bowen (who wrote the score), used to design websites. A Facebook friend recommended him to me as a designer, not knowing Jeff doesn't do it anymore. Jack saw the recommendation on my wall and thought it was so random and not possible that he suggested his own totally inappropriate web designer, but also phrased it with the exact same amount of syllables so the joke landed deliciously. Here are the lines in succession:

SETH: Does any know someone who can take over my website?
EDWARD: What about Jeff Bowen?
JACK: What about Jan Maxwell?

I cannot tell you how many times over the last week I've laughed because of that. Completely obsessed.

Speaking of which, I've always wanted to be in the approval matrix at the back of New York magazine. It's an actual matrix about pop culture with "Highbrow" and "Lowbrow" and then "Brilliant" and "Despicable." Someone can be Highbrow Brilliant or Highbrow Despicable or Lowbrow Brilliant or Lowbrow Despicable. The Broadway medley I did with Sarah Silverman made it into Lowbrow Brilliant. I still got it...ish.

And finally, Happy Thanksgiving!

Mutchnick & Seth
November 28, 2011

Attention readers, my new young adult book is finally available! Ah! So exciting! It's called "My Amazing/Awful Popularity Plan" and it's published by Random House. #Fancy *P.S. The sequel is now available as well! It's called "The Rise And Fall Of A Theater Geek" and features the same characters. I'm not saying the lead character is based on a younger version of me, but suffice to say it's about a Jewish teen who's obsessed with theater and constantly tries to manipulate situations to his advantage only to have them backfire horrifically. He's basically a 15-year-old gay Lucy Ricardo.*

Now to the more mundane. I have *eight more hours* on this train. That's right, I'm in hour three of my *11-hour* train trip to Canada. I was asked by Jack Latulippe to do a master class in Montreal. He's had people like Shoshana Bean and Stephen Schwartz up to teach, and his goal is to bring lots of Broadway people and shows to Montreal. I was so excited when he asked me to *visiter*. When I asked James and Juli to come with me, James thought it would be a fun "adventure" if we all took the train up and back together. The nice part is it goes up along the Hudson, and the scenery is beautiful. The not nice part is there are eight more hours of scenery and not-the-cleanest bathroom ahead. Anyhoo, I'm going to make the best of it and get some writing done.

So, let's start with last Monday. I've been friends with Anne Martin ever since we went to Usdan Performing Arts Camp together when I was 14 and she was 13. Her close friend from high school is Eric Hyman, who is now married to Max Mutchnick, the creator of "Will and Grace." Turns out, Max is a fan of my radio show and asked Anne if we could all go out to dinner. Fun! Of course, as soon as I meet a celeb, I immediately ask them to be on my radio show, so here's a recap of the dinner *and* his appearance two days later on *Seth Speaks*. First of all, the name "Max Mutchnick." When he arrived at college, he wanted to reinvent himself, so he changed his name from Jason to Max. He added that "reinventing" was his code word for coming out. I suggest he might have wanted to can the Mutchnick as well (believe me, I know what it's like lugging around "Rudetsky"), but he said he liked the alliteration. After graduating college, he started working as a staff writer on various sitcoms. Warren Littlefield asked Max and his writing partner to come up with a new "Mad About You" type show, and they wrote one about a couple in San Francisco who were friends with two other couples, one of which was a gay guy and his straight girlfriend. Warren felt that Max and his writing partner had the biggest affinity for the gay/straight couple and told them to write a show centering on them. It, of course, turned into "Will and Grace."

Weirdly, Megan Mullally had actually auditioned for the role of Grace months before but didn't make an impression til her Karen audition. And, by "didn't make an impression," Max said he has no memory of her audition. I know the feeling. Over dinner, I told Max that *I* had auditioned a few year ago for the sitcom he wrote based on his relationship with Eric. He stared. Then I said I auditioned for the part based on him. Staring. I told him I had my audition in New York. Stare. I clarified that my audition was filmed and sent to L.A. He's still staring.

I also recently interviewed the out recording artist, Matt Zarley, whom I met in the 90's when he played Mike in the *A Chorus Line* tour through Europe. However, at one performance he almost had to go on for another character because he was the only one who could sing high enough. Who was the character? Richie. That's right, the one who sings "Gimme the ball, gimme the ball, gimme the ball." And, quite frankly, the one character who has an actual line clarifying that he's *black*! Normally, if a white guy understudies the role, the script says to change the line from "...and I'm black." to "...and I'm straight." Unfortunately, the guy playing Richie injured himself in the middle of the show and it was after he made it clear to the audience that he was black. It's sort of a racial spin on the Mary Ingalls character on "Little House on the Prairie." Remember? She was on the show for years and suddenly her character went blind. Fortunately, the actor playing Richie was able to finish the show, so the non-traditional production never happened. But I asked Matt for more musical theatre mishaps, and he told us that once, when doing *Cats*, the dance captain was walking around backstage and tripped over a wire. Simply a wire. Well, it not only caused *all* of the sound system to cut out, it also caused a complete blackout in the theatre. I don't quite understand how one wire controlled everything, but I love it! It's such an extreme version of dominos. Matt has a new CD out, and you can get it and hear clips at MattZarley.com. Brava!

Now I'm on hour two of our 11-hour train ride back home. Montreal is a city that speaks French and English, but in many places French is dominant. As soon as we arrived, I walked into our hotel and said "hello" to the receptionist. She pointedly said "Bonjour" back to me with a "You are in a *French*-speaking city" attitude. I ignored the vague hostility and instead became excited to try out my French, so I immediately said "Ca va" to her. This time, instead of speaking French, she pointedly responded, in English, "I am fine." In other words, her attitude began with "How dare you greet me assuming English is my native language?" followed by "How dare you think your French is good enough to converse with me?" That's right, she was angry I spoke English and then angry I spoke French. I was not deterred, however, and kept hauling out my French throughout the trip. Jack Latulippe, who brought me up to Montreal, was a great host and actually told me that I spoke with barely an American accent. He chose not to comment on the fact that I can only conjugate in the present tense and only with verbs ending in "er."

On Saturday night, we begged Jack to take us to an authentic Montreal restaurant. Unfortunately, he did. It was a very hip and popular restaurant that served Italian food with a Montreal spin, meaning the menu was full of "delicious" items like tripe, rabbit and wild boar. Despite the horrifying majority of food choices, the dinner actually wound up being delicious (I got fish, James pumpkin ravioli and Juli meatballs) and afterwards, Jack took us out to a dessert place that's an entire restaurant dedicated to chocolate. It was mind-bogglingly good. The next morning, however, there was a call back to the time in England when James got the black pudding thinking it was chocolate and discovered it actually consisted of intestines. This time I got a bagel at a buffet and saw little plastic cups with some kind of cream cheese inside. I decided to clarify and asked what kind of cream cheese it was and discovered it wasn't cream cheese at all. It *looked* like cream cheese but was instead a "Montreal specialty": ground up beef and pork. And *coupe*!

Next Monday and Tuesday is the *Gypsy of the Year*, and I'm hosting for the fourth time. It's one of my favorite things to do, and I can't wait to stand in the wings and watch all the acts! *This event happens every year so get thee!* Alors, au revoir, mes amis....a la semaine que prochaine!

Neil Sedaka Talks About His Hits
December 5, 2011

Greetings from Logan Airport. I just did the Sunday matinee of Andrea Martin's show in Provincetown and I was planning on flying out Monday morning. However, I made the flight plans before I knew I was hosting Gypsy of the Year Dec. 5-6. I decided that it was too nerve-wracking, even for me, to fly to New York on the morning of the event so I decided to try to get a flight home Sunday night. I found one through United that leaves at 8 PM, but I still had to find a way to get from P-town to Boston. This is where "social networking" is fabulous. I went to my Facebook and Twitter account and asked if anyone was driving from P-town to Boston on Sunday. Within minutes, someone from my fan site volunteered! It was so easy. This never would have happened before the internet. I guess I would have had to put a note on the Equity board to have them call my "service." I would then "call them in the morning, or my service would explain." Pam Myers? Anybody? Everybody!

I told Andrea that I had never met the person picking me up and she texted me frantically during my drive to Boston because she was afraid, she admitted in a text, that I was being driven by Jeffrey Dahmer. I then texted back that my driver, Amy, was a woman over 50 accompanied by her Labrador retriever. Andrea was immensely relieved. And then, of course, *I* began to think of Stephen King's "Misery." Regardless, she was a great driving companion and I made it to the airport with plenty of time to spare. But speaking of Andrea, she's been doing her shows in Canada with another pianist because I told her I didn't want to travel so much this year. At the end of the show in P-town, she introduced me and told the audience, "I could not do this show without Seth." I then gave her an incredulous look and she added, "Although I have...and it's actually gone pretty well." Brava on the honesty.

This week I saw Patti LuPone and Mandy Patinkin's show on Broadway. They've both completely kept their ranges and Patti's voice especially sounds exactly the same. The next version of *The Picture of Dorian Gray* should star her larynx. It was so enjoyable to see such solid actors do not just songs, but classic scenes from shows together (they do sections of *South Pacific* and *Carousel*). Of course, during the *Evita* segment I had to hold myself back from crying. The tears were because I was so moved seeing them recreate something I was completely obsessed with when I was a little boy. The tears were also because of unresolved anger toward my mother for relentlessly getting me tickets to a show right *after* all the original leads had left. *Annie, A Chorus Line, Ain't Misbehavin'* — no matter what, she waited 'til every contract expired before calling for tickets. Speaking of my mother, I took her to the Patti/Mandy show, and while she was flipping through the Playbill she commented that she couldn't understand why there was a new show starring Louis Vuitton and Christian Dior. I looked over her shoulder and told her that she was looking at an ad for Bloomingdales. I'm not joking! The woman next to my mother didn't even try to conceal her laughter.

Mandy mentioned that it was his 59th birthday, and a gaggle of leggy ladies dressed in black came out during the curtain call. They proceeded to sing and dance a sexy version of "Happy Birthday" that obviously took Mandy completely by surprise. They were all adorable. After they ran off, Patti told them to come back and do it again! This time, Mandy joined them in a kick line. Let's just say that when he searches through Backstage, he should skip the "singers who dance" auditions and focus only on those for "singers who move." Regardless, it was a very special thing to witness from the audience and Mandy remarked, "I can't wait to see what happens when I turn 60!"

On *Seth Speaks*, I interviewed one of my idols: Neil Sedaka. I'm obsessed with his amazing composing and beautiful alto voice. Literally alto. He actually said that he feels his voice is androgynous and that's what contributed to his success: girls would buy his records thinking he was a guy and boys would buy it thinking he was a girl! I asked him if there was any castrati incident in his past and he remarked, "I am still intact." Phew.

He's from Brighton Beach and started out as a classical pianist with a scholarship to Juilliard prep (I auditioned for that same scholarship...and was summarily rejected). I told him how much I loved his composing, and how I could tell the song "Superbird" was influenced by the Bach A-minor invention.

He remarked that being a studied musician gives him an advantage over other rock composers who can only play four chords. Sass!!! I love his voice so much and he told me he never had a voice lesson. As a fellow Jew, I then asked him how he sounded when he sang from the torah for his Bar Mitzvah. He recalled, "Not a dry eye in the house." Hilarious. He said that afterward the Rabbi wanted to make him a Cantor, but his mother put the kibosh on that because she wanted him to be a concert pianist. Of course, he wound up being neither because, soon, one of their neighbors asked if Neil would write music if her son, Howie, wrote lyrics. Neil told them he could only play classical music, but Howie Greenfield convinced Neil to try... and they wound up writing 300 songs together! "Where the Boys Are", "Calendar Girl," "Love Will Keep Us Together" and *many* more.

Neil and Howie were two of the first people in the famous Brill building which was a place that young songwriters would work from 10 AM to 5 PM, five days a week. He started as a teen, and they had hit songs like "Stupid Cupid," but by 1959 RCA was going to fire him because he had a few flops in a row. Well, this is where Neil is brilliant; he looked at a copy of Billboard and bought the records of all the No. 1 songs from all the countries that were listed. Then because he's a "very good sleuth," he wrote down what all the songs had in common. He noticed they all had a girl's name in the title, a certain vocal riff, guitar riff and drum beat and he put it all together and created "Oh, Carol." He looked at my audience and summed up his efforts by saying, "Three million copies." Brava! P.S. He put the name "Carol" in the title because of Carole King, whom he dated, according to him, "for around one minute." *There is a reference to that at the beginning of BEAUTIFUL!*

Suddenly, The Rolling Stones and The Beatles became popular and Neil stopped having hits. Fourteen years later, in the '70s, Elton John contacted him and said he was going to make him a star again. Elton had a new record label and produced Neil's album and Neil came back on the charts with two No. 1 hits: the slow version of "Breakin' Up Is Hard To Do" and "Laughter in the Rain." By the way, when the song goes to "Ooh...I hear laughter in the rain..." the chord underneath the "ooh" is what he calls the "drop dead" chord. He says you need to have a chord that's out of the ordinary and special that gives the song a lift. I asked him about his big hit "Love Will Keep Us Together" and he told me that he wrote it by combining many different homages: The signature vamp at the beginning is based on The Beach Boys, the augmented chord is from Al Green and the vocal line is a la Diana Ross! He compares himself to a clothing designer who takes many different swatches and then combines them to create something new.

At the end of the interview, I mentioned the song "Solitaire" and he remembered that he wrote it because his friend told him he hadn't yet written "the great one." He told me that the song was influenced by Roberta Flack and I assumed he meant the chord changes or the vocal line. He responded: "the tempo." So specific! Listening to his music is like looking at a Hirschfeld drawing and trying to find all the different Ninas! I brought Farah Alvin to sing "Solitaire" and when I told him, he yelled, "I love her!" He first saw Farah sing at an Actors Fund salute I put together years ago. This time he was prepared and, before she sang, he begged for tissues because he knew he'd be crying (!). And then after she belted that crazy high F at the end, he hugged her and called her "a songwriter's dream." Brava! Look for the video on Youtube!

O.K., I have to rush and get ready for Gypsy of the Year so peace out and Happy December!

After Gypsy of the Year, a Quick Getaway to Dublin
December 12, 2011

Hello from Gate 86 at Newark airport. I'm on an airplane, but I'm not on my way to do a gig. I'm going away for two days and this is the first time in a *long* while that I'm out of town purely for fun. A few months ago when I hit 25,000 frequent flyer miles, I got "Elite Access". As I mentioned before, it's so great because I now get upgraded to First Class whenever there are seats available, and it happens all the time. James had around 2,000 miles left to fly before he got Elite Access and he had to get them by Dec. 31 or else they wouldn't count. We didn't want to spend the next year traveling with me being upgraded and him sitting in the back, next to the scullery maid, a la "Upstairs Downstairs." So, we decided to find the cheapest flight we could take where he'd get the miles before the end of the month. Cut to: Dublin, here we come! Right now it's Friday night at 7 PM. We leave in a few minutes and land at 7 AM, Dublin time. We're staying Saturday and Sunday and high-tailing it back Monday morning. Since this is also supposed to be a romantic weekend where we don't worry about work, I decided to leave my cell phone at home. No cell phone! iPhones don't work in Europe anyway *the old days!,* but I still miss the security of having it in my pocket. It's so weird not to have it constantly one inch away from my hand!

This past week began with the 2011 Gypsy of the Year competition. It was my fourth time hosting and, yet again, it was so much fun. The whole opening number featured a reunion of the original cast of *Grease* to celebrate their 40th anniversary. Everybody looks amazing. Adrienne Barbeau still has a fabulous figure (and muscular arms), and backstage I mentioned her twins and she told me she gave birth to them when she was 51! Yowza! The whole cast sang portions of "Summer Nights," "There are Worse Things I Could Do," "Mooning," "It's Raining on Prom Night," "Born To Hand Jive" and "We Go Together."

Right after the number, I made my first entrance for the show trying to hold back tears because I was so moved while watching from the stage-right wing. It was a combination of the thrill of seeing a group of actors recreate so many classic Broadway moments and remembering being a kid in the '70s, watching that *Grease* commercial over and over again. I pulled it together, did my opening bit (getting some delicious larfs) and the competition began.

The numbers were introduced by me or by a voiceover, and once in a while an actor would go out for a special section (like introducing the judges). Halfway through the show, right after one of the numbers ended, I didn't hear a voiceover, so I ran onstage to introduce *How to Succeed*. In the middle, I heard noise from offstage. It was very distracting so I turned to glare and then saw it was Tom Viola in the wings, motioning me stage right. Aha! I remembered that there were a few intros I was supposed to do away from center stage in order for the crew to set props. So, I moved to the right and continued my intro. Then I heard *more* noise. I'd had it. Right before I hauled out my supersonic glare I saw that I wasn't being told to go stage right, I was actually being told to get *off the stage*. That's right, I wasn't supposed to be introducing *How to Succeed* at all. I had come out at the wrong time. P.S. Not only did I come out at the wrong time, but the moment I upstaged was Judith Light's incredibly moving introduction of the moment of silence. That's right. The one truly somber and tender moment in the whole show began with me a.) babbling center stage, b.) babbling stage right and then c.) babbling as I fled the stage. As I clanked my way offstage, a regal and glorious Judith Light entered the stage and gave her impassioned and moving speech that led to the moment of silence. The only reason I wasn't 100 percent mortified about my onstage clunkery is because I remembered that Daniel Radcliffe is now on Broadway and I hoped he somehow put a forgetting spell on all the muggles in the audience. *P.S. I did the SAME THING the following year!*

Speaking of Daniel Radcliffe and my mortification, they went hand-in-hand at the next day's performance, Dec. 6. On Monday night, my dog Maggie had an upset tummy and woke me up a few times during the night to let her outside. The next morning, James took one look at my puffy sleep-deprived eyes and told me I had better wear some make-up at that afternoon's performance. When I got to the theatre, I saw one of the off-stage vocalists and I asked her if she had any kind of under-eye concealer. She did, and I asked her to put it on for me in the hallway. When I was done, I joked that we didn't have a mirror and it would be hilarious if she made me up to look like a clown. At least, I thought I was joking. Well, the two-hour show was almost over and Hugh Jackman, Bernadette Peters and Daniel went onstage to announce the winners. I remembered that Juli is obsessed with Daniel and decided to corner him when he left the stage. So, after the show I ran up and asked him to take a photo with me for Juli. We got the shot. When I looked at it, I was surprised that there was some glaring light shining on my face and yet not on his. Then I wondered why it was only around my eyes. *Then* I realized that the concealer put around my eyes wasn't so much "concealer" as it was "clown white." Why did *no one* told me I looked like a crazy albino raccoon during the whole show!

Now we're in Dublin and I'm looking at the Irish Sea outside the window of our hotel. We landed at 7 AM, took a bus and a train and got to the Royal Marine Hotel at 9:30 AM. After a four-hour nap from which I almost had a breakdown trying to wake up, we went out to lunch. We saw lots of stores we wanted to check out but by the time we decided to visit them, they were closed. Yay! I forgot that in Europe no one feels the need for anything interesting after 6 PM. I accepted that the stores were not an option anymore, so I decided to get some coffee. We walked over to the coffee café and *that* was closed. And, the mind-boggling part is, the coffee place was called "Insomnia." *Insomnia*? What nerve! Don't claim you have insomnia if you're asleep by 6!

This week on *Seth Speaks* I interviewed Rachel Shukert, who recently wrote *Eight Days More*, the story of Chanukkah as told through the songs of *Les Miz*. For the last two years I've played Moses in *Everything's Coming Up Moses*, her story of Passover as told through the songs of *Gypsy* (hilarious) and now I'll be Judah Macabee in her recent excursion. I'm obsessed with her opening lyric, which was inspired by the time she played Brigitta in a touring production of *The Sound of Music*, when she was a little girl. One day the kids were sitting around backstage and somehow they realized that the lyrics of "So Long, Farewell" fit perfectly with the lyrics of the prologue of *Les Miz*. You know...the part that goes "Look Down, look down, don't look them in the eye..." can be replaced by "So long, farewell, auf wiedersehen, adieu, etc..." In the Chanukkah *Les Miz* version, the show starts with Jewish prisoners singing.

ALL: Oppressed, oppressed,
we'll always be oppressed.
Oppressed, oppressed
It's what the Jews do best.

SOLO: The sun has gone to bed and so must I.

ALL: That's not this show
It's by another guy....

O.K., it's now my last night in Ireland and I have to get to sleep because we have to wake up super early in order to catch the 6:10 AM shuttle to the airport so, "So long, farewell, auf wiedersehen, goodbye!"

Merry Christmas From *Avenue Q*'s Christmas Eve, Ann Harada
December 19, 2011

It's not even Christmas Eve yet, but I celebrated it with Ann Harada already. Last Monday was her third annual *Christmas Eve with Christmas Eve*. Yet again, the writing, performing and direction (by Alan Marouka) were amazing. It's so hard to do a one-night event and land every joke because you often need an audience to tell you what works and what doesn't, and yet every year her show never has a clunker. Brava! The concept is that Christmas Eve (the character Ann created for *Avenue Q*) has one wish for Christmas: to sing duets with Broadway's leading men...and make them take off their shirts. This year, Santa gave her an option — have her wish come true or get two house seats to *The Book of Mormon AKA The Dear Evan Hansen of its day!* She struggled with the decision, but decided to do the duets. The first man to come out was Norm Lewis who was in the middle of tech rehearsals for *Porgy and Bess* but was able to make it. Of course, Christmas Eve went crazy over his sexiness and then "accidentally" dropped her pen so Norm was forced to bend over to get it. Inappropriate ogling ensued. They then sang "Wheels of a Dream," the Coalhouse and Sarah duet from *Ragtime*. Norm sounded so fantastic and Ann pushed Christmas Eve's Japanese accent to new heights. When Coalhouse sings "We'll go down South and see your people...," Sarah responds, "See my folks!" Of course, when Christmas Eve heard that Coalhouse would take her down South to see her people, her Japanese accent made her enthusiastically respond, "See my forks!" I texted Ann after the show and she wrote back that she herself is still laughing about that line. There were so many other highlights but one that stands out in my mind was she and Marc Kudisch singing "Anything You Can Do" from *Annie Get Your Gun*. They changed the lyrics from time to time, and at one point he was towering over her and sang, "Anything you can be, I can be taller." *Silence* from her. One of my other favorite moments was when she and Daniel Jenkins sang a full medley from *Big River* together. I had never seen him play Huck Finn in the original production on Broadway, I had only heard the record, and it was so cool to see him looking like an adult, but still having the same voice. I, of course, had full tears in my eyes as soon as he hauled out "Look out for me...Oh, muddy water...." If you've never seen Ann in action, look for our Playbill *Obsessed* on youtube!

This week on *Seth Speaks* my guest was Ana Gasteyer. We were both, yet again, raging about auto-tuning. Where is the outrage? It's literally changing what people think is the sound of singing - AH! Of course, this also always brings up Ana's mother. As I mentioned before, her mother was a classical music snob. When Ana was a teen violinist, she was forced to spend her summer vacation at the Gettysburg Chamber Music Camp. She remarked that it was more boring than it sounds. According to her, they spent their time sweating in un-air-conditioned practice rooms doing chamber music or watching Civil War re-enactments. Her one highlight was that it was the summer she learned how to lip-synch. When they had parents' day, her classical-music friend's mom visited, and her friend gushed about how extremely talented Ana was. Her friend's mother then asked Ana to play something, to which her friend responded, "Not at the *violin*, at lip-synching 'Funky Town'!"

Ana spent many years doing *Wicked*, but before then people were always surprised she could sing. She claims that I'm the only one who wasn't surprised. That was because we both worked at "30 Rock." Not the show, the location. When she was on "Saturday Night Live," I was a comedy writer on "The Rosie O'Donnell Show." There were TV monitors in our offices and we'd get the live feed from "SNL" rehearsals. I heard Ana doing a Celine Dion sketch, and when I later saw her at the NBC gym, I told her that I noticed she was belting an F and she sounded amazing! Hence, fast friends.

I also interviewed the hilarious Jackie Hoffman, who is starring in her own Jewish version of *A Christmas*

123

Carol, called *A Chanukkah Charol*. I asked her to do one of my favorite bits about one of her old Hebrew school compatriots calling her when she got *The Addams Family*. He left her a message in a thick Yiddish accent on her cell phone: "Hi, Jackie, this is Chaim from yeshiva. I heard you're in a show. Good for you. Tell me when the show is and I'll come see it." She was raging. "In a show? I'm in a *Broadway musical*! I don't tell *you* when the show is, you call a stranger and pay lots of money to come see the Broadway musical!" She then remarked that she's positive Bebe Neuwirth doesn't get calls like that, but then she went into an imitation of Bebe's response doing an amazing imitation of Bebe's calm tone and slow speech: "Hi, Chaim. It's Bebe. My show runs Tuesdays through Saturday at 8 PM, with 2 PM matinees on Wednesday and Saturdays and Sunday matinees at 3 PM. Now, Chaim, I have to hang up. I have a *lot* more calls to make."

Then I had my sister Beth as a guest on *Seth Speaks* because I have recently become obsessed with a song she wrote a while ago. She composed it back when she was the singer/pianist at "Burt Bacharach's." Not his actual house, but the restaurant he owned! Of course, back then she didn't realize the "beauty" of the name Rudetsky and kept changing her name. At one point, she used her middle name as a last name and went by "Beth Diane," sounding like she was a soft porn star. Then she used my mom's maiden name and went by "Beth Sheerin," sounding like she was an Irish washerwoman. Regardless, I decided she's a quadruple threat because she writes the lyrics, music, sings *and* accompanies herself! The song is called "Empty Projector," and Beth said that she wrote it before people were taking Prozac, so one's only option was to write a downer song. You can find the video on Youtube.

Finally, I interviewed lots of cast members from Broadway's *Godspell*. Hunter Parrish plays Jesus and the cast recalled a recent show where the crucifix set piece didn't lower down to the stage, so Hunter had to do the whole last 15 minutes of the show with his arms out in a crucifixion position but with nothing supporting him. Ow! I then commended him for doing what everyone did in the '80s when we were doing Jane Fonda videos. Anybody remember those horrible arm exercises where you held them straight out and did circles? Still hurts. Then I asked Hunter about his time in *Spring Awakening*, in which he had to expose his butt at the end of Act One. He remembered that Daniel Radcliffe, who was doing *Equus* at the time, came backstage and asked him how he keeps his butt so hairless! Apparently, Daniel had to wax what the Brits call his "arse." *Depilatory-ous*!

Happy Holidays everyone — and go see a show!

Visiting Sutton Foster Backstage; Loving Linda Lavin; the Return of *Chatterbox*
January 3, 2012

I am writing this end of the year wrap-up/looking-forward-to-the-new-year column in Provincetown at the lovely Anchor Inn Beach House with my fireplace a-burnin'. Ahhhh.

The week began with my adorable nieces visiting NYC with my sis and her husband. Eliana (the younger one) and I went to see *Anything Goes* and loved it. After the title song, Eliana was so completely breathless that she literally wanted her inhaler. I don't know if she was over-excited from the amazing Broadway dancing or if she inherited the patented Rudetsky co-dependence — connecting too deeply/emotionally with the out-of-breath dancers that she herself couldn't breathe. Either way, I'm passing along the number of my therapist. After the show, we went backstage and chatted with Sutton Foster about the TV pilot she recently filmed. It's called "Bunheads" and she plays a Las Vegas dancer who hits bottom when she tries out for the Vegas production of *Chicago* and doesn't get it. She goes on a bender, marries a random guy, moves to his small town and finds herself teaching at the local dance studio. I asked her if she had to audition and it was sort of yes/no. In other words, she had to fly out to L.A. for an audition *but* she was the only one being considered for the role. Brava! She knew she had to take the pilot because it was written by Amy Sherman-Palladino, who created TV's "Gilmore Girls," which is Sutton's favorite TV show. Sutton took a picture with me and Eliana after the show completely *sans* make-up, or, as she told us, "keeping it real."

I interviewed Linda Lavin on my *Seth Speaks* radio show and found out she's from Portland, Maine, like Andrea Martin. Who knew that town was a hotbed of future Tony winners? Linda made her Broadway debut in *A Family Affair*. Even though she was in the ensemble, she got a great mention in the New York Times. I asked if that jump-started her career and she said it actually did nothing whatsoever. *But* doing that show started a great professional relationship between her and first time director...Harold Prince! Up until that point, he had produced, but never directed. A few years later, Linda was trying to find a job. When Hal found out, he offered a gig in the ensemble of *She Loves Me* on Broadway. Unfortunately, on the day she was supposed to begin, the show closed. Yay show biz. I myself was supposed to learn the keyboard book to the Cy Coleman musical *Welcome To The Club*, and when I showed up, I could not figure out how to get the stage door open. I finally figured out that it wouldn't open because it was locked — because the show had just closed. Excellent.

Linda and Hal continued their good relationship and she felt so comfortable with him that she had no shame in campaigning for a big role in his musical *It's a Bird...It's a Plane...It's Superman!*! She had photos taken of her looking like Lois Lane (in phone booths, etc.) and she sent Hal a mocked-up "Superman" comic strip starring herself, and asked him to consider her for the role. He told her a flat-out NO...but he followed that statement by telling her that he wanted her for another role — the sassy sidekick, Sydney. That was the show in which she got to introduce the song "You've Got Possibilities."

Linda talked about the ups and downs of the business and how arbitrary it is. The TV show "Alice" was based on the film "Alice Doesn't Live Here Anymore" (a struggling singer working as a waitress while she raises her son), but the script was not being turned into a TV show because they couldn't find anyone to star in it. Alan Shayne, who was a casting director, and then became head of Warner Bros. TV greenlighted the script and told them to hire Linda Lavin. Everyone had told him that the show wasn't funny, and he said Linda would make it funny. She got the gig and her whole life changed. It's one of those "there's stuff going on you don't even know about" stories because when Alan was a casting director, he had apparently seen her work throughout the years but had *never* called her in for anything.

Yet he wound up calling her in for the biggest gig of her life! Linda said that throughout the series, and to this day, women come up to her and tell her that they struggled with issues similar to Alice and would find strength from watching the show. Essentially they would say, "If Alice can do it, so can I." The show also tackled social issues from the get-go. On the second episode, a football playing buddy of Mel (the diner's owner) goes out on a date with Alice. He doesn't want to kiss her and finally tells her that he's gay. She then has to deal with her own homophobia issues because she's uncomfortable letting her son go on a fishing trip with him. This was in 1976! Brava!

Linda starred in Neil Simon's *Broadway Bound*. I told her that I heard he can be cranky. She said that wasn't true and that he's always been wonderful and, in *Broadway Bound*, he wrote her a beautiful 16-page monologue. I said that a 16-page-monologue actually doesn't sound wonderful, it sounds stress-producing. Well, it obviously wasn't to her because it won her a Tony Award! But that show was also the site of a classic mishap for her. During the show, she was able to go offstage during one scene and it always timed out to be when "Designing Women" was on TV. She always had enough time offstage to watch a scene up until the commercial break and then she'd go back onstage. Well, one night "Designing Women" was particularly riveting and she somehow found herself watching the next scene. Suddenly, she was snapped out of her reverie when she heard Jonathan Silverman and Jason Alexander on the monitor saying, "Boy, I wonder where Ma is..." She had a mug of tea in her hand and she remembers hearing it shatter as she dropped it. Then she said she felt like a kid who's late for school and decides maybe it's better to not even show up. She thought, "I'm already so late for the scene and it will be so mortifying when I come on...perhaps I'll just skip it." Then she changed her mind and ran like a lunatic up the stairs to the stage. When she got onstage, Jason and Jonathan sassed her by asking, "Gee, Ma...where were you?" She babbled something about a neighbor needing help and the show went on. After that story, *I* needed Eliana's inhaler!

This weekend I did Ana Gasteyer's fantastic show in Provincetown. In it, she sings *such* fun songs and they're all in such crazily high keys. Literally belting F's. However, besides the belting, I mentioned before that my other fave part is her reading of Barbra Streisand's "My Passion for Design." Ana reads it while making seemingly supportive comments that are hilarious. She talks about how the book is inspiring for everyone, no matter what amount of free time you have or what your income level is. For instance, Ana says, showing a picture from the book, if you need a little pick me up, why not do what Barbra did and build an entire millhouse? She then talks about the underground mall Barbra built beneath her house and the "store" completely filled with dolls. She adds, "And I, for one, cannot think of *anything* more appropriate in a vast, childless house than an entire basement filled with dolls."

And on that note, Happy New Year! And I hope you keep your New Year's resolutions slightly longer than my friend Adam Pascal, who's starring in *Memphis* and always amuses me with his Facebok postings. At the beginning of the day, his Facebook status was: *My new year's resolution (it will be hard) no more negativity on Facebook. Its ugly...mouth shut! mouth shut!* That was followed a few hours later by: *Well I'm off to a bad start. Hey morons, a play is not a movie. When you talk to us while were working, we can hear you. It's horribly distracting. Shut the f**k up you stupid uncultured fool!* Yay! Now I can feel better about breaking any of my resolutions. Peace out!

The Team From *Lysistrata Jones*, Plus Eve Plumb
January 9, 2012

This week was chock full of fun interviews beginning with the cast of *Lysistrata Jones*. Unfortunately, they had just gotten their official closing notice. I say "official" because they had the heads-up the day after opening. There was a cast meeting and the producers told them that they would definitely stay open...if they sold out *every single show* Christmas week. Of course, the cast said they looked into the audience at their next show and saw 35 people. (Not *really* 35, but you get it.) It's one of those mystifying things where a show can get a *great* New York Times review and still not sell tickets. I asked Douglas Carter Beane why they chose to open the show in the winter, which is a notoriously hard time to keep a show running, and he said that it's impossible to get a theatre in the spring. *Lysistrata Jones* had actual people for producers whereas, according to Doug theatres are being requested in the spring "by Disney and General Motors."

For those who've done a Broadway show, we know that when a cast is forced to assemble onstage for an "important meeting" with the producer, it's usually a horrible sign indicating imminent closing. Unfortunately, almost everyone in the cast was making their Broadway debut, when the producer called the meeting after Christmas week, one of them thought, "Yay! We're being told the show's gonna run forever!" They said that the first sign that perhaps it wasn't going to be a happy announcement was the fact that the theatre was freezing and the producer was dripping sweat. The cast had so many talented people, and Josh Segarra *who in a few years would play Emilio Estefan in ON YOUR FEET* was so funny during his *Chatterbox* interview. He talked about the show having so much basketball choreography, and how the balls continually flew into the audience, especially during its summer Off-Broadway run. Josh said that most of the time when a ball came at someone, they would catch it. But some people in an audience forget basic life skills, and they would just literally stare at the ball in horror as it approached and eventually hit them. After the show, he'd see people who got hit by the ball and say, "I'm sorry...," followed by a muttered, "...but you're an idiot."

Jason Tam who was brilliant as Paul in the *A Chorus Line* revival played Xander. I asked him about *A Chorus Line*, and he told us that unlike the original production, the orchestra wasn't in the pit, it was in another room and the sound was then pumped in. One night, they were at the part in the opening number where it builds and builds and Zach finally says, "Let's try the whole combination facing away from the mirror," Zach then yelled "5, 6, 7, 8!" and everyone in the audience was psyched to hear the band come blasting in as everyone danced full out. But for some reason there was only one orchestra mic working. So, everyone onstage turned away from the mirror and danced up a storm... to only *one* instrument. And it literally sounded like a toy piano. Was Schroeder the only pit musician that day? You decide.

The end of *A Chorus Line* features a kickline to "One" that is supposed to symbolize the chorus line going on forever. There's no actual ending to the kickline, the lights dim to a blackout as they kick. Well, Jason said that one night the lights didn't dim. So, they were all forced to just kept kicking. Endlessly. Well, not all of them. He seems to remember Broadway vet Charlotte D'Amboise (Cassie) realizing it was going to be endless and making the smart choice to simply stop. Perhaps the audience thought that her character took the "don't pop the head" advice many steps further and ceased moving *any* part of her body. Brava subtext.

Douglas Carter Beane, who wrote the book to *Lysistrata Jones* is a hilarious person to interview. He used to be a stage doorman for *many* years and has so many stories associated with those days. He was always in the middle of writing some play while he was working. During his doorman duties on *Ah, Wilderness!*, Colleen Dewhurst asked him what he was writing and he told her it was a play. They never really discussed it again. *Years* later when he had his first play produced, she sent him a card with a picture of the *Ah, Wilderness!* theatre on the cover and inside she wrote, "Next time, write me a juicy part." I love that she remembered!

Speaking of the late Colleen, he'll never forget the time he had to operate the elevator up to Jason Robards' dressing room carrying what I call the "basses of Broadway." Yes, in the elevator was Colleen Dewhurst....Lauren Bacall...and Elaine Stritch! Doug does an amazing imitation of them greeting each other. Essentially three incredible low, smoky voices getting lower and lower in pitch: "Hey, girl!" "Hey, girl!" "*Hey, girl.*"

He also told the *Chatterbox* audience that I have "stealth fame." I cocked my head Scooby-Doo-style until he explained. First, he recalled the recent time he gave a fundraiser at his apartment for Music for Autism and Kerry Butler was the celebrity asked to sing. She called me to play for her and we were waiting on the sidelines before the performance. Doug told the audience that when the mother of the head of the organization heard I was there, she physically pushed Kerry Butler out of the way so she could meet me. Hilarious. That's right! Bypassing the celebrity to meet the "celebrity."

At my radio show *Seth Speaks*, I interviewed Eve Plumb, who's currently starring in *Love, Loss, and What I Wore*. I asked her what TV shows she did before playing Jan on "The Brady Bunch," and she rattled off a slew of '60s faves including "Lassie" and "A Family Affair." And, in almost every guest appearance, she had to cry. She then listed every depressing situation she was in, per show, including playing a girl who dies of cancer in "Family Affair." The title of the episode? "Christmas Came Early This Year." It did?!?!? Not for her character.

I'm seeing *Porgy and Bess* this week and this time, I'm prepared with a full pocket of Kleenex. Have a good week and stay warm...and/or cool depending on what Global Warming is doing this week. Peace out!

The *Follies* of Jan Maxwell and Deconstructing for Free
January 16, 2012

Oy! And, now, I have a month of crazy busy-ness! In one week, my new young adult book comes out, and I'm doing a reading/signing/performance at Barnes and Noble (86th and Lex.) on Jan 23. The day before all of that, *Disaster*, the musical I wrote based on all of the amazing 1970's disaster movies, opens at the Triad! We start today (only seven days of rehearsal), so I don't know if it's going to be one of those "Wow! We pulled it off!" or "What were we thinking?" experiences that becomes a hilarious story once the devastation wears off. I guess that's the excitement of putting up a new show. It's also why people turn to "dolls."

This week I saw *Porgy and Bess* for the second time (first time was in Boston). I still cannot get over the amazing singing, specifically Audra McDonald, Norm Lewis and Josh Henry. I cannot *wait* for the CD! Of course, after the show, I eavesdropped on audience members, and two women obviously knew Audra only from "The Practice." One confidently commented that Audra plays a doctor "married on the show to Tie Diggs." Yes, she pronounced Taye as Tie. Then the other one commented, "Yeah! You could tell on the TV show that she was talented." Then she pointed to the Playbill, "...but not *this* talented." Had they never seen Audra on Broadway? Are four Tony Awards not enough to get in the public eye? *Soon to be two more!*

Anyhoo, I had Jan Maxwell on my Chatterbox this week and she was such a great guest. First, I asked her about *Follies*, and she told me that they started rehearsals with a read/sing-thru for Sondheim. I had a panic attack hearing that, but she remembers being relatively calm. I asked her why she didn't have (what we called in the 70's) a "nervous breakdown," and she said it's because she lives by the theory, "Respect everyone. Revere no one." Uh-oh...I've made a career out of worshiping people. Now what?

Speaking of which, I was having a game night at Andrea Burns' apartment, and she was doing a hilarious lip-synch of a singer who clanks numerous times on a phrase. Andrea re-enacted it, adding her own subplot that while the singer was fading out on a note in the recording studio, she starts gesturing to the booth asking for another take. I, of course, then became the recording engineer in her improv, pointing to my watch and mouthing, "We don't have time to do another one." After we deconstructed it twice, Andrea told me that the night was so "meta" because if people knew I was doing it, they'd probably ask, "Wait! That's your actual job... you had a night out with friends and you spent it deconstructing?" She thinks it's so funny that people don't realize that deconstructing is what I've *always* done with friends, literally since elementary school. The job part came later. And, P.S., the job part pays me pretty much the same as what I get deconstructing with friends.

Back to Jan Maxwell. I told her that everyone was shocked she was such a musical theatre sasstress in *Follies*. She said that she had always done musicals, especially in summer stock. She started rattling off shows (she played Evita in *Evita*!) and then she mentioned *Anything Goes*. "Who did you play?" I asked. She couldn't remember the name and said, "You know...the person!" We figured out she played Reno Sweeney, and the horrifying part is they told her at the last minute that they wanted her to tap in the big "Anything Goes" number. The problem was, they told her a half hour before the show, and she didn't know the dance or even how to tap! She was panicked in the rehearsal room at 7:30, trying to figure out what to do, when her best friend walked in. He advised her to "just smile a lot." Cut to, after the performance, she saw her boyfriend. Jan asked him what the dance looked like during the title song, and he replied, "I don't know... but I've never seen you happier!" It worked?

Her first Broadway musical was as an understudy in *City of Angels*, which she said was a terrifying experience. There was a moving treadmill that went across the stage that she had to walk backwards (!) on, but she never had a chance to practice on it during rehearsal because it would have been too expensive to hire a crew to operate. It was actually dangerous, and she remembers that before each entrance, a crew member would tell her what to do for her safety, and it was terrifying instructions like, "Make sure you move to the side or else you'll have something enormous slam into your head" or "Keep your arms next to you the whole time or else you'll be killed." Literally. Where was the fun part? I guess surviving with her life.

Speaking of surviving, she's been injured off and on during *Follies*—including being hit by a van (!)—but has refused to stop performing even though a doctor told her to take weeks off. Jan said she did the ol' chestnut of going from doctor to doctor until she found one who said she could continue doing the show. Yay quacks!

Her first big musical job was touring in *Annie* as the Lily St. Regis understudy. She flew down to Atlanta and, because she didn't know anyone, she started exploring different neighborhoods by herself. One afternoon, a police car screeched up next to her, and the policeman asked where she was from. She muttered, "New York..." Then he asked where she was staying, and she said, "Uh...the hotel?" He told her to get in the backseat of the police car because he thought she was a prostitute! She stammered that she was in town with the tour of *Annie*. The policeman said, "Oh, I'm so embarrassed...I just bought a ticket to see it tonight!" Turns out, though, Jan was still in rehearsal and therefore wasn't in the show yet, so she told us that he probably got to the theatre, looked at the Playbill and yelled, "That whore!"

In terms of bad auditions, she talked about going in for *Parade* and feeling like her career was over because she had just given birth a few weeks earlier and she was exhausted. Plus, she happened to have made good money that year doing voiceovers (she said it was the only time she ever made good money), and she found out she owed $10,000 in taxes! She was devastated and decided to not get dressed up because she somehow thought it was for a student director of Hal Prince, but when she walked in she saw it was for *the* Hal Prince and mega-producer Garth Drabinsky. She then decided her career really *was* over. She turned her devastation into being cranky, and basically couldn't stop herself. Whatever they asked her, she had a whiny, annoyed line reading that, when she re-created it, was hilarious. The dialogue was:

HAL: Have you seen the sides?
JAN: Have I *seen* the sides? Of course, I've *seen* the sides!
HAL: Do you have questions?
JAN: Yes!!! What's this play about????
HAL: You play the mother of a little girl who was murdered in the South.
JAN: She's *Southern*??!?!?
HAL: Yes.....
JAN: (Overwrought) Do you want an accent!?!?!
HAL: Uh...sure.
JAN: When did it happen!?!?!?
HAL: In the 20's.
JAN: (Exasperated) Not the *time period*! When I read this scene, how much time has passed since the murder?!?!?
HAL: Uh...a few weeks.

Jan did the scene, and then Hal told her the show was going to go to Philadelphia. She replied, with great consternation, "Philadelphia?!?! For how long?" He told her five days. She replied, completely overwhelmed and annoyed, "Five days!?!?" I'm obsessed with that part, because literally however many days he said would have irritated her. Well, for some reason, they offered her the role and later on Hal's assistant told Jan that Hal had written on her audition sheet, "Awesome!" Then "Hostile?" Hilariously accurate.

And speaking of Jan, I just saw *Follies* for the second time. It was the Actors Fund performance. I cannot recommend seeing an Actors Fund performance enough! The cast is always so amazing because the audience is extra enthusiastic filled with fellow gypsies, and it's star-studded! Just in my area I saw Audra McDonald, Marilyn Sokol, Norm Lewis, Tom Hanks, David Alan Grier, John Benjamin Hickey and Victor Garber. And now, peace out!

The Story of My New Book
January 25, 2012

Last week when I interviewed Mario Cantone, he said people are always surprised about some aspect of his career: People who know him from Broadway ask, "You do stand-up?" while people who know him from comedy clubs ask, "You act?" And then there's a mixture of both groups who ask "You sing?" It's very similar to what happens to me, but, unfortunately, people ask me, "You act?" after seeing me in an actual play. Rude. Regardless, my pit musician friends don't know about my performing career, and a lot of my radio listeners don't know I played the piano on Broadway for years. And then there's the crossover group who don't know I've written some books. So, since "My Awesome/Awful Popularity Plan" (my first young adult novel!) is being released this week, I thought I'd give a little back-story on my writing.

My mom at my book release.

My first big writing attempt was a play I wrote in fourth grade called *Killer Girlfriend*. I'm not saying I was already heavily influenced by Broadway, but the so-called killer girlfriend's name was "Miss Mazepa." Nothing came of the play even though I had ample copies of it due to the fact that I was able to use my father's rexograph machine (anybody around from the '70s?). Cut to the year 2000; I was in a bookstore and saw a copy of the novel "The Nanny Diaries" on the shelf. I thought that if people were interested in the inside world of nannying, then there would also be people interested in the inside world of Broadway! That night, I started writing my first novel, originally called "Subbing." I decided to write about a Jewish piano player on Broadway who worked as a sub ("write what you know," people!). After each chapter, I would send it to various friends for feedback, especially my best friends Tim Cross, my *Disaster!* co-writer and best friend, Jack Plotnick, and currently starring as the Nun in *Disaster!* (and Yale alum and beltress), Anika Larsen. Then I started bringing it to the theatres where I was playing in the pit. During *The Full Monty*, I would haul it up to Andrea Burns' dressing room, as well as giving it to various fellow pit musicians so they could be distracted and miss cues. I decided to contact Charles Busch's partner, Eric Myers, because he and I were friendly through Charles and I knew he was a book agent. He read the first chapter and was crazily enthusiastic. He told me that comic novels were very rare and that I wrote exactly as I spoke and that could be a big plus. He kept on me to finish the book and I finally did by doing most of my writing after I came home from playing a Broadway show (aka 11 PM).

I was so happy to finish, and immediately started spending my publishing advance money in my head. Eric took it to three publishing houses that he thought would be the best match. I knew it would be difficult to choose between three and hoped that one offer would be astronomically better than the other so I could make an easy decision. It wound up being a very easy decision to make because all three rejected it. Wowza. Three out of three ain't bad. Actually, yes it is. Eric told me not to worry and then said, "Listen, worse comes to worse, we can always go to 'Clanky Publishing House' (not it's real name)." Well, ten rejections later, he then called to tell me that "Clanky Publishing House" *also* rejected the book! I was mortified. Finally, Eric said with little enthusiasm, "Well, you could ask this publishing house I know, but it's basically self-publishing." I wanted him to do it for me but he said since they really don't pay much, I needed to do it myself. Oy. I swallowed my pride and sent them the book. Can you guess the rest? That's right. Rejected. From a place that is basically self-publishing! Why was my book so repellant? Eric told me that most publishing houses aren't fond of publishing books where the lead character is gay. That was so weird to me, because the book isn't about the lead character, Stephen, coming out or anything specific about his gayness. It's about Stephen not being satisfied with career/love life because of his co-dependant relationship with his narcissistic mother.

Regardless, after years of rejection, a new editor (Joe Pittman) took over at one of the publishing houses that rejected me (Alyson). After reading the first three chapters, Joe asked to read the rest of the book. I then got the delicious call from Eric I'd been waiting for: "How you would like to get your book published?" Yay! It was so thrilling. First, Joe made me change the title to "Broadway Nights." Then came the part I hate: re-writing. I completely dreaded it. But, Joe gave me great notes and after forcing myself to start, I wound up being super happy with the result. And, to all the publishing houses that rejected me, my first novel is now in its fourth printing! Ha! Of course, each printing is probably 20 books, but brava nonetheless. P.S. Alyson went out of business and now Vantage Point has taken over the publishing. It has a fancy new cover and a new intro by Audra McDonald. Sass!

The nice news is, people would sometimes mail me after they read the book and request a sequel, but I never got around to writing one. One day, Eric (my agent) called me and mentioned that as hard as it is to get an adult book published with a lead gay character, the *young* adult world is clamoring for one. What!? Publishing a novel without having to beg? Yes! I immediately sat down and started writing. I wanted it to be about dating, so I knew the kid couldn't be too young. I settled on 15 years old. I decided, yet again, to base him on aspects of myself, so I made him an overweight teenager (based on my "fondness" for Husky brand jeans) and I added a so-called Jewfro. I thought of the name Justin for him but wanted a last name that inherently sounded awkward: Goldblatt. Ow.

I wrote the first three chapters super-quick and my agent sent them to Schuyler Hooke, a fabulous YA editor at Random House. Schuyler loved it and said that in order for Random House to buy it, he'd need the whole book. And thus my writer's block/laziness began. I just couldn't get myself to write more. Every time I'd run into Eric, he'd ask how it was going. *Silence.* Then I'd see Schuyler sitting in the audience at my *Chatterbox* shows and *he'd* ask the same devastating question. Eventually, two years passed. Really! Finally, James told me that he ran into Eric, and that Eric asked him to get involved and convince me to finish it. I felt like I was in an episode of "Intervention," but it worked. I decided I was going to write every day until I finished. So, I sat at my desk overlooking Manhattan Avenue (this is when I lived in Harlem) and every night I would show each chapter to Anika and Jack as usual and then I'd show James before we went to sleep. I took all of their advice and finally finished it in January 2010. Eric sent it off to Schuyler and *three weeks later* we had an offer from Random House! It took almost two years to get "Broadway Nights" a deal, and just three weeks for my YA book! Since I'm using initials, I'll add *WTF*!?!?!

First, Random House asked me to change the title. It was called "Surviving Sophomore Year" but that went the way of "Subbing" and became "My Awesome/Awful Popularity Plan." Schuyler sent back my manuscript with a bunch of notes, but they were all great and I started to rewrite it. Then I suddenly found myself doing *They're Playing Our Song* with Sutton Foster and right after that I got cast in *[title of show]* in New Jersey. Suddenly my deadline for revisions came and went. I got a crazed email from Eric asking where the revised manuscript was (maybe it was "where the H" or "the F"), and I wrote that it was almost done. If "almost" means one page out of 300, then I wasn't lying. I started frantically rewriting on the train to and from the George Street Playhouse in New Jersey but I was stuck on a plot point Schuyler wanted clarified; if Justin is so savvy, why would he possibly think he has a chance with

Chuck, who is so obviously straight? Oy. I didn't know! Then I flew down to New Orleans to film "Varla Jean and the Mushroom Heads." While on set, I kept my computer open so I could write when I wasn't filming. Suddenly, during a take I wasn't in, I came up with the plot point that explained it all and I ran to the computer and typed up a storm. Phew! This is a classic example of adult ADD; I need an extreme amount of pressure and a past deadline to get anything done. That's why it's "fun" to live and/or work with me.

I remember when Eric first told me the release date it seemed so far off (two years!). But now it's here! I was so thrilled when I got my first copy. *And* because I'm so modérne, the new novel is also a Nook book. Brava! Here's the description of the book from Random House:

Justin has two goals for sophomore year: to date Chuck, the hottest boy in school, and to become the king of Cool U, the table in the cafeteria where the "in" crowd sits.

Unfortunately, he has the wrong look (short, plump, Brillo-pad curls), he has the wrong interests (Broadway, chorus, violin), and he has the wrong friends (Spencer, into Eastern religions, and Mary Ann, who doesn't shave her armpits). And Chuck? Well, he's not gay; he's dating Becky, a girl in chorus with whom Justin is friendly.

But Justin is determined.

In detention one day (because he saw Chuck get it first), Justin comes up with a perfect plan: to allow Becky to continue dating Chuck, whom Becky's dad hates. They will pretend that Becky is dating Justin, whom Becky's dad loves. And when Becky and Justin go out on a fake date, Chuck will meet up with them for a real date with Becky. Chuck's bound to find Justin irresistable, right? What could go wrong?

Seth Rudetsky's first novel for young adults is endearingly human, and laugh-out-loud funny, and any kid who ever aspired to Cool U will find Justin a welcome ally in the fight for popularity.

My musical *Disaster!* opened at the Triad on Sunday and was *amazing*. So thrilling. I have a ton of stuff to write about dealing with getting the show up (that's what she said) but will write it next week. Peace out!

From Texas to *Disaster!*
January 30, 2012

I'm on a flight home from Houston because I was down here for a big high school/college theatre festival called TheatreFest 2012, a project of Texas Educational Theatre Association. They take theatre *seriously* in Texas. A local woman told me (in full Texas twang) "It's football, cheerleading, then theatre." Brian Stokes Mitchell was supposed to perform the first night, but he suddenly got strep throat. So, at the last minute, Donna McKechnie flew down and did a fantastic interview with David Michaels (I know him from his producing of West Coast Actors Fund events). The kids went crazy for Donna, especially when she ended by performing "The Music and the Mirror." She's still got it!

On Saturday morning, I did a reading of my new book ("My Awesome/Awful Popularity Plan") at the Blue Willow Bookstore and it was so fun! The book existed for years only on my computer, and now, suddenly, people are reading it and writing to me about it. I love the fact that even though it's considered a "young adult" book, so many adults are reading it. I'm telling anyone who loved my earlier novel "Broadway Nights" to get "Awesome/Awful" because it's essentially a prequel. The leading character is pretty much exactly the same, just 20 years younger. They don't actually have the same name, but apparently I'm only capable of writing one lead character (neurotic, scheming, slightly overweight Jew) and I'll stick him into whatever genre I'm writing. Next up: a period romance featuring a neurotic, scheming, slightly overweight country squire.

On Saturday, I also did *Deconstructing Broadway* for the festival. Before I performed, David Michaels interviewed Alice Ripley. He talked about her show-stopping performance as Amy in the Kennedy Center production of *Company*. When she was first working on "Getting Married Today," she was doing very over-the-top Carol Burnett-style physical comedy including hanging from the set and singing a whole verse upside down. She happened to try out that staging at a rehearsal attended by Stephen Sondheim. Afterwards, he told her simply: "Don't do that…just sing the song." Alice was happy to get that advice. Just hearing the story gave me an anxiety attack. She also felt that she did the right thing by going so far in rehearsal. She feels you have to go all the way in one direction to know what it's like — and then you can tone it down. Because you've had the experience of pushing it, it adds to your performance. She remembered doing *Side Show* and having her director, Bobby Longbottom, come backstage and tell her that her big second-act solo had to be cut. He was, literally, on his knees (!) apologizing. She, however, was thrilled. "Are you kidding me? Thank you! One less difficult song to sing!" But, because she had the experience of singing the song during previews, she could add that experience to her character's journey. She also told the students to always have some sort of creative outlet. While she was playing Diana in *Next to Normal*, she began to focus on playing the guitar in her spare time to bring her back to herself. She then performed a song from *Next to Normal* on the guitar, but it was a song that the character of husband sings in the show. She told us that singing it really helped her see his perspective in the story.

Speaking of creative outlets, I thought I'd tell the story of my musical *Disaster!* One of my first jobs when I came to New York was playing piano for *Forever Plaid*. When I first joined the show, Frankie was played by Drew Geraci, who had recently played Paul in the final Broadway company of *A Chorus Line*. Drew and I became good friends and wound up traveling all over the place and setting up various companies of *Forever Plaid*. Off the top of my head, I remember we did the Toronto, Vancouver and Las Vegas companies. Also off the top of my head, I remember I threw my back out in Toronto because for some reason suitcases didn't have wheels in the early '90s. When we got to Toronto, the cab dropped us off a few blocks away from our hotel and I had to carry my suitcase, causing a back spasm. I know the internet didn't come around 'til the late '90s but why was it just as difficult to think of wheels for suitcases? Back to *Disaster!*: Drew and I were always thinking of different shows to write. One was about two guys: One is gay and obsessed with the other, who is straight. The gay guy decides to get a sex change so the straight guy will like him, but unfortunately the straight guy *also* decides to get a sex change to get the gay guy to stop bothering him. Cut to: They're now both women and arch-rivals. And then they both get offered the title role in *Mame* in competing Broadway productions. I have no more memory of what else happens to them, but if the rest of the plot was as brilliant as that, I'm glad it remained unwritten. A better idea we had was to write a musical version of a 1970s disaster movie. We had both loved "Poseidon Adventure," "Towering Inferno, "Airport '75," etc. — and even clunkers like that movie about snakes called "S-s-s-s-s-s-s." Anybody? Anybody with a lateral lisp? We wanted to feature a new disaster that hadn't been in a movie, so I thought it would be funny to do a whole show about the New York City blackout of 1977 because it's such a soft disaster. Where's the scary part? For the music, we wanted to use actual '70s songs. Well, like many things I've planned on doing (leading all the way up to this morning in terms of putting away my clean clothes), it went completely undone. For more than 15 years! Finally, last year, I was asked to do a benefit for Only Make Believe, which brings theatre to hospitalized children. I've performed in their annual gala many times and I had done an evening of *Deconstructing Broadway* for them the year before. They told me I could do any type of show I wanted. I decided to employ the Charles Busch trick: give yourself a deadline to force yourself to write something. Back in the '80s, he got a date to perform at the Limbo Lounge in the East Village and then wrote *Vampire Lesbians of Sodom*. So, I picked a date in late May and told Only Make Believe we'd be doing *Disaster!* Cut to a blank computer screen. Ah! Writing it was the hard part. The one thing I changed right away was the idea of the blackout being the disaster. I thought it would be more exciting to incorporate *all* of my favorite disasters from those 1970s films.

Drew and I met to discuss various plot elements, but we're both Pisces and there was a lot of procrastination and dreaminess. Plus, he was working a full time job and we were on opposite schedules. Cut to: It's mid-February and I'm in Palm Springs playing for Audra McDonald at a fancy benefit for Desert AIDS. They gave me a great hotel room so I invited one of my best friends, Jack Plotnick, to stay with me. He loves being creative, so he asked if he could brainstorm the show with me. I was telling him various ideas and he was loving them. *Then* I told him the show was scheduled to happen in three months and nothing script-wise had actually been written down. He had a panic attack and forced open my computer so something could actually be *written*. We became a team. By April, Jack and I had written the show, with Drew adding extra hilarious material. Then I began casting. I wanted to replicate another aspect of Charles Busch and decided to surround myself with friends onstage, so I called/emailed/texted people I've known forever and asked to play different parts. All the roles are archetype disaster-movie roles. To name a few, I was able to get Anika Larsen (who I've known since she was doing *Zanna, Don't* and I was doing *Rhapsody in Seth*) to play Sister Mary Downy, the nun with the gambling addiction; Kathy Fitzgerald (who I met when we were both doing *The Producers*) to play Shirley Summers, the older lady with the heart condition; and Lauren Kennedy (who I've known since I interviewed her right after she understudied in *Side Show*) to play Jackie Sylvestri, the lounge singer who has terrible taste in unavailable men. *For the Broadway company, Rachel York asked if we could change it to Jackie Noelle...we agreed it sounded more like a sexy lounge singer.* And, a la Charles Busch, I gave myself a great part! That's right, I cast myself as Professor Scheider, the disaster expert.

So, May 23 came, the benefit show went fantastically and we then got some funding to do a two-day reading. The next step was rewriting some stuff and then doing an out-of-town tryout. Out-of-town? No joke, when my friend Traci Lyn invited me to her wedding, I said I'd only go if it was scheduled for a Wednesday between shows *and* located in a church on my block.

In November, I went out to lunch with James and was complaining about having to take the show to a regional theatre when he suddenly pointed across the street: Yes, the theatre where I first saw *Forbidden Broadway* and then did *Forever Plaid* would be *perfect* for *Disaster!* I called my manager, Orin Wolf, who also produces, and he agreed to help us get the show going.

We began rehearsals on Jan. 16th and I have never felt more like I was in a Mickey-and-Judy film. Jack told me a theory that when you try to put something creative out into the universe, every day something will try to stop it. *BOY* was he right. Among the obstacles: we got news that we suddenly needed *thousands* of dollars we didn't know we needed. And we had to get approval from various unions or we'd have to shut down. It's been crazy. Yet, so much fun. First of all, we're doing a show in a theatre that seemed crazily cramped with a four person cast (like *Forever Plaid*), yet we're a *15-person cast*! We're doing full production numbers so close to the audience that if I didn't have such an awful extension, I'd kick someone in the teeth. And we not only have everyone on stage performing, we also have a full rock band. Now I know what my Grandmother felt like in steerage when she came here from Russia.

The fun-nee Kathy Fitzgerald in costume as Shirley in Disaster!

Last week, we started rehearsals on Monday and did our dress/tech (and first run-through) on Sunday afternoon, leading up to the 7 PM curtain. Suddenly, in the middle of Act Two, we found out that we hadn't properly timed the tech and we had to leave the stage so the theatre could be set up and prepped for an audience. Not only had we never, ever run the show, but we had never done the last 20 pages of Act Two with any props, costumes, band, etc. While we were backstage waiting to go on, Kathy Fitzgerald tried to cheer us up by saying, "It's like summer stock. You know, where you put up an enormous show in 10 days!" Lauren responded simply, "But we didn't have ten days." Ouch.

Well, the show went *so* well. I watched the audience while we were doing the finale ("Hooked on a Feeling") and was terrified that I might see a sea of blank faces. But even though our first show ran long, they were all smiling. *I would see the same thing on Broadway! That show was so much fun to do!*

Caroline Rhea, Nick Jonas, Tony Sheldon
February 6, 2012

Let me start with fun stuff from this week: I went out to brunch on the Upper West Side this Sunday and, when I entered the Fairway cafe, I heard my name called. Turns out, Caroline Rhea was sitting down to brunch and called me over. We hadn't seen each other since her daughter was a baby. She immediately pulled up a photo on her phone, but told me not to make fun. She wasn't nervous that I'd make fun of her daughter, she was nervous I'd make fun of her cellphone. Wowza. It was such an old-school phone that I wound up being miffed I didn't see the cord that plugged it into the phone jack. She had even lost the phone recently and when she went to get a new one the store told her she could have an upgrade — but she insisted on getting the one she'd always had. They went into shock because it pretty much looks like that same one the kids used when they sang "The Telephone Hour" in *Bye Bye Birdie*. She won't get an iPhone because she tried one once and told me that after she pushed one letter, out came a paragraph. She told me that "since she refuses to get lipo on her fingers," she's keeping this one.

At *Seth Speaks*, I interviewed Nick Jonas who's currently starring *How To Succeed in Business Without Really Trying*. First of all, hopefully nobody from Juli's school will listen because I picked her up from 6th grade for "an appointment" right before the taping and then dropped her back at school two hours later. I didn't keep it under wraps very well because I wound up letting Juli ask him a question during the interview. She asked him what the craziest thing a fan had ever asked him and he immediately remembered the time a fan approached him and asked him...to punch her! He refused. I, however, wonder if it was Lea Michele asking him to audition for the film version of *Spring Awakening* (Whipping scene? Anyone?) By the way, *How to Succeed* is not his Broadway debut; he did *Beauty and the Beast*, *Annie Get Your Gun* and *Les Miz* many years ago when he was just a little boy (AKA ten years ago). As a matter of fact, his Broadway gig is what made him a pop star. Every year Broadway Cares/Equity Fights AIDS puts out a CD called "Carols For a Cure" which features cast members from different Broadway shows singing holiday songs. When he was 11 and doing *Beauty and The Beast*, "Carols for a Cure" featured a song he wrote. One of his neighbors showed the song to a record executive and that got Nick his first record deal when he was 13. I pointed out that at age 13, I was simply getting my bar mitzvah. But, on a side note, I'm sure my bar mitzvah performance had 80 percent more scooping and vibrato than his first two CDs combined. *Liza with a Cha'i*?

Speaking of vibrato and pop music, Betty Buckley did an amazing Twitter rant about "American Idol's" constant dishing of Broadway and vibrato. There is a myth that rock/pop singers don't use vibrato and it's a total *lie*. My favorite quote of Betty's is "Broadway is a place, not a style." Brava!

Back to Nick: In the '90s, he was cast in a small role in Madison Square Garden's *A Christmas Carol*. He was also an understudy for Tiny Tim but it was assumed he'd never go on. Cut to: he had to go on and had no rehearsal. He knew his part but when the lights hit him, he got so nervous that he didn't sing for around 16 bars of music. That day, he told us that he made a solemn vow to never to be nervous again. He was 7. Really? When I was 7, I vowed never to pee in my pants again. The vow lasted two days.

P.S. I also busted him because I watched the *Les Miz* 25th anniversary video and he relentlessly hauls out a not-since-Madonna British accent! Nick revealed that he was told to sing in a British accent! Even though the show takes place in France. *And* he's from New Jersey.

I was back at *Seth's Broadway Chatterbox* this week with all three male leads from *Priscilla Queen of the Desert*. Tony Sheldon (Tony-nominated for playing Bernadette) grew up in Australia with a super-famous musical theatre star mother, Toni Lamond. Add to his pedigree…his aunt is Helen Reddy! I asked him about a role we both played: Arnold in *Torch Song Trilogy*. He did his in Australia and his experience proved that much of a show's success is about the marketing: in the first city, the poster featured a picture of him in drag and underneath it said, "Meet Arnold. You may have more in common with him than you think." And…the show tanked. Then another producer came along, moved it to another city and the ad campaign featured *no* drag and instead featured other cast members like Laurel (the pretty girl dating Arnold's boyfriend) and Arnold's mother. He said the ad had something written on it like, "Aren't families wacky?" Cut to: it ran for two years!

I asked him what his most mortifying audition was, and he remembered auditioning for some pop musical in Australia being directed by Tom O'Horgan (*Hair*, *Jesus Christ Superstar*). Tony researched the Beatles and decided to do "With a Little Help From My Friends." He got to the theatre and saw that the pianist was in the pit. He bent down to give him the music, but the guy was so far into the pit that Tony had to literally lie on his stomach on the stage and then reach his hand all the way forward. So, he laid down, handed him the music and stood back up again. The vamp began, he sang, "What would you do if I sang — " and suddenly heard "THANK YOU!"

Literally one measure! Tony wanted to flee but instead he had to get his music. Meaning he had to *lie down again*, reach his hand out, get his music and *then* flee. And flee he did. He's hoping to stay here in America. Brava! *He stayed and recently starred in AMELIE!*

Tears and Laughter, and a Rave
February 13, 2012

This week I did *Seth Speaks* on SiriusXM and I interviewed Tony Award winner Alice Ripley. Naturally, I asked Alice about a lot of her past jobs, including being a "'Hee Haw' honey." If you were mercifully spared knowledge of that show, it was a TV variety hour featuring country music and comedy. I had *zero* interest in it when I was child and yet in the mid-'70s, despite the myriad "Bugs Bunny" and "Charlie Brown" options, my mother bought me a "Hee Haw" lunch box. To this day, I am miffed, mortified, confused and mind-boggled. What was she thinking? The only country music I like is *The Best Little Whorehouse in Texas* but I assume *that* lunch box was too risqué for me to carry around my Yeshiva. Regardless, before Alice got the "Hee Haw" gig, the show had been on the air for 26 years. She told me they decided to re-format it and hire all new people including Alice. It was then immediately cancelled. We also discussed her work at various theatres before she starred on Broadway. One of the theaters was in San Diego and it sat directly underneath the flight path for jets landing at the airport. The sound when the airplanes approached obliterated everything else, so the theatre had an ingenious system worked out: All the actors onstage could see three traffic lights that were stationed in the pit. The show went along as usual when the green light was on. When it went to yellow, the actors knew they had to prepare for a jet. When it finally went red, they had to stop whatever they were singing, freeze, let the jet pass, and then resume. Seriously. She had soprano leads, and essentially the audience would hear "Sweetheart, they're suspecting things..." (Big finish) "Peo-ple will sa-a-a-a-y, we-e-e-e-e're.... " (Silence, then the sound of an enormous jet for 10 seconds....then) "in lo-o-o-o-ove!" Applause?

As I write this, it's 5:30 AM Los Angeles time and I'm on my way back to NYC. I came out here for the Steve Chase Humanitarian Awards, which is a fundraiser for Desert AIDS. Jack Plotnick drove me down from L.A. and we spent the day together. This event had celebrities like Wynonna, Peter Gallagher, Joan Rivers and Queen Latifah, so basically nobody knew who I was or if I was even invited. My first sign that something was amiss was when I was at rehearsal and one of the people running the organization came up and introduced himself to me. Unfortunately, the "me" he introduced himself to was Jack Plotnick. He shook Jack's hand and called him Seth. I informed him that *I* was actually Seth and he re-introduced himself.

Once that happened, I went into a panic about what was scheduled for me that night: the red carpet. That's when you walk the paparazzi line and there are tons of flashbulbs going off and people clamoring to interview you. *If* you're a celeb. Sometimes there are Broadway fans on the press line, but I knew this one was going to be mortifying. Just to make it super awkward, I decided to shave the last minute but realized I had forgotten my razor. The hotel sent one up to my room and it was one of those "Buy 20 Razors for a Dollar"-types which always cut my face. I actually wound up being late to the red carpet because I was bleeding from so many places on my face. I walked down to the lobby with a towel pressed against the bigger cuts and when I was ready to go, I didn't know what to do with the towel. I went to the concierge and asked him where I could get rid of it. He looked at the bloody towel and said, "Hold on one minute." Then, "Let me get the incinerator." Brava on the sense of humor! The first person I saw interviewing people on the red carpet was Michael Costello, who's currently on "Project Runway All-Stars." I always watch that show and was excited for an opportunity to be interviewed by him. He was holding a big microphone in his hand that I saw him use to interview the celeb before me. I approached him and as soon as I introduced myself to him, I saw the microphone drop to his side. As in, "This won't be needed." I wound up fleeing the red carpet and went to the dinner/show, which was great.

Queen Latifah sang "I Know Where I've Been," Wynonna sang "I Wanna Know What Love Is" and Joan Rivers was a hi-larious host. She talked about a charity she claims to support that brings sex to homebound seniors. She claims it's "Feels on Wheels." *I felt so lucky that I got to interview her a few times before she passed away. She was a great lady!*

I was at the event to play for Megan Mullally. We first worked together on *Grease!* back in '94 when she played Marty and I played piano at rehearsals and subbed in the pit. For this benefit she sang "Happy Days Are Here Again," and at the end went up to an E flat and the crowd flipped out.

Right after the event, I took a car to L.A., got to bed by 12:30 and woke up at 4:45 to catch an early flight back to NYC so I can do *Disaster!* Which brings me to the thrilling part of the week. Last week's performance of *Disaster!* was hard for everybody because we've always been able to run the show in the afternoon before a performance, but we weren't able to last Sunday. It's really difficult to do a full musical with six whole days between performances. So, a whole week had gone by and we were all shaky and forgetful. So many things went wrong that I was backstage in a full depression whenever I wasn't onstage. For example, at one point I'm supposed to run out into the group of survivors and announce, "People! I have an announcement!" The bad guy is supposed to tell me to "Can it!" and we have an argument. Well, for whatever reason, the bad guy forgot to come in with his line. So, the audience saw me come out and yell, "People! I have an announcement!" This was met by a wall of silence onstage. I wanted to cue the next line somehow, so after a good amount of silence went by, I panicked and implored, "Let me speak!" It literally made no sense. Who wasn't letting me speak? The air?

The show was chock full of clankity-clunky moments like that. I wasn't that upset afterwards because I knew it was only our third performance and we'd be able to run the show the following Sunday afternoon. Well, who happened to be at the clankity-clunky show reviewing it? The New York *F-ing* Times! My Off-Broadway play, *Rhapsody in Seth* ran for six months before they reviewed, but for this they waited two (2!) performances and then showed up! It actually wound up being a perfect situation because a.) I had no idea they were there so I felt no stress; b.) I didn't spend a week frantically checking to see if a review came and hoping it was good/worrying it was bad; and, most miraculously, c.) we got a *rave*. We were all in shock. It's like being told you won the lottery when you didn't even know you bought a ticket.

The most perfect "full-circle" aspect of it is that the day the Times review came out in the paper is the day I was in Palm Springs with Jack doing the 2012 Desert AIDS benefit. As you remember, Jack and I first started writing *Disaster!* in Palm Springs, at the 2011 Desert AIDS benefit! We were able to walk by the spot where we first opened my computer and started the first scene exactly one year ago. The first line of the review: "While the Giants were winning in Indianapolis, another triumph was unfolding on West 72nd Street." It says that the script "doesn't pause for refueling"; it calls the show "irresistible"; it calls the cast "exuberant" and "indefatigable." The only devastating part? The reviewer calls me a "seasoned multi-hyphenate (Actor-pianist- playwright-satellite radio host)." What does "seasoned" mean? I'll tell you: old! Anyhoo, the cast was joyous and as soon as I know what the next step is, I'll tell you!

Love, Loss... and Change Your Hair
February 21, 2012

Hello, again Playbill readers.

On to L.A. I'm out here because I'm playing for Andrea Martin's show (coming up in Palm Springs) and because I'm doing *Deconstructing Broadway* (Aka *Seth's Big Fat Broadway Show*) at Jason Alexander's "Reprise" which is the like the west coast version of Encores. I'm very excited because I'm sold out. I still got it!

Last week I was on my SiriusXM show and talked about coming to L.A and staying with Marissa Jaret Winokur like I did last year. If you don't remember, we all stayed with her and her adorable family last February, but because she actually doesn't want overnight guests, she doesn't have an extra bed. That's right, she has a pile of pillows/couch that she calls "The Pit," and quite frankly it *was* the pits. The house is amazing, her son adorable, but I had to get three (3!) massages because my back went out from the gelatinous sleeping area. So, I was mentioning my aching back on SiriusXM and the next thing I knew, I had an email waiting from Max Mutchnick (creator of "Will and Grace"). Max's husband is Erik Hyman, who is the best friend of one of my childhood best friends, Anne Martin, with whom I went to musical theatre summer camp (USDAN), and that's how I met Max. Max told me that he would not allow me to stay at a "poor actress's" house and that we had to stay at his place. Meanwhile, Marissa is anything but a "poor actress". It wound up becoming a battle of the 1%. At the point Max told us he had a separate guesthouse, I stopped returning Marissa's phone calls. I'm writing this column in his backyard, overlooking his pool *and* tennis court and listening to the sound of his stone fountain while I smell the jasmine in the air. So pretty. TV definitely pays a *lot* differently than Broadway. Especially TV in "the day." I was doing Andrea's show last weekend and Sean Hayes, Dan Bucatinsky ("Web Therapy") and his partner Don Roos came. I was fawning all of over Don because I'm obsessed with one of the films he wrote and directed called "The Opposite of Sex." He told me that it was easy to fund independent films when he made the movie, and we were talking about ways to make money nowadays. His advice was: "Make a sitcom...in the '90's." Hilarious!

Disaster! is going so great but I'm beginning to hate how crowded my apartment is. What do I mean? Well, this show is so Mom and Pop that every week we have to move the set out of the theatre and store it. Where you ask? My living room. And here are the set pieces that are in our tiny NYC apartment:

-the railing of a ship

-a slot machine

-a wall that's been in an explosion...and more!

More L.A. Even though I refused to throw my back out again at Marissa's place, we still got to hang out. She brought her family *and* her enormous family eight-seat car to Costa Mesa and drove me, James, Juli and Andrea Martin to the San Diego Zoo. Marissa won the Tony Award for *Hairspray,* but for the last few years, she has pretty much stopped acting and begun to do hosting gigs/reality TV like "Dance You're A** Off," "Dancing with The Stars," "The Talk," etc. Well, last summer she played Tracy in *Hairspray* at the Hollywood Bowl and went out to eat afterwards with Jeff Garlin from "Curb Your Enthusiasm." He told her she needed to stop doing reality shows, get back to acting, and stop having blonde hair. He claimed that "nobody could recognize her." She took his advice and went back to being a brunette. And she told me she hasn't stopped working since! She just finished a season on the sitcom "Retired at 35." *And*, right when Jeff told her to stop the reality stuff she was about to sign a contract for "Celebrity Wife Swap." Wowza. I'm sure that wouldn't have been a career low. Not since "I'm a Celebrity, Get Me Outta Here." P.S. I know she's the queen of hair extensions so when I looked at her brunette curly locks, I asked, "How much of your hair is fake?" She immediately replied, "All of it." Brava.

This morning, we were told by the house cook that breakfast would be served at 8:30. So fancy! We all came to the main house and met Max and Erik's two twins, Rose and Evan. They are not even three years old and are already being completely immersed in Broadway. Rose sang (with all the wordy lyrics) her own version of "Don't Rain On My Parade" (with raised arms) and Evan, not be outdone, hauled out "My Man" with amazing sustained notes during "Fore-e-e-e-e-e...ve-e-e-e-er...mo-o-o-o-re!" Maybe they'll be able to trade off the role when the revival finally happens. *P.S. I love that there's so much Max Mutchnick in this book which is coming out right when WILL AND GRACE is coming back!*

This afternoon I'm heading to Kevin Chamberlin's house. He is graciously letting men use his house for a get together of the L.A. friends that I always want to see whenever I'm out here, but never do because I always run out of time. We're meeting at five because he said the sunset is beautiful from his place. Yay!

Andrea Martin got two great reviews at her Costa Mesa show even though she forgot her lyrics to the beginning of her encore. We couldn't stop re-creating the moment because we loved the fact that it was *such* a big set up for a song that was then followed by nothing. She told the audience, in a somber way, that she wanted to sing "Laughing Matter" because "I think it's so beautiful... and because it truly sums up my philosophy of life." The audience sat back to watch and...nothing. Finally, I fed the opening lyrics to her and she sang but we're obsessed with her whole attitude of "I'm at peace and let me show you how you can be at peace, too" in the introduction and then the complete silence.

My young adult book "My Awesome/Awful Popularity Plan" is thankfully selling well amongst adults, and I just found out I'm going to do an audio book as well! I'll be taping it in NYC in two weeks and it'll coming out on Audible.com. My first novel, "Broadway Nights," is also on audible.com and stars me, Kristin Chenoweth, Jonathan Groff, Andrea Martin and more. Now, peace out!

West Coast Reunion, Plus a *Disaster!* Disaster Averted
February 27, 2012

I'm writing this on an east-bound airplane, about two hours away from New York. I was in L.A. for 10 days and I'm finally heading home. I started my West Coast excursion by doing Andrea Martin's show in Costa Mesa, CA, which is around an hour from L.A. She jokingly informed the audience that she's hitting all the hot spots in this leg of the "Andrea-Martin-I've-Run- Out-Of-Options-Tour." Juli's vacation coincided with the week I had to be in L.A., so she and James flew out to be with us. We went to Knotts Berry Farm and, thankfully, Jack Plotnick came along because even though James is willing to go on *some* scary rides, Jack will go on everything. I literally feel nauseated on *anything* so the only "ride" I went on was a glass-enclosed room that lifted gently in the air. Its main function is to give people a view of the park so they can decide what rides they want to go on. I saw all the rides and I chose nothing. It was a similar experience to getting your college course catalog and not signing up for any classes. Or, taking the courses I did my freshman year at Oberlin: piano, ballet and mime (and French which I dropped after a month).

I'm very thankful we spent the week staying as the guests of Max Mutchick and his husband Erik Hyman. They're both so high-powered it's crazy. Max just had a pilot picked up and was in the middle of final casting and Erik is an entertainment lawyer who represents everybody. We'd have breakfast with them every morning right before they'd rush off to their respective offices and I've never felt lazier and less connected.

However, the one cool Hollywood thing was I was *offered* a part on NBC's "Smash" with no audition!

All right, now I shall clarify what really happened. The "part" I was offered didn't have a lot of lines. Actually, the "s" is unnecessary at the end of the word "line." That's right. It was for a person who says one line! I guess they know I'm an expert at the ol' one-liner. Anybody? *And*, though it's my first TV offer since my unplanned appearance on "Cash Cab," I turned down the role. Why? Because I have a better offer? No, dear. Because I have jury duty! I've already postponed and I'm too terrified to do it again. The "good" news is I have jury duty on Tuesday...which is also my birthday!

I mentioned last week that Kevin Chamberlin, who's out here starring in the TV show "Jessie," threw a party so I could see all of my L.A. friends at one time. Marissa Jaret Winokur, Christopher Youngsman and Jen Cody were there (we all did *Grease* together on Broadway). Jen and Kevin were regaling us with stories of *Seussical*. Jen said that at one point someone got fired every day, so at night they would haul out their video camera and play "Seussical Survivor." In other words, they would meet after dinner and each would show the camera a piece of paper where they had secretly written down the name of the person they thought was going to get fired the next day. Of course, Jen was always right.

Kevin is loving doing a show on the Disney channel. First of all, they do 30 episodes of "Jessie" per season (!) and when you sign a TV contract with them, you also sign to do four films. *Plus* Kevin gets to direct one episode of "Jessie" per season! He let us come to the set to watch filming and we loved it, especially Juli.

As for *Disaster!*, we had a cra-za-zy weekend. First of all, Chil Thorn plays Tony, who is the antagonist of the musical. He owns "The Barricuda" which is the casino that floats in the Hudson River (attached to a pier) and he ignores my warnings that he's drilled the pier directly into a fault line. I found out Friday that Clif had a family emergency and couldn't do the show. Because we're basically a Mom and Pop

Me as Professor Scheider, Paul Castree as Scott and Jack in the middle as Tony!

show, we have no understudies. So, Jack took the red-eye from L.A. and arrived Saturday to learn the part for the Sunday show. We also had one more problem: Kathy Fitzgerald plays Shirley, the older lady who's on vacation with her husband to celebrate his retirement. Kathy is currently rehearsing to play Mama Rose in Arizona. She asked the cast to switch their day off in order for her to fly in Sunday morning and do the show Sunday night. The *whole* cast voted yes, but the union said that a day off cannot be switched during tech week. So, we had no Shirley. Well, many years ago when I was first talking about this show with my friend Drew Geraci (from *Forever Plaid*), we joked that he would play an older lady in the show. And, on Sunday night, that joke became a reality. That's right, Jack was on for Tony and Drew was on for *Shirley*! What's even more crazy is that Shirley's husband in the show is named Maury (played by Tom Riis Farrell) and Drew played Maury the first week because Tom wasn't available. So, Drew has gone on for both halves of the married couple! There was an announcement made before the show telling the audience there were two last-minute cast replacements. The show began and, around 8 minutes in, I was backstage and heard the audience go *wild*. We didn't know what happened and turns out it was because Drew made his first entrance. He literally stopped the show when he came on in a blonde wig while wearing a Mrs. Roper muumuu. Drew had a week's notice but Jack only had two days. I told him to carry his script but he was completely *off book*. It was amazing. The performance played on a deeper level to us because Drew and I had conceived the idea for the show years ago, and Jack and I wrote it, so it was so meaningful to have us all on at the same time.

P.S. When we transferred Off-Broadway the following year, Drew had to go on for Shirley again and he was amazing...and Jack took over the role of Tony for a month. If it ain't broke...

Peace out!

Judy Kuhn Belts, Alan Menken Times Three, *Disaster!* Re-Casting
March 5, 2012

Greetings from XNA! That's the airport code for the Northwest Arkansas airport. I flew down Friday to go to Fayetteville and the Walton Arts Center where I put on a show announcing their 2013 Broadway season. I've started getting bookings as a Broadway representative who goes from theatre to theatre to tell subscribers why they should sign up for the upcoming season. I deconstruct songs and video clips for each show and point out what I think it "amahzing" (yes, I'm still hauling out that word). Next up: Rochester and Sarasota. I'm so glad I have gigs, but it's actually a ton of effing work to put together each presentation. Who knew there were so many Broadway shows that could be booked around the country? Why can't every theatre stick to one universal season? So, this week, besides having to put together a show highlighting *Stomp, American Idiot, Hair, Billy Elliot, Memphis, Shrek, Anything Goes, Catch Me If You Can* and *War Horse* (!), I've also had to divide up my book for audio recording next week. Audible.com is going to do "My Awesome/Awful Popularity Plan" as an audio book. And instead of me reading the whole thing, I'm doing it like a radio play with all of the roles assigned to different people. I'm playing Justin; my meddling mother is Andrea Burns; the high school football player I'm "in love" with is Will Swenson; the school bully is Josh Gad; the girl I date as a beard is Megan Hilty; her obnoxious father is Marc Kudisch; and my best friend is Jesse Tyler Ferguson. So, I had to go through the entire book and find what each character says and then make a script for each person so we can record this week. You may think it's easy to do but you probably don't have adult ADD! Ah! So not fun.

But I'm excited about my cast. The other exciting news about the book is Random House just offered me a contract to write a sequel! Yay! Now, all I have to do is write it. *Silence.* And...immobilization. *I finally wrote it and it's out! It's called The Rise And Fall Of A Theater Geek. Look for it online or in any bookstore...if there are still indeed bookstores.*

This week I interviewed the great Judy Kuhn. I was a classical piano major at Oberlin Conservatory and all throughout college I would listen to Judy, and I obsess not only about her amazing voice but about the fact that she also went to Oberlin. She was a voice major, which means opera, and she said it wasn't until after college that she knew she could belt. Seriously. She was doing a summer stock show and her character was supposed to hit a B flat. She did it, Oberlin-style, and the music director asked her to belt it. He demonstrated and she tried it. She remembers thinking, "I've never sounded like that before." All I can say is, "*Thank you,* summer stock music director! Because of you, I've listened to the title song from *Rags* repeatedly for the last 20 years." Speaking of *Rags,* Judy was starring in that show when she auditioned for *Les Miz.* They called her back for the role of Cossette but she didn't go because *Rags* was about to open on Broadway. However, she was soon available because *Rags* opened on a Thursday and closed on Sunday! The *Les Miz* people called again and she got the role of Cossette and hit my favorite high B flat on Broadway. Of course, I'm also obsessed with what a know-it-all Cossette is...always one-upping Marius. For instance, he sings, "Do I dream?," and she trumps him with, "*I'm* awake." Take a gander on youtube for my *Les Miz* deconstruction featuring the passive/aggressive behavior of Cossette.

Since *Rags* had such a short run, no one knew that she belted up a storm in that show. She was known as a soprano ingénue. Then *Rags* and *Les Miz* were both nominated as Best Musical. Teresa Stratas (the star of *Rags*) was going to sing on the Tony Awards but dropped out right before the telecast. Judy was asked to sing instead so she wound up being the only actor to sing in *two* Best Musical nominee performances on the Tony Awards! Trevor Nunn, who directed *Les Miz,* knew her as a sweet high soprano but when he saw her *Rags* performance, he was shocked that she could belt and suddenly considered her for his next Broadway show...*Chess*! So brava Teresa Stratas for dropping out because it allowed Judy to make a cast album I've *also* listened to obsessively for the past 20 years.

Judy's *Rags* Tony Award performance has a great story attached that I must write about. She was nominated for Best Featured Actress in a Musical for *Les Miz* and, luckily, her category was first so she was able to dress up and sit in the audience. Frances Ruffelle wound up winning and Judy wanted to go backstage right afterwards to practice for her *Rags* appearance. It had been months since she did the show and, even more scary, they had shortened the song for the telecast. They dropped certain sections and then put them back in until finally they were satisfied, but Judy knew she had to review it to remember exactly what was out and what was in. The Tony Award people told her that someone would come get her from her seats and take her backstage to get ready. Well, the show kept going and no one came. She didn't know what to do because she didn't really know how long the awards ceremony was. Should she wait? Did she have plenty of time? Finally, she decided she was going to go backstage and prepare even if she was super early. She ran out during a commercial break, terrified the show would begin again and catch her scurrying through the aisles. When she walked backstage someone yelled, "Where have you been!?!?! You're about to be on!" The next thing she knew, she was grabbed into a dressing room, thrown into a costume/wig and pushed onstage. She was completely frazzled and had no time to practice the new version of the song. She began it, but one third of the way through she thought, "The orchestra is off!" Then she thought, "Wait...the orchestra is on tape...*I'm* off!" Luckily, within four measures she was back on track. *And* if you watch it, you can't even tell. Unless you realize that she repeats the lyrics "Dreams...you gave me dreams..." twice. Look for it on Youtube. It's fascinating to see how she recovers *and* how the late great Dick Latessa goes along with her mistake.

On Thursday at the *Chatterbox* I interviewed Alan Menken. We discussed the original film version of *Little Shop of Horrors* and I asked him if he remembered Rick Moranis auditioning for Seymour. He didn't, but he remembered another actor who wanted the role very badly...Tom Cruise! Who knew?

Disaster!, my musical at the Triad, was extended and Felicia Finley just took over the role of Jackie. One of my favorite Felicia stories happened when she was a little girl. She's from down South and when she was very young they did a nationwide audition for *Annie* replacements. She auditioned and got cast! She was set to start on a Monday and told everyone in her school she wouldn't see them for a while because she was headed to Broadway. Of course, all the kids in her elementary school thought she was lying. Felicia was all set to fly to NYC when her Mom got a call that *Annie* had posted its closing notice. Ah! So devastating. But even *more* so considering she gave a lengthy and dramatic goodbye to everyone in her school on Friday...and then showed up for classes on Monday. Felicia told me everyone called her a big liar and subsequently beat her up. It's "fun" to have to deal with your Broadway dreams being taken away while getting kicked repeatedly by a 10-year-old girl.

Jack Plotnick came to NYC to help put in the new actors and after the performance, we went to a late-nite diner for some delicious pancakes. While we were sitting there, Fred Armisen (from "SNL") walked in. I've met him a few times (and we peripherally knew each other as kids because he grew up right near me). I'm also a huge fan. Anyhoo, I greeted him a big smile and he was friendly/wigged out. I chalked it up him being a TV star and me being a crazy fan who vaguely knows him. Then I got home to get ready for bed, and when I looked in the mirror, I saw that I hadn't fixed my crazy "I've just been in an earthquake/tidal wave etc..." hairstyle *and* make-up. And Jack let me go out in public without telling me to wash it the hell off! No wonder Fred was on the verge of calling 9-1-1. Peace out!

Wrangling Megan Hilty and Jesse Tyler Ferguson; Rita Moreno in the Studio
March 12, 2012

Brushing up to soon play the role of Becky on the Audible.com version of my book!

We all sprang forward! And now we're all exhausted. I was always able to justify losing an hour of sleep when I was a kid by telling myself that it was a signpost that the school year was almost over. Now, it just feels like a major inconvenience *and* a set-up to make me late to work because I've forgotten to set my clock. As a matter of fact, I had to work all day recording the audio version of my young adult book "My Awesome/Awesome Popularity Plan." Sunday was TV-star day because it's impossible to plan on meeting someone who works on TV during the week because they don't know their schedule 'til the last minute. So, first I met with Megan Hilty, who plays Becky, the girl my character winds up dating as part of his popularity plan. We met at 10 AM and yet she looked stunning. I asked her about "Smash" and she said she's having an amazing time. She told me it combines the best aspects of doing a TV show *and* a Broadway show. I don't need a combination...I just want one of the two.

My first choice for the part of Spencer, my character's best friend, was "Modern Family" star Jesse Tyler Ferguson. I told him he was perfect for the part because the character has red hair and so does he. He then reminded me it was an audio book. Hmph. Regardless, he immediately said yes, but then we spent literal weeks going back and forth with emails every day trying to find a time to record. At one point, he was so excited that he was going to be in New York on a break...until we realized it was the exact days that *I* was going to be in Los Angeles. And then when I returned to New York, he had to be in L.A. It was like a boring bi-coastal version of "The Gift of the Magi." Finally, he told me that he doesn't film on Sundays so I asked Audible.com if there's a recording studio in L.A. he could use. There is (!) and then I asked if I could record dialogue with him while I was in NYC and he was in L.A. They said they could do it and we finally decided on this Sunday after what Jesse called "officially the most difficult meeting of the minds of 2012."

On Wednesday I did my SiriusXM talk show with Rita Moreno! Of course, I immediately brought up the fact that she's won an Emmy, Tony, Oscar and Grammy and she commented that it was "not bad for a Puerto Rican girl." Which led me to ask, how did she get started? Turns out, she was doing a dance recital as a teenager in New York, and a Hollywood scout saw her. Essentially, what we've all dreamed about happening while we've done rickety-rackety recitals and cabarets actually happened to her! He asked her and her mother to come to a meeting in his hotel penthouse to discuss a contract. However, because she and her mother didn't have a lot of contact with wealthy people, they were flummoxed when they got to the hotel because they didn't know what a penthouse was. Luckily, they figured it out and Rita had her meeting with...Louis B. Mayer! She told us that she always tried to wear her hair like Elizabeth Taylor and when Mr. Mayer saw her he said, "She's like a Spanish Elizabeth Taylor." Perfecto! P.S. If he had seen my hair as a teenager, he would have said, "He's like a Jewish Dorothy Hammil."

Rita became a Hollywood contract player. To tell you how long she's been in the business, let me just say that when I mentioned *The King and I*, she remarked, "That was *so* long after I came to Hollywood!" (It was 56 years ago!) Of course, I really wanted her to talk about "West Side Story." She remembers having a great audition where she sang and then did the dramatic candy store scene. But Jerry Robbins (whom

148

she knew from "King and I") told her she'd have to really dance at her next audition. He said she'd have a few months to get ready and she immediately signed up for non-stop classes. She had danced all of her childhood, but it was Spanish dance and she had no real training in jazz. P.S. When she mentioned Jerry Robbins I said, "Everyone said he was a cranky ass." She immediately said, "No!," and I thought I went too far. She then finished her thought and said, "That's way too kind." And then furthered it with, "He was sadistic." Yowtch. Regardless, she wanted that gig! Right before the auditions, she decided to contact a friend who had done the show and learned the dances. Unfortunately, they didn't have much time and she was only able to learn one section of "America" and one section of the Mambo. Rita showed up at her audition and the assistant choreographer showed her a section of "America"...and it was the same one she already knew! She "learned" it and then he showed her a part of the Mambo...and, yes, she had already learned that one, too. Nonetheless, she had him "teach" her the steps and then danced it for him. Apparently, he called Jerry Robbins and told him, "She doesn't have a lot of technique, but she's got style...and she's an *incredibly* quick learner!"

The hardest part about filming that number was the very last pose. All the ladies had to jump on the guy's shoulders and it always worked in rehearsal. However, the reason it was easy was because Rita would wear a cotton rehearsal skirt and the guys had cotton t-shirts on. Cut to the day of shooting where they wore their costumes which were silk and the fact that Bernardo's shoulder sloped downward. Suddenly, every time she landed, she was on a sliding pond. Take after take, and *finally*, on the 30th take, she aggressively hooked her foot into his back and managed to balance. And...Academy Award!

Rita had tickets to see a play and her publicist had said she needed to leave my show right after her interview, but she wound up not only staying for the whole show, but became my co-interviewer during the Paul Shaffer segment. Paul told us that he's Canadian and went to play for a friend's audition for the Toronto company of *Godspell*, and, like many other times before and since when someone has brought someone else along, *he* wound up getting the gig. Here's a mini-list of this occurrence: Ted Sperling playing Vicki Clark's audition for *Sunday in the Park* (he got the gig as the pianist) as well as Lea Michele offering to accompany her friend to the *Les Miz* audition (Lea got young Cosette). Note to everybody: don't bring *anyone* to an audition! It will backfire!

I ended the interview with Clark Oliver who's starring in *Disaster!* as Ben and his twin sister, Lisa. Clark has three songs in the show and each one literally stops the show. *Plus*, in the New York Times review that gave the show a rave, *none* of the actors was mentioned...except for him. Hmph. *By the way, this has continued. Off-Broadway, Jonah Verdon got non-stop amazing reviews, on Broadway Baylee Littrell got an Outer Critics Award nomination and in London Bradley Riches won a Best Actor award!*

Over the weekend I went to see *Spring Alive* starring my friend Spring Groove with whom I did *Grease!* back when she was plain ol' Wendy Springer. The show is about her evolution from Broadway gal to busker. No, not the star of the ill-fated *Busker Alley*. She literally travels the world and does street festivals singing and playing her guitar. The show had great music, and all the people I was with loved the songs and Spring's great personality onstage. The only scary part for me was when she sang a call-and-response song in Sanskrit. She told us that repeating the same phrase over and over again is supposed to release positive chemicals in you. My only problem was that I was singing the Sanskrit in Spring's octave, so it was really high in my voice. The whole audience was singing along so no one noticed that I was singing in a completely inappropriate range, but I kept fearing that the audience would pull a "Blubber" on me. Remember that Judy Blume book? The whole elementary school chorus decides to meanly drop out during a song so the title character sings an unintended solo? *And* it's on the word "breast"? *And* the girl rolls the R? Devastating.

All right, this week I'm finishing my audio book with Andrea Burns, Ana Gasteyer and Josh Gad. Three comic masters! Peace out!

Shut Your Mouth, Susan Blackwell!; Take Your Shirt Off, David Turner!
March 19, 2012

I just came from a delish dinner with fellow vegetarian, Kerry Butler. James and I were walking up Ninth Avenue when we saw someone who looked like Kerry wearing more makeup than Tammy Faye Bakker. Then I realized that it was between shows on a Saturday, and Broadway girls don't want to have to reapply their makeup for the evening show, so they walk around with their faces proudly sporting the make-up scheme of a contestant on *RuPaul's Drag Race*. The three of us decided to have an impromptu dinner at Zen Palate, and I asked Kerry about her new role in *The Best Man*. First of all, this is her first play on Broadway! She's done lots of musicals but never a play, and she's thrilled because she's starring opposite so many fantastic actors, including two titans of the theatre: Angela Lansbury and James Earl Jones! She said Angela is so much fun to work with and will break into impromptu dances (as will Eric McCormack). And, she heard a great story about James Earl Jones' dedication to acting that took place during *Driving Miss Daisy*. He was going through the script and noticed a new moment he wanted to explore, so he scheduled a rehearsal with Vanessa Redgrave. When did this happen, you ask? During the *last week of the show*! That's right, he only had a few performances left but he was still mining the material. He says that an actor is constantly striving to find the humanity of the character. Really? I'm constantly just trying to get a laugh.

This week I interviewed the whole cast of *Now. Here. This.*, which also happens to be the whole cast of *[title of show]*. Their new show features a lot of material from their various childhoods, but one story that used to be in the show is now out! I first saw a version of the show on the R Family Cruise, and I was obsessed with Susan Blackwell's childhood trickery, so I must write it for you. Susan remembered that, when she was a kid, she never wanted to go to school or, quite frankly, leave her mother's side. One morning when she was around eight, she slipped on the ice and when she got up, her parents asked her if she was hurt and, for some reason, she didn't go with the "I sprained my ankle" or "Ow! My back!" routine. Instead, she looked at her parents, and because her mouth happened to be open, she proclaimed, "I can't shut my mouth!" That's right, she pretended the fall had somehow hurt her jaw and made it impossible for her to close her mouth. So, actually, her "I can't shut my mouth" sounded more like "I cahn shu m' mou!" Both of her parents went with her to the hospital (!) and Susan remembers sitting in the ER wondering, "How is this going to play out?" Finally, the doctor called her in his office. He touched her chin, then he touched the outside of her jaw. Finally, he said calmly, "Susan? Can you try shutting your mouth for me?" And... she did. Yes, the jig was up that quickly. She's so mortified thinking back on it because her parents didn't have much money, and they both took off from work *and* took her to a hospital even though they had no health insurance. A horrifically expensive attention-getting device. Yet, the story is still hilarious.

Everyone in the cast had his or her own stories of trying to get attention with injuries. As a matter of fact, Hunter Bell told us that he was always so jealous of people having casts on their broken bones in school because people always flocked to them and everyone would sign their casts. So...he would repeatedly try to close the door on his foot to break it. It didn't work, but the door slamming gave him excellent practice for any future farces he might appear in. I myself had a bout of severe "stomach aches" that lasted all through sixth grade with no known cause ever discovered. Why did we all have to concoct these elaborate ruses instead of simply saying, "I want attention"?

I also interviewed Kate Clinton, who is right now going around the country with her *All Fracked Up* tour. Turns out, she began as a teacher, but her friend got tired of her talking about doing stand-up comedy and eventually signed Kate up for an open-mic night. And thus, started her career. I asked Kate how her friend knew she was funny, and she told me some antics she pulled while teaching. Apparently, one day her pantyhose were bunched up near her ankles and she knew her whole class was looking down there and not concentrating on the lesson. So, to prevent them from staring at her lumpy l'Eggs, she got into a wastepaper basket and moved around in it for the remainder of the class. She also said that one spring day the whole class was ignoring her and looking out the window at the grass being mown. So, she left the classroom and literally got on the electric mower and rode it around, waving.

At *Seth's Broadway Chatterbox* I interviewed David Turner, one of the leads from the now-defunct *On A Clear Day...* revival: I asked David for an onstage debacle, and he talked about a mortifying performance of *On a Clear Day...*. Normally, the scene is supposed to begin with Harry Connick Jr. as a psychiatrist giving a lecture about hypnosis. David, in the lecture hall, comments that *he'd* never be susceptible to hypnosis and, of course, as soon as Harry Connick snaps while demonstrating, David falls asleep. Harry then tells the class that once a patient is asleep, one can add a post-hypnotic suggestion like "When I say the word Wednesday, you'll take off your shirt." He then snaps his fingers and David wakes up. At the end of the scene, Harry tells the class, "See you next Wednesday," and David immediately starts taking off his shirt. Audience laughs and end of scene. There are then two more Wednesday references throughout the show. Cut to, one night, Harry got mixed up on lines and *forgot* to say the part about Wednesday and taking off the shirt. David didn't know what to do but felt he had to play the scene as directed. So, when Harry told the class, "See you next Wednesday," David stood onstage and started taking off his shirt. The audience was silent, horrified *and* mystified. Why did a main character randomly start taking off his shirt? David was mortified and ran backstage to plan how they could cut all of the future Wednesday references. Unfortunately, he was never offstage when Harry was offstage, but he assumed someone would tell Harry how they were going to change the script. Well, when you assume...AKA David came out for the next scene, now as Harry's patient, Harry put him to sleep and right before he woke up, Harry added this line: "And, uh, just for kicks, when I say the word Wednesday, take off your shirt." He then said "Wednesday," and David was forced *yet again* to take off his shirt for an audience that was once again silent, horrified, mystified and now not just turned against David, but completely judging the psychiatrist character for shockingly unethical behavior. "Just for kicks" you're making your patient take off his shirt? See you in court, Doctor.

Peace and enjoy the beginning of spring!

"Ghosthunters," Ana Gasteyer and Getting Ready for Florida
March 26, 2012

It's Spring Break so I'm heading to Florida! Normally that applies to a fun-loving college kid, heading to Miami to soak up the sun and drink from a keg with a fraternity. *My* version of heading to the white sandy beaches in Florida is doing shows in towns with a vibrant retirement community and my traveling companion is not my fun-loving fraternity pal but instead my mom who, let's just say, can confidently order alcohol without a fake ID. Yay? If you don't know, my Mom is always so much "fun" to travel with. When she was in San Diego before we got on an R Family Cruise, she was outraged that it was 11 AM and her hotel room hadn't been cleaned yet. She tracked down the maid who only spoke Spanish, but that didn't stop my mother who repeatedly pointed to her watch and said "mas tarde!" First of all, that doesn't mean "very late" it means "more late" so I'm sure her babbling was met with a blank stare. Made even more so by the fact that my mother hadn't yet changed her watch into the Pacific Time Zone so in fact it wasn't *11* AM, it was *8* AM. Mas moron.

This week I took my sister Beth to see *Jesus Christ Superstar*. At first I was disappointed that Josh Young wasn't on for Judas, but then excited because Jeremy Kushnier went on instead. He was great and so was the whole cast. King Herod (Bruce Dow) added some great comedy moments and Jesus (Paul Nolan) had so many high notes that he could also be the matinee Evita. I've always loved that score. To me, it's like *Hair* and *Pippin*, meaning every song is fantastic. There's no "Henry Street" to make you frantically run to your record player and pick up the needle to skip to something, *any*thing. Beth actually wound up crying during the show because she was so moved. I cried because I didn't hear any of the amazing string section that sounds so thrilling on the original recording. Devastating. I beg producers to stop cutting string sections!

Then I headed to SiriusXM to do *Seth Speaks* with Ana Gasteyer who is promoting her upcoming Joe's Pub performance of *Elegant Songs from a Handsome Woman*. Her show is *so* enjoyable...really funny and her song choices are so eclectic. I happened to mention that I recently watched on old "Brady Bunch" episode and it was the one where the whole family (plus Alice, for some reason) went to the Grand Canyon. First of all, not only were three people proudly in the front seat not wearing seatbelts, but Cindy, the youngest and most vulnerable, was in the middle! The lack of safety awareness we all had in the '70s is hilarious. Ana chimed in and told us that her friend recently told her his family's car in the '70s had seat sensors and could tell when someone was sitting. The car then wouldn't start unless all seatbelts were on. His mother couldn't bear to wait for the sensor to detect if the people seated were wearing seatbelts so she had a system for tricking it into thinking no one was in the car but the driver. The family would pile into the car and the Mom would immediately announce, "Asses *up!*," and they would all hover over their seats until she could start the car. I guess that was much easier than having to wait an extra five seconds. Then, Ana started talking about kids, and she told us that she just threw a birthday party for her four-year-old son, Ulysses. She lives in a hip, wealthy area of Brooklyn and was first trying to make it an enormous soiree. Her son wanted it to be "Star Wars-themed, so she started researching all these elaborate ways to push it to the level of the Liza/David Gest wedding. Then she decided there was no way she was going to pay $700 for a party for a four-year-old, and wound up getting cake and inflatable light sabers that all the kids hit each other with. One of the "I'm-a-rich-perfect-SuperMoms" walked over to her during the party, looked around and said, "This party is so old-school." Translation: Judgment.

Later, Ana and I delved into our love/hate relationship with Twitter. I told her I'm obsessed with this comic named Caprice Crane. Her tweets are hi-lar. First of all, she advised that if you are annoyed by a friend's email or text, it's fun to respond with "unsubscribe." Brava! And I so identified with this tweet: "If you ask for one of my fries, sure, I'll give you one. But don't think for a minute that I'm not FURIOUS about it." Yes!!! And "Few things can elicit the level of self-loathing I feel when I'm forced to say 'grande' or 'venti' at Starbucks." I agree 100 percent. Ana is fascinated by the creepy aspect of Twitter: She recently tweeted that she had been shopping at Marshall's and it had brought up bully memories, "…as it is the store from whence I purchased my heavily-mocked Sassoon knock-offs." Immediately after posting that she received a tweet from @Marshalls. Literally the "store" tweeted her a reprimand! Essentially, it said that they did *not* sell knock-offs and demanded that she retweet the truth. How can an inanimate store scold you? It's like "1984," but the shallow version. It's not Big Brother who's watching, it's a chain store with a two-for-one sale on leggings.

Then I had Adam Berry on the show. I first heard him sing in Provincetown a few years ago when he was around 20. Amazing voice. Now, he's still pursuing musical theatre, but his "day job" is as a ghosthunter on…"Ghosthunters." I decided to watch an episode before interviewing him. Um…it was supposed to be an episode, but it seemed to me like footage they decided not to use. It was basically the ghosthunters in Alexandria, VA, checking out three different locales where there had been unexplainable activity. The bulk of the show was the ghosthunters walking in dark areas saying, "Did you see that?" and another ghosthunter saying "no." Then there was a lot of "Hello?"…. Hello!?" I confronted Adam on all of it and he invited me to come to an actual ghosthunting with them. I agreed, assuming it meant he was buying me tickets to *Ghost*. *Now he's in Kindred Spirits on TLC!*

I'm playing Moses again in Rachel Shukert's *Everything's Coming Up Moses*, which is the story of Passover as told through the story/songs of *Gypsy*. My sister Nancy saw my last Jewish holiday musical (*Don't Cry for Me, Achasveros*) advertised in her weekly Jewish newspaper and immediately sent it to me. She thinks it's hilarious because the top of the article says that it stars Jackie Hoffman and Seth Rudetsky and then there are two pictures of us and right underneath mine it says "Scott Rudetsky." Nancy is obsessed that literally four inches away from the photo it says "Seth," but it was apparently too far to make a lasting impression. So many people call me Scott by accident. There was also the awkward time right after my parents' divorce when my Mom brought her current beau to house and he said with fervor, "How ya doin', Shaun!" I glared. He moved in soon after.

OK, hope to see you in Florida this weekend and you can hang out with me and my Mom. Or better yet — my Mom! Peace out.

Manatees, *Nothing Like a Dame*, a *Disaster!* Injury
April 3, 2012

Greetings from somewhere over Florida. I'm on my way back from Sarasota where I previewed the upcoming season at the Van Wezel Performing Arts Center. When I introduce the titles of the show, I do a lot of guessing games with the audience to see if they can figure out what's coming and the Sarasota folks were very knowledgeable. Although, my friend Ben was in the audience and he told me that when I played the classic opening notes from "The Addams Family" TV show, the man next to him nodded and said knowingly to his wife, "The Munsters." I began my foray by flying down to Ft. Lauderdale. My mother and I arrived in Newark airport and I immediately got annoyed with her crazy over-packing. Her choice for Florida's 85-degree weather? Not one, not two, but *three* coats. Crazy. Then, her signature bizarre comments started. When I said our flight was at gate C110, she said, "C110? I've never heard of such a gate." Why would she have *ever* heard of it?

Before I left for the south, I saw *Nothing Like a Dame*, the Actors Fund Benefit for the Phyllis Newman Women's Health Initiative. This year there were so many women over 80 who sassed it! Marilyn Maye sounded fabulous as usual and I can't wait to see her at Feinstein's later this month. Polly Bergen came out and told everyone that she met Phyllis Newman doing a musical version of "Pride and Prejudice" years ago when they both very young (she's now 83). She then qualified it by saying, "Well, one of us was very young. I was 18 and Phyllis was in her mid-30s." Hi-lar and totally not true! By the way, that reminds me of the fact that when my mom told me when she sits in the audience at my Florida shows, it's the only time she feels young.

This week is the third annual *Everything's Coming Up Moses* performance. This year it's at the 92nd Street Y in Tribeca. The show is the story of Passover as told through the songs of *Gypsy*. Rachel Shukert has written such a brilliant parody and it parallels the story of Mama Rose incredibly closely. Here's part of my big breakdown from the 11-O'clock number, "Moses Turn":

I had a dream...
I dreamed it for you, Jews...
It wasn't for me, Aaron...
And if it wasn't for me, then where would you be?
Dead! In the Red Sea!!!!!!!

This week on *Seth Speaks* I interviewed comedian Jim Gaffigan. Jim and I met when I first began doing stand-up comedy back in 1996. His signature bit was all about the manatee. I asked him why, and he said he had visited Florida and noticed that everyone there is obsessed with manatees. There are streets and a town and tons of other things named after them and, P.S., last weekend in Florida I indeed saw a Manatee Memorial Hospital and found out the local community theatre was called The Manatee Players! He said he loved that fact that manatee is the proper name but they're also called "sea cows." His bit would always feature a sweet manatee being a guest on "The Ricki Lake Show," and some hostile person from the audience would always get up and say, "Yeah, what up? I got something to say to the sea cow..."

"I'm a manatee."

"Yeah, whatevah. Listen, sea cow, you need to get a *job*!"

Jim is taking a page from Louis C.K.'s business model and he's filmed his own comedy show that he's selling from his website. During my show, he was talking about food and how nobody admits to buying McDonald's, yet there are over four million hamburgers served. I haughtily told him that I don't eat so-called Big Macs because I'm a vegetarian. He then asked why I sounded like I wanted praise for it. "Being a vegetarian doesn't mean you work in a homeless shelter." Touche.

I also had Kurt Peterson and Victoria Mallory on the show. They first met at AMDA in the late '60s and then got cast opposite each other as Tony and Maria in the City Center revival of *West Side Story*. They then got cast in *Follies*; he was young Ben and she was young Heidi (aka "One More Kiss"). They've now reunited (40 years later!) and just did a big concert for Broadway Cares/Equity Fights AIDS which is out on CD. Kurt definitely knows how to put on a good concert. He was the one who produced that "Sondheim Evening" in the late '70s whose CD cover has the crossword puzzle and featured essentially everybody. He started that whole trend of doing one-night Broadway events (aka the bandwagon I jumped on for my Actors Fund concerts of *Dreamgirls*, etc).

Kurt has an amazing history of Broadway highs and notorious cult flops like *Dear World* with Angela Lansbury and *The Baker's Wife* with Patti LuPone. One of the most amazing things about Victoria's past is that during *A Little Night Music* she played Anne, who begins the show married to Frederik (Len Cariou) but, at the end, runs off Mark Lambert who played Henrik, Frederik's son. Well, cut to: She was dating Len Cariou at the beginning of the run of the show and, later on, wound up marrying Mark Lambert! They then had a daughter named Ramona. The crazy part is, when *A Little Night Music* was revived, Ramona auditioned and got the role of Anne! Talk about passing the torch.

At my *Chatterbox*, I interviewed some cast members from *Godspell* and found out that Lindsay Mendez's big break happened in high school when she entered a California arts competition. During the finals, it was between her and another boy…Adam Lambert! And she won! She didn't bring the video, so I don't know who sang higher or wore more makeup. I, of course, asked about devastating auditions and Uzo Aduba told me about one where she forgot her words. Not to a wordy section of the song, by the way. She started out singing, "I don't know how to…" and was stumped. Finally, the pianist sang "…love him!" It's pretty bad when the lyrics you can't remember form the actual title. *P.S. This was before she was cast on Orange Is The New Black and won the Emmy award!* The same thing happened to Priscilla Lopez when she was starring in *A Day In Hollywood/A Night in the Ukraine*, for which she won the Tony Award. She had taken a week's vacation and when she came back, everything was fine 'til her big song, "Best in the World." She said she sang the first verse and got to the part where she sings "Papa said you're the best. You're the best in the world." All she remembered was "Papa said…" And then she faded out. Finally, someone offstage loudly whispered, "…*you're the best!*" Hmm…maybe "Papa" needs to re-think his praise.

The whole week began with the final performance of *Disaster!* at the Triad. The first act was amazing! Until the very end. I have an entrance where I run onstage with Felicia Finley and try to warn everyone that an earthquake is coming. I turned to run onstage and as soon as I stepped down on the floor, I thought Felicia had kicked me in the calf. With a pair of pointy shoes. *Really* hard. I thought maybe my calf bumped into her because I was too close to her as we were running. I kept thinking the pain would dissipate but it *really* hurt. I then realized it wasn't Felicia, it was something I did when I stepped down. I finished the last small scene at the end of the act, took four Advil (!) and told everyone I could finish the show if I could lean on something. The only cane they could find was an old broom. Seriously. So, I did the first scene leaning on the broom and then realized I looked crazy and/or like Elphaba, so I decided I would just limp for the rest of the act. I knew I looked crazy limping through the whole show and prepped myself for a slew of *"What happened?"* from my various friends in the audience after the show. Cut to: People came up to me after the show, I prepared my story ("I put aside my pain for the sake of the show") and *no one asked*! When I finally confronted one of my friends in the audience, he told me he thought it was part of the show. That's right, the limping happened after the earthquake hits, so people thought it was a so-called character choice. Annoying! I wanted sympathy! Anyhoo, I saw an orthopedist and he said I ruptured my something or other in my calf and it will take a maximum of six weeks to heal. It actually feels a million times better already. The thing that helps me the most is that I have to wear compression socks. They're black and end right under my knee. Yes! I finally get to wear Liza Minnelli's half-stockings from "Mein Herr." And on that note, I now have to go walk around the plane for a bit to prevent what my doctor lovingly calls "deep vein thrombosis." Horrifying. And I'm out!

P.S. This happened on the other leg a year later. Yay?

***Everything's Coming Up Moses*, Patti LuPone, Melissa Errico and More**
April 9, 2012

Oy! Time to loosen ye olde belt. And I don't mean Patti LuPone's high belt. I mean the one cutting into my gut. Yes, last night was the Seder — and, boy, are my pants tight. I had it at my place and it was full of the usual side comments while the Haggadah was read. There were a lot of old chestnuts bandied about but a new one was added by my mother. When she read the section about the Jews having to cast their sons into the river and only keep their daughters, she whispered to me, "The beginning of drag queens." True 'dat! Speaking of Passover, on Wednesday I played the title role in Rachel Shukert's *Everything's Coming Up Moses*. The Jews in the audience went crazy for the first lyrics of "You Gotta Get a Gimmick." Normally the song starts with, "You can pull all the stops out, 'til they call the cops out...," but in this version Matt Cavenaugh sang, "You can stand and sing 'Aleinu', 'til they shout 'Dayenu!'" Brava. In the afternoon, when we were staging "Some Hebrews" (aka "Some People"), I told Michael Schiralli (the director) I needed something to take off the wall at the end of the song (to sell), like Mama Rose does. So Rachel added two lines before the song to set up the ending. I looked at the wall and said, "Aaron, that's a nice mezuzah. How much do you think I could get for it?" Aaron yelled, "Moses! That's my retirement mezuzah!" The *Gypsy* fans in the audience got the reference and I loved it because it made no sense. What's a "retirement mezuzah"!?!

Speaking of *Gypsy*, I called the most recent Tony Award-winning Mama Rose and left her one of my signature babbling messages and signed off with a quick, "Peace out, Patti! Take it up the octave!," just because I love her high belt. Later that day I got a message, "Seth. This is Patti. I got your message." Then, she carefully asked, with every word articulated, "Did you say 'take it *up* the octave'?" *Pause*. Uh-oh. I didn't know what was going to follow: A lecture about how taking something up the octave could potentially hurt your vocal cords? A curt, "I will *not!*," followed by a click? Instead, she burst into signature Patti LuPone laughter. Phew!

On Wednesday, I had *Freestyle Love Supreme* on *Seth Speaks* on SiriusXM. Lin-Manuel Miranda started the group years ago and their shows are made up of totally improv'd hip-hop music, based on audience suggestions. I asked Lin about his current writing projects and he said that right now *Bring It On!* is touring, but hasn't come to Broadway because there's a lack of theatres available. That's always my problem when I write Broadway shows. Where are the theatres!?! And, because he can't stop creating, he's currently working on a musical about Alexander Hamilton, in which all the songs are hip hop. Natch. *I think that worked out for him... And* he's getting ready to do the concert-cast recording of *Merrily We Roll Along*. I had heard that Stephen Sondheim called Lin and asked him to play Charlie in the *Merrily* Encores! production. Well, on Thursday at my *Chatterbox*, I interviewed Lin's co-star, Colin Donnell and he told me that Sondheim did indeed ask Lin to play the part but the offer was followed by James Lapine calling Lin and saying something to effect of, "As amazing as Sondheim is, he still doesn't get to cast my production." Snap! So Lin had to audition, and of course, he got the role! Back to *Seth Speaks*. I also interviewed Melissa Errico, who's married to Patrick McEnroe, the tennis champ and sports commentator. Melissa said sometimes it's hard to be around tennis people who only know her as Patrick's wife. She finds herself muttering, "I've kinda done some shows on Broadway. I sort of have my own CD and stuff..." But, P.S., she said she has no shame calling herself Melissa McEnroe when she goes to Wimbledon. Then, it's a lot of "Right this way, Mrs. McEnroe" and "Here are front row seats, Mrs. McEnroe." Delicious.

Melissa also talked about how tennis technique can be applied to theatre. First I glared, but then when she explained, I totally got it. She told me that she once was using all of her arm effort to slam balls over the net until Patrick told her that tennis balls actually go the fastest when you hit them with a relaxed arm. Who knew? It's the same with singing: Relax and you can get the high notes. She also said that when you miss a ball playing tennis, you have to immediately forget about it. You can't miss a ball and start thinking, "Why did I miss that? Usually I have an amazing forearm. Wow. Maybe I need to work on — " And...you missed the next ball. It's the same thing with performing. If I miss a laugh, I can't be devastated and obsessed about it or else the rest of my performance clanks. Melissa also brought up how sports stars lose all the time. She was in the elevator with Venus Williams at a recent tournament and was totally star-struck. She later mentioned it to Patrick and he remarked that Venus had just lost her round and gone home. Melissa was dumbfounded but she began to realize that great sports stars lose all the time and then they move on to the next tournament. It's the same with actors.... auditioning every day and constantly being rejected. Speaking of which, my favorite/most depressing rejection happened to my good friend Kristine Zbornik years ago. She tried out for this headache-y Off-Broadway revue. Right after she sang, they gave her details about the contract. She then realized she couldn't do the show because it paid so little. With the new gig, she wouldn't be able to make rent. Once she found out, she apologized in the room and told them that she couldn't do the show because she couldn't afford it. The next day she got a call from them telling her that they weren't casting her in the show. What the — ? She already told them she couldn't take the job!!! I guess they were just clarifying that even if she could, they were rejecting her.

On Saturday, I saw the matinee of *The Best Man*. It's amazing that it was written more than 50 years ago and it's still so relevant. *And* the cast is so star-studded. James and I especially loved Candice Bergen. I've never seen her live and I thought her acting and comedy were amazing. Backstage, we visited Kerry Butler (who looks beautiful in the show and gets her signature laughs) and we noticed that there was food on every landing of the backstage area leading all the way up to her dressing room. Turns out, Kerry organized an Easter potluck buffet and the whole cast brought in food. Delish! *And* she was in the process of hiding eggs all over the theatre for a kids-and-adult Easter Egg Hunt. *She did the same thing during DISASTER! on Broadway. Cast Kerry Butler in your show if you want Easter egg hunts or to have your dressing room decorated for Valentine's Day!*

I will close with something that is typical of my friendship with Ana Gasteyer. I've written about this before, but if you don't know, we've had many real-life, sitcom-style mix-ups. Here's another one...this year on my birthday, which was just two weeks after my sweet doggie Maggie passed away, I got two emails from Ana. The body of the email was blank but each had an attachment: a picture of Maggie. So shocking! Why did I need to be reminded? I didn't know what to make of it until I got this hilarious email from Ana. Here it is:

Subject: OMG! One of our classic F-ups!

*Please forgive me. I was resending the pictures of dear Maggie to my mom so she could work on a BEREAVEMENT card for you and I just realized I sent them to YOU. ON YOUR BIRTHDAY. So, a horrible painful image with no message. I am SO SORRY if I made you any sadder on your birthday and God, I hope you find the humor in this classic f***up. Xoxo*

Of course I found the humor and a few months later, her Mom mailed me a beautiful sculpture she had done of Maggie!

On that note, happy Passover/Easter and, P.S., if you want to adopt an animal, Spring is a great time! PetFinder.com!

I Hit EW's Bullseye; Corbin Bleu Is Jesus; Melissa Errico Does Yale by Mail
April 16, 2012

Countdown to Cleveland! Yes, I am returning to the city that I flew into many times while I was a piano major at Oberlin. I'm doing *Seth's Big Fat Broadway* on April 26 at Playhouse Square and it's not only a return to the state of my alma mater, but it's a return to the state where I music-directed *Forever Plaid* back in the mid-'90s. I have a strong visual image of the name Playhouse Square because a few years I was cleaning out an old wallet and found a check from them that I hadn't cashed, ADD-style. Of course, it specifically stated it was valid only for 90 days but I kept looking at the front and back of the check over and over again to see if there was another section that said it was valid for more than ten years. There wasn't.

Entertainment Weekly!

The exciting news of the week began with a Facebook posting. Someone congratulated me about being in Entertainment Weekly. Huh? Sometimes I can't tell when a posting was put up, and I'm constantly seeing news about an upcoming event that I then find out was posted six months ago. It's making me crazy. Anyhoo, I had been in Entertainment Weekly last year so I thought the posting was old and/or the person was one of those folks who are a year behind on everything (aka my mother: "I hear they're going to make a film version of *Chicago*"). I asked for clarification and he wrote that I was in the Bullseye *again*. Ah!!! If you don't know, the Bullseye is inside the back cover of EW and it lists "pop culture's hits and misses" for the week. Well, my new book was a hit! There's a photo of the cover of my YA novel, "My Awesome/Awful Popularity Plan," and EW states, "All the awfulness and awesomeness of being a teenager wrapped up in a great young adult novel." So amazing!

This week was chock full of fun interviews. First, I met with Corbin Bleu, who's about to star in *Godspell* as fellow Jew, Jesus Christ. I asked Corbin about his name and he told me that his parents were big fans of U-2 and his dad wanted to name him Bullet Blue after one their favorite songs: "Bullet the Blue Sky" (I was completely lost after the phrase "U-2", but I nodded). His mom allowed the "Blue" but not the "bullet," and thus Corbin Bleu Reivers was named. He dropped the last name when the family moved from Brooklyn to L.A., where Corbin studied dance at Debbie Allen's Dance Academy. He said that Debbie has two (!) canes that she brings to class; one named Debbie and one named Allen and when you were doing something wrong, she'd give you a "love tap" (aka hit you). She's old-school.

I asked Corbin about auditioning for *In The Heights*, and it turns out he was originally brought in for Benny because he's half black/half Italian and not Hispanic. But at his audition, they asked if he spoke Spanish and he told them that he grew up surrounded by his parents' friends, who were Hispanic, so it was very much part of who he was. They ixnayed the idea of him playing Benny and he made his Broadway debut as Usnavi, the part created by Lin-Manuel Miranda. He said that *Godspell* is the completely opposite in terms of staging. In *In the Heights* there were so many characters walking in and out of scenes and/or dancing inches away from you that it was vitally important to know your specific placement on stage. There are numbers on Broadway stages that help people know where to be during dances; 0 is in the center and then it goes 2, 4, 6, 8, 10 towards the right and the left. Dancers have to know what number they're supposed to be on during songs so they don't block the person in back of them or crash into people etc. Corbin said that in *In the Heights*, people doing straight acting scenes *also* had to know what number they were on or they'd have someone crash into them! However, in *Godspell*, everything is pretty free-form. Throughout the whole show, he's been told to pretty much go wherever he wants. Of course, he's overwhelmed by the lack of boundaries now, but he knows he'll love the freedom once he gets into the run.

Corbin and I talked about "High School Musical," and I asked if he saw the recent pictures of Zac Efron with his shirt off. Corbin laughed and told me that he often has pool parties so he's used to seeing Zac look like that. He then told me I could come to his next pool party. When I awoke from my immediate coma, we concluded the interview and I wished him luck on his *Godspell* opening.

At *Seth's Broadway Chatterbox* I had Melissa Errico as my guest. She's a Long Island native and remembers the moment when theatre became her dream. She saw the Broadway revival of *On Your Toes* at the Virginia Theatre in the early '80s and during the show, she started weeping! Her mother didn't know what was wrong, but Melissa said it was because she was so moved by all the different aspects the show...singing, ballet, tap and wanted to know who those people were and how they got to do that. She was completely riveted and obsessed with it. Cut to: Her first lead on Broadway was ten years later....*at the same theatre!* The stagehands heard how obsessed she was with *On Your Toes*, and one day she came to her dressing room and found that they had gone to the basement and retrieved the original giant placards that were outside the theatre and decorated her room with them!

Melissa got her big break when she was on her way to Yale (yes, she's a smarty pants). She was auditioning the summer before freshman year for both Theater By the Sea and Ringling Bros. Barnum and Bailey circus. Seriously! I asked her what the H she wanted to do in the circus and she said the audition notice in Backstage said you had to be able to stand on an elephant and she was confident she could do that. 'Natch. Also, she wanted to be one of those women who hang on a rope from the ankle and spin. Who doesn't? Thankfully, before she auditioned she was spotted in the hallway by Richard Jay-Alexander, who asked her to come in and sing for *Les Misérables*. She thinks his interest in her was based on her long curly hair, which gave her a *Les Miz* quality. She sang "A Heart Full of Love" (which features the difficult pianissimo high B flat at the end) and he asked her if she could start in ten days as Cosette on the national tour! Of course, she said yes immediately. Actually, no she didn't! She started arguing with him and said that her B flat wasn't very good. He then said, "You should hear what we've hired in the past." Compliment? Insult? Both? Regardless, Melissa decided she could do it but then had to call her parents and ask if she could put off going to Yale. Yikes! They said yes and she wound up doing her first-year courses via correspondence, or as she called it, "Yale by Mail." She wound up spending so long on the road that she missed a whole year of school. I asked if that meant she had to graduate late and she hemmed and hawed. She finally admitted that she was able to graduate with her class because she began Yale as a *sophomore*. That's right, she had enough smarty-pants classes/test grades to place out of freshman year! But all of her smarts didn't help when she forgot the lyrics one night to "In My Life." Normally it goes:

In my life
There are so many questions and answers
That somehow seem wrong
In my life
There are times when I catch in the silence
The sigh of a faraway song.

Unfortunately, she panicked one night and could only remember the title. So she sang, "In my life, in my life, in my life, in my life....in my life etc..." I guess the audience sure remembered the name of that song. The most awkward moment for her was during Jean Valjean's death scene. She comes onstage at the end of Act Two with glasses for drinking, puts them down and starts to sing a soothing song. Unfortunately, one night she dropped the glasses. The sound of breaking glass wasn't the horrible part. That particular moment came when she started to sing soulfully to her dying father and three stagehands dressed in black came onstage to pick up the broken glass. With a broom? No, dear. With a loud, battery-operated portable vacuum cleaner! I'm sure the audience felt they were right in the middle of France circa 1800s when all the bourgeoisie used "Le Dustbuster."

We then talked about her first Broadway show — *Anna Karenina*. She had a song where she's supposed to put on a hoop skirt while she was singing. One night, the hoop skirt got caught on her head and she couldn't get it off. She sang the whole song with her face peeking out the hoop-skirt opening and then had to exit with the skirt around her face. Mortifying. Who was in the audience that night? The Weisslers! They were producing *My Fair Lady*, and instead of boycotting her from ever auditioning for wearing a costume as a wig, they asked her to come to the callbacks for Eliza. After 11 auditions (!), she got the gig opposite Richard Chamberlain! Unfortunately, her experience was marred by a vocal injury on the road. Eliza screams when she's forced to take a bath. The director really wanted the show to be dark, so he wanted the shrieks to be terrifying. In order to save her voice for an eight-show-a-week run, they pre-recorded her screams. Unfortunately, they asked her to record them late at night after an all-day rehearsal and when she let loose with some blood-curdling screams in the recording studio, she burst a blood vessel! She was out of the show off and on during the national tour, but thankfully came back with full sass for the Broadway production.

My fave story, however, doesn't involve Broadway. She was cast on the TV show, "Central Park West," and her character was pretending to be pregnant to trick her boyfriend. She remembers that she had some crazily-written line where she told her doctor that she needed to have a baby already. It was something like, "I'm not a rhino. I can't gestate for 15 months!" She didn't really know how to make that line work (understatement) and right before she filmed it, Lauren Hutton (who was also starring on the show) came over and gave her some advice. She whispered, "If you ever have a line that you can't make sense of, just say it while crying." In other words, the subtext will be, "I'm so hysterical, I don't know what I'm saying." Melissa turned on the tears and it worked!

OK, everyone. This week I'll be seeing some of the slew of new Broadway shows that seem to be opening every day — and enjoying the amazing spring weather. Peace out!

Stars Come Out for "Awesome/Awful" Audio, Plus Unlikely Couple Len Cariou and Dr. Jane Goodall
April 23, 2012

"My Awesome/Awful Popularity Plan" is finally out as an audio book. I spent two weeks recording it and then someone edited all of the various takes and now it's officially available. The characters, the actors who play them and the premise follow.

In a shocking act of nepotism, I cast myself as the lead character, Justin Goldblatt who's an overweight, unpopular 15-year-old who sports a Jewfro. Justin is sick of being the school loser and decides that this year he will become popular and somehow start dating Chuck, the school quarterback played by Will Swenson. Chuck is dating Becky (played by Megan Hilty), one of the most popular girls in school and one of the prettiest. One day after detention, Becky's blustering father (Marc Kudisch) makes them break up because Becky is destined to become a doctor and Chuck is a dumb jock. Since Justin is a bio whiz whom Becky's father approves of, Justin comes up with a scheme where he'll pretend to date Becky so she can secretly keep dating Chuck (and Justin can secretly try to win over Chuck!). The plot gets very convoluted because even though Justin becomes popular with all the so-called cool kids, he loses the real friends he's had for years like Quincy Slatton (played by Paul Castree) plus he has to avoid his annoying, meddling mother (Andrea Burns) and, worst of all, he has to deal with his disapproving and vegan best friend, Spencer (played by Jesse Tyler Ferguson...recorded via Skype from L.A.). And always the character actress, Ana Gasteyer, plays the teacher who complains about her maladies non-stop, earning the nickname "E.R." as in Emergency Room. Ms. Horvath is her real name, but she's called E.R. because every time a student passes her in the hallway she can be heard loudly complaining about her "bum fibula" or telling someone about her acupuncture and that "those painful needles are simply not helping my colon do its job in a timely manner." Get it all on Audible.com

Now, let me give you a directive to go see the feature film "Chimpanzee." I just interviewed Dr. Jane Goodall on *Seth Speaks*, and she told me that Disney donated a portion of the profits to The Jane Goodall Institute, which helps save chimpanzees. It was so cool interviewing her because she's such a pioneer. Back in the early '60s she got funding to observe chimps in the wild even though they had never been observed before (they always got spooked and ran away). Of course, at first the chimps didn't trust her and kept running away, and I asked her how she had the patience to keep coming back every day. She said (in her British accent), "Hmm...let me give you an example of my patience." She then proceeded to tell me that when she was four (!) she went to a farm on a little family vacation and her job was to collect eggs. She knew the hens were responsible for the eggs but had no idea where they came from on the hen's body. She kept asking but nobody would tell her. So, she sat in the hen house and waited until a hen laid an egg so she could find out. She was four years old and she sat there expectantly for...four hours! So, to her, going back into the wild day after day and hoping the chimps would finally act normally around her wasn't a big deal. Because she was finally able to observe them in their natural habitat, she was the first person to find out that chimps made and used tools! No other animals had been observed doing that. And chimps were always thought of as being vegetarians, but she observed them eating meat. Horrifically, that went even further and she also saw them be cannibals. Horrifying. She's a vegetarian (like me!) and I asked her if she cooks for herself. After I asked that, I got British sassed: "How can I cook when I'm on the road 350 days of the year?!" Ok! Ok! She's in her 70s and looks amazing and when I told her that Juli loves chimps and wildlife she recommended her organization called Roots and Shoots. It's for young people and combines nature conservancy and community service. Brava!

Besides Dr. Goodall, I had the amazing Len Cariou as a guest. We went back to his first Broadway show, *Applause*, and he told me about the gypsy run-through (a dress rehearsal where members of the Broadway community are invited). It was held in the afternoon. After the bows, he stayed onstage and spoke to various audience members milling about. One of the cast members came over to him and asked, "What did Hal think?" Len responded, "Who's Hal?" His fellow cast member said, "That guy who was talking to you." Len asked, "You mean the guy with the glasses on his head?" His friend, annoyed, said, "Yes!!!! Hal Prince!" Len is Canadian and this was his first show so he hadn't met any Broadway bigwigs yet. He freaked out when he realized that Hal Prince was the guy who came over and told him that he was one of the best leading men he'd seen in years! A few years later, Hal sent Len the script to *A Little Night Music* (no songs yet...just script) and asked him to audition...for Carl-Magnus. Len felt he had played that type of part many times and wasn't interested in doing it again. But he wanted to read and sing for Hal and Stephen Sondheim so he went to the audition. Afterwards, Hal gave him a new script that now had lyrics. There were no songs, but there were lyrics (that Len thought were terrific) but now he extra-dreaded telling Hal he didn't want the part. Hal called the next day and Len got ready to drop the bomb when, instead, Hal dropped one first: he offered Len the role of Fredrick. Len told Hal, "I'm 34! The script says that Fredrick is supposed to be 50!" Hal dismissed his concern with, "Meh! It's a period piece." And, for those that don't know, here's the classic *Night Music* story: The 11-o'clock number for Len hadn't been written yet and rehearsals were well under way. Len and Glynis Johns felt that their characters would act differently than what was in the original script because the show had evolved, so Hal suggested that they improvise a scene and have Sondheim watch it so he could finally write Len's big number. Len called Sondheim and he came and watched them do the scene they improvised. The next day, Sondheim came in and gave good news and bad news: The good news was he finally wrote the big 11-o'clock number. The bad news (for Len) was... the song was now for Glynis. Ouch! Yes, it was "Send in the Clowns," and became Sondheim's most well-known song.

This week I saw *Ghost* with Juli and once again I'm obsessed with Caissie Levy's voice. So good! We went backstage afterwards and, life imitating art-style, we saw that Caissie has a potter's wheel in her dressing room. She said she prepares the clay herself because it has to be a certain way or she can't work with it. I was nervous taking Juli to the show because the story has some scary parts, but nothing was as scary as what happened at our own apartment recently. James called my name in a panic a few days ago because, in our backyard, was a *rat*! Not running. Just walking around, strolling you might say, in broad daylight. We decided to let Sonora out because she's part rat terrier and we thought she'd scare it off. Well, her version of scaring it off was running and grabbing it in her mouth! I heard James screaming but was too scared to look. He said Sonora picked it up, dropped it and the rat tried to escape...by desperately clawing against our glass door! At that point, James was screaming up the octave. Suffice it to say, the rat is still at large, James has vocal damage and we don't let Sonora lick us anymore.

David Garrison to the Rescue, Plus Megan Hilty Is a Smash
April 30, 2012

This week, I had a jam-packed *Seth Speaks* at SiriusXM and it was delish. First, I had Andre De Shields as a guest, and I told him that I was obsessed with *Ain't Misbehavin'* when I was a kid. He talked about when it first opened in Manhattan Theatre Club's 1970s location, which was all the way on the East Side. He didn't know if it was going to be a big hit or just play out its initial run, until one performance when he noticed someone in the audience. He told us her name with a five second pause between each segment: "In the audience was…Jacqueline… Bouvier….Kennedy…Onassis." That was the first clue that they were going to be a mega-hit, then he noticed big-time Broadway producer Gerry Schoenfeld and then Manny Azenberg. It finally transferred to Broadway, where this little five-person show won the Tony Award for Best Musical!

Juli in drag.

Andre's first big break was in *The Wiz* and before it opened they kept asking him to audition for either the Lion, the Scarecrow or the Tin Man, but he told them he *only* wanted to play the Wizard. He got the gig and told me he had an amazing entrance where he walked down a giant staircase in crazy, enormous heels. He learned how to do it without falling down because the director Geoffrey Holder gave him specific instructions that involved rolling your foot forward to feel the edge of the step. Who did Geoffrey learn it from? The glamorous Lena Horne! And so it is passed down.

Speaking of glamour, Juli won a free makeover at The Body Shop on Saturday. We don't let her wear makeup (except lipstick when she sees Broadway shows) but we allowed her to get a full face of makeup for fun. Look at the picture and tell me if you're surprised that her favorite TV show is "RuPaul's Drag Race." Seriously!

I had Will Swenson (who just recorded my audio book!) as my co-host on SiriusXM because Christine Pedi was out of town. I asked him about onstage injuries and he told me that when he was playing Berger in *Hair*, he severely hurt his ankle because he did an extra high jump for fun during one performance. Apparently, no one in the cast was surprised because he was constantly causing injuries or near-injuries with his hijinx/hyperactivity. Case in point: almost breaking Sasha Allen's nose one night when he did a sassy turn. The cast got so used to the carnage he wrought that they made up a phrase for it: "Getting Bergered." As in, QUESTION: Why is your arm in a sling? ANSWER: I got Bergered during "Aquarius."

Cutie Will Swenson.

At *Seth's Broadway Chatterbox* I had David Garrison as a guest. Last week I wrote that *On Your Toes* was the show that made Melissa Errico want to perform on Broadway. For David, it was seeing *Hello Dolly!* No, it wasn't the fact that he and Carol Channing had the same vocal range. Instead, what sold him was seeing the train onstage for "Put on Your Sunday Clothes." *That train is featured again in the 2017 revival!* Right after college, he got cast at Arena Stage in Washington, and then the first American production of *Joseph and the Amazing Technicolor Dreamcoat* with the amazing David Carroll as Joseph. David Garrison, however, was Camel Number 2. Regardless, he wound up getting cast in the "Milliken Breakfast Show," which was a yearly event for retail store buyers and other textile industry professionals where the best of Broadway would put on 13 performances of a full musical to promote the Milliken products (which were mainly polyester clothes). And I mean, the *best* of Broadway! I was looking online and the 1978 show starred Ann Miller, Phyllis Diller, Donna McKechnie, Chita Rivera, Cyd Charisse Dorothy Loudon and more. They also had "Millikiddies" — which were a group of talented young people (Jane Krakowski) or, if need be, short people (Baayork Lee). Directed by the best (for instance, Michael Bennett), written by the best (Burt Shevelove) and using a full orchestra. They were major extravaganzas. David starred in one and was then recommended to Tommy Tune to play Groucho Marx in *A Day in Hollywood/A Night in the Ukraine*. He told me that he tends to be very last-minute at preparing for auditions, and the night before he finally started practicing and then went to his neighbor's apartment at 2 AM to see if she thought he was good. I asked him how he knew she would be awake and he said, "She wasn't."

He got the show and I loved it so much that I saw it twice when I was a kid. Obsessed! If you don't know, Act One takes place at Grauman's Chinese Theater and the whole cast play ushers. Act Two is a full-out Marx Brothers movie/musical, which is hilarious. I wrote a few weeks ago how Priscilla Lopez once forgot the lyrics to her big song in Act One because she had taken a one-week vacation. David, however, had an even bigger gap from doing the show. After he left the production, he got a call one day while at rehearsal with Priscilla for (the ill-fated) *Gallery* by Ed Kleban. The guy who had replaced David in *Hollywood/Ukraine* was sick and the understudy hadn't shown up! They still had David's costumes and asked him to please, please, please go on for the matinee. David told them that there was no way he could do the show because it had been three months! Then...Priscilla Lopez dared him. That was all it took. He left rehearsal, went to the theatre and they made an announcement to the audience telling them what was going on. The opening number featured the cast singing "Just Go to the Movies" and walking in and out of the doors of Grauman's Chinese Theater. David walked onstage, got entrance applause.... and immediately turned the wrong way and crashed into someone. Still it went well. Every time he was offstage, he was able to review the next section of the show with the dance captain, Albert Stephenson (now John Kander's partner). Then came intermission. All the Groucho lines in Act Two come fast and furious. David was in his dressing room getting his mustache on and running lines. The problem was, he would remember the first three...and would then draw a complete blank. He was in a panic and told everyone he flat out couldn't do it and wouldn't go on. They told him it would be fine. (Huh? Based on what?) Well, apparently they were psychics, because David told us that even though he didn't remember the show when sitting in his dressing room, as soon as he got onstage and started doing the blocking his body remembered it and the lines came out. Terrifying but amazing! *Just like the Christine Ebersole story about CAMELOT!*

His next big gig was taking over the lead in *Torch Song Trilogy*. He had the "fun" task of taking over the leading role the day after the show won the Tony Award for Best Play *and* the day after Harvey Fierstein won the Tony Award for Best Actor in a Play! David was terrified. The day he had to go on, he was in the lobby and heard a woman arguing with the box office. "What do you mean Harvey's not in the show anymore? He just won the Tony!" Then Harvey happened to enter the lobby and the woman accosted him. "I came up from Florida to see you in this show and now you're not in it!" He explained that he had to leave to go to Boston because he was writing *La Cage Aux Folles*. Then Harvey told her that an excellent actor would taking over named David Garrison. And, look...there he is, sitting in the lobby! Harvey pointed at him, the woman squinted, then said full volume, "I don't know him!"

Maybe she'd know Michael Urie who's starring in the revival!

A Starry Surprise Party for Mom
May 8, 2012

This has been a big week for me. Last Sunday was the culmination of weeks of planning. A few months ago I ran into Stephen Spadaro on the Upper West Side. Stephen is one of the company managers of *Chicago* and the partner of one of my best friends, Paul Castree. He asked about my Mom, and when I mentioned that her 80th birthday was coming up, he suggested I put on a show for her. I loved the idea so I rented Don't Tell Mama and asked my Mom's favorite Broadway singers to come and sing at what I decided should also be a surprise party. When Sunday came, I told my Mom and sister Beth (who was in on it) to take the 11 AM Long Island Railroad train to Manhattan, calculating that it would get them to Don't Tell Mama at noon for the big surprise. Of course, when I told my mother the train schedule, she immediately said to Beth suspiciously, "When has Seth ever told me what train to take?" Why is she suddenly Miss Marple? Then, my Mom was taking a long time getting ready that morning and Beth panicked and told her they had to make the train. My Mom said, "What does it matter? Seth is always late." Yikes. Almost foiled by my horrific reputation.

Thankfully, they made the train and my Mom got to NYC thinking we were meeting for brunch. Then Beth got a (pretend) text from me saying that I was having a little rehearsal at Don't Tell Mama and to meet me there before we went to the restaurant. Beforehand, when I would mention the surprise element of the party to people, a few made jokes like "I hope her heart is strong!" I began to have horrible visions of everyone screaming surprise and then my Mother keeling over, so I told all the Broadway guests we were going to do a "heart-attack prevention" surprise party. What dis that mean? Well, I met my Mom out front, brought her to the back room where I was supposedly still rehearsing and opened the door to the party room. When we walked in, nobody yelled SURPRISE!!!!. Instead, the door opened, my Mom saw everyone standing there and everyone literally did a low-energy, sotto voce, whispered, *surprise*. Hilarious. And heart-healthy.

The party was much fun and the show was amazing! It started with my friend Lauren Mufson, who I know from my piano bar days (and who was the star of *Mamma Mia!* on Broadway), singing "Me and Bobby McGee." The song was always playing in the car when my family and I would vacation together when I was a little kid. Lauren has been to many Seders with my family and introduced the song by saying, "Sally, when I'd see you passing the bitter herbs or ladling out the charoset, I never figured you for a Janis Joplin fan." Well, she is! Anika Larsen sang "A Little Less Conversation"! The great Tituss Burgess pre-Emmy Nominations for Kimmy Schmidt sang "Get Here," the song my mother loves to hear him sing. Not only did he sing it in Oleta Adams' key (she's a woman) but he took optional *higher* notes. Amazing.

My ex, Aaron Dai, did an amazing piano piece he wrote that consisted of all of these high-falutin' classical variations on "Happy Birthday." So funny and so creative. Charles Busch sang something that my Mom has spoken of for years: his rendition of "Bill." So simple, beautifully acted, and moving. My sister Beth sang the first song she wrote (in '79!), which is my Mom's favorite out of all of Beth's songs. Beth announced it by saying it's one of her less depressing songs but, true to her style, the subject is nonetheless someone who was just unceremoniously dumped. She claims she writes songs with manic-depressive themes, and I told her she forgets the manic part. Farah Alvin recreated her amazing performance of "Solitaire" that my Mom heard at the Actors Fund salute to Neil Sedaka. Beautiful! My friends from *Forever Plaid* (Paul Castree, Tim Cross, Drew Geraci and Clif Thorn) sang James Raitt's arrangement of "No, Not Much" from the show.

167

Then, my Mom's favorite 6-foot-plus lady, Varla Jean Merman, did a hilarious number based on a "I Need A Hero" called "I Need A Hair Fan" which ends with someone running up to the stage with one of the those giant leaf blowers which rips her wig off and her blows dress up all the way up. Hi-larious!

Near the end, I had two people show up whom I had thought wouldn't make it: Nell Snaidas, my friend with the amazing coloratura, had a singing job that morning but got there just in time to come onstage and sing Mabel from *Pirates of Penzance*. But, because it was for my Mom, she sang the version she once had to perform...in Yiddish! She noted that the original lyrics are "Poor wandering one. Though thou hast surely strayed," but the Yiddish lyrics are typically Jewish and translate to mean something like "Poor idiot who will amount to nothing." Perfect for my Mother's temperament. Gavin Creel had told me he was rehearsing a reading of Tom Kitt's new musical and would try to come by on his break. He arrived in the middle of my Mom's show and I announced to everyone that he graciously came during his rehearsal's lunch hour. He then countered by telling everyone, "Actually, I wound up not having rehearsal today. I'm just late." Brava on the honesty? And finally, Darius DeHaas performed "I Am Changing" from *Dreamgirls*, ending the show with his fantastic singing. Happy birthday, Mom!

Last weekend I saw *Leap of Faith* and I loved the crazy high belting of the choir! Hopefully, they get a group discount for prednisone. And I've never seen leading lady Jessica Phillips. Brava! Her acting was excellent and very real. And, of course, Raúl Esparza is so in his element playing as a faith healer whose meetings always evolve into an enormous production number. It actually reminded me of his sassafrass as the Arbiter when we did *Chess* for the Actors Fund. *Watch their performance on the Tony Awards!*

And finally, I had Sandra Bernhard as my guest at *Seth Speaks*. She always sings in her shows, so I asked her about her musical-theatre aspirations. She told me that in the early '90s she was being considered to do the Broadway revival of *Funny Girl*! It was, sadly, the first of many cancelled revivals of that show. I then asked her to sing, and she did a rendition of "Before the Parade Passes By" because it's from the first show that she became obsessed with. Sandra saw it on tour when she was a child in Michigan and cried on the car ride home. When her mother asked why, Sandra said she was sad because she thought her Mom was going to arrange a backstage meeting with Carol Channing. Years later, when Sandra moved to New York, she told herself she'd know she made the right move if she saw Carol Channing somewhere in NYC. Well, right after she got there, she was walking around the West 50s and she saw her! Later on, Carol saw one of her shows, came backstage, hugged her and said, "You are my soul sister." Delicious.

I was telling Sandra how much I loved her first CD, "Without You I'm Nothing," and especially the story she tells of her step-Mom having a coughing fit after eating one of those candies that restaurants have near the cash register. After she stopped coughing, she slowly said, "There must have been dus-s-s-s-t on those mints." Well, cut to: Sandra sang with me and then cracked a little on a high note and asked me to start again. Right after she cracked she looked at me and slowly said, "There must have been dus-s-s-s-t on that song." Brava! *And years later when my best friend Tim (also a Sandra super-fan) had surgery on a brain abscess (he's totally fine) I had Sandra make a recording for him. Naturally she said, "There must have been dussssst on that brain abscess!"*

Happy pre-Mother's Day and peace out!

Andrea Martin Gets Prickley; Laura Osnes Goes from Soprano to Belter
May 14, 2012

My June 18 benefit is sassing up! It's called *Not Since High School*, and I'm having people sing songs from (inappropriate) roles they did in high school. I just added one of my faves to the line-up: Norbert Leo Butz. When I wrote to Norbert and told him what the theme was, he replied: *"I did a lot of bad work in high school. The choices are endless...."* I'm right there with him. Joining Norbert are Mandy Gonzalez, Josh Henry, Melissa Errico, Chris Jackson and Lisa Lampanelli (!).

Right now, I'm in an exit row and loving the extra leg room. Delish! This time I'm flying from Chicago after spending Mother's Day weekend with Andrea Martin doing her show. We have one day off, and then Tuesday we start a full eight-show week in Wilmington, Delaware. Exhausting. What's that you say? When did I first perform in Delaware, you ask? Well, *years* ago I was doing the *Grease* revival on Broadway, and the national tour needed a pianist for one night. The Amtrak ride is very short, so I was able to go back and forth in one day. It was all uneventful except for one thing. First of all, you should know that if you play in a Broadway orchestra pit, sometimes you wear headphones because it's not always easy to hear the instruments you're supposed to hear (depending on where you're sitting). For instance, you always want to hear the drums so you can lock into the rhythm, but you won't be able to do so if the drum set is completely behind Plexiglas. My point is, during *Grease* the rhythm section all wore headphones so we could hear each other. Besides having a volume control for guitar, bass, etc., there was also a control to hear the vocals onstage. Most pit players on Broadway don't turn that volume up because they just want to hear their fellow musicians, but I, of course, am always obsessed with how people were singing. And, I was especially excited to hear the cast of the national tour after hearing the Broadway cast for years. All new singers! The first big song in the show is "Summer Nights," and I remember freaking out when I heard the girl playing Sandy. She had *such* a good voice! I wasn't able to meet her that night in Wilmington, but I heard she was the sister of someone I knew in the Broadway cast. Months later, she came into the Broadway cast as a replacement for a few weeks, and I was finally able to meet the guy-who-played Roger's-younger-sister...Sutton Foster! She not only sounded great, but she added so many funny moments as Sandy that, when she went on, it was known as the Carol Burnett version of Sandy. And now, she's a proud owner of two Tony Awards. And, I'm a proud watcher of the Tony Awards.

Edith Prickley and Jr.

James and Juli came with me to Chicago. During the Mother's Day performance, Andrea came out as Edith Prickley and added a special moment where she introduced her "daughter," Penelope Prickley, AKA Juli. Juli came out in full leopard print and said, "Happy Mother's Day, Dear!" followed by her version of the Edith Prickley laugh.

This week I interviewed the lovely Laura Osnes at *Seth's Broadway Chatterbox*. She's gearing up to do her first solo show at the Café Carlyle but, of course, I had to ask her about doing "You're The One That I Want," which was the reality show where they cast Danny and Sandy for the *Grease* revival. It's also what got me my first job on Playbill.com because I was hired to write a recap each week that then led to my current column. We talked about "Grease Academy," which was the so-called training school where 50 contestants were whittled down to the final 12. It was so awkward to watch them get cut; all the Sandys stood in a room singing the same song, in unison, as the heads of the show walked around "listening" and then tapped people on the shoulder to reject them, saying, "You're *not* Sandy." Laura said that it may have been brutal for the at-home audience to watch that awkward two-minute segment on TV, but in real life it took them *two hours*! They had to keep setting up camera shots to catch the reaction of the people being destroyed by rejection. Laura was supposed to get married in March right after the TV show ended, but NBC decided to extend the TV show by two weeks, so she had to postpone her wedding to the summer. She wound up winning (so it all worked out), and I asked how she was able to move from Minnesota to NYC to do *Grease*. She said that NBC moved all of her belongings for her and gave her an amazing apartment. Oh, I'm sorry. Actually, NBC gave her $2,000 in moving expenses (a.k.a., enough for one suitcase) and "graciously" connected her with a broker. Wow! I guess it saved her the time of typing in www.CraigsList.com.

On *Seth Speaks*, I interviewed the gay couple team from Season 10 of "The Amazing Race" known as Tom and Terry. I first met them because Rosie O'Donnell brought them on one of her cruises, but at that point I had never seen the show. I'm now obsessed with "The Amazing Race," and it was so much fun getting inside scoop. First of all, the whole show is taped over five weeks and when you're chosen to do it, you're only allowed to tell three (!) people. You have to sign something saying that if you don't adhere to the rules, you can be sued for ten million dollars. Yowtch! Their respective bosses knew why they were leaving for five weeks, but none of their co-workers knew the reason. Tom's co-workers thought he was adopting a baby. Terry's co-workers, however, thought that the five-week leave was because he was getting a sex change(!). The horrible part is that because the season before theirs didn't do well in the ratings, the producers decided to make their season based on "Survivor," so the contestants never had enough food to eat, and they had to beg for money on the street. AKA, they were living the lives of actors. Tom and Terry lasted for a lot of episodes until they got to Vietnam. They were told they had to spend the day and night at the Hanoi Hilton, which is the nickname for the horrific prisoner-of-war camp where people like John McCain were held. Tom couldn't understand why the contestants were dreading it because he's not that knowledgeable about 1970's history. He literally thought they were all going to Hanoi and would be staying in an actual Hilton Hotel. He was horrified when he and Terry had to sleep on a plank in a rat-*and*-roach infested outdoor area. The next day's challenge was to row to another location, and they wound up rowing for three hours in the wrong direction! In total they rowed for *eight* hours, and they were the last team to check in. Tom and Terry said they weren't allowed to tell anyone the outcome. Unfortunately, when the show started airing, Tom's mother chose the night of their elimination to have a dinner party and view the episode with all of her friends. She called Terry and said, "I know you're not eliminated tonight because I just saw a coming attraction for next week, and I see you and Tom running in the background." Turns out, when "The Amazing Race" films coming attractions they put doubles of teams in the background so viewers can't figure out who's coming back.

Tom and Terry didn't go home right away when they were eliminated. Instead they checked in with the other eliminated teams in Portugal but under fake names. Why? Because there are "Amazing Race" stalkers who travel the world trying to find contestants and events while it's being filmed. Bizarrely, at one point, Terry was doing a task in Beijing and running across a park when he heard his name called. Turns out a co-worker was on vacation *in Beijing* and saw him! Of course, he couldn't say why he was there or else the dreaded $10,000,000 lawsuit. They both told me that James and I should come on the show as a team, and I told them that as soon as I'm stressed while traveling, I turn into a horrible person and am incredibly mean to anyone with me. They obviously suspected that because they immediately said, "Perfect! That's what the network wants!" Great. I'll be the Broadway version of Omarosa. I'm out. Speaking of "out," peace out!

Music Director Steve Marzullo, Plus Remembering My Salad Days at Oberlin
May 22, 2012

Greetings from Wilmington, Delaware. I've been traveling back and forth all week doing Andrea Martin's *Final Days: Everything Must Go*. The DuPont Theater is the longest operating theatre in the U.S. (100 years!) and the lobby has pics from past productions. The *Bye Bye Birdie* tour came through in 1991 and the cast featured a lot of people I became friends with later on in the '90s: Paul Castree, Jessie Stone, Susan Egan, Marc Kudisch, etc. When I arrived in Wilmington I got a Facebook posting from my friend Spring (who was known as Wendy Springer when we did *Grease* together) saying that she's in Europe and had recently downloaded both of my books ("Broadway Nights" and "My Awesome/Awful Popularity Plan") to her iPad. She wrote that she just finished them and loved them both. Cut to: Right after I read that posting I went to the DuPont lobby, and directly outside the main doors is a big picture of Tommy Tune — and off to one side is Wendy Springer! No wonder Facebook traded at such a high price last week; it can foreshadow what photos you run into.

This week I interviewed Steve Marzullo, whom we all call "Marzullo." He has a new CD called "Show Some Beauty" that features amazing singers like Rebecca Luker, Andrea Burns, Terri Klausner and *many* other folk. Marzullo is also a pianist and conductor (he did my recent *Disaster!*) and I subbed for him on *Grease*, *Seussical* and *Mamma Mia!* Usually, people get sick of shows that they play for a long time, but Steve has been playing *Mamma Mia!* since it opened in 2001 (more than 3,000 performances) — and yet when he cleans his house, he listens to ABBA! Either he loves it or he's the first musician to have Stockholm Syndrome. He relayed a story that I call "Back at'cha": When he was music directing the original *Once On This Island* he felt that cast members were adding too many riffs and starting to change melodies from the Ahrens/Flaherty score. He firmly asked everyone to sing *only* what was on the page and to not add any embellishment. Well, the song "Mama Will Provide" was then being rehearsed, and Kecia Lewis-Evans sang her part as usual. At the end of the song, she went up to the E as written. But, right before the song ended as she held the E, she quickly popped up to a G sharp, just to sass Marzullo. Well, instead of being irritated, Marzullo gave her a "right back at'cha" and told Kecia he loved it and she should sing it eight times week! Busted. And now, it's officially in the score!

In academia news, I'm very excited to be heading back to my alma mater in a few weeks. Yes, Oberlin is having its first conservatory reunion. Usually, Oberlin has reunions in three-year clusters (in other words, everyone who graduated in 1991-1993 comes for a group reunion). This year is the first reunion for anyone who *ever* went to the conservatory. Back in the day, I was a classical piano performance major and I'm flying out on Saturday, June 14 with a vocal performance major — Judy Kuhn! I'm going to interview her/have her sing some of her classic songs and that night I'm going to co-host *Mock Students*. It's a comedy/variety show that happens every spring at the conservatory. The acts are always super funny and very inside. My senior year, I hosted it with voice major Cindy King (who was hilarious). I remember that for our opening, we prepared a whole slide show making fun of fellow students and teachers. First, we showed a picture of the *very* old harp teacher and told the audience that she's about to star in a spin-off of "thirtysomething" called "ninetysomething." FYI, it was the '80s, people...very timely. Also, there was a flute major named Pierre who was really tall and really skinny. We showed a picture of him and congratulated him on winning the "I Look Like My Instrument" Award. Hmmm...maybe you have to be a classical musician to find that funny. Or 21 years old. Anyhoo, if you went to the Oberlin Conservatory (or "con" as we call it), come to the reunion in June! There'll be plenty more jokes like those. Wait...that's not an incentive?

My *Not Since High School* benefit just added Corbin Bleu!). I asked him to haul out a song where he would bust a move. He mentioned doing a song from the musical *Footloose* and I was mortified to ask if he was in high school when that show came out (because I, decidedly, was not). He emailed me back and said he wasn't. Phew. Then I realized that *Footloose* came out *before* he was in high school! Holy botox!

Peace out!

Interiors by Andrea Martin; Leslie Uggams Explains "June Is Bustin' Out All Over"
May 29, 2012

Happy unofficial start of summer!

I'm writing this surrounded by stacks of books, boxes and a general mess. No, I'm not moving again (I've literally moved three times in the last three years), I'm actually in the process of redecorating. Well, *I'm* not actually redecorating. I'm not allowed to. The only person allowed to make decisions is Andrea Martin. Not joking. If you don't know, James and I are not the stereotypical gay guys with amazing taste. Quite the opposite. We buy clothes every few years (I still wear the shirt Betty Buckley bought me 15 years ago) and we decorate like we're still in college. Remember the old "I can use these milk crates to hold my books" style we all had freshman year? The only thing that's changed for me from those days is that my jeans have an added elastic waistband. Andrea, on the other hand, has a stunning apartment in New York and a beautiful house in Toronto that feels so inviting as soon as you walk in. Everything is placed ju-u-u-ust right and appears casual yet perfect. She's always told me she could help my place look nice but we've both always faded out on the follow through. Cut to: She came over on Tuesday to have a "look around" at 12:30 in the afternoon. She didn't leave that day 'til 5:30. Suddenly, things I had bought with pride for the apartment were going into the trash.

Actual conversation:
Me: Can I keep the carpet?
Andrea: No, dear.

Then on Friday, James rented a Zipcar and we drove to Ikea. She was supposed to meet us at 10 in the morning after she had a training session at the gym. She told us that she was incredibly anxious/excited the night before, and when she woke up she went right to the gym at 9 AM, paid her trainer for the session and left for our apartment at 9:01 AM. She didn't leave that night til *9 PM*! Twelve hours of bossiness. She was in a rage that we put our TV on the wall and said we *had* to get a small table for it instead. Ikea's prices are so cheap and we easily found one for $20! While we were waiting on line to check out she told me seriously that I can't keep going to secondhand furniture stores and buying crappy things. She looked at me earnestly and said, "You've come to the point in your life where you deserve nice things. Nice, well-made, high-quality objects." Then she pointed to the box on the conveyor belt. "Like this $20 table made of particle board." Busted.

I went to do my radio show for a little while and when I came back, she and James had already taken three furniture pieces to Housing Works. Then she insisted that the two of them put together the new table we got for the living room. I said I'd take down all the books in the bedroom so it could be painted. After 15 minutes, I heard her and James muttering about me and then, in what was supposed to be a lighthearted voice, Andrea called out, "How's it going in there, sweetie?" So transparent. I completely busted her for attempting a casual check-in when the simmering subtext was, "What the hell is taking you so long to empty a bookshelf?" She owned up to it immediately. But, P.S., still wanted to know what the hell was taking me so long.

After spending Friday's day and night with us, she bid us goodbye for two weeks; she had a trip planned and was leaving the next morning from JFK. Cut to: At 9:30 AM Saturday she was at our apartment, lugging her suitcases and begging to buy us some lamps before she had to go to the airport. She found something amazing at Jonathan Adler. But before she left she told me and James that we are forbidden from buying anything for our apartment until she gets back. The only thing she will allow us to purchase are (no more than) four placemats for our new table. And even that she reluctantly granted us. I have to say, though, that it already looks *so* much better. Turns out, if an apartment gets no sun because it's on the garden level, you shouldn't fill your living room with dark furniture that absorbs the smattering of light you get.

This week at *Seth's Broadway Chatterbox* I had the amazing Leslie Uggams as a guest. Firstly, I told her how amazed I was when I was in the pit of *Thoroughly Modern Mille* when she played Muzzie and I heard how high she was belting. She told me that her voice got *higher* as she got older. What the —? She began singing at a very young age, touring around with people like Louis Armstrong and Ella Fitzgerald. Seriously! At the time, she was going to the Professional Children's School which was all the way downtown from where she lived in Washington Heights. I asked how she got there every day, and she shrugged and said she took the subway. By herself. Starting at age *eight*! She stopped performing when she entered her awkward teenage years but one day she was watching "Name That Tune" and decided to enter a contest where viewers could send a list of songs and if a contestant could guess each one, the viewer could team up with the contestant on the show. Well, she sent a list, they read Leslie's song choices, the contestant got them all right and they called and asked Leslie to join the show. She was just a teenager but she knew a lot of pop songs and her partner knew a lot of classical/legit ones so they were a great team and kept winning. The first week, the host asked Leslie what she did in her free time and she said she was a singer. He then asked her to sing something, which she did. Suddenly, the network got a ton of fan letters. From then on, she was asked to sing every week. Mitch Miller had been trying to get his show "Sing Along With Mitch" on the air for years, but no network was interested. Finally, it was picked up. Because he heard Leslie on "Name That Tune," he asked her to be the singer on his show. When it finally aired, it was a hit *but* the South wouldn't carry it because it featured a black singer. The network was losing money from all those Southern networks and they asked Mitch to cut Leslie. He said no. Then they asked if he'd give her a week off. No. Then they asked him to just have her sing one song (so her segment could be removed in the Southern broadcast) and he still said no. I asked her if she felt stressed knowing that the network wanted her off the show and she told me that Mitch kept it from her and her family! It wasn't until way later that she knew how strong he was in the face of all that pressure. It's doubly amazing because it took him four years to get the show on TV and yet he was still willing to stand up to the network.

Finally, the show was such a hit that the South couldn't take being left out so they started airing it! The fabulousness of the show trumped their racism. Brava!

Even though she studied acting and dance her whole childhood, she didn't do her first musical until she was in her early 20s. She played the lead in *The Boyfriend* in Berkeley, CA. This was in the '60s and it was a big coup that she got the part because it was played on Broadway by Julie Andrews…and, FYI, Julie isn't black. This version of *The Boyfriend* wasn't done in the Pearl Bailey all-black-cast style, they just cast Leslie and kept the rest of the cast as is, including giving her white parents! Then *Hallelujah, Baby!*, a new musical by Jule Styne, Comden and Green and Arthur Laurents, was about to come to Broadway, but its star, Lena Horne, had a falling out with Arthur Laurents. Leslie got the part, her first on Broadway…and won the Tony Award!

I asked her about "Roots," the miniseries from the 1970s. She auditioned to play Kizzy but they wanted to screen-test her to see if she could play the character at 80 years old. The makeup people didn't know what to do because Leslie didn't have any wrinkles. Poor thing. They put tons of latex on her face and she wound up looking like a mummy for the screen test. She knew she didn't get it, and she told her husband/manager that she bombed. He got on the horn and tracked down the makeup guy who did

"The Autobiography of Miss Jane Pittman." Leslie went over to his house, where he tried out some makeup. The "Roots" people let her screen test again and she got the part...*and* they hired the makeup guy for the entire series! The network didn't have a lot of hope in the success of the miniseries and thought no one would be interested enough to watch it over a few weeks (like all miniseries ran back in those days) so they aired all the episodes over one week to get them all over with. Turns out, the ratings went through the roof and the network was hailed for its brilliant idea (which had actually been done to get the show out of the way). As a matter of fact, Leslie was in Vegas when it started airing and on the third night, Ann-Margret called her and said she had to change the time of her show because there was no audience when "Roots" was on!

Finally, I had to ask Leslie about..."June Is Bustin' Out All Over." If you don't know, it's a clip famous within Broadway circles because Leslie sings a string of wrong lyrics, relentlessly. I finally got the story; Leslie said that she was hired to sing in a live TV concert on the White House Lawn. All the lyrics were on cue cards so she could read them. Unfortunately, it rained the night before the concert *and* the morning of. When the song started, everything was fine...until the cue card man slipped in the wet grass...and never got up again! It was live TV, so Leslie had no choice but to keep going and "fake it." And that she did. Making up crazy words, nonsense syllable and only solidly landing the phrase "just because it's June!" She was horrified, but after the concert she ran into the conductor. He didn't say anything. Then she saw her husband. He didn't say anything. Her friends didn't say anything. She thought, "OMG! I got away with it!" Until a few years later, a friend came up to her and said, "Do you know you're in every gay bar in America?" She said, "Doing what?" He said, "Singing 'June is Bustin' Out All Over.'" She said, "Oh, lord, I've been busted!"

Peace out!

Everything's Up to Date in Kansas City, Plus Kate Wetherhead and Andrew Keenan-Bolger
June 4, 2012

What time did my alarm go off, you ask? Why, 3:50 AM, 'natch. That's right, I'm doing one of my signature early-morning flights. This one leaves at 5:32 from Kansas City and if this column were on Skype right now you would be slathering Maybelline's "Under-Eye Bags Go-Away" to your computer screen. Anyhoo, I flew out here to see the Music Theater for Young People production of *Chicago*, and to do my show. I know Julie Danielson from NYC (I hired her to play bass on the MTV *Legally Blonde* reality show) and she told me about the children's theatre training program that her mom runs. Well, I came out to see their senior production (all the kids are 18 years old) and it was great!

First of all, I want to say this wasn't the new trend of having kids do "junior" versions of shows, with truncated scenes and songs which sometimes makes me feel like I'm watching a day of 16-bar auditions. This was the full-length *Chicago*. How long did they rehearse, you ask? *One week*! Not since I did summer stock in the '80s! They began last Sunday and had their first performance on Saturday night. I thought it would be one of those productions where the songs aren't very staged except for a couple of sassy moves at the end of every number. Cut to: it was fully choreographed, and I mean *fully*. I was watching the back-up dancers for "All I Care About Is Love" and they had moves every other beat. And they were all together! Usually, when I watch a show that's just started performances, I have anxiety from the anxiety of the people onstage who are constantly thinking "I don't know what's next" (aka, the first two weeks of my show *Disaster!*). Well, the only anxiety I felt was because all the kids have 28-inch waists and I had just bought an enormous package of trail mix that was supposed to last me the entire day, but I had finished all 20 grams of fat by the time I was in baggage claim. *I still do this. Trail mix is evil...and delicious.* Never felt fatter. My point is, these kids were as confident as if they'd been doing the show since the '96 revival began. P.S. That Tony-winning revival opened two years after these kids were born. Never felt older.

The trick is that they rehearse from 9 AM til 9 PM every day, 12 hours a day! I told the kids they needed to get a union but, of course, they *love* rehearsing non-stop and would actually prefer a *24*-hour-a-day schedule. Wowza. Not since the workhouse boys that inspired "Oliver Twist." It was one of those shows where there were different levels of talent on the stage, but everyone was at the same level of commitment. I had tears in my eyes more than once throughout the show because I kept getting that feeling I get when something is really theatrical, like everyone hitting a sassy pose on the button of a song at the same time. Of course, one of the things I love the most is that MTYP also uses a full orchestra. That's right, no pre-recorded music which many theatre groups use, no "piano, bass and drums" to cut down on costs. Whatever the original Broadway show used, they use. So, how come when shows are revived on Broadway, half the orchestra is usually cut? Why does Kansas City realize how much better a full orchestra sounds? Anybody?

I began the week by playing for Colleen Ballinger's alter ego, Miranda Sings. Miranda Sings the "youtube sensation" who is a horrific singer but thinks she's amazing. And when I say sensation, I mean it. She has hundreds of thousands of views. *Now in the millions!* Her concert was hilarious, and featured Adam Pascal, who, as usual, sounded great. Miranda joined him in a duet of "Light My Candle" from *Rent* and there were so many amazing moments. Because Miranda "doesn't say bad words" she wound up singing "They say that I have the best tush below 14th Street."

Speaking of TV, I began the week with booking Bravo's "Watch What Happens Live," hosted by Andy

Cohen. Random House got me the appearance to promote "My Awesome/Awful Popularity Plan," but it wasn't my first time with Andy because we did a pilot together a few years that was like a version of "The View" (the show was decidedly *not* picked up). The pilot ended with a clip from Judge Glenda Hatchett's show, where she told a defendant, "So what if you paid child support! What you want? A biscuit?" It was such a bizarre expression that they asked me to write a whole song about it. Well, "Watch What Happens" asked me if I would write a song about the "OC Housewives." I said yes, but meanwhile had never seen the show. I got a list of all the highlights from this season plus a DVD of the newest episode, which I watched with Juli. After watching, Juli's comment was, "They remind me of the girls at my school" (the girls at her school are 11 years old). Regardless, I wrote a whole song and had the best time singing it. My fave lyric was about Heather: "When Brianna got married, Vicki was a mess. And Heather stole my gig as the first O.C. Jew*ess*!"

At *Seth's Broadway Chatterbox*, I had Kate Wetherhead and Andrew Keenan-Bolger, who both created the webseries "Submissions Only." Right now, Andrew is playing "Crutchie" in *Newsies*, but he first performed on Broadway as a kid. He played Chip in *Beauty and the Beast*, and I immediately asked him about any mishaps. He claimed nothing much happened to him, but he did hear about another Chip who was firmly ensconced in his teacart when it began to roll toward the audience. If you don't know, the boys who played Chip weren't able to use their arms or legs because they're essentially in a fairy tale version of an iron lung. Finally, someone in the cast stopped the cart before it landed in the pit or crashed on an audience member. Beauty and the Lawsuit? Kate Wetherhead talked about the inappropriate roles she played as a young person. When she did *Once Upon a Mattress* in school, she couldn't get cast as the Princess or Queen because she was an underclassman. So, they gave her the role of the minstrel. They boldly did non-traditional casting, putting a girl in the boy's part, *but* they didn't make much effort past that — no change in keys. That's right, her big song stayed in the original key, so she was forced to sing it an entire octave up. Not since Minnie Ripperton's "Loving You." Then, when she was in her first summer stock show, she was cast in *Working* and hoped for the waitress song. Instead she was given the song "If I Could Have Been," normally sung by an older woman who has lived many, many years and is now filled with regrets. Kate was 20. The director "solved" the problem by writing her a monologue to recite before the song that essentially was, "You know, my *mom* sure isn't satisfied with her life. And I think that someday, I, too, will look back on my long life of missed opportunities. I'll probably feel like this..." Cue song. As well as crickets.

Peace out!

Joan Rivers, Matthew Broderick, The Tony Awards
June 11, 2012

OK, I'll get to the Tony Awards after a little weekly re-cap. Next Monday is my benefit called *Not Since High School*, where celebrities recreate roles they did in high school. I just had a rehearsal with Lisa Lampanelli who was a teen-aged Reno Sweeney in *Anything Goes*. She told me that two weeks before the show opened, the director told her that he rethought the role and she needed to lose weight. How much? Twenty pounds! Her response? Deep-fried food at every meal. Not only wouldn't she lose weight, she was determined to gain it. Brava! Speaking of the benefit, I just added one more performer: Susan Blackwell who starred in *[title of show]* is going to recreate one of her high school roles. Was it appropriate casting you ask? Well, she's white, from Ohio, and not trained as a dancer. Therefore, she starred in *West Side Story* as Anita. 'Natch! She will be doing a duet of "A Boy Like That" with a very unlikely Maria who had to spray her hair black until it looked like a shellacked shell...Lisa Lampanelli's other high school role! Seriously!

The much-missed Joan Rivers.

I interviewed the late great Joan Rivers for my radio show *Seth Speaks* and couldn't stop quoting my favorite Joan lines to her. First I hauled out, "My body is falling so goddamned fast my gynecologist wears a hardhat." Then, I mentioned one of my favorite Royal Family bits where Joan makes fun of the Queen for not keeping herself up. "Listen! If you own England, *and* Scotland, *and* Ireland, for Christ's sake, *shave your legs*!" Hi-lar! What's crazy is that Joan is one of the very few Americans who was invited to the recent royal weddings. After those comments!?! Weren't people in England beheaded for less? Speaking of comments about Elizabeth, I did ask her about the Elizabeth Taylor jokes she used to make all throughout the '80s. This was after Elizabeth Taylor had gained a lot of weight and Joan would say things like, "She puts mayonnaise on an aspirin"...or that Elizabeth Taylor puts food in the microwave and then screams, "Hurry!!!" Turns out, she and Elizabeth Taylor were both friends with Roddy MacDowell and Joan told Roddy to tell Elizabeth that if she thought the jokes were too mean, she would stop. Well, Roddy asked and Elizabeth said, "Tell Joan that those jokes don't hurt me where I live." Joan thinks it's because Elizabeth had a very healthy ego and always thought of herself as beautiful. Of course, Joan always thought of herself as ugly. In her new book, "I Hate Everyone...Starting with Me!" she writes that she was so ugly when she was young that a rapist would grab her and say, "Can we just be friends?"

On *Seth Speaks* I also interviewed Matthew Broderick and I asked if he still has the ability to talk to his fellow actors onstage without being picked up by his body mic. He first feigned that he didn't know what I was talking about, but I kindly reminded him of various moments that Nathan Lane had told me about. One was during the first big scene between Nathan and Matthew in *The Producers*. Bialystock (Nathan) tells Bloom (Matthew) that there are two rules to being a producer: "Number one, never put your own money in the show." Bloom then asks, "And number two?" and Bialystock yells, "*Never put your own money in the show!*" Well, when the show first opened, that second line would bring down the house. Crazy laughs. By the second year, the audiences had stopped being so "inside" and the laughs dried up. Literally not a peep. Many bits were tried to make that joke land a laugh (including adding reverb to Nathan's mic), but it got crickets. And yet, Nathan still had to play it big and broad. Right before Nathan would yell the second line, Matthew would look at him and whisper, "Here we go..." and wait for the joke to bomb. Matthew told me that he finds nothing funnier than someone onstage giving all they've got to get a laugh and then getting nothing in return. He needs to see some of my live performances.

Matthew then told me that in his current show, *Nice Work If You Can Get It*, he often won't run into Kelli O'Hara backstage. The first time he'll see her is onstage. So, onstage he'll give her a "Hello! How are you?" using his signature talking-so-that-the-audience-can't-hear-him style. Matthew and I also spoke about his love of Ethel Merman. When I was doing *The Producers* with him, he would listen to Merman recordings before he went on to get him in the Broadway mood. Back then, when I was working in the pit of *The Producers,* I would often ask him to add a little Merm to his performance — and he would do her signature brassy style during one section of "I Wanna Be a Producer." Cut to: I went to see *Nice Work If You Can Get It* and texted him during intermission. I did a dramatic reading of our texts during the radio show. They were as follows:

ME: It's Seth! I'm in your audience and I demand to hear an Ethel Merman note like you used to do for me during *The Producers*.

MATTHEW: I usually do one in Act 1 and I didn't bother today...I'll try and find one in Act 2.

After the show, and a decided lack of Merman notes, I got another text.

MATTHEW: My integrity as an actor did not allow me to put Merman into Act 2. That's how dedicated to craft I am.

Tony Awards night, June 10, began with me planning a major Tony party at my apartment and ended with me not even being in my apartment. As I've mentioned, Andrea Martin has been overseeing/bossing around the entire redecoration/painting/de-cluttering of our place. I was excited to debut it on Sunday to a gaggle of friends. Slowly they began to fade out...one had to go to Ithaca, one had a migraine, one wanted to watch it in her apartment so she could turn it off whenever she wanted, one had a daughter who was too tired to stay up... finally, it was just Andrea Martin who was going to see our newly decorated apartment. Of course, we knew the reveal would be less exciting since she herself had decorated it.

Well, on Saturday Andrew complained that her jaw hurt and I immediately knew what it was; a result from teeth grinding. My dentist told me I grind my teeth and I've periodically woken up with my jaw killing me. When James came home, I asked him if his jaw ever hurt from teeth grinding and he backed me up completely. Andrea asked why she'd suddenly start grinding her teeth later in life and we told her it can happen at any time. We told her to get a mouth guard and it would clear up. Cut to: Saturday night she couldn't sleep at all and by Sunday morning her entire left side of her face swelled up! She got an emergency appointment with a doctor and found out she has a raging infection and needs to be on antibiotics. So, the first thing we realized is that James and I are not qualified to do a medical diagnosis. Secondly, Andrea had to recuperate all day and therefore couldn't leave her apartment. So, my big party at my newly decorated apartment turned out to be me, James and Juli taking a cab ride up to Andrea's apartment and then watching the Tonys with her lying prostrate on her couch. It did wind up being a lot of fun, though. And it was cool to watch the Tonys on her TV while seeing her actual Tony Award sitting right next to it (she won for *My Favorite Year*). It was also so great to see Audra McDonald win as Best Actress in a Musical. I've known her for so many years (I played her audition for his first agent as well as her Juilliard Senior Recital) and now she has *five* Tony Awards *soon to be six!* A few months ago, I asked

Will Swenson (her fiancé *now husband*) where Audra keeps her Tonys and he told me he could tell me where three of them are. I wanted to know why he couldn't tell me where the fourth one was and he said it's because Audra can't remember what she did with it. That's right, she has so many Tony Awards, she's actually misplaced one.

I just did Julie Klausner's *soon to be starring on "Difficult People"* podcast called "How Was Your Tonys?" with Ana Gasteyer and we had a great time. We were saying how happy we were that Christian Borle won, and Ana remembered first meeting him at a reading of *Shrek* years ago. She thought it was going to be casual and take place in someone's living room while she read a variety of parts. Turns out, it was incredibly high-powered, took place in a fancy studio, Dreamworks execs were there, and it involved non-stop rehearsals. And since she had just starred in *Wicked* on Broadway, she thought she'd probably play one of the many funny roles. Instead, she was in the female ensemble. She wound up being seated on a stool against the back wall and all throughout rehearsals she kept leaning back and, by accident, turning off all the lights. Hilarious. *OMG. Re-reading this literally brought tears to my eyes from laughing!*

My Passion for Patti LuPone
June 18, 2012

Last weekend, I went back to Oberlin College for the very first reunion of the conservatory. In other words, instead of having a reunion for a certain graduating year, *anyone* who had gone to the conservatory could go. I had a great conversation with a woman who graduated a little before I did... in 1944! On Saturday night, I did a show with fellow alum Judy Kuhn and it was so much fun. We were introduced by the current dean, we then took a bow and I played her first pitch. She then inhaled and started singing the aria "Batti Batti o bel Masetto" from *Don Giovanni*. After around 6 bars she said "Cut!" and we both stopped abruptly. She laughed and told the audience that the show was going to be all Broadway but I forced her to try to trick everyone into thinking it was a serious classical concert. She revealed that she had sung that aria at her senior recital...and hasn't sung it since. She then admitted that it was also the last time she sang anything classical...*or* in a foreign language.

She started the show with a song from *Rags*, the first Broadway show in which she had a leading role. The score is probably Charles Strouse's most brilliant and she was confident the show would be a hit, despite the troubled tryout period. Well, opening night happened and Judy was so busy during previews she didn't have much time to clean her house. The day after opening night, she decided to finally tidy up. While she was vacuuming, she was watching the news and saw the logo of *Rags* come on the screen. "Oh, goody," she thought, "they're going to talk about the show!" Well, they did indeed talk about the show, but what they said was "*Rags* which opened yesterday, will close tomorrow." And that's how she found out she would be playing her first Broadway lead for only four performances. If you've never heard her brilliant singing on the title song, watch my deconstruction on youtube!

On Tuesday night I saw Patti LuPone in her amazing show at 54 Below. Holy S***! Her voice is so amazing! My head was coming off the whole time. Every song was in such a high key and she nailed every note. *And* Joe Thalken, her amazing pianist/arranger, told me that Patti had spent the whole previous week doing her show, *and* a reading *and* performing on the Tony Awards. Yet her voice was so incredibly solid. Patti told me that she's placing her voice better than ever due to her teacher, Joan Lader. Brava!

The other thing I was crazily impressed with is how every song had tons and tons of lyrics and Patti was so completely confident singing them. I was sitting with Jane Krakowski, and after Patti sang "Come to the Supermarket in Old Peking", Jane was in a state of shock over how many verses there were. I was sitting with Scott Wittman, too, who directed the whole thing and I told him how much I loved it. At the end of the show, Patti performs a request taken from Twitter. She asked for a "Ronnie," in the audience who had requested "As Long As He Needs Me." She asked him to raise his hand, but it turns out he wasn't there. Then a woman, whose name was Ronnie but that wasn't the requester, piped up. Patti asked what she requested and she named some obscure song called "Baby Loves Me." Patti asked what that was. The woman told her that it was once a hit in England (?!). Patti said, "What makes you think I sing that song?" The woman said, "I know you don't sing it, but I thought you'd sound great on it." Patti was hilarious and told her "That's actually not a request. It's a suggestion." Brava!

Patti then performed "As Long As He Needs Me" and sang the whole last phrase without a breath. In other words, "As long as he-e-e-e ne-e-e-e-eds me-e-e-e-e!" It was so good! I met with her the next day to rehearse our show for Provincetown and asked her about her amazing breath control. She said she's always had it and that when she was at Juilliard, the whole acting company had to get x-rays to see what kind of breath capability they had. The doctor looked at her lungs and told her she could be an opera singer. I wasn't surprised but couldn't get past the part where her acting class was forced to have their chests x-rayed. "OK, people! We're starting the morning with warm-ups, then trust games and, after lunch, MRI's!"

Patti was talking with me about being short (she's 5-foot-2) but on Tony night she told me she was like a giantess because she was joined by two other Evitas who are shorter than she is! She, Elaine Paige and Elena Roger were all chatting — and Patti was essentially the Tommy Tune of Evitas. Jackie Hoffman was in the audience at Patti's show and I was chatting with her director (and my old friend) Michael Schiralli. We were laughing because Jackie was the first performer at 54 Below, but all the press said that the room was opening with Patti LuPone. I remembered how Jackie's show started with a recording of a supposed phone conversation between the owners of 54 Below. One of them mentioned how excited he was that Patti LuPone was going to open the room. The other one said, "What? We can't have a performer of that stature perform here without testing it first. What about the sound? What about the air quality? We need someone so desperate and so low on the celebrity totem pole that she'll try out the room before an actual star does." Then, "Ladies and gentleman, Jackie Hoffman!" She's still got it!!

What Show Tune Did You Sing in High School?
June 25, 2012

Ahhhh. I can relax a little. Last Monday, I did my benefit for the Chesapeake Bay Academy called *Not Since High School* and there was a *lot* to do to get the show ready. Usually, when I do a benefit, I book the singers and have them sing a great song. Deliciously simple. This required all the performers to sing a song from a role they did in high school *but* I knew that if they just sang the song as is, it would be enjoyable for 20 seconds and then become a live version of Ambien. So, every song had a concept attached and that's where the headachy-ness came in.

The whole show began with Christine Pedi singing a song from her first show, *Godspell*, which she did at her all-girls high school. She gave us a sample of "Save the People" up the octave with the horrible soprano straight tone she used as a 15-year-old. After a few measures, she stopped and asked me who *my* ideal female cast would be and she then did her amazing imitations to create an all-star version of *Godspell*. She did Patti LuPone singing "Day By Day" and then Judy *and* Liza doing "All For The Best." It was perfect to have Liza do "Don't forget that when you get to Heaven you'll be blessed. *Yesh!* It's all for the best!" She also did a hilarious version of Bette Davis doing the finale, which was simply a Bette line-reading on "Oh, God, I'm dying." Then "Oh, God. I'm dead."

Next up came Norbert Leo Butz. He told everyone that he was too embarrassed at first to do theatre in his school because he was a jock, so he would go to neighborhood all-girls schools and volunteer himself. He literally called it "making the rounds" because he rented himself out to so many of them. First he did his Harold Hill for us and sang a jazzed-up version of "The Sadder But Wiser Girl." So good! Before the concert, I asked him to sing "I'll Know" from *Guys and Dolls* (because he played Sky Masterson), and I emailed him to tell him that my friend Melissa agreed to sing it with him. When we began rehearsal, I brought Melissa onstage. He got *so* excited because he didn't realize that "my friend Melissa" was, in fact, Melissa Errico! He kept telling her that he had no idea she was doing it and that he was thrilled. Then, as soon as she sang her first note, he interrupted and said, "I can't believe I get to stand here and listen to you sing this!" My initial concept was to have Melissa tower over him because Norbert was an especially short leading man in high school. He actually still is, but he told me that people don't realize it when they've seen him in shows. He said that fans have met him and been shocked that he's only 5-feet-7-inches tall. They've told him "You looked so tall in *Rent* and *Wicked*." He said, "Yeah, that's because Daphne Rubin-Vega is really short and Kristin Chenoweth is even shorter. Of course I look like a giant next to someone who's 4-foot-10!"

Next, came Lisa Lampanelli who was a teenaged Reno Sweeney. We dueted on "Friendship" and ended each verse by telling the audience about a school friendship that went terribly wrong. Hers was about her best guy friend who she wound up making out with and then never hearing from again. She revealed that he was one of the many guys she "turned gay." I told a story about my friend who told me, with a huge sympathetic smile, she was getting me a sweater for my bar mitzvah because all the ones I wear "are so ratty."

Next up was Christopher Jackson from *In the Heights (now "from" Hamilton)*, who told us that his first onstage role was in *Oliver!* as The Artful Dodger. He was the only black kid in the show and sassily commented that casting him as a thief was racist. He gave us "Consider Yourself" once through, sung as he did as a kid (with a Cockney accent) and then he performed it as he would as an adult...R&B style. It sounded great *and* completely inappropriate.

Next, Corbin Bleu came onstage and sang a song from *way* back when he was in high school. Five years ago. I knew he had gone to a performing arts high school (with Fergie, FYI!) as well as attending Debbie Allen's dance school, so I asked him to do a song in which he could "bust a move." He did "I Can't Stand Still" and not only danced great, but his body looked amazing. I told him how in shape he looked and he said, "You should have seen me months ago," which I took to mean "I was so out of shape and I'm so proud of how far I've come." He actually meant, "You should have seen me months ago because I was in *better* shape." Hmm. "Thank you" would have sufficed.

Susan Blackwell came onstage and told everyone that when she was in high school she was cast as Anita in *West Side Story*, causing her to "hit the tanning bed pretty hard and spray my blonde hair black with Halloween bullcr*p." She launched into "A Boy Like That" but spoke over every musical break and it was hilarious. At one point she informed us, "Because my high school was so small, they had to cast most of our gang members from the middle school. So, in the second act, when Anita nearly gets raped by the Jets, I was so much bigger than most of Jets, it looked like I could have easily raped *them*." At the beginning of the song, she told the audience that if they were shocked she played Anita, just wait 'til they find out who played Maria in another high school production. During the part where Anita sings "Just wait and see, just wait Maria! Just wait and see!" she sang "Just wait and see who played Maria, just wait and see!" and the audience suddenly heard a high soprano singing "Oh, No Anita no! Anita no!" sung by…Lisa Lampanelli! That's right! Lisa "sang" some more and then took a break to tell the audience that she went to high school in Connecticut, even though she is Italian, she was cast as the Puerto Rican Maria. She said, "That's because Italians are the Puerto Ricans of Connecticut." Brava!

Melissa Errico came back onstage and told us of the many roles she played at French Woods Summer Camp including the title role of Evita at age 11! Who was her Che, you ask? Why, it was that fiery Latino, Jason Robert Brown! Jason *Roberto* Brown?

Melissa's mom would always mail her costume pieces. Melissa remembers singing "Don't Cry For Me, Argentina" in her mother's nightgown. She asked, "Why? Was Evita supposed to have woken from bed?" Then she told us that she played the sexy, sexy role of Carlotta in *Nine* when she not very much older than the title age. Well, she was 14.

Finally, Mandy Gonzalez came out and told us about playing Maria as a teen in *The Sound of Music*. Her high school rehearsals consisted of her teacher plugging in a TV and playing the movie. The cast was told to copy what was onscreen. Seriously! Mandy played Elphaba last year in *Wicked*, so at the end of her rendition of "I Have Confidence" we immediately segued into "Defying Gravity" because the songs have a similar "I-still-got-it" attitude. She sounded so great on her soprano and then thrilling on her high crazy belting!

In other news, does anyone have a sequel to my book they can lend me? Mine was due June 1. If not, peace out!

Seth Is On Demand as Andrea Martin Opens a New Window
July 2, 2012

Can you believe it's July? Don't forget ye olde sunscreen.

This week I saw *Peter and the Starcatcher* and loved, loved, loved the theatricality. It makes me so happy to see an audience break into laughter and applaud for something as simple as an actor wearing a rubber glove and flapping around like a bird. Or Celia Keenan-Bolger "flying" by being on a board that tilts upwards. I tried to analyze why audiences react so strongly to things like that, and I think it's because people appreciate cleverness on a very deep level. And they identify with the people onstage. Meaning they think, "Wow! Someone just like me achieved a really cool special effect by being smart!" and it makes them feel connected to the people onstage and the people around them. As opposed to appreciating technology, which makes audiences think, "Wow. A computer and/or machine just did a special effect. Cool, but I'm not that surprised. Machines can do anything." To me, the reaction the audience had at *Peter and the Starcatcher* is the essence of theatre. There's nothing like seeing people in the flesh doing something magical, right in front of you.

On *Seth Speaks* this week, I interviewed Marissa Jaret Winokur, who just started Season Two of "Retired at 35" as the daughter of Jessica Walter and George Segal. She told us that in the past, she wouldn't memorize lines for TV auditions because other actors told her it looked needy, but she decided she *was* needy and was going to try as hard as possible to get the "Retired at 35" gig. She's most proud that the character breakdown was simply for a woman under the age of 40. AKA, anybody. The people running the show told her that as soon as she walked in, they knew she was perfect. Of course, that theory has some holes in it since they made her come back eight times.

Andrea Martin is *almost* finished redecorating our apartment. She's completely transformed it, and whenever people come over they think we bought tons of new stuff when the reality is we just bought a few things, cleared things away (AKA, Andrea threw them out), and rearranged the rest. She also could not be working harder on it, simply to help us. I've never seen someone run around town more. She's constantly texting me from home furnishings stores. She transported a new rug from ABC Carpet, carried it in (!), laid it out in our living room, and let us keep it for a few days to decide whether we liked it. Finally we said no, so she took it back for us and picked out three rugs from Pottery Barn! We brought them back to our apartment, she laid them out and we all chose one. After another day, we decided it wasn't 100% perfect, so we returned them, and she got *another* one from ABC Carpet all the way downtown. This one looks amazing and brightens up the whole room.

P.S. She's been doing all of this while recuperating from her sickness that made her cancel her 54 Below performance. She has an insane amount of energy. And OCD. She had a breakdown that our windows looked dirty, so she hauled herself up on the ledge in our bedroom and started cleaning. *And*, she did the outside as well by climbing onto the storage unit in the backyard, keeping one hand on the window gates and spraying window cleaner and wiping. We're most obsessed with the fact that her "cleaning outfit" is a pure white dress. Excellent for not showing dirt. P.S. She could not be funnier. We were out to eat at a fairly sleazy diner and, as she looked around the room, she surreptitiously pointed to the various waiters and asked, "Why is it that every waiter has a lovely selection of herpes above their lips?"

I went to see Brian d'Arcy James' show and was most impressed that Brian's "patter" was the most unscripted I've ever heard. I always get a little uncomfortable when I hear people do material between songs that I know they've been doing "off the cuff" for the last two years, but he really seemed like he was making it up on the spot. He talked about being on his high school's basketball team (!) and having to make Sophie's Choice: going to "the" game against his Catholic school's arch rival… or a Billy Joel concert in nearby Ann Arbor. He was completely 100% obsessed with Billy Joel and didn't know what to do until his follow-the-rules parents told him that they'd actually back him up if he said there was a "family emergency" that night that prevented him from going to the game. He skipped the game, saw the concert and was blown away. However, the coach somehow found out his family emergency was less emergency and more two hours of non-stop songs like "Movin' Out" and "She's Always A Woman." Sadly, Brian was benched for the rest of the season. But, he said, that concert laid the groundwork for his first New York City act 30 years later, and indeed it did, because almost the whole thing was Billy Joel songs! I didn't know many of them, but they were all so good, and I thought, "There should be a Billy Joel musical." Not to brag, but I'm obviously a psychic whose specialty is reading thoughts that happened ten years ago to Twyla Tharp.

OK. I have to go ASAP. Why? Because Andrea Martin is standing in back of me and wants us to return the pillows we just got from Gracious Home and get another set in green. She is exhausting me!

Patti LuPone in Provincetown; High Flying, Adored!
July 9, 2012

Greetings from the high seas! Actually, from the Hudson River. I'm on The Broadway Cruise and as I type this we're leaving the pier at 53rd Street and 12th Avenue. Goodbye burning hot sun of New York City! Hello burning hot sun of Bermuda. I'm here with Juli, James, his mom and my mom. But on my mind right now is this week's two-day trip to Provincetown with Patti LuPone. It was one of the most amazing experiences of my life. It all began when I was 13 years old. My friend, Allen Hahn, got me two albums for my Bar Mitzvah; the soundtrack to "All That Jazz" and Broadway cast album of *Evita*. I distinctly remember sitting on the couch in the den, opening *Evita*'s two (!) record set, taking out the included lyrics and listening to it for the first time. It's so weird when you first hear it ("...to inform the people of Argentina, that Eva Peron, spiritual leader of the nation, entered immortality...") but after non-stop listening sessions, I became obsessed. I loved the music and lyrics... but it was Patti's singing that riveted me. The tone and power of her voice and, most importantly, the incredibly high belting. I had *never* heard a woman belt an E, F and then a G! Unbelievable! Of course, my mother continued her tradition of only taking me to see Broadway shows *after* the original stars had left so I eventually saw *Evita* starring someone else. Not just the replacement, mind you...the replacement's matinee cover. My point is, my dream has always been to hear Patti sing my favorite *Evita* songs live. A dream I thought was 30 years too late to ever happen.

Cut to: I asked her to do my Broadway Series at The Art House in Provincetown, MA, and she said yes. Her three shows immediately sold out, so we added a fourth. I told her it was going to be a casual show consisting of me interviewing her and then running to the piano to play. I mentioned that I wanted her to sing some *Evita* songs and she seemed game but we wound up not rehearsing anything in New York because she got sick during her acclaimed run at 54 Below. Also, she had to perform her show with Mandy after the Provincetown gigs so I knew she shouldn't push herself. I thought maybe she'd haul out "Don't Cry For Me, Argentina," but would limit her belting. Yet, a few days before the gig she emailed me and wrote that we should rehearse a few songs, just for fun. She said we could run through "Rainbow High" and then she added: "And let's try 'High Flying, Adored' just to see if I can still hit that note. What is that note?" (FYI, the sustained note is a D and then it goes up to an E, but I didn't want to tell her in case it freaked her out.) Well, I showed up for a quick sound check and nervously took out "Rainbow High," worried she'd tell me to forget it. Not only did she not say that, she suggested we lead into it with "High Flying, Adored" since that's how it is in the show. Really? Both songs? Was my dream about to come true? I thought I'd give her an out in case she wanted to save her voice, so I tentatively asked, "Original key?" Instead of asking to try it a few steps down, she shrugged and said, "It's the only key I know." Brava! I started playing the vamp and Patti launched into both songs. With all the top notes. She had certain inflections that are so uniquely hers that it took me right back to listening to her sing those songs on my record player all those years ago. I was literally holding back tears as I was playing because ever since I was a kid, I'd always dreamed of one day hearing Patti sing these songs live. Now, not only was I hearing her sing them, I was playing them for her! It was more than I ever expected.

Well, we had two shows the first night and Patti said we had to do the *Evita* songs at the second one. Why? Because Ryan Murphy (who created "Nip/Tuck" and "Glee" and is a big *Evita* fan) had gotten married that afternoon and was, naturally, spending his wedding night at Patti's show. We did both songs and the audience went crazy. Before the songs, I played a recording of her singing the "Rainbow High" modulation ("I'm their savior!!!") from the original cast album and then compared it to Madonna singing the same section in the film. Let's just say, it doesn't compare favorably. When Patti finally sang that part of the song live, she got full out applause in the middle of the number. So thrilling!

After that performance ended, she did the requisite "I'm pretending the show is over, but I'm coming back to do an encore" chestnut. She did a fantastic "Don't Cry For Me, Argentina" and we exited. The theatre is pretty small and once you leave the stage, you have to walk outside. We were standing outside the theatre and chatting for a minute and suddenly Patti became the Broadway version of "The Bionic Woman." She cocked her head to the side because she was hearing something. A cry for help? A kitten caught in a tree that needs rescuing? No. Something more important. She looked at me and said, "They're still applauding." That's right, even though we were completely out of the theatre, she was able to use her supersonic hearing that is acutely tuned to cries of "Brava!" and "Encore!" After she heard it, she looked at me with a mischievous smile and said, "Do you wanna do B.A.?" *Yes*! I was so excited because "B.A." is *Evita* talk for "Buenos Aires"! That's another song she hasn't done in around 30 years. Yet again, she did it in the original key and killed it! So good! After the show, Mark Cortale (who runs the Art House) saw Ryan Murphy and asked him if he liked the show. Ryan responded with, "Are you kidding? It's like crack." True 'dat!

Patti was so forthcoming. The interviews were as exciting for me as the songs. She talked about the bad experience of doing *Oliver!* which was on Broadway but directed by a British director. First she started off by telling the audience, "Let's get this out of the way; Americans can't do Shakespeare and the Brits can't do musicals. Over and out!" Blimey! She told us that there was an associate director who came over before rehearsals and cast the show. Then the director showed up for the first day of rehearsal and within a few hours *fired* the little boy who played Oliver! A late revenge for the revolutionary war? Patti also un-fondly remembered "As Long As He Needs Me." First of all, she wanted to sing it in a higher key because the original key was for Georgia Brown who had a much lower voice. The music director, however, refused to raise the key so she was forced to sing in Bea Arthur's key. After the show opened, she met Lionel Bart (who wrote the whole show) and he told her that she could have sung it in any key she wanted! Yet again, *blimey*! She also recalled the staging of the number which went completely against her instincts. As she was singing the incredibly exciting ending section, the director wanted her to *back up...* and as she held the last note, he asked to her exit the stage. She said, "So...when the song is over, you don't want me onstage to get applause?" Answer: "That is correct." After telling the story, she got up and sang the entire song in a higher key than Georgia Brown *and* stood center stage the whole time. So satisfying!

We talked about *Gypsy* and she remembered that Arthur Laurents was very into giving line readings to the cast. She, Laura Benanti and Boyd Gaines were concerned because they wanted to put their own imprint on their parts. Patti said that Arthur finally let them explore their roles and allowed them to develop their own interpretations. I so agreed with what she said about line readings, which is that a lot of directors think "if it ain't broke, don't fix it." Meaning, if a line always works with a certain cadence, keep it that way. I've done a lot of Broadway shows where replacements have come in and tried to make a role their own and, in doing so, lost tons of the laughs because they want to do it their own style. However, she feels that an actor shouldn't just imitate the inflection. He/she has to understand what the line means and what the character's motivation is when saying it so even though the ending result the actor comes up with might sound exactly the same as the initial line reading, the actor has to have meaning behind it to make it truly work. Yes!

The most exciting thing happened the final night. We finished the show and did the requisite encore. We walked out of the theatre and I kept one ear to the stage because I hoped there'd be the demand for one more song. There was a ton of applause so Patti went back and did "Buenos Aires." We took our bows, Patti and I left the theatre and went back to our (shared!) dressing room. I turned my back as she got into her casual street clothes and waited for James to knock because I knew he wanted a picture. I kept checking outside the dressing room for him to appear. The third time I looked out I saw Shelley, our excellent sound person, come out of the theatre. The dressing room is on the ground level and she was exiting the tech area so she was at the top of a long flight of stairs. She looked at me with a "what do you think" face. What did I think about what? How the show went? I looked back with a "what?" face and she yelled down: "They're still clapping!" That's right! In all the time it took for Patti to exit the theatre, walk to the dressing room *and* completely change out of her outfit, the audience was still clapping! I got her out of the dressing room and she went back for a third encore. So, after the fourth show she did "Blow, Gabriel, Blow," then "Buenos Aires" and *finally* "Don't Cry For Me, Argentina." And this time, during the part when she breaks down and can't sing anymore, the audience suddenly started humming just like the *Evita* ensemble does during the show. It sounded beautiful!

There's so much more to tell, but I have a cruise meal to overeat. So peace out and I'll write to you next from dry land!

Having Faith in Prince and Celebrating the Genius of Gene Kelly
July 23, 2012

I'm now officially in my summer travel mode. Every week I'm going to Provincetown for the Broadway Series at the Art House and this Thursday and Friday I'll be with Faith Prince! Everybody knows she won the Tony Award for Adelaide in the '90s *Guys and Dolls* revival. But many people don't know the iconic role she *almost* created. Back in the '80s she auditioned for the original *Little Shop of Horrors* and got a callback for the role of Audrey. Finally, she got the phone call telling her she got the part! But...she was contracted to do an IBM industrial that happened to conflict with the show. P.S. If you don't know, industrials are shows that corporations put on for their workers. Usually, they feature big musical numbers with lyrics changed to be about the product. Hunter Bell and I did one for Rite-Aid in Baltimore where we touted "RAPTAR," an acronym that all Rite-Aid workers are supposed to remember. It stands for Recognition, Appreciation, Praise and Respect. Our industrial offered parodies of famous TV shows; the finale was based on "Everybody Loves Raymond" and was called "Everybody Loves RAPTAR." It featured Hunter (in a black wig) as Ray Romano and me (in full old lady drag) as Doris Roberts. Lemme just say, we didn't hold the audience rapt(ar).

Regardless, Faith told the folks running the industrial that she got a leading role in a new musical, and would like to please be released from her contract. They told her no. She remembers she actually got down on her knees and begged...and they still said N-O! So, the role went to Ellen Greene and the rest, as they say, is her-story. But some interesting side notes: Faith has no bitterness about what happened. She told me that a little later she was at the Goodspeed Opera House doing a show and there was a big New York Times feature on Ellen as Audrey. People in the show were trying to hide it from her but Faith was totally at peace about it. She felt that the whole thing was meant to be and would work out for both of them. And *Guys and Dolls* is what was waiting for her! Faith thinks she wouldn't have gotten Adelaide if she had been known for playing Audrey because the roles are similar. And, on another side note, two of the stars of *Guys and Dolls* almost worked together before Jerry Zaks cast them. Yes, Faith almost played Audrey and, if Lee Wilkof hadn't accepted the role of Seymour, the next choice was...Nathan Lane! Faith did wind up playing Audrey during the NY run as well as in L.A. so it's "all good".

On a shallow note, this morning at Starbucks, I had an uncomfortable "I refuse to speak Italian for no reason" face-off with the Starbucks counterperson when I ordered two shots of espresso.

ME: Two shots, please.
COUNTER PERSON: Doppio?
ME: Two shots.
COUNTER PERSON: Doppio?   *Pause.*
ME: *(Barely perceptible conciliatory nod).*
COUNTER PERSON: *(Barely perceptible triumphant nod).*

On *Seth Speaks*, I had Chris March and Jesse LeNoir who were former contestants on "Project Runway." Or, from what they told me, "Project Prison." When they got on the show, they had to sign a contract saying that the producers could portray them in a negative light as well as altering their image *and/or* alter their voice! Plus, the show owned their life story *forever*! Chris said the contestants worked non-stop and the only break they got was after a judging. I asked if he meant they got a day or two off. He said he meant they got an *hour or two* off! The judgings, where they stand on the runway, would last *seven hours*! And if one of the contestants argued, they'd go back and forth with the judges for at least an hour. That's why a lot of them would just agree with whatever criticism came their way. The contestants also had severely restricted access to the outside world. Jesse said that they only reason they knew Michael Jackson died was because they were in a car going through Times Square and saw it on the newsfeed. Chris has been asked by many people why he cried when Sarah Jessica Parker came on the show. He responds "Because I had gotten eight hours of sleep...*in four days*!"

Also on *Seth Speaks* was Patricia Ward Kelly, Gene Kelly's third wife and now the trustee of his estate. She tours around the country showing people his genius, screening clips of his films and sharing information about his artistic choices. This summer would be his 100th birthday and she's trying to show people how relevant he still is and what an innovator he was. I went to see her lecture/dem at Lincoln Center Friday night and it was fantastic. Because Gene was such a wonderful performer people forget that he was also a brilliant choreographer and director. I always hear dancers speak of Jack Cole and Bob Fosse as geniuses of modern theatre dance, but Gene is rarely mentioned. However, when you watch his film clips, you see what a trailblazer he was in American dance. Patricia said that while Fred Astaire continued the European style of dance, Gene wanted to develop one that was distinctly American and athletic. I'm also obsessed with how so many of his big musical numbers were done with barely any camera cuts. In other words, he'd dance continually, like in a Broadway show.

Patricia told us that when he filmed "On the Town" they were on location in New York and tried to avoid the mobs of fans eager to see Frank Sinatra. Gene, Frank and Jules Munshin would travel to and from each locale (filming without a permit, by the way) and make Frank lay down in the back seat so he wasn't seen. It wasn't until they did the last section of "New York, New York" at Rockefeller Center that people figured out who was there.

I also did a show with Shoshana Bean last week and someone in the audience told her how he impressed he was that she didn't take one sip of water. She revealed that she challenges herself, hydration-wise, at every show because a while back someone told her how cool it was that she sang five songs in a row without water. Now, she tries to see if she can go a *whole show* without water. I don't exactly understand why she needs to build that stamina, unless she's preparing herself for The Mojave Circuit. *I experienced that same thing with Chita Rivera later on. I'm going to start screaming "Drink some Evian" at various Broadway stars the same way people yell "Eat a cheeseburger!" at skinny models.*

My agent called me a few days ago about two auditions; The first was for a Sandra Bullock film. Yay! I then found out my character was in one scene and his name was listed as "Choking Victim." Even though I wanted to do it just to see what the audition would consist of, I passed. Then I was asked to audition for a Martin Scorsese film. I said yes! I was also told it was starring Leonardo Decaprio. I reiterated yes! Then I was told there was an orgy and nude scene. *Silence.* I read the script and decided the nudity was "tasteful"...and went in! The film takes place during the '80s Wall Street boom and I was auditioning for the role of a butler to a big financier. I decided to wear my red button down shirt that I love to wear because it's so comfy and I think it looks great on me. Well, I did the audition (no nudity...yet) and the casting director was very nice. And, at the end of the audition she complimented my shirt. Yay! However, she should have stopped after the first sentence.

This was the conversation:
HER: I love your shirt!
ME: Thank you!

HER: It's perfect. So-o-o-o-o-o '80s.
ME: *Mortification*
P.S. I didn't get it. However, you can rent "Wolf of Wall Street" and see who did get my part.

Tonight I'm yet again hosting and music directing the New York Civil Liberties Union benefit at the Skirball Center. It's chock-full of Broadway folk. And on that note, peace out!

Faith Prince, Lea DeLaria, Jerome Robbins and a Duck
July 30, 2012

I can't believe it's about to be August! Let me start this week's column with last Wednesday, when I did *Seth Speaks* with Lea DeLaria, *Pre "Orange Is The New Black"* who was a hilarious guest. She told us that she began doing stand-up in San Francisco in the '80s and her stage name was simply "Big Fat Dyke." She wound up being a hit but had to get rid of the stage name and go back to being Lea DeLaria because when she'd walk down the street people would yell from their cars, "Big Fat Dyke!!!" She didn't know if they were fans or if they were harassing her. In the late '90s, she flew in to NYC from California when she was asked to audition for *On the Town* — and she got the role of Hildy, the brash cab driver. She only had experience doing TV and film so when they started dress rehearsals she told someone, "I can't wait to see what the make-up person does with my make-up!" She then found out that Broadway ain't like TV and the make-up person's name was Lea DeLaria. The show opened in Central Park and she and her manager hiked it down to the New York Times building at 2 AM to get the review on the night it came out. Lea said she started reading the first paragraph and saw that it was about her. Then the second. Then the third. At this point she sat on the sidewalk to keep reading. There were seven paragraphs lauding her! Soon, "I Can Cook, Too!" became her signature song and she was asked to sing it at many events, including the big Leading Ladies concert at Carnegie Hall. Lea was freaked out to be performing with so many big stars until she saw Audra McDonald backstage. Audra walked by and told Lea that she was a nervous wreck. Lea then thought, "If a Tony winner is nervous, then it's OK that I'm nervous," and that made her calm down. I remember that night because I played for Audra who did a version of Barbra's "Down With Love". Look for my deconstruction on Youtube!

And speaking of Audra, Lea said she knew she had to share a dressing room at Carnegie Hall with one of the other ladies and hoped it was with Audra. Because she's a fan? Lea said, "No, because she's HOT!" Lea's wishes weren't exactly granted. She didn't get to share a dressing room with Audra, but she did get to share one with another great lady of the theatre, but one who is perhaps not as "hot": Elaine Stritch.

Varla Jean Merman!

Speaking of dressing rooms...on Thursday I flew up to Provincetown and did two shows with the fabulous Faith Prince as part of the Broadway Series at the Art House. We used the same dressing room that Jeff Roberson (AKA Varla Jean Merman) uses to get ready for his/her show. The subject of the Off-Broadway musical *Lucky Guy* came up because Jeff starred in it last year and always jokes about how proud he is that he made the actual cover of the New York Times...even though the article was a picture of him as Varla with the headline: "*Lucky Guy* loses at least two million dollars." Faith then told Jeff that she did an earlier version of *Lucky Guy* in the '80s...and, turns out, they both played the same part! Faith's show was about to begin so, luckily, there was no catfight.

At our show, Faith and I told the audience that we know each other very well even though it was our very first time doing a whole evening together. How do we know each other so well? Because we spent every Monday night, for *years*, in the same group therapy! We started back in '91 on Wednesdays and I remembered that we changed it to Mondays when she got *Guys and Dolls*. Now that I've done a lot of

Broadway I told her that I couldn't believe she was in this major hit show, with tons of pressure, and she spent her one night off in group! She laughed and said that her husband Larry asked her the same thing. He would say, "Can't we go away to the country for a break each week?" She told him she felt that if she didn't dedicate herself to group, the two of them wouldn't be together in five years. She wound up staying in group every Monday and they've been together for 25 years! Brava!

Faith went to Cincinnati Conservatory of Music and when she graduated she was voted "Most Talented." But it still took her ten years to get to Broadway! When she first moved to New York, her mom came to visit and Faith took her to see a little Off-Broadway show called *Scrambled Feet*. I saw that show when I was a kid and loved it. It was like a precursor to *Forbidden Broadway*, with comedy songs and quick black-out sketches. Faith went to see it because her college friend, Jimmy Walton, was the understudy and he was going on. The show starred three men and one woman, and at intermission her mom turned to Faith and said, "You would be good in this show." Since her mom was not a Mama Rose-type, Faith really listened when her mom would say something like that. As opposed to *my* mom, who would take me to *Ain't Misbehavin'* and ask me why I didn't audition. Back to Faith; during Act Two, she watched and imagined herself in the show and decided she *was* right for it. After the bows, there was a question-and-answer session with the cast because theatre students from Colorado were there. Faith, who is normally very shy, suddenly got up the courage to raise her hand. When she was finally called on, her question was, "Do you need another girl?" The actor onstage was taken aback but then asked her "Do you sing?" "Yes!" she answered. Then, since everyone in the show had to play piano (they accompanied each other), the actor asked if Faith played. "Absolutely!" she said.

He told her to leave her picture and resume with the stage manager. She auditioned... and was asked to open the show in Boston! The one thing I forgot to mention is that it starred three men, one woman and one *duck*. Seriously. The duck's name was Hermione and her understudy was Fred. The woman in the show would come out in an evening gown, start singing an operatic song and then the duck would come onstage. The song would then switch to a lament about never performing onstage with children or animals. Well, throughout her nine days of rehearsals, Faith was trained on how to scoop up the duck at the end of the number. She was told to scoop with her arms wide because the duck had a six-foot (!) wingspan. Cut to Faith's first night in the show. Everything went perfectly. Then she began her opera song, the duck came onstage and suddenly made a beeline for her hemline and grabbed onto her thigh... and bit it! Faith freaked out and flung the duck away from her. Of course, the duck then took off in flight over the audience... with its full six-foot wingspan! Faith stood onstage helpless and screamed, "Will someone please get the duck?!" Finally, the men in the show came onstage (in their tuxes for the final number) and scooped up Hermione and brought her backstage. Faith was devastated because it was her first Equity job and she was sure she would be fired. After the show, the producer came into her dressing room. He had tears streaming down his face, and instead of firing her, he told her it was the *funniest* thing he ever saw and asked her if she could do it every night! After that, they changed the blocking for the number and had the duck chase Faith around as she sang!

I also asked Faith about the first Broadway show I saw her in — *Jerome Robbins' Broadway*. She reminded me that people auditioned for months and months, they got a 60 person cast and, even though most Broadway shows rehearse six weeks, they rehearsed for *six* months! I've heard a lot of stories about Robbins being mean, so I asked her about her experience with that. She remembered rehearsing the scene before "You Gotta Get a Gimmick" where she was Tessie Tura, the stripper. It was now the fifth month of rehearsal. They would run the scene and song almost every day. In a studio with no audience. As the scene was being done, she heard Jerry Robbins snapping his fingers in the back indicating they needed to move faster. She stopped, turned to him and said, "No. This moment needs a pause to get the laugh." He told her no, it didn't. She said it did. He told her it didn't. Finally, she said, "Well, sir, there's no way I'd know that because we've been rehearsing the same thing over and over again for months and months *with no audience*!" Paul Gemingnani, the famous music director, turned to her and whispered, "You have the balls of God." Rehearsal ended and, like the duck fiasco, she thought she'd be fired.

That night, Debbie Shapiro was throwing a Christmas Party. Faith showed up and the first person she saw was…Jerry Robbins. Uh-oh. They looked at each other and finally Faith said, "Merry Christmas." Jerry looked at her and said, "Merry Christmas, Faith." Then he continued. "And listen… the next time we have a fight, can we talk about it right away? Because I've been upset all day long." Turns out, the show should have been called *Jerome Robbins: Softie*. Peace out!

Mario Cantone in P-Town
August 6, 2012

I'm on a JetBlue flight back from Boston. I was up at 5 AM (!) to catch my 6 AM Cape Air flight to Boston from P-Town. I know that seems like last-minute, but Cape Air is so Mom and Pop that you can saunter up to the counter to get a boarding pass at 5:45 and there's an "it's all good" attitude. I came up to New England to do two shows with Mario Cantone at the Art House on Saturday and Sunday nights. Mario was great. The show featured him singing and me interviewing him, which was really just me asking a simple question that would launch him into a hilarious ten-minute tirade. One of my favorite things he said was about Paula Deen. He was raging about how everyone turned on her when she got diabetes. He couldn't understand the anger coming towards her. He yelled, "*She* has diabetes. She didn't give *you* diabetes!"

He performed in Provincetown only once before, when he was 19 years old, for the summer. But he was traumatized from being heckled and didn't come back 'til now. I asked him what his comedy was back then and he said he did imitations, like Julia Child. He did an amazing version of her voice and her late-in-life bent over body, telling the audience "My hump is actually made of pecorino and parmesan." Then he started miming putting a cheese grater on his back. "Say when!"

I asked him what he watches currently on TV and he instead told me what he would *never* watch any shows featuring "The Housewives." "They're *who-o-o-o-o-o-ores*! The Housewives of *Who-o-o-o-o-o-ore*-ange County!" He also raged about the teen parents in his own neighborhood. Twice, he's rescued a baby carriage on 9th Avenue that was rolling into traffic because the mother wasn't paying attention. One of the young ladies was standing with her boyfriend and kept apologizing profusely.

"Oh, Tito! I'm so sorry. I'm the worst mother. Tito! I'm so sorry!" Then her eyes widened when she recognized Mario from TV.

"Oh! I remember you..." she said

"You remember *me*!?!?!" he yelled back. "Remember your *child*!!!"

He grew up loving musicals but was only interested in seeing the original cast. When he was 12, his sister told him she got them tickets to *Chicago*.

"And," she said, excited. "Guess who's in it?"

"I know who's in it." he replied. "Chita Rivera and Gwen Verdon."

"No!" she said. "Gwen Verdon has been replaced by...Liza Minnelli!"

He glared at her and said, "Then I'm *not going*!" Seriously! He refused to see it because it wasn't the original cast. I love it! *What's hilarious is the reason I found out Mario is such a good actor is because I saw him in LOVE! VALOUR! COMPASSION!... in which he REPLACED Nathan Lane!*

We talked about him doing "The View" and he busted Barbara Walters for loving Justin Bieber so much. He told her she had no right being obsessed with someone who was born *after* she received her lifetime achievement award. He continued with, "I know why you're so into him, Barbara. Because he's a compatible donor!" Hi-larious!

A few months ago, my sister Beth was on Facebook and was "friending" her favorite mystery writers. She started a little correspondence with Zoe Sharp, one of her favorite British writers. Beth told her that she was a composer/lyricist/singer and sent Zoe one of her songs. Zoe *loved* it and asked Beth if she would write music and lyrics for a promotional "trailer." First of all, I've never heard of a so-called book trailer. However, when I was four years old ('til I was 6), my family spent the summer in Montauk *living* in a trailer. Two parents, four kids, one dog. So much fun when I was a kid. Would kill myself before doing it as an adult.

Anyhoo, apparently a book trailer is like a movie trailer, but for books. It's a video that has scenes from the book, or at least scenes that represent the tone of the book and there's music throughout it all. So, Beth got Zoe's book ("The Fifth Victim") and wrote a song called "The Victim Won't Be Me," based on what the book is about. She went to Millrose Music recording studio and played/sang the song along with cellist Mairi Phaneuf-Dorman. Zoe had the trailer made with Beth's song and it got great comments and reviews. Then, J. Carson Black, another mystery writer, saw the video and asked Beth to write a song for her newest book called "Icon." I love how Beth has created the *most* specific niche for herself. Beth wrote a song called "Vengeance" based on that book and recorded the piano/vocals and orchestrated it for Mairi and Karl Kawahara on violin. When Zoe Sharp did the video for her book, it was produced and filmed in England. This newest one was set to be done in the U.S. and Beth was suddenly in charge of producing it! She got Mark Ezovski (who films all my *Obsessed* videos) and hired Jessica Phillips (from *Leap of Faith*) as the lead actress. Then she hired a lead actor who I'm very familiar with...James! That's right, old school nepotism. They filmed in NYC (even though it takes place in an Arizona desert) and it came out great! It's so weird for me to watch James and Jessica as a couple. It seemed very real and now all I want to do is dye my hair red because apparently that's what James prefers.

On my SiriusXM show, I celebrated the release of the video with Beth, Mairi and Karl performing the song live! And it was a brava! And, thanks to the miracle of the phone, I was able to interview them all along with J. Carson Black, who lives in Arizona. Look for the video on Youtube!

Last week, I did a master class and *Deconstructing Broadway* at French Woods Performing Arts Camp. I knew that my friends Melissa Errico, Andrea Burns and Jason Robert Brown went there so I was excited to finally see it. I also found out that three of Maroon 5 met there! Well, I've now decided I must send Juli there next year. It's amazing! Not only a wonderful theater program (where the musicals use *full* orchestras) but an enormous music program (classical and rock), art (ceramics, silk screening, animation), film, roller skating, circus (!) and a ton more. I want to actually live there. I also love what a stereotype it is in terms of typical obsessed theatre teens: I watched a rehearsal of the current musical and, of course, I saw a bunch of 15-year-olds doing *Company*. It was so fun seeing a teen Joanne say "Sometimes I catch him looking and looking. I just look right back." I wound up getting so emotional watching it because I *also* was 15 when I did *Company* in high school (I was Harry). It was like reliving my youth. P.S. I was really impressed with them. They were doing "Side By Side," which had tons of dancing and yet when they'd run by me in the middle of a dance step, I could hear they were all singing full out. It's such a bust on Broadway producers who add pre-recorded vocals to their shows claiming that it's difficult to dance and sing. Really? Then why can non-professional 15-year-olds do it!?!?!

And on that valid question, peace out!

Remembering Marvin Hamlisch, and the Way He Was
August 13, 2012

This past week began with the sad news about Marvin Hamlisch's death. He was an idol of mine because his music — both Broadway and pop — was such an important part of my childhood. Not only did I love his chord changes and melodies, but I especially loved his music because when it was at the height of popularity, I was a young pianist and his songs always seemed to feature the piano. *A Chorus Line* began with that famous piano line "*da da, da dum dum dum* — Again!" And the piano was prevalent throughout so many other songs in that show: the beginning of "Nothing," the famous "One" vamp and all throughout "At The Ballet," which was played on that incredibly cool 1970s electric keyboard, the Fender Rhodes. Then, pop-wise, there was that great piano intro to "The Spy Who Loved Me" and the beautiful vamp that starts "The Way We Were." When fellow SiriusXM host Christine Pedi interviewed Marvin, he said that vamp represented church bells chiming on the campus where the characters played by Robert Redford and Barbra Streisand went to college.

Speaking of SiriusXM, my regular Saturday show that I do with Christine ("The Dueling Divas") was expanded this week to include some of Marvin's co-workers sharing their memories; Don Pippin, (the original *Chorus Line* conductor and vocal arranger), Priscilla Lopez (the original Morales) and Donna McKechnie (the original Cassie). Before we played the song "Nothing" on the radio, Priscilla and Don talked about when the song was written. Priscilla remembered when Marvin and lyricist Ed Kleban first played it for her. She said she wept because they had taken one of the worst things that happened to her and turned it into one of the best things: a fantastic solo in an upcoming Broadway show! However, one day after rehearsal, the whole cast was sitting onstage getting notes and between mundane ones like, "Everyone make sure your kicks are the same height," and "Try to sing out throughout group numbers," Michael Bennett also said, "Oh, and 'Nothing' is cut." Priscilla was devastated! She knew it was a great song. What was wrong? Well, Don Pippin then took over telling the story because he played an important part in getting it reinstated. Turns out, "Nothing" was originally staged with all the dancers in back of Priscilla acting out what was happening throughout the song. Don told us that after the song was cut, he was in a meeting with the creative team and right before he left (he remembers his hand was on the doorknob) he said, "You know, 'Nothing' is a comedy number. There are so many people onstage that it's difficult to hear any of the lyrics." Michael Bennett asked him to repeat what he said. Don did, and left. Michael then cut everyone else from the number and suddenly the number worked! And Priscilla loved the fact that it's the first time in the show that someone is onstage alone. The only other times it happens is with Cassie and Paul.

As much as we were all lauding that show, we also talked about how disappointing the film was. Before *A Chorus Line* transferred to Broadway (it started at the Public Theater), the character of Cassie would turn up *after* the whole opening number. She entered in a fur coat, asking if anyone had change for a cab. Donna told us her line was "Does anyone have change for a ten?" Well, until Priscilla reminded her it was a five. I love that Priscilla remembered! That entrance wound up turning the audience against Cassie because it made her look like a diva and separated her from the other dancers. It was opposite the whole point of the show, which is that dancers are all the same. They all need to dance because they love it. So, Cassie was then added to the opening number. Cut to: Years later Donna went out to lunch with Cy Feuer who was producing the *A Chorus Line* film and when she read the script, she was horrified to see they were using the old Cassie entrance! She and Priscilla laughed as they told us it was as if the scriptwriters took all the moments that hadn't worked (and were cut) and put them in the film. In fact, they said it seemed like they took the original *A Chorus Line* script before any changes were made and used it as the film script.

Donna and Priscilla remembered that, at one point, Michael Bennett was going to direct the film. He wanted to keep the show's feeling of urgency and desperation for a job, so the film was going to be about a bunch of actors trying out for the *Chorus Line* film! It was going to take place on a soundstage and there'd be all different people trying out for each part. Sadly, it never happened. When the real film went into production, all the originals were given a chance to audition, but Priscilla felt it was only so Sir Richard Attenborough could say, "Well, I saw them all and they weren't right for the film." As a matter of fact, when Donna tried out, he asked her to do it again and condescendingly told her, "You know, this is film. You don't need to speak so loudly." Donna said, "But isn't Cassie onstage? Talking to a director all the way in the back of the audience?" Touche! *And now there's great documentary, Every Little Step, about auditions for the most recent Chorus Line revival!*

Don and Priscilla were reminiscing about doing the show all the way downtown and remembered one particular rainy night spent with Kelly Bishop (Sheila) and Thommie Walsh (Bobby). Kelly lived on the Upper West Side and didn't have time between shows to walk her dog (Venus) so she'd bring him to the Public Theater and they'd take a cab home. Well, because it was raining that night, they couldn't get a cab so they decided to take a subway. But how? Dogs aren't allowed. Well, *most* dogs aren't allowed. That's right, they decided to pretend that Venus was a seeing eye dog! Because of Priscilla's fondness for character acting, she volunteered to pretend she was blind. First, she took off her rainbow poncho (it was the '70s) and put it over Venus so people couldn't see there wasn't a harness. Then she put on her sunglasses and they all went down the subway. No one stopped them and they got on the train. After a while, Priscilla began to have an anxiety attack because she saw a cop get on the train! Finally, at 59th, she told them they had to get off and walk the rest of the way before they got busted. As soon as they stepped onto the platform, Venus was so happy that he went bounding towards the exit. Of course, everyone in the train station was horrified watching that poor blind lady being dragged up the stairs by her guide dog.

Speaking of the run at the Public, they remembered that *A Chorus Line* used to have a different ending each night! Michael Bennett wanted the actors to really feel like they were auditioning for a show, so Robert LuPone (Zach, the director) would pick a different cast each night. Eventually, the script changed and the ending became set: who would make it and who wouldn't. In the Public Theater run, Cassie wasn't cast in the show. *A Chorus Line* got applause, but no standing ovations. One night, Neil Simon's wife Marsha Mason came (Neil was doctoring the show) and told Michael Bennett that Cassie *had* to make the show because it was too devastating for the audience to see her be rejected. That next night the ending had Cassie getting the job and the show got a standing ovation! Donna said she'd get letters from fans who loved the show because her character represented second chances. She'd hear from businessmen who'd been fired and were so moved to see her able to start again. We asked Donna what Cassie would have done if she hadn't been cast and she said, "Well, first, hopefully get some therapy."

Besides being a musical genius, Marvin was so warm, supportive and extremely funny. This is something I wrote a few years ago after an interview with Marvin. I thought was timely again now:

Marvin works with Barbra Streisand a lot and, turns out, they're very similar. They both want things to be *perfect* and once they're done, they move on. He said that he would be the worst pit piano player because he'd have a breakdown having to play the same thing every night. I actually enjoy doing the same things over and over again (see my stand-up act for the last ten years. Perhaps it's time to retire those Janet Reno jokes?). Anyhoo, he wrote the theme to "The Way We Were" and was watching a run of the film with a test audience and was mortified to see that there was no crying from the audience in the last scene. He, being Jewish, blamed himself. He knew if the music was right, the tears would flow. Marvin had underscored the moment when Barbra brushes away the hair on the forehead of Robert Redford with the *secondary* music theme of the movie, not the title song. Perhaps, he thought to himself, he was wrong? He discussed it with his orchestrator. Marvin said he didn't want the audience to hear the same theme 30 times in the same movie because it could seem tacky. The orchestrator explained that it may play 30 times, but the audience would "hear" it around three times. Only the composer is that honed into the music in the background throughout the whole film to really notice. Marvin decided to re-record that moment and bring in the main theme from "The Way We Were." However, the movie studio said NO WAY. They weren't going to pay for more musicians to come in and do any more playing. So…Marvin paid for it himself! That's a lot of cash-ola…it was a 55-piece orchestra! He re-recorded it, got it put in the movie and went back to another screening. He watched Barbra touch Redford's forehead…he heard the music play….and one woman sniffled. Then another. Then a bunch. Finally, Marvin heard the crying he was looking for! P.S. If he wanted so badly to hear crying in the mid-'70s, he needed only to visit my house every afternoon when I returned home from school.

That same year Marvin became an international celebrity because of the Oscars. He won Best Musical Adaptation for "The Sting," Best Score for "The Way We Were" and Best Song for "The Way We Were." That's right, he won THREE Oscars in one night! Speaking of "The Sting," for those of us who grew up as pianists, that was Marvin actually playing "The Entertainer" that we all listened to on that recording and tried to emulate. I asked him if he cheated and recorded each hand separately to make it easier…and he said he DID! Aha! But not on "The Entertainer." Only on one of the rags because, he said, it was a really hard stride left hand and busy right hand and there were other musicians playing with him. Marvin knew that if he made even one mistake, everyone would have to start the whole piece over from the top and he wanted to save them all the annoyance of having to do that.

Right after he won the three Oscars, Michael Bennett contacted him. Marvin was an incredible fan of his. When Marvin met Michael years earlier, he told him that he wasn't going to file Michael's phone number in his address book under B for Bennett, but under G for Genius. Michael called and asked him to fly to New York because he had an idea for a show. Of course, Marvin's agents were completely irritated. He was the only composer that was being booked on national talk shows…he could have any high-paying gig he wanted. But the pay wasn't important to Marvin, he wanted to work in theatre. He went to Michael's apartment and saw that it was all black. Marvin realized it was because Michael had special lights on all of his awards and the black really made them stand out and glimmer! He met with Michael and was incredibly excited to hear the idea. Michael sat him down told him: (pause)… "It's about chorus kids." Marvin sat and waited for the beginning, middle and end. Silence.

Marvin went home and, even though it was not the way he was used to working, he knew he had to say yes. Marvin thought that one of the reasons Bennett hired him instead of one of the Broadway reigning greats of the time, is because he was a Broadway newcomer and Michael knew that he could have more control that way. Tricky! And it worked!

When they first workshopped it, the show was five hours long. Yikes! After they did a run-through, Michael asked Marvin his opinion and Marvin said he could only comment on the first two hours. Brava. Marvin said that he really didn't get the show for a long time as he was working on it…until Michael drew the line on the floor and said it was about people "on the line." Then it became clear to him. Marvin also said that if you're composing a show, you shouldn't work very hard on the opening number. The original opening number for *A Chorus Line* was called "Resume." The only thing that remains in the opening we all know now is the melody of "I really need this job" and the cast holding their 8x10's in front of their faces. Marvin advised that composer/lyricists should essentially just write a dummy version of an opening because it's going to change later on. He said that you have to write the bulk of the show and then you'll be able to really see what the show is about. That's when you write the opening. He said that both "Tradition" from *Fiddler on the Roof* and "Comedy Tonight" from *Forum* were both written *after* the bulk of the show was in place. He and Ed Kleban wrote all of *A Chorus Line* and then went back and wrote the opening.

I'll conclude by saying that I knew I was such a fan of his, but I didn't realize in how many different ways he influenced me. As most of you know, I've been desperately trying to finish the sequel to my first young adult novel, "My Awesome/Awful Popularity Plan." I wrote around half of it and even though I knew what was happening plot-wise, it took me that long to finally start to understand the themes. So, I went back to the beginning and started re-writing it once I understood more about the book. I realize now that I felt so comfortable doing that because I remembered what Marvin had told me about writing a show and then going back and writing the opening. I internally knew that going back to the beginning was the right thing to do. So, thank you, Marvin, for everything you brought to the world. And, thank for helping me finish my sequel that was so overdue. Last Wednesday night at 10 PM, I sent it into Random House!

Charles Busch, Varla Jean Merman and Margaret Cho in P-Town
August 20, 2012

Greetings from Provincetown. Rainy, chilly Provincetown. I'm about to go to a tech rehearsal for Charles Busch's show at the Art House, but I'm avoiding walking over to the theatre because I don't feel like starring in the final scene from *110 in the Shade*. Oops, I should have prefaced that with "spoiler alert." Anyhoo, this whole week has felt like a vacation. Why? Because I finished "The Rise And Fall Of A Theater Geek" which is the sequel to "My Awesome Awful Popularity Plan" and therefore I don't have a horrific weight bearing down on me. Delish! Let me come out of my leisurely pace and write about *all* the interviews I've been doing lately. Last Sunday, I dedicated a full hour to Audra McDonald on *Seth Speaks* and we had a great time. And by "great time" I mean every five minutes we challenged each other on our memories of things that have happened to us. She claims she met me when she auditioned for the Bucks County Playhouse's 1989 production of *Evita*. I completely deny that since I *never played those auditions*! However, I will say that my ex-boyfriend Tod and I were obsessed with belting back then and he went to go see that production because one of our favorite belters, Noelle Player, got the title role. Audra told me she was cast as the understudy. Apparently, the fact that one of my ex-boyfriends saw someone else play the role that she covered is the same thing as me playing her audition. *P.S. We just did our show in London and she is STILL sticking to her story. You have to admire her tenacity. And faulty memory.* The *actual* way we met was when I was the audition pianist for an industrial and she sang something from *Dreamgirls* (and got the gig). Right after she auditioned, I asked her if she would sing at one of my volunteer hospital shows ("Hearts and Voices" brings entertainment to AIDS wards) and she said yes. We began working together a lot and one of the auditions I played for her was at Lincoln Center for *Hello Again*, which led to her getting *Carousel* and her first Tony Award.

I also remember her coming over to my apartment and me telling her that I had a call back for *Master Class*. I was up for the classical pianist and I knew she'd be right for the soprano. I called the casting person and told him he had to see her. Of course, just like Leroy and his friend at the "Fame" audition, I didn't get cast and *she* won another Tony Award.

I also interviewed the fabulous Denis O'Hare. Turns out, when he was in college at Northwestern, he was studying opera! Who knew? He told me that he auditioned with a German art song and immediately forgot the lyrics. Thankfully, he covered up by making up nonsense German words. The song ended and one of the professors auditioning him stared and finally said, "You are aware that we all know the correct lyrics, right?"

Denis talked about his experience doing *Sweet Charity* on Broadway and shared one of his most horrific onstage experiences. He played Oscar opposite Christina Applegate's Charity, and at the end of Act One, they both get stuck in an elevator and he has a panic attack. Normally, he'd gesticulate a lot and get some great laughs. Well, one night he stopped getting laughs. *Why?*, he wondered. He started making bigger and bigger gestures. Nothing. Uncomfortable silence. Turns out, he had cut his hand at the beginning of the scene, and he was so into the scene that he didn't realize it. As soon as the audience saw the blood on his hand they stopped laughing. Then, when he started gesturing wildly, he didn't get the laughs he was trying for, but he did succeed in splattering blood all over the elevator, the front of his shirt, *and* Christina Applegate. Hence the audience's silence and terror.

All right, now it's a beautiful Sunday in Provincetown and I'm sitting on the deck of the Anchor Inn Beach House, looking out at Commercial Street. Charles Busch did his first show last night and it was so great.

When we were rehearsing he was talking to me about "not being a household name" and he remembered his aunt once telling him, "If I didn't know you, I wouldn't know you!" Charles began the show by remembering the time he visited Provincetown as a very, very young man with an older, sophisticated gentleman who taught him the ways of erotic love. Now that Charles is back in town, he decided to look up this former lover... until he did the math and realized the gentleman is now 102 years old. Charles said that he spent a brief moment considering contacting him, since everyone now says 102 is the new 90, but then decided not to disturb him.

His show was so diverse and fun-nee. He did a dramatic reading combining the posthumously published autobiographies of Bette Davis and Joan Crawford. Bette Davis recalled that Joan Crawford had three sizes of fake bosoms that she wore and "when we did that final scene on the beach, she wore her biggest one. I had to fall down on top of her and I nearly had the wind knocked out of me! It was like landing on two footballs." He read from Arlene Dahl's memoir and quoted the part where she asks various movie stars what they like in a woman. The movie stars she looks to for advice? Tony Perkins, Rock Hudson and Noel Coward! Literally a slew of gay men.

Charles also did a section as a character he created named Miriam Passman who was the predecessor to the character Linda Lavin played in his big Broadway play *The Tale of the Allergist's Wife*. Miriam is a French teacher in Westchester who is finally making her cabaret debut at Don't Tell Mama where she proudly proclaims her showtimes and they are always horrific ("Mondays...at 4:30")! She goes off on a tangent about her mother who wouldn't allow Miriam to pursue singing because she had another dream for Miriam; "That dream involved Teachers College." Miriam tells the audience that she's finally accepted that her mother could not express love. "Actually, that's not true. My mother loved her white-haired Persian cat, Princes Caroline. Princess Caroline was the most pampered, over-fed, indulged mean-spirited cat.... And that cat lived to be *29 years old!*"

Varla Jean Merman made a guest appearance in the show a la Ethel Merman appearing during Judy Garland's show. Varla suddenly appeared in the audience singing, "You don't need analyzing..." and claimed to be "down the hall filming the Red Skelton Show." Those being the exact words Ethel said when she "surprised" Judy Garland on her show. Varla (aka Jeff Roberson) wound up telling a true story onstage about the first play he ever did which happened to be Charles' big Off-Broadway hit, *Vampire Lesbians of Sodom*. Jeff said that when they began the run, his co-star had recently been arrested for drugs (!) so all of his costumes included a beautiful flowered wrap around his lower legs...to cover up his court-mandated ankle bracelet!

The brilliant Margaret Cho.

Speaking of drag, I also saw the brilliantly funny Margaret Cho do her show at the Art House and she told us that this year was the first time she did male drag. She played Kim Jong II on "30 Rock" (and got an Emmy nomination). She was horrified to find out how much she naturally looks like him. She said she didn't put anything on her face to change into him, she simply took *off* her make-up and the likeness was perfect. Her show was so incredibly funny. I can't print most of it, but she did do a hilarious section about Madonna being a lot older yet still trying to show "I still got it." Margaret said she watched that big dance Madonna did at the Super Bowl Halftime Show and thought, "Madonna... you should be doing those moves underwater." Amazing reference to senior pool aerobics.

And finally, what would summer be without lemonade? Juli has started selling homemade lemonade and her stand is doing phenomenally! It's also a beacon for Broadway performers. Literally within minutes both Andrea McArdle and Evan Pappas happened to walk by and bought some.

Peace out!

Close-Up at *Closer Than Ever*, Plus Megan Mullally, Kristine Zbornik
August 27, 2012

This week began with my sister and her family visiting from Virginia. On Monday night, we hauled it over to the East Side to see *Closer Than Ever* at the York Theatre's home at Lexington and 54th. First of all, the whole experience reminded me of being a kid… in the sense that I used to get cast recordings, memorize them within a year and *then* see the show. In this case, I got the cast recording for *Closer Than Ever* on cassette tape and listened to it on my signature Walkman for a whole summer. I memorized it as usual, but instead of seeing it within a year I wound up not seeing it until *23* years later! There was something so thrilling about finally getting to see the staging for something I had listened to again and again.

Anyhoo, I loved it. A lot of musical revues I've seen have actors that come off looking generic because there's no dialogue to solidify their characters. Or the actors come up with a lot of shtick to make themselves unique. In this production of *Closer Than Ever* everyone is so likeable without resorting to non-stop bits and each has a distinct, different energy (or "flava" as the kids say). After the show, I saw Richard Maltby, Jr., who wrote the lyrics and directed it and I complimented him on how great the staging was and how each actor was able to shine without pushing. He told me that he told the actors they each have an interesting story to tell and to remain modest. Hmm…it sounds like a combination of a screenwriting class and Parochial school, but it worked. During the show, I was sitting next to my 15-year-old niece, Eliana, and my sis Nancy was sitting in back of us with her husband. Throughout the show, Eliana and I kept hearing sniffing every ten minutes because Nancy kept holding back tears. I was totally right there with her, tears-wise. The tears in the eyes weren't because the songs are so sad, but because of the humanness of each one — plus the delicious harmonies!

By the end of the show, Nancy had an enormous crush on Sal Viviano, one of the actors. We went backstage and Nancy introduced herself with typical Rudetsky-no-boundaries-style. "Hi! I'm Seth's sister…" she said while shaking his hand, "and I think I totally want to marry you." *And* to add to the awkwardness of that comment, she remarked while gesturing to the person in back of her, "this is my husband Allan." Brava.

On Tuesday, I took Eliana to see *Bring It On* and I'm completely obsessed with Ryann Redmond's voice. Sass! *She performed in our Atlanta Concert For America and is now in her third original cast Broadway show!* On Wednesday, James and I saw the Shakespeare In the Park *Into The Woods* and I first have to say that it's so beautiful to be sitting in the middle of Central Park watching a show. You feel like you actually *are* in(to) the woods. Secondly, I was so proud of my friend Kristine Zbornik. Kris and I worked in Rose's Turn piano bar for years and we've done tons of comedy shows together. She plays Jack's mother and was such a stand-out. So funny and then so real in Act Two. Watching her I got my signature tears in ye olde eyes. Also, I'm now obsessed with Sarah Stiles. Brava on the Little Red Riding Hood comedy!

On Thursday, I high-tailed it up to Provincetown to do three (sold-out!) concerts with Megan Mullally for my *Broadway at the Art House* series. People think of Megan as a comedy actress only, but I first met her (almost 20 years ago!) when we did *Grease* on Broadway. She played Marty and I was the sub pianist. Or, as she said during our interview, "janitorial services." But before she was an actress and singer, she began as a ballet dancer! She was in a ballet company in Oklahoma City (as a soloist) and spent the summers studying at the School of American Ballet. This was during the time when ballet stars were celebrities. She remembers being in the ladies locker room and seeing Gelsey Kirkland constantly running in with smeared make-up and "crying about something Barishnikov did."

Megan's music teacher in high school discovered she had a good voice and asked her to perform for the students. She did "Don't Rain On My Parade," "People" and "Razzle Dazzle." Unfortunately, the only time everyone in the school assembled was for morning mass (it was an Episcopal school) so, as she described, she was "doing fan kicks inside a chapel and basically giving the principal a lap dance."

Cupping Megan Mullally.

All she wanted to do was go to NYC after high school, but her mom asked her to apply to one college. If she got in, she had to go. But if not, she could go to New York. Megan remembers sitting on the floor of her bedroom and putting no effort into writing a moronic college essay for Northwestern. She was then *outraged* to find out that she got accepted! After college she lived in Chicago and did a lot of theatre and grew her hair all the way down to her waist. She said there were many days on the Chicago T where she'd have to turn to the person next to her and say, "Excuse me, sir… you're sitting on my hair." She wanted to move to NYC but her boyfriend asked if they could try California for a month. She wound up getting a great agent right away and stayed. Her first big film audition was for the lead in "Risky Business." "Spoiler alert," she said, "I didn't get it." But then she auditioned for her first pilot and was cast on "The Ellen Burstyn Show" (1986-87). Her mom was played by Ellen Burstyn and her grandma by...Elaine Stritch! They wound up becoming friends and staying in touch since then. As a matter of fact, when Megan was in *Young Frankenstein* and got two tickets for opening night; she gave one to her husband and one to Elaine. Megan said that she was bowing onstage for an extended curtain call and when the curtain finally came down, Stritch was somehow standing onstage. Megan was giddy from the thrill of opening night and, of course, was still in full costume. Stritch hugged her and said in her signature voice, "Megan you were wonderful." One second pause. "The show is *horrendous*." Happy opening?

Megan first came to Broadway in 1994 because she had gone to college with Jeff Calhoun (the director of *Grease*). He asked her to try out and Megan reminded him that *Grease* takes place in high school and she was 34! He didn't care and she got cast as Marty. However, a few weeks into the run, they asked her to start understudying Rizzo (played by Rosie O'Donnell). Megan completely didn't want to because her mind doesn't work that way (learning new staging, reversing dance steps, etc…) but she had no choice. "Don't worry," Rosie told her, "I never get sick." Cut to: A few days later, Rosie gets laryngitis and is out for a week. The horrible part for Megan was listening to the intercom in her dressing room. She'd be getting into her Rizzo costume and hear "The role usually played by Rosie O'Donnell will be played by Megan Mullally." Megan remembers that the announcement was always followed by angry cries of "Son of a-!!!!!" mixed with "This *sucks*!" and then the sound of Playbills being flung on the floor and seatbacks flying up as people stormed out and demanded their money back.

After *Grease* opened, our friend Paul Castree told Megan she'd be perfect for the role of Rosemary in *How to Succeed in Business Without Really Trying*, so Megan tried out…and got it! She starred opposite Matthew Broderick, which was fun, but the bad part was that from the very first rehearsal people kept saying, "You're going to win a Tony for this!" The producers knew that Glenn Close was probably going to get the award for *Sunset Boulevard* and they wanted to give Megan a chance to win, so they took her out of the leading lady category and put her in "Best Featured Actress." Well, that was the year that

Smokey Joe's Café opened and *all* of those women got the featured nominations...so not only didn't Megan win a Tony Award, she wasn't even nominated!! *And* if she had stayed in the Leading Actress category, perhaps she wouldn't have won, but she would have at least been nominated because that year the *only* nominees were Glenn Close and Rebecca Luker! Literally two. Megan said that was the year she stopped caring about awards. It was so stressful that it wasn't worth it. Cut to: Years later she's doing "Will and Grace" and she was not thinking about the Emmy Awards at all. She was on vacation at a place with no internet and her agent called on her cell phone. He excitedly told her that she was nominated for an Emmy and because it wasn't on her radar she first thought he meant an award given by Emme, the plus-sized model! Seriously! Megan was like, "Really? I mean, I'm not a size zero, but I'm being nominated for being overweight!?!?!?" She realized it was the Emmy not Emme awards and then won...twice! *And now "Will And Grace" is back on the air!*

And now, as the song says, "See you in September!"

Michael McGrath at the *Chatterbox* and Alice Ripley in P-Town
September 4, 2012

Hello from Logan Airport. I just left Provincetown, and it is definitely the end of the season. The streets were hardly filled, one of my fave coffee places was closed, and the weather seemed to say, "Take care, summer. I'm out." Everywhere was chilly, grey and drizzly. It was essentially a live version of Christine Ebersole singing *Grey Garden*'s "Another Winter In A Summer Town" without the Tony Award.

I interviewed recent Tony Award winner Michael McGrath (*Nice Work If You Can Get It*) at the *Chatterbox* a few weeks ago. One of the crazy stories he told me involved doing *Grease*. He had played Doody many times back in the 80's, and one day he was in his house in Massachusetts and got a call from a director he worked with before. She told him that the guy playing Doody in her current production got injured, and she asked Michael if he could go on that night. He said yes. She then said the production was in *Wisconsin*. It was already mid-afternoon, so he raced like a lunatic to the airport, got a late afternoon flight, flew to the Midwest and when the plane landed, it was 7 PM!

However, Wisconsin's Fire Side Theater is so popular in the town that there was a police escort from the airport to get him there as fast as possible. There was also a dance captain sitting in the backseat to go over the show. Michael knew the lines, songs and dances, but the guy kept saying bizarre things like, "Enter at noon. Exit at 3 o'clock." *What*? Finally, Michael was informed that the show was being performed *in the round*! The actors knew where to enter and exit from by thinking of the stage as a big clock. Michael got to the theatre and there were thousands of people in the audience because it was a "star package," meaning the show had a headliner; Danny Zuko as played by *The Brady Bunch*'s Barry Williams. Thankfully, everything went fine. Except that no one warned Barry Williams that Michael usually adds a split leap over the head of Danny Zuko during "Hand Jive." So Barry came out of a crouch a little too fast, and the top of his head connected with the bottom of Michael's crotch. But, the good news is, the damage was apparently minimal because Michael still fathered a daughter.

I also got to do a show with Alice Ripley in Provincetown. We first talked about *Side Show*, and Alice said that she and Emily Skinner were side-by-side eight hours a day in rehearsal for weeks and that's why, no matter what, they'll always share a special closeness. However, eight hours a day, side-by-side, also resulted in a different end of the day than what Alice was used to. Usually, when rehearsals end in the late afternoon, Alice will hang out with her fellow actors. Instead, she and Emily were like, "It's 6 o'clock. *See 'ya!*" They needed severe breaks every night. Alice said they were both like, "I've been smelling your sweat all day long. Take care."

Speaking of closeness, she and Lea DeLaria shared a dressing room during *The Rocky Horror Show*. Lea played Dr. Scott/Eddie. And when Alice played Daisy Mae in *Li'l Abner* at Encores!, Lea played Marryin' Sam. Alice said that one day she came into the dressing room and gave Lea a kiss on the cheek and thought, "Wow! So smooth. Lea really got a close shave today." *Then* she thought, "Wait. Lea's not a man."

Speaking of which, when I was in Provincetown, I saw two amazing performers: Varla Jean Merman (Jeff Roberson) and Miss Ritchfield 1981 (Russ King). Varla did an amazing version of "Que Sera, Sera." The first verse was *(As Varla) When I was just a little girl. I asked my mother what will I be? Will I be pretty? Will I be rich? Here's what she said to me...*

(yelling as her mother) How the *hell* would I know? I'm not a psychic! (pause) Get me a vodka. (Then

back to her sweet singing voice.) *What will be, will be*.

Miss Ritchfield 1981 came out and immediately told everyone how happy she was to be in "Providence-town." Then she added, "I guess I love Maine!" She was so hilarious when she talked to the audience. She told one woman to stand up, and as soon as she did, Miss Ritchfield looked at her hair and said sympathetically, "I know...the humidity." Then she asked for single people in the audience to raise their hand. She found one named Jim from Staten Island who was retired, and she tried to set him up with another single in the audience named Matt. Matt wasn't interested because he said he didn't like people from New York. Miss Ritchfield then told him, "Well, you're in luck because most people don't consider Staten Island part of New York." Then she told Jim he was probably still single because he's picky. "Jim, face facts; you live on Staten Island, you're on a fixed income...my advice? Settle!"

Happy back-to-school!

Re-Playing *Chess* With Judy Kuhn in P-Town
September 10, 2012

I'm sitting on my deck at the lovely Anchor Inn Beach in Provincetown and there's a rainbow over the bay. So beautiful! Before I start writing about this week, there's a moment I forgot from last week that Juli insisted I print because she thought it was hilarious. On the second day of Alice Ripley's show at the Art House, Alice pointed out someone in the audience and introduced him. "Everyone! I'm very happy that in the audience is my very first boyfriend!" (applause) "...with his husband." Of course, everyone applauded more!

 Secondly, I forgot to write down another amazing Michael McGrath understudy story. His first big Broadway musical was *My Favorite Year* where he was in the ensemble and understudied the leading role ("Benjy Stone") played by Evan Pappas. Well, *right* after the show opened, Evan started to get sick. Of course, Michael hadn't had any rehearsal and he was so busy learning his own stuff that he hadn't worked on Benjy. He went home after the show knowing that he might very well have to go on the following night. He sat down with his wife (the fabulous Toni DiBuono from *Forbidden Broadway*) and started going through his lines while she held the script. They were there for a few hours and got to a scene that began with one of his lines. He was silent. She waited. Silence. Finally, Toni closed the book and told him, "You just don't know this part. I'm sorry but I have to go to bed." Michael wound up staying up by himself 'til around 6AM (!) reviewing everything and finally went to sleep. The next morning, the stage manager told him he was definitely on! Michael told us that the thing that saved him was being the fight captain, meaning he was in charge of keeping the sword fights correct. He thinks that if he didn't know the fight stuff, there would have been no way for him to go on. Cut to: He did the show and it went great! So great that at the end of the show, Michael prepared to do the regular bows in this order: the cast, then him and Tim Curry and then just Tim Curry. Well, when he was about to leave the stage to give Tim the solo bow, Tim grabbed his arm and told him to stay. Tim then got down on one knee, crossed his sword over his chest and presented Michael to the audience. Of course, Michael started crying when it happened...and then so did I when I heard the story!

Speaking of *My Favorite Year*, it also happened to be my first Broadway show. And I was also an understudy. I was the sub piano player for the regular pianist, the fantastic Joe Thalken. However, I only got to play it a few times because the run was so short, so I always call it *My Favorite Week*. Anybody? One of the other understudies of note was a young blonde who covered the romantic lead and whose regular part had her coming out during the show-within-a-show's commercial break. I can't remember her specific costume, but it was a giant letter or a peacock...something that covered her head so she was unrecognizable. Now she has two Tony Awards... Yes, it was Katie Finneran!

I kept insisting to Michael that Casey Nicholaw was also in the ensemble. He kept saying he wasn't. I kept saying he was. Someone then looked it up and found out he wasn't. Finally, I conceded and told Michael he was right. He said, "I am. And you know why? Because I was *in the show*!" Good point.

I'm here in Provincetown with Judy Kuhn, whose voice, composer/lyricist/conductor David Friedman told me, is "the healthiest on Broadway." It's true. It's clear as a bell and sounds exactly the same way it did when she starred in *Les Miz*. I asked her how she got her Equity card and she said she hadn't thought about that for a long time but remembered waiting in a lo-o-o-o-ong line during the winter for an audition for a Theaterworks production of *Rapunzel*. She said it was freezing and the line went down flights of stairs and down the block. She couldn't take it anymore and was about to leave when a friend walked by. They chitty-chatted for a while and suddenly Judy was much further on the line. She decided she might as well stay, so she read the audition scene, thought it was hilarious, auditioned, and got the gig *and* her Equity card. She often thinks, what would have happened if her friend didn't stop by? She then remembered auditioning for a show that asked for a high soprano excerpt so she sang the end of "My Lord and Master" from *The King and I*. It was one of those auditions where the door was open and everyone in the hall could hear. As she left the audition room, a woman stopped her and asked if that was her singing. Judy told her it was and the woman said they were looking for a new Tuptim understudy to do the national tour. She asked Judy to come in and sing for Yul Brynner. Judy came back the next day and got the gig! Again, she points to the arbitrariness of the business. If she hadn't sung "My Lord and Master" and that woman didn't eavesdrop from the hallway, then Judy wouldn't have gotten *The King and I*. I guess the message is to keep auditioning because everything leads to something else. P.S. It's not surprising that the *Rapunzel* script was so funny; it was written by David Krane and Marta Kauffman who then went on to create "Friends."

Judy and I also spoke about *Chess*, which I was lucky enough to see when I graduated college. Judy thinks the reason the show didn't work was because the set was so overwhelming and oftentimes didn't even function properly. Trevor Nunn wanted the show to be cinematic…meaning he wanted no blackouts and for people to be able to walk down hallways and then enter a room during a scene. Therefore, there were enormous columns onstage that moved all around and could create doors and walls, etc. Well, Judy told us that inside each column was actually a stagehand! He would have a compass (!) so he'd know where he was going and he'd move his column around the stage following cues from his headset. The headset had to be specially made to be able to work inside the columns and, unfortunately, they would often stop working. Judy said that in the middle of scenes people onstage would hear frantic knocking coming from inside a column and then a muffled voice yelling, "John! I'm out!" Someone would then come on the stage and push the column where it was supposed to go. Or sometimes, they'd be doing a scene and there'd just be a random column wandering around the stage, trying to find its place. At one point, Judy was doing a very serious scene with the late, great David Carroll, and out of the corner of her eye, she began to see an enormous column heading straight toward her. She kept signing and when the column got incredibly close, she kept going with her lines but thrust her arm out to the side and stopped it. Judy said that David Carroll was obsessed with the image of little tiny Judy Kuhn stopping a massive column with the flick of her arm. The stagehands were onstage all the time so they felt very connected to the actors. Judy said that for years she would walk through Shubert Alley and someone would run up with a big smile and a Brooklyn accent and say, "Judy! It's me! Tower three!"

From Varla's dressing room.

Judy and I were in Varla Jean Merman's old dressing room. I took a photo of what remained on his/her counter and sent it to Varla: Cough drops, hair spray, Listerine, Urine Destroyer and a withered old eyelash. Varla wrote back a frantic message: "That's not all mine! I never use Listerine." Brava!

This week James and I went to 54 Below, the cool club underneath Studio 54 and saw Marin Mazzie's new show. She invited the audience to the town she grew up in Rockford, IL (P.S., along with Joe Mantello, Paul Castree and Jodi Benson) and her song choices were all related to her childhood. I was especially obsessed with her acting on "That's the Way I've Always Heard It Should Be." So good! I decided that song is essentially Mother from Act Two of *Ragtime* transplanted to the 1970s. My favorite part of the show happened when she sang "Evergreen" and explained that she performed it in her Catholic High School during the "blessing of the class rings" ceremony. First of all, what? There's a special blessing for rings? Who's the patron saint? Liberace? Anyhoo, halfway through her 54 Below performance of the song, she stopped and explained that the following lyrics were a problem with Sister Ann Patrice (or SAP, as she admitted everyone called her). SAP thought "You and I will make each night a first. Every day a beginning..." was inappropriate. Marin tried to explain that it could easily pertain to her and Jesus, but SAP was unyielding. Therefore, when that section came, Marin switched from the lyrics to 16 counts of Barbra's signature humming, ooh-ing and ah-ing and then continued with the rest of the song. Marin demonstrated how she did it and told us, in her hilarious serious tone: "And a crisis...was averted."

Peace out.

Adam Chanler-Berat, Lance Bass, Varla Jean Merman Plus Seth TV, In Magical Colors
September 17, 2012

On Thursday, I went with my mom and my ex, Aaron, to go see the Actors Fund performance of *Book of Mormon*. It was hilarious as usual. During intermission I showed Aaron the Playbill, which had a big ad for Bloomingdale's that said "Starring" followed by lots of designers names like Michael Kors and Bill Blass. I pointed to the ad and told him the story I've mentioned before, "My mother saw this the last time we were at the theatre and was in a rage that all of these designers had the nerve to be starring in a new Broadway show." My mother then looked over and said in an annoyed tone, "Well, why *are* they starring in a show," yet again not realizing it was an ad for Bloomingdale's. At least her irritation with the world is consistent.

This week I interviewed Lance Bass on my SiriusXM radio show. He was in high school when Justin Timberlake's vocal coach recommended him to be a member of the newly forming group. Lance sang a lot in school in their show choir but never thought he'd have a singing career because he's a bass. He obviously never heard the original cast album of *Applause* starring Lauren Bacall. All the boys in 'N Sync are actually great musicians and, turns out, they never lip-synched in performance! So many pop performers do live concerts that are lip-synched even though they think they're tricking people by wearing a body mic right next to their mouths. Lance said that when they got popular they did tons of TV shows, but he felt they didn't officially make it until they were on "The Rosie O'Donnell Show."

I interviewed Adam Chanler-Berat at *Seth's Broadway Chatterbox*, and I asked him about his high school theatre experience. He told me that his teacher took him aside and told him, very seriously, "I can count on my hand the number of students I've felt could pursue theatre professionally." She then held up four fingers, keeping her pinkie folded down. She stared at him. "I can now add one more." Then, as she said, "Go for it!" she lifted her pinkie so all five fingers were extended. Comedy? Dramedy? You decide.

I will start the next section by going back many years. When I was 22, I was hired to be assistant music director on a new musical out of town. It was going to be at the Studio Arena Theater in Buffalo...in the winter! I knew it would be freezing, but it was one of my first job offers, so I was very excited. I met with the composer and music director, and the meeting was decidedly not fun. First, I mortified them because when I met the female composer, I did my signature, "Hi, sister." They were not amused at my casualness. Then I asked what kind of say I'd have as an assistant music director. The response? "Hopefully none." I was there to do what the music director, told me to do. The music director also warned me to call the theatre because they were notorious for taking advantage of musicians - I needed to make sure there weren't endless hours of rehearsal and there were definite breaks throughout rehearsal.

I called the number he gave me. Of course, I stammered when the phone was answered. "Hi..." I asked, nervously. "Are you the producer...guy?"

I then heard, angrily, "I am *the* producer."

Excellent. "Oh, great!" I continued. "I was just hired as the assistant music director. I wanted to ask about the rehearsal day."

Silence.

"How long is it?"

"We rehearse *until we are done*!" he responded, just as angrily.

The conversation didn't get much better and a few hours later I got a call from the music director. "Well, Seth," I was told, "you managed to offend a lot of people today!"

"What?" I asked. "You told me to call that guy and ask about breaks and rehearsal length!"

"You're fired!"

Oy! I was, of course, very depressed from the whole ordeal. Well, the years went by and I found out that the theatre went bankrupt. Yikes! It reopened on Friday night for the first time in four years with a new name: the 710 Main Theatre. Let me simply say it was a delicious feeling that the show chosen for their grand opening was *Seth's Big Fat Broadway*! That's right… two decades later, instead of sitting alone and depressed in my Brooklyn apartment after being fired, I was standing center stage in front of a sold-out 600 person audience!

And now, for my fellow Jews, Happy New Year!

Shields & Yarnell, Ann Hampton Callaway & Barbra, Michael Cerveris & *Tommy*
September 24, 2012

Wah! I'm on the flight home from Provincetown. This weekend was my last performance until New Year's Eve. James and I came up for the weekend with Juli to celebrate Juli's 12th birthday. We stayed at the lovely Grand View Inn, which was great because it had a giant freezer where we kept Juli's Ben and Jerry's ice cream cake. At the end of my show (where I deconstructed 1970s variety shows) the whole audience sang "Happy Birthday" and we served them ice cream cake and an enormous sheet cake, too. I recalled spending my 12th birthday at a depressing bowling party and was mildly resentful of Juli the entire time. Speaking of '70s variety shows, on Saturday afternoon a man came over to me and asked me what Shields and Yarnell clip I was planning on using in the show. I told him it was one from "The Sonny and Cher Show," where they're dressed up as Sonny and Cher. He then revealed that he was the director/choreographer for the "Shields and Yarnell Variety Show"! How random is that? He just happened to be in Provincetown at the same time as me. Or, should I say, the same *mime* as me. Anybody?

On *Seth Speaks*, I had the fabulous Ann Hampton Callaway who's performing her all-Barbra show at 54 Below and then touring it everywhere. She loves Barbra like I do, but unlike me she's actually written for her! Barbra heard some of Ann's songs and loved her lyric writing. Through her "people," Barbra asked Ann to put lyrics to a song that someone else had written the music for. Ann decided to write what she thought Barbra was feeling toward her then-fiancé James Brolin. Barbra loved the lyrics and asked Ann to make a recording of the piano part because she was having a "gathering" in a few days. Turns out, Barbra wanted a recording of the piano track so she could sing along with it. Why? Because the "gathering" she was having was actually her *wedding*! That's right…it randomly worked out that Ann happened to write a song about Barbra and James Brolin and then happened to finish it two days before their wedding. Barbra told her later, "It's lucky you wound up singing it in my key!"

I also interviewed Bob Fass on *Seth Speaks*. Bob is a fascinating guy who's the focus of the new documentary "Radio Unnamable," playing at Film Forum in Manhattan. Back in the early '60s, he asked WBAI if he could have a radio show that started at midnight and lasted through the night. They told him that there was nothing on TV or radio during those times because nobody was awake. He told them that there is actually a whole bunch of people all around the city doing the night shift! They gave him a show…which then lasted for 40 years! The documentary features actual recordings from his shows because he saved them all. And they're really amazing. There's one with his buddy Bob Dylan (!) and one day he also had Arlo Guthrie come on and debut his new song called…"Alice's Restaurant"! He was the predecessor of so many radio shows (including mine) because he didn't want his show to have any particular style. He played whatever music he wanted. He was the first to have live phone calls from people. Plus, he didn't have a call screener. He just answered the phone. Scarily, one of the calls was from a man who wanted to commit suicide. As they spoke, Bob found out the guy had already taken a ton of pills and was in the process of falling asleep. This happened in the days when tracing a phone call took *hours* and the tracing itself could only pinpoint a certain area of town. Bob kept the guy on the phone the whole time and after a few hours, the guy fell asleep. You can actually hear him deep breathing on the air. Bob kept yelling his name to wake him up but the sleep was drugged so he couldn't be awakened. Finally, the call was traced but there was no way to know exactly where the guy lived, so Bob put a record on the radio at a crazily high volume so it'd be heard through the guy's apartment door! The police were then able to find him, the man was saved… and he wound up getting a job writing sexy letters for Penthouse. I was shocked! Not because the man's life was saved, but because I always thought those letters were real. Not cool.

My guest at the *Chatterbox* was Michael Cerveris and we went back to his first big break, which was playing the title role in the La Jolla Playhouse production of *Tommy*. Well, when the show was going to Broadway all of the cast members had to audition again. Rude. Michael felt a lot of stress about the audition, and, on top of that, he had a cold. He was living in L.A. and the producers agreed to fly him to NYC for the audition but, probably to save money, they got him a flight that was actually going to San Juan but had a layover in New York. When Michael got to the airport he told them that he would be leaving the plane in New York and they told him that he would be allowed to do that, but his luggage would have to go to San Juan! It was a Sunday and he tried to track down the people who bought him the ticket but he was only able to reach Des McAnuff who told him to buy a new ticket and he'd get reimbursed. Michael finally got a flight, but it left *much* later. So, he arrived in New York with a cold *and* completely exhausted. He stayed at the music director's apartment but found out when he arrived that there were cats and he's allergic. So, the next day he was exhausted with a cold *and* severe allergies. He started the audition by playing for himself on guitar and after two songs they asked him to sing from the show. Well, by the time he got to the second song ("I'm a Sensation") he had no voice left. At all. The creative staff had seen him play Tommy of town, so they knew how he could sing, but there were lots of producers there who hadn't seen him and were decidedly not impressed.

Michael resigned himself to not getting the role and a few days later Des and Pete Townshend asked him out to dinner which Michael assumed was a consolation prize. It wasn't until way into the dinner that Pete said casually, "It's so funny that we saw hundreds of people for this show and the one person who gave the worst audition of all is getting the title role." It wasn't until that moment that Michael then realized it wasn't a consolation dinner, it was a congratulations dinner! He starred in *Tommy* on Broadway and then starred in the German company for a long run. The biggest adjustment for Michael in Europe was getting used to the crew in Dusseldorf. Michael said the crew people weren't trained like in New York. They were just guys who applied for a job in a variety of places (restaurants, factories) and the one they happened to get was at the new theatre being built for *Tommy*. They had to be firmly told that since they were in charge of dangerous things like making sure Michael was flown on and off the stage safely, they must promise to not be stoned before *or* during the show. On top of that, they weren't versed in musical theatre...at all. During the first run-through, the girl playing Sally Simpson had to run backstage really quickly to get to the other side. She wound up banging into a stagehand who was standing in the way. The guy was told not to stand there because Sally had to make a quick cross. The next night she ran backstage again and...slammed into the same guy again! Why? Well, he was told the night before not to stand there so he moved. The night before. He wasn't informed that he couldn't stand there the next day. In other words, he had no idea that the show stayed the same each night!

This week I'm doing a show with Andrea Martin and, as you know, we're always talking about our mutual obsession with food. She recently texted me about a Food Inspection Grade she was ignoring. "Even the airport bakery's Grade C (i.e. rats) won't stop me from getting a croissant." Brava! Happy fall and peace out.

Carol Burnett Brings Seth to Tears
October 1, 2012

Hello from my Atlanta to NYC flight. I just came from Knoxville, TN, and since flights to New York are not direct on weekends, I had the privilege of flying *further* South before I fly back to NYC. Yay! It's fun for the second part of my trip home from Tennessee to be longer than it would have been had I simply flown direct. Anyhoo, so much has happened this week. First of all, I was offered a part on "Smash"!!!! That's right! *Offered*! No audition. I'm "offer only" from now on. And I mean "offer only" as in: I'll "only" get one offer. Regardless, the last time I was offered "Smash" it was a role with one line: the curtain came down on a show and I would be in the audience and say, "That's it?" Well, I had jury duty on the day I was supposed to film so I couldn't do it. Now, I have 200 per cent more lines! That's right, this role has *three* lines! And, I'm not certain how SAG/AFTRA defines a line, but if "Tom! Tom!" counts as two lines, than I have four total! The extra-cool thing is I'm playing...Seth Rudetsky! Literally. At one point, someone points and says, "Karen is talking with Seth Rudetsky!" Of course, it seems obvious that they would cast me as Seth Rudetsky, but let's go back to the mid-'90s; My friend Marco Pennette created "Caroline in the City" and came to see my weekly piano bar gig at Rose's Turn. He then told me he was going to write an episode featuring a pianist who works at Rose's Turn...named Seth Rudetsky! Yay! A part tailor-made for me. Hmm...not really. Not only did I not play the role but I was also not even asked to audition for it. It was the opposite of "offer only." Something I like to call "rejection completely." P.S., I know it seems like a joke, but look it up! The role of "Seth Rudetsky" was played by Dan Futterman! I guess they decided they just needed someone with an equally headache-y last name. Well, I finally get to debut as myself and will fill you in on details next week.

Last week, on *Seth Speaks*, I interviewed Dean Pitchford. The first knowledge of him that I had was when I saw, and LOVED, the film "Fame" (he wrote the lyrics). Turns out, he began as an actor and stood by for the role of Pippin and eventually took over during the original production! I asked him about that amazing full orchestra, and he remembered it so distinctly because he was barefoot for the whole show and the stage had a section that was directly over the pit. He said he loved feeling the deep vibrations from the musicians right through the floor and up through his feet! He played the title role opposite Betty Buckley and they've remained friends ever since. As a matter of fact, she was his date for the Oscars. He remembered a time in the '70s when they were both in a cab and someone asked him how old he was. Dean said he had to think for a minute because he was always saying he was younger than he actually was. Betty looked at him seriously and asked, "Is there anything you've done that you're ashamed of?" He thought about it and said no. Then she said, "Then why would you not tell your age? You should be proud of every year you've been alive!" Ever since then, he's always 'fessed up. I love that a woman in show business was the one that convinced him to be proud of his age. He said that Betty was a feminist from the very beginning and I remember her telling me she was a charter subscriber of "Ms." Brava! Or should I say Brav-(gender-neutral vowel).

As for his songwriting career, Dean said that he started writing with Michael Gore who was the music supervisor for "Fame." Michael wasn't hired as the composer, but he could submit anything to the director (Alan Parker) to see if he liked it. So when Michael found out the inside scoop that the title of the film was being changed from "Hot Lunch" to "Fame," he called Dean. They wrote a song together and Michael was able to submit something that just happened to have the exact same title as the film! I asked Dean about the final song in the film ("I Sing The Body Electric"). The director wanted something that encompassed all the different art forms that the Performing Arts school taught; Acting, singing, choral, dancing, rock and classical. Dean thought about the first lyric and decided that since it was graduation, the character of Bruno would base the song on a poem he studied in English class. Dean thought that since it was high school, they probably studied American poetry. Dean then decided that "I Sing the Body Electric" was perfect because it had "sing" for singing, "body" for dance and "electric" because Bruno was into pop music. P.S. The first solo is sung by Laura Dean and she sounds so stunning!

Speaking of Laura Dean (who played Sue, the nice girl, in the workshop of *Carrie* by Dean and Michael Gore), we discussed his ill-fated thriller musical and where it went wrong. Pitchford said that the contract they signed with the Royal Shakespeare Company (who produced it) stipulated that the writers would not be allowed at rehearsal. Hence, they didn't know how the show was being directed. I'm sure it was a "pleasant" surprise when they saw that the high school students wore gym outfits that looked like white togas. What was even more horrible is the way it all ended; the show opened to not great reviews but the cast was called in for a talk from the main investor/producer. He told them the show would remain open and they would get past the negative reviews. Yay! Everyone was overjoyed. The investor/producer then left in his limo, told his business manager to close his bank accounts and flew back to Germany! Not only did the show close right away but no one was paid! Fast-forward to 2012 and a revised *Carrie* revival, Off-Broadway that's now being done all over the place.

Last week was very exciting because a new DVD came out featuring tons of episodes from the original "Carol Burnett Show." I was scheduled to talk with Carol, Vicki Lawrence and Tim Conway on *Seth Speaks*, but first they were booked for a special show where lucky SiriusXM viewers got to come in and ask them questions. The cast was in the large studio that has enormous glass windows and there were listeners inside and crowded into the lobby as well. James came with me because he also grew up obsessed with the show, and we stood in the lobby and listened to comedienne Amy Schumer interview them. *I remember Amy saying that she was about to get her own TV show. Boy, did she hit it big right after this!* I was hoping to entice Carol and Vicki to sing something when I interviewed them and Amy must have been told to see if they'd be willing to sing. Unfortunately, she was told to do it during her show! So, as I was watching the interview in the lobby through the glass windows, I heard Amy mention to Carol and Vicki that there was a piano behind her. Carol and Vicki acknowledged seeing it. Then Amy asked if they'd be willing to sing. Carol and Vicki both asked who would play the piano. Amy told them that the producer didn't quite tell her that part. There was a pause and I turned to James and asked, "What should I do? Should I run in there?" Two seconds later, I pushed past the crowd, went into the studio, hit a starting pitch and started playing "I'm So Glad We've Had This Time Together." Carol and Vicki joined in and it was fabulous.

Well, as they were walking out, I was semi-freaking out because I grew up loving that show so much and couldn't believe I was finally going to get to meet them all. First, though, they had to go to another interview. Carol came up to me and thanked me for playing and asked my name. I said "Seth" and another producer told her that she was going to be on my show later that afternoon. Suddenly, her face lit up and she said, "Seth!?!?! Oh! I listen to your show all the time!" I could *not* believe she knew who I was. Of course, tears immediately came to my eyes because I was so happy. Who would have thought when I was a little boy on Long Island watching her show (I was 11 when it went off the air), I would one day meet her and she would tell me she listened to *my* show!?!?! All three of them then sat down with me for a chitty-chat and, of course, right after my initial question Tim Conway asked if he was also required to speak that fast. Hmph. Carol revealed that the biggest compliment she can get is when people tell her that they watched her show as a family...with their parents or grandparents. And, P.S., that's exactly what James told her. Hers is the show that always reminds him of his grandfather because they watched it together. I asked her about doing *Once Upon a Mattress* and she said that when the show closed Off-Broadway the entire cast picketed in front of their theatre (in full costume) looking for a new venue. They moved to Broadway and went from the Alvin to the Cort to the St. James to the Winter

Garden. She said that Neil Simon quipped, "Have you seen *Once Upon a Mattress*? Don't worry. It'll soon be coming to a theatre near you." I brought up the character of Eunice, and Carol, as usual, mentioned that the "Family" sketches were her favorites. I told Tim that I loved how he always spoke to "Mother Harper" like she was deaf, and I told Carol and Vicki how obsessed James, Juli and I are with the sketch where they play "Sorry." Suddenly Carol and Vicki immediately recreated it for me on the air. Carol went into her character voice and screamed: "*It was a seve-e-e-e-e-e-e-en!!!!!*" Then Vicki, as Mama, said calmly "Eunice seems to be of the opinion that it was a seven. So I will just move the yellow man back seven spaces, then I will move my blue man ahead seven spaces...landing on your green man sending him back to start. *Sorry*!!!!"

And now, peace out and Happy October!

Seth Gets "Smash"-ed; Audra McDonald and Will Swenson Get Hitched
October 8, 2012

This week started with me filming "Smash" for NBC!

First, I was so happy it was being filmed right here in Manhattan instead of Astoria, Queens where lots of TV shows are shot. I'm notoriously lazy and hate traveling out of my neighborhood for anything. Anyhoo, the episode takes place at the opening of *Liaisons*, the musical version of *Les Liaisons Dangereuses*. I got the script on Thursday and memorized my lines in the same amount of time it took to speak them: 10 seconds.

My fancy trailer!

When I got to the set, it was a combination of being treated like a guest star (here's your personal camper!) and like a glorified extra (bring your own clothes). The camper (they don't call them trailers) was parked on Broadway right outside the Letterman theatre. When I walked up, I saw the name "Seth" on the door. The PA who greeted me told me that she had first written my character name on the door, which she didn't realize was also my actual name. Apparently, people walking down the street recognized it, and she decided to get rid of the "Rudetsky," obviously to prevent a crowd of rabid fans from forming. P.S. I looked up the definition of crowd, and it says "a large group of people"; I say two to three people is large. My camper was great with a TV, sound system and a mystifying bathroom. I say mystifying because I drank a lot of iced coffee and used the toilet but then had *no idea* how to flush it. I spent an inordinate amount of time walking around the bathroom thinking that various light switches would flush the toilet. *Finally*, I saw there was a foot pump underneath (!) that flushed it. What a fun way to spend my time before filming!

Anyhoo, since the episode was about the opening of *Liaisons*, it was filmed at the Broadway Theatre, which has been empty since *Sister Act* closed. I had heard I was filming the scene with someone name "Cat," and I thought it was Cat Deely from "So You Think You Can Dance," but turns out it's the nickname for Katharine McPhee! Who knew? I guess it's spelled "Kat." I went over to the theatre and when I got there, I was delighted to see that Casey Nicholaw was the director! I met Casey in 1986 (!) when I was a 19-year-old music intern at The Equity Library Theater, and he was in the chorus. Since I was playing myself, I asked if I could make the lines more in my style. He said yes, and I made some changes including turning "Can we talk off the record?" into "Can you give me some inside scoop?" as well as shoe-horning in the word "a-mazhing." Yes, that old chestnut. Not since Carol Burnett's Tarzan yell. The other actor in the scene was Christian Borle, who I've known forever, so I was very relaxed when we rehearsed. We ran the lines and went to do hair and makeup and to get into our costumes... or more accurately stay in my own clothes.

The really fun part was when the PA asked me what I wanted for breakfast, and I was able to give her an order for the on-set chef! Mmm...delicious! Well, I'm on a diet, so let's just say, mmm...egg whites. After a half hour, the PA told me they were ready to film, and when we walked back to the theatre, there were a ton of extras dressed in their opening-night finery. I stood in the lobby of the Broadway Theatre, which was glammed up to look like a big Broadway opening and saw a pile of souvenir programs for *Liaisons*. The cover photo had the cast (including Sean Hayes and Megan Hilty) in full period hair and make-up, and I was excited to open it and read the mock bios. However, once I turned past the amazing cover photo, I saw that the inside stayed what it originally was: a full issue of *Us*! TV trickery! I had my mic put on, got powdered down a little, and we started to film the scene. Suddenly, I was nervous! For the first few takes, my body was having its signature physical reaction: left leg shaking. Hopefully, the final version won't look like I'm nervous but simply that I'm going through a severe drug detox.

The middle of the week involved a fun *Seth Speaks* with Andrea Martin and Michael Urie. Andrea Martin was there to promote Gilda's Club for which she's done a lot of fundraisers. If you don't know, Andrea Martin first met Gilda Radner when they both starred in the Toronto production of *Godspell*. In the 80s, Gilda passed away from Ovarian cancer and now Gilda's Club is a great organization that helps not only people with cancer but any of their friends and family. James and Juli got so much help there when James' mom had cancer, and I highly recommend it for their programs, chat groups or to simply stop by and relax in their library.

Finally, Michael Urie came on and we chatted about when Bernadette Peters was a guest star on "Ugly Betty" (I'm sure she wasn't asked to bring her own outfit). Michael had racked his brains trying to figure out a way to talk to her. Finally, he approached and told her he was thinking of getting a dog, which, he informed us, was a complete lie. The next day, however, she showed up with two dogs so he could choose which one he wanted! Busted! He picked one he named "Sprouts," and now he travels with him back and forth from L.A.! I love that Bernadette took his (faked) interest in getting a dog and took it 1,000 steps further by bringing two actual doggies to the set! He had no choice but to adopt one. In improv terms, she "Yes and'd" him to the 10th power.

At Audra and Will's beautiful wedding.

On Saturday I hiked it upstate to Audra McDonald and Will Swenson's house for their wedding. The wedding was outside and Audra kept sending Facebook messages to the invitees warning us that there would be tons of mud. Of course, I went into a panic and opted for dark jeans and black boots. Cut to her version of a "dress for mud" outfit was a stunning white dress. Yes, her backyard was dry as a bone and we decided her "dress for mud" messages were simply so we'd all look horrible and she'd look stunning. When I confronted her with my theory, she claimed that the backyard had been very muddy and that certain areas still were. She then pointed out a one-inch patch of moist dirt. When I asked her why she was allowed to look gorgeous and I was in seven-year-old boots, she lifted up her dress to reveal her shoes, which were indeed rickety-rackety mules. Regardless, the ceremony was beautiful, and she and Will read their own vows which were so moving and talked about their love and their promise of loving each other's children. Speaking of children, Will's sons (Bridger and Sawyer) and Audra's daughter (Zoe) sang an amazing version of "All You Need Is Love" with Zoe soloing on the alto sax! Then four friends who were in *Hair* (with Will) did a gorgeous arrangement of two folk songs, and I immediately booked them to do it on *Seth Speaks*. *No joke: it never happened because of scheduling issues and this just reminded me I have to book them ASAP.* Afterwards, all the guests went to an outdoor tent for delish food. Andy Gale made a great toast and at one point asked, "Does anybody remember the film 'The Best Years Of Our Lives'?" I thought, "Boy...that's a really old film," and right at the moment I heard someone say, "I do!" Not surprisingly, it was Zoe Caldwell (age 79).

Speaking of Broadway stars, I saw Lonny Price before the meal and he told us the wedding cake was delicious! How did he know since it hadn't been served yet? Well, turns out the so-called wedding cake was created by Zac Young, a "Top Chef Desserts" winner and was, in actuality, an enormous structure of donuts. Lonny thought they were put out for noshing before the ceremony and grabbed one as soon as he arrived. It wasn't until after he was halfway through scarfing one down that someone told him he was eating the first slice of wedding cake. Speaking of Lonny, he gave a great toast and joked that Audra had broken up with him in order to marry Will. He pointed to himself and then to Will (who's from Utah) and said, "She could have had *Fiddler on the Roof* but instead she chose *Book of Mormon*."

Peace out!

Apple Picking With Audra, and Making 'Em Laugh With Andrea Martin at 54 Below
October 15, 2012

This week always reminds me of *Kiss of the Spider Woman*. Why? Because my niece Rachel Sarah's birthday is on Oct. 15, and when my sister first started contractions, I was playing keyboard in the *Spider Woman* orchestra. That was 17 years ago! Yowza! I remember calling the hospital room during intermission and talking to her husband, Allan. Nancy was in labor and I could hear her caterwauling in the background. Allan told me to check in later because she was about to get an epidural. I called back after the second act and, because of the epidural, the contrast was *crazy*; Nancy picked up after one ring and not only was there no more screeching and screaming, I simply heard a calm "Yello?" Huh? Was this the same Nancy who was bellowing an hour before? I said a tentative, "Nan?" She responded with a matter-of-fact, "Yep. What's up?" I guess "epidural" is code for Xanax.

This week began with a trip upstate along with James, Juli and Audra McDonald, plus family, to go apple picking. It brings up the philosophical question: if you go to pick apples and there are no apples, are you still apple picking? The orchard was basically barren! Not since Anatevka. Apparently the weather was too warm this summer for apples (thank you to people in denial about global warming) *and* the apples that happened to grow were snatched up by families who got there earlier than us. We finally were able to scrounge up a few apples but every time I picked one up, I found myself doing the same face and gesture Mary Tyler Moore makes during the opening "Mary Tyler Moore Show" credits when she picks up that package of meat.

On Tuesday I did the first of three shows with Andrea Martin at 54 Below and performed a section where she told the audience why she had to cancel her shows back in June. The publicist sent out a release saying she had bronchitis but that's because no one really knew what was wrong. Remember when I told you her jaw hurt because she was grinding her teeth? Well, it took nine days at Lenox Hill (!) and a four-hour surgery to discover that she had a strep infection that led to another infection deep inside her throat that had to be taken out. Thankfully, she's completely fine now but the whole thing was nerve-wracking...and hilarious. She told the audience about having to take various MRI's. "If it hadn't been for the years of meditation technique, I don't think I would have survived it. I kept breathing calmly, counting, thinking of my sons and how grateful I am....and occasionally why Katie Finneran got the part of Miss Hannigan and not me." The audience loved it! P.S. Andrea wrote a hilarious email during this time period and after she described the MRI she wrote, "When I finally was taken off the table, I said to the technician that the procedure was torture, and he replied, 'I'll tell you what torture is, having dinner with my son.'" Dr. Borscht Belt? Andrea also shared with the audience that Debra Monk was with her every step of the way and when Andrea was heading into surgery Deb held her hand and whispered, "I'm cancelling everything tomorrow to be with you." Andrea said that she suddenly snapped out of her drugged state to angrily ask, "What the hell do you have planned for tomorrow?" Andrea then shared: "Deb showed me her calendar, and sure enough she had cancelled her walk."

This all led to a song that Scott Wittman and Marc Shaiman wrote for her a few days before the concert. The premise was that after the hospital experience, she re-examined her priorities and called her agent to tell him that she no longer wants to do comedy parts. She told him she wants to show her dramatic chops. This is supposedly the conversation between Andrea and her agent. (Sung to the tune of "Make 'Em Laugh"):

BE A CLOWN! BE A CLOWN!
DON'T YOU KNOW ALL THE WORLD LOVES A CLOWN?

I SAY MY "BLANCHE" WOULD CAUSE 'EM TO WEEP
HE SAYS "YOU AIN'T MERYL STREEP!"
GIVE ME SHAW! GIVE ME INGE
HE SAYS "DO YOU WANT BRANTLEY TO CRINGE?"
MY HECUBA WOULD LEAVE THE PUBLIC GASPING FOR BREATH
I TELL HIM I COULD REALLY SCORE AS LADY MACBETH
HE SAYS HE'D RATHER SEE THAT PART IF IT'S PLAYED BY SETH
BE A CLOWN, BE A CLOWN, BE A CLOWN....

Hilarious!

So much of Andrea's show has amazing videos: slides of the original Toronto Cast of *Godspell* (Victor Garber, Gilda Radner, Eugene Levy, and Paul Shaffer), her first headshots, videos of her first commercial, her amazing appearance on Johnny Carson, etc. Well, in the middle of the first show, the computer crashed! Nothing! Of course, there was an hour left to the show and we couldn't leave the stage. Andrea just kept going and simply described things ("Here's the part where I show a picture of me in "My Big Fat Greek Wedding" as a 45-year-old Greek woman... then I show a picture of me at my senior prom *looking* like a 45-year-old Greek woman"). It was like a workshop performance of the show. But, because it was so spontaneous, the audience loved it!! The last show had Victor Garber, Deb Monk, Nathan Lane, Shaiman and Wittman, Brooks Ashmanskas and Christopher Fitzgerald in the audience. Essentially, if 54 Below had blown up, Broadway would only be able to do straight plays for the next two years.

I had the cast from the current *Forbidden Broadway* (Natalie Charlé Ellis, Scott Richard Foster, Jenny Lee Stern and Marcus Stevens) at *Seth's Broadway Chatterbox* and they were *so* funny. Before any singing, however, I confronted Natalie on her middle name "Charlé." Literally with an *accent aigu* over the e. Turns out, her mom named her "Charle" after her grandfather (pronounced like "Charles" without the S) and Natalie always hated it. But when she was doing a beauty pageant as a 'tween, the announcer read her name wrong and called her "Charl-ay." Voila! Thus her middle name became a tip o' the hat for people who change "Target" to "Tar-jay." The other woman in the show, Jenny Lee Stern, is super-funny. When she told me that she and her husband (Broadway's Jeremy Kushnier) have two kids, I asked her, "How do you stay so thin?" She immediately answered, "Drinking and anorexia." She then followed that with "Hey, if it ain't broke...it's a tried and true combination." Brava!

On *Seth Speaks* I had Jeffrey Roberson (aka Varla Jean Merman) who's starring in Carlo Menotti's *The Medium* which is opening at the Marjorie S. Deane Little Theater near Lincoln Center. Jeff told me, "My character is a medium who has a daughter and is also a conniving, drunken scam artist." He sighed. "It's a hard role for me to play...'cause I don't have children."

I also had Joey Mazzarino who's been the head writer on "Sesame Street" since 2009. He's also married to the fabulous Kerry Butler. I asked him what it was like being married to a Broadway star and he laughed and recalled being in Toronto when Kerry was opening as Belle in *Beauty and the Beast*. Joey saw all the Disney top brass at the after-party and he felt very cool and like an insider. As a photo was about to be taken of everyone, the photographer walked over to Joey and asked, "Can you step out of the photo, please, Mr. Butler?" Joey was obsessed with the double bust: not only "step out of the photo," but "Mr. Butler."

Peace out!

Wedding Bells for Seth and James
October 22, 2012

Our honeymoon in Portland!

It's official! James and I got married last week and it was *amazing*. Before wedding details, I thought I'd give a little history first. James and I met almost six years ago after my long-term relationship had ended. Right after the break-up, I immediately joined every single dating site possible (Match.com, Jdate.com, OKcupid.com, DesperateAndAging.com, etc...). I had been off the dating market for ten years and planned on spending the next year making up for it. I couldn't wait to have non-stop dates with all different people and was elated when I got an email from DJ Salisbury (a sassy director and choreographer) who wrote that he had seen my dating profile on Match.com and recognized my name from "the business." He then invited me to a game night for singles! I love games (and was lookin' for singles!) so I immediately said yes. It was at a Chelsea restaurant and there were around eight other guys there. Frankly, I was interested in every single one and planned on asking them all out (see DesperateAndAging.com).

Meanwhile, unbeknownst to me, James had just moved back to NYC from Texas with his recently adopted daughter. He was raising her as a single dad. Since it was Christmas time, his mom was visiting, and that allowed him to have a much-needed night out at a movie. Afterwards he stopped by the game night just as we started playing "Apples to Apples," a game where everyone has cards that contain lots of different random nouns, like "The First Day of School," "Madonna" or "The Cold War." Then one person who's the main player for that round puts down an adjective like "Ugly" or "Distressing" and everyone else puts down the card from their hand they think most describes that adjective. The main player then chooses one card he thinks is the most appropriate adjective. The adjective James put down was "important" and I chose the card from my hand that said "Israel." James looked through all the nouns in the pile and rejected mine. I immediately said, "Who's the anti-Semite that just joined the game?" Of course, that *could* have upset him, but instead he laughed. Brava for getting my (alienating) sense of humor! After the game, he mentioned that he had a daughter and I recommended that they come on the R Family Cruise for gay parents and their kids. Five days later, on New Year's Eve, I emailed him and asked if he had looked into the cruise. He wrote me back a really nice four-paragraph email, and since I was in a very "I'm-going-to-date-everybody" period, I asked him out. At that point, I just assumed he'd be one of the many, many people I'd be dating that year.

We met at Café LaFortuna on West 71st Street and when he walked in, he was carrying a book on how to be more proactive promoting social justice. Uh-oh. Tugging at my liberal heart strings. I refused to be too interested because I had a year of playing the field to look forward to. We had a very nice time and that night he wrote me *another* very sweet email. Later on, my mom called me and told me that she couldn't come into the city the next day to see the *Les Miz* matinee like we had planned. I knew James loved Broadway and would want to go, but thought it was too soon to see him again. Finally, I ignored the age-old advice I've read in numerous Cosmo articles ("Do You Like Him? Then Don't Call For At Least 24 Hours!") and invited him to *Les Miz*. Afterwards, I took him backstage and Norm Lewis (who was playing Javert) kept giving me eyes with the subtext of "Brava on the new boyfriend!" I kept glaring back, trying to convey "Cut! He is not my boyfriend. He is one of *many* boyfriends I plan on having for the next

12 months!" James and I had two more dates, and soon I was a combination of elated and devastated. Elated because I knew I found someone I knew I wanted to be with forever and devastated because I never got my year of starring in *The Best Little Whorehouse on the Upper West Side*.

A few years later, we got engaged but wanted to wait until it was legal in NYC. When it finally became legal, our ADD set in and we could not figure when to have the wedding. We were completely overwhelmed by the planning, even with the simplest of what date to get married; First night we met? First official date? Date we got engaged? Finally, while eating breakfast at Fairway, a couple of weeks ago, James suggested we just do it at City Hall ASAP and go right to the honeymoon. I checked my calendar for a four-day period I'd have free and we decided we'd get married on Monday, Oct. 15 and then take a honeymoon through Thursday night. On Monday we got up super early and we both played out our most annoying aspects. First, we headed down to City Hall...45 minutes later than we planned on leaving. Then, when we got there, I told James to go ahead without me and get on line at the marriage bureau with Juli because I had something very important to do: order a grande iced soy latte at Starbucks. Of course, when James got to the head of the line at the marriage bureau I was nowhere to be found and the man at the check-in counter was having a fit. Apparently, for some strange reason, in order to for two people to get married, both people have to be there.

Finally, I sauntered over with my iced latte and tried to avoid the obvious second thoughts that were clearly readable in James' eyes. Then as we waited to go into the marriage room, James went into a panic because he couldn't find the marriage vows he had written the night before. I tried to force myself not to say, "You constantly, constantly, *constantly* lose things," and succeeded. But I couldn't help a few involuntary eye-rolls and judgmental shakes of my head. Hopefully, he thought they were cute. After around 20 minutes we got called into the room for the ceremony and, typical me, I decided to take that opportunity to look for someone to videotape the ceremony. That's right, I waited until the moment the ceremony was about to begin to figure out how to get it videotaped. I asked random people in the waiting room and no one was available. James was standing with everyone in the room and suddenly looked around and realized his groom wasn't there. I, yet again sauntered in (this time without coffee), and gave my iPhone to James' mother who volunteered to videotape. Unfortunately, she turned it on right away and the video caught the "charming" comment from James about where I had been and then my defiant justification. Let's just say, I'm glad videos can be edited.

Regardless, the ceremony was so great and both James and I were in tears during our vows. Afterwards, we took photos in front of the amazing/tacky backdrop they have of city hall and then we hightailed it to breakfast. We sent Juli to school (chaperoned by James' mom) and my mom went back to Long Island. James and I hopped in a cab to JFK and flew right to Portland, ME. We chose that city because it's a short flight and we love the ocean and bed-and-breakfasts. Unfortunately, we didn't realize it's pretty much a summer community. Every day, we'd hear about a place that sounded great, drive an hour to get there and then arrive to see a sign that said, "Thanks for a great season! See you April 4th!" Still, had a fantastic time and did non-stop laughing. The most frustrating thing was the natural disaster that occurred. If you know me, you know that I grew up obsessed with tornados/tsunamis/earthquakes, etc. I've always wanted to experience one...without any of the death/injuries or destruction.

So, last Tuesday we decided to go to a highly recommended (and basically deserted) coffee place. We planned on having dinner at our bed and breakfast at 7:30 but at the last minute postponed it to 8 o'clock. We got back to the bed and breakfast for dinner and found out that Portland had just experienced an *earthquake*! And we didn't feel a thing! The epicenter was in a neighboring town but the coffee place we had been in didn't shake — it was as immobile as the botoxed forehead of (insert

Hollywood actress' name). Yet *everybody* at the bed and breakfast (where we would have been had we not moved our dinner reservation) couldn't stop talking about how the whole house shook! *Then* I checked my Facebook page and saw that my friend Elizabeth Higgins put up a status about her whole house shifting during the earthquake. She doesn't live in a neighboring town. She lives in Boston! That's right. She felt it hundreds of miles away and we were *two blocks* to the left and felt, a la Elaine Stritch, *Zip*!

When we got back, we saw *Closer Than Ever* at the York Theatre (for the second time) and it was fabulous. Every lyric by Richard Maltby, Jr. tells a complete story, and the David Shire music is so gorgeous. My two friends Anika Larsen and Marya Grandy (who have both done the R Family Cruise many times) are the new ladies in the show and they sounded great.

On Saturday, we scooted to the East Side and saw Betty Buckley's new show at Feinstein's. It's called *The Other Woman: The Vixens of Broadway*, and I was so excited when each song began! So many of my faves... "When You're Good To Mama," "I Cain't Say No," "Unusual Way" — and I especially loved "The Miller's Son."

And finally, for those who are wondering, it really does feel different to be married. There's a delicious feeling of permanence and I love knowing that we chose each other and committed officially. FYI, while we were in Maine, there were political signs everywhere because Maine is about to vote on allowing marriage equality. I'm happy to say that there were a lot of signs that read "Yes on 1!" Hopefully, there are enough people that live there to make a difference — that they're not just the people planning on returning April 4th. *And now it's legal across America!!!*

Peace out and call me Sadie!

Hurrying Home for the Hurricane; Marin Mazzie Talks!
October 30, 2012

What a nachtmare! Let's start pre-Sandy: Last Thursday I flew to Pittsburgh's City Theatre to do *Seth's Big Fat '70s Show* (aka *Deconstructing '70s Variety Shows*). As I just mentioned, I'm obsessed with natural disasters, and I was getting more and more excited that Hurricane Sandy could come to New York. My first performance went fantastic and I wound up getting a delicious review. However, soon things began to get stressful. The storm was going to cover much of the East Coast and, not only could it be really dangerous for everybody, I began to get nervous that my flight after my Sunday matinee was going to be cancelled and I wouldn't be with my family.

James thought that LaGuardia Airport was more likely to have cancellations (because it's so near the water), so he suggested I get *another* reservation, but for a flight to Newark...just in case. I used my miles to get a flight that was scheduled to leave right after my matinee so I felt I was covered. Two different flights, two different airports. Cut to: right after my Saturday matinee I got an email telling me my flight to Newark was cancelled and re-scheduled to Monday! What? I knew the hurricane would be in NYC by Monday and there was no way the flight would leave. Then I got *another* email telling me my re-scheduled Monday morning flight was cancelled and moved to Monday afternoon. I knew that my other flight to LaGuardia was probably going to be cancelled as well (it was), so I consulted with the theatre and they kindly let me cancel my Sunday matinee so I could fly back that morning. I got a 6 AM (!) flight and arrived back at my apartment by 9 AM.

That afternoon, however, things got much worse. I saw the signs. I knew she would probably arrive by Sunday afternoon, and I was right. I didn't know if my apartment could take the brunt of her, but I knew I had no choice. As I predicted, by late afternoon I was enduring the full impact of...*my mother*! That's right, Hurricane *Sally* made landfall at 5 PM Sunday. She arrived with her two shi tzus, with whom she has a very special relationship. For one thing, she insists they won't eat unless she literally hand-feeds them. That makes sense because, as we all know, dogs do not eat when they're hungry, they only eat when coerced by an 80-year-old woman speaking baby talk.

All right, let's go back to before the storm and reflect on last week. I had the fabulous Marin Mazzie on as my radio guest "Dueling Diva" because Christine Pedi, my regular co-host was out of town. Marin played the mom in the recent revival of *Carrie* and we were discussing the moment that she had to stab Carrie (played by Molly Ranson). She told me that she was always scared she would actually stab her. I didn't understand why, since those fake knives retract on contact. Turns out, Marin told me that those fake knives don't always retract; they stab people! *Marin* had the nerve to say she was scared? What about Molly? Which would you rather have: The emotional wound that comes from stabbing someone by accident, or the wound that comes from a knife embedded in you?

   We talked about her childhood and I mentioned that I loved the story she told in her act at 54 Below, about the time she sang "Evergreen" at her Catholic School's "Blessing of the Rings" ceremony and Sister Alice Patrice made her change the "inappropriate" lyrics. I knew that her school in Rockford, IL, had a lot of Broadway folks come through it (Paul Castree, Jodi Benson, Joe Mantello), but she added to that list by telling me that the pianist for "Evergreen" was Robert Greenblatt — the current head of NBC! *And Broadway producer of lots of shows like Dear Evan Hansen and Mean Girls!*

Marin and I were talking on the air and I brought up her husband, Jason Danieley, who's currently starring in *Sunday in the Park With George* at Chicago Shakespeare Theater. I told her that, now that I'm married, it's weird for me and James — we've always celebrated our anniversary as the anniversary of our first date, but now we probably have to switch it to our wedding anniversary. Marin told me that we can celebrate both; she and Jason commemorate both their wedding anniversary as well as the date they "got together." I thought she was referring to their first date until I asked how she celebrated the day they "got together." She smirked and muttered, "Well…," and I immediately cut to a song.

I then brought up *Passion* (which is to be revived Off-Broadway this spring with Melissa Errico and Judy Kuhn), and I made her tell my listening audience one of my fave stories: At the beginning of Act One, the curtain would come up and Marin would be sitting, *nude*, on Jere Shea's back. Well, Jere's back was aching before one performance so he put something on it to ease the pain. Unfortunately, he didn't wipe it all off before the show began. So, at "places," Marin got on his back, the curtain went up, and soon she began to feel something in her nether regions. What did she feel you ask? How about the burning sensation of *Ben Gay*! Imagine what Ben Gay feels like on your skin and now imagine what it would feel like on (fill-in-the-blank). Marin finished the opening number and ran backstage and asked her dresser for cold, cold water. She said she was literally running around singing the *Sweeney Todd* song "City on Fire." Of course, she changed "city" to a word that starts with a P and ends with a Y. Then she sang it on the air. I thought it was hilarious 'til I got a tweet from someone telling me her four-year-old is now running around singing that song. With the new lyric. Hm…maybe she thinks it's about a cat on fire?

I taped a special Halloween version of *Seth Speaks* called "Seth Shrieks," and it was super-fun. My first guest was Rosie Perez, who was promoting *The 24 Hour Plays,* and I asked her about her childhood Halloween memories. Turns out, she never went trick-or-treating because she grew up Catholic and it was considered pagan/evil. She told me that every time she ate a piece of someone's Halloween candy, she would cross herself. I loved hearing that, and thought, "*Finally*! A fun holiday Jews enjoy that Catholics are jealous of!" And don't tell me that Jews have plenty of fun holidays. Name me one Catholic School girl pining to celebrate *Simchas Torah*.

I also had Jim Faro on the show. He is one of the creators of "Blood Manor," one of those scary houses that's filled with actors who jump out and terrify you. I went to one of those when I was a teenager and I screamed like a crazy person the whole time. He said that often there'll be a macho guy forcing his girlfriend to come with him into the house. She'll be begging to not have to do it, but the guy will laugh and insist. Then Jim will watch them both on the video monitor and within minutes he'll see the guy hiding in back of the girl. I'm dying to see the video feed and deconstruct it! He also told me that he has a deal telling customers that if they lose control of their bladder, they get a free t-shirt. Seriously. And every day he gives out at least three free "I P*ssed Myself at Blood Manor" shirts. Wonderful?

During "Sandy," James and I watched many episodes of "Homeland" because we had only watched half of the first season. So, now we're finally about to start Season Two. It's so good!

Peace out and stay dry!

Pitching In After the Hurricane, Plus *Annie, Drood* and Lizz Winstead
November 5, 2012

I feel like I'm living in *A Tale of Two Cities*. It was the best of times, it was the worst of times. I live on the Upper West Side and was not affected *at all* by Hurricane Sandy. Yet, there are so many areas nearby that were devastated. It's so eerie to be in a city where a few miles means the difference between keeping the status quo or the complete loss of electricity and possessions. James, Juli and I are taking a cue from Jen Cody and Hunter Foster who have been going out to Staten Island and helping out every day. We're going to haul ourselves over there on Election Day since Juli's off from school and it will be a welcome distraction from the stress of the election. *And I thought THAT election was stressful!*

Just on a side note, please don't be impressed that I quoted *A Tale of Two Cities*. It's one of the three assigned reading books I actually read in high school. I love reading *so much*, and I read constantly, but all the books assigned in school were always snoozefests. However, I lo-o-o-o-oved *A Tale of Two Cities*. Such a great plot and amazing ending! All of the other assigned books I "read" by using the Cliff Notes. If you don't know, they were small booklets that give you a synopsis of the plot plus lots of info to talk about in class. As a matter of fact, Cliff Notes helped solidify my hate-filled relationship with my AP English teacher: When I went in for my private meeting with her to discuss my first term paper (on *The Three Sisters* by Chekhov), every plot point she brought up was met with a blank face by me (I had just bought the Cliff Notes but hadn't gotten around to reading them yet). On the way out of the meeting, my Cliff Notes literally fell out of my notebook and landed at her feet. Suffice it to say, from then on our relationship consisted of moments such as her wagging her finger at me and intoning, "They warned me not to put you in this class!" And me responding, casually, "Well, now you've learned your lesson." Hence my college major: Piano performance.

This week I did an Election Day special edition of *Seth Speaks* with Lizz Winstead who co-created "The Daily Show." First the name. I busted her on the extra Z and she told me it was because of her sorority in college. There were five Lizzes (!) so each one had to be different. Since there was already a Liz W she became Lizz with two Z's. (The sequel to Liza with a Z?)

Lizz started out as a stand-up but didn't get political 'til the early '90s. She actually remembers the exact moment when it happened. Lizz told me that she was on a blind date with a guy, and she immediately knew that he was a moron because when she suggested they see a movie at the Film Forum he asked, sounding devastated, "Isn't that in black and white?" Despite her misgivings, they saw the film but she passively/aggressively got back at him by eating popcorn and then, with her greasy fingers, touching the sleeve of his satin Yankees jacket. Because she felt guilty about that, she agreed to go with him to a bar after the film. When they walked in, the TV was tuned to the news. The Gulf War had just begun and she remembers that the screen was full of graphics, green lights and people standing on roofs reporting on the war. She felt the war wasn't being reported, it was being sold. Her date stared at the footage and said, "This is *awesome!*" She thought, "If he's watching and thinking that, how many other people are?" She then decided she wanted to focus on how the media gets news to us and it became part of her act.

She worked for a little while on Jon Stewart's talk show, and after it was cancelled, she was brought into Comedy Central to help think of a new one for him. The idea of a show about the news came up and she told them that it should be like an actual news show: theme music, graphics, fake correspondents, field reporters, etc. Comedy Central agreed and Lizz said they were able to hire people who had worked for years on actual TV news show so they knew exactly how to do it to make it look real — how to light it, what kind of music to play. It was so interesting for me to hear about the formation of the show because when I see a finished product that's great (like a brilliant Broadway musical), a part of me thinks that's the only way it could have been. I forget about the *years* of workshopping and non-stop changes during previews, etc.

I just saw *Annie* on Broadway and as I watched it I thought about the development of that particular musical. At first, the original concept was for Annie to be played by...Bernadette Peters! Yes, it would be an adult Annie. Also, the show could have been an adventure about the Little Orphan Annie we all know from the comics, but instead the writers wisely made it about how she *became* the Little Orphan Annie we all know from the comics. P.S. There's so much talent on that stage! Special shout-out to Anthony Warlow who took a role I never really like (I spent my childhood constantly picking up the needle whenever "Something Was Missing" began to play) and not only sounded great, but added some great laughs!

Of course, I always love Katie Finneran in anything, but my experience was clouded by the knowledge that someone in my generation is playing Miss Hannigan! I still think of myself as a Tessie...*possibly* a Duffy. I can't believe my peers (and I) have graduated to the adult roles I knew as a child. And, speaking of children, Lilla Crawford (who plays Annie) is great. Great actress, smoky Andrea McArdle-esque speaking voice and delish vibrato. She was "swung out" of the show last week (they put her understudy on to give Lilla a rest) and wound up coming to the taping of *Seth Speaks* because she and her mom are fans! She's adorable.

On Saturday we saw a great production of the operetta *The Medium* starring Jeffrey Roberson (a.k.a. Varla Jean Merman). He plays the title role (which was written for a woman) and sings the whole thing in the correct keys! Except for one song, which was taken down a step. The introduction for the song is two notes descending...and they added one more note to take the key down. Jeff said that at one performance the first two notes played, then the third one played, which indicated the song was being lowered. As soon as the third note played, he heard a *loud* guffaw from the audience. Devastating. Then he had to sing. *The Medium* is running in rep with Well-Strung, the singing string quartet. They play classical music *and* pop music *and* sing harmonies.

On the home front, I've been getting so many nice congratulations from people for my marriage. Will Swenson sent me this text: *Wanted to send you and James a huge congrats. So f-ing great. Old, married theater nerds rock!*
I responded: *Very sweet! What the f is with the "old"?*
He wrote back: *Apologies. I turn 40 this week so I'm slight age-paranoid at the moment.* Then, he added, *Also...we're old.*

Hilarious!

Only Make Believe! Disneyland! *The Book of Mormon* in L.A.!
November 14, 2012

OK, here we go. First of all, my devastating travel stories usually involve me almost missing my plane and it's often because I'm late or I've gone to the wrong airport or some other "I Love Lucy"-type plot. This time, I got a cab with plenty of time to spare. Delish! However, halfway to JFK, my driver suddenly pulled over to the side of the road. He got out and told me that he suspected the engine needed anti-freeze. I then saw why he was slightly concerned; there was smoke pouring out from underneath the hood! I don't know much about cars, but I assumed that more smoke than Act Two of *Wicked* wasn't a sign of a healthy engine. After he poured in anti-freeze he told me he wanted to stop at a gas station and buy some more. Why? Because there was *still* smoke pouring out.

He stopped at a station, poured more in and I assumed everything was fine...until a car pull up alongside us and I saw the driver pointing frantically at the cab with a horrified expression. I don't understand sign language but I do understand the universal sign for "There is something *crazy* going on with your cab!" I told the driver and he said that the anti-freeze was probably dripping out of the car. He put on the hazards...and then promptly got on the Van Wyck Expressway! It was "fun" to be on a fast highway and not know what it means to have no anti-freeze... were we suddenly going to stop in the middle of a lane? Were we about to blow up? I tried to think back to the Drivers Ed course that I took senior year but not only did it take place in 1984, it was also at 7 AM in the morning. I was constantly half-asleep. The only thing I retained back then was water from my high sodium diet. Maybe it was nothing? While I was worrying whether I should be worrying, my cab pulled over and hailed *another* cab to finish my ride to JFK. I paid the first cab driver and he gave some cash to the second driver. I arrived at the airport on time but frazzled from my near-fatal or not-at-all-a big-deal experience. I went into a guilty panic because I didn't know if I needed to pay the new cab driver even though he got paid by the first one. I got out of the cab, thanked him and he drove off without complaining. Delicious! The deliciousness faded away quickly when I then realized, because of my frazzled-ness over whether I owed money, I got distracted and left my backpack in his cab. Which contained my CD *and* the DVD for the show I was flying to California to do. It also, sadly, contained my laptop. And because I didn't pay the second cab driver, I had no (zero) receipt. Yay! I got out of paying extra cash for the second cab and because of that lost a $1,500 computer. What a fair trade-off!

Young Iain Armitage!

Last week began much better with the annual Only Make Believe benefit on Broadway. Only Make Believe brings theatre to hospitalized kids. The benefit performances played the Bernard B. Jacobs Theater, an exciting location because the Tony Award-winning *Once* is playing there. However, the set of *Once* is not ideal for a benefit. Who wants to do a splashy joyous benefit in a dark, hasn't-been-cleaned-for-years Irish pub? It all wound up being fine, however, and the show had some fantastic acts. I sat in the audience before I went on with Ashley Brown and Kerry Butler. Right before it started, an *adorable* four-year-old boy came up to me and said, "Excuse me, sir... I love listening to your radio show!" I said, "Thank you so much!" and asked, "Are you an actor?" He looked serious and responded, "I'm not an actor *or* an actress." Obsessed! I then saw my friend Lee Armitage (whom I met on the R Family Cruises) and she told me that Ian is her (and Euan Morton's) son. And, P.S., Ian *is* an actor. I had recently seen a video of him in a cabaret singing a song that most four-year-olds know by heart: "Stars" from *Les Miz*. *And boy, is he now an actor! He starred as one of the little who is accused of being a bully in "Big Little Lies" and is now playing Sheldon on the new "Big Bang Theory" spin off!*

Matthew Broderick opened the show, and before he went on I asked him how he fared during Hurricane Sandy. He told me that his house lost power and I asked how Sarah Jessica Parker's "beautiful, beautiful hair" was. Matthew said that they got a hotel on the Upper East Side, so her hair held out. We talked about the lack of audiences right after the hurricane and he told me there were about 200 people in the house when *Nice Work If You Can Get It* started up again. Matthew looked through the curtain and begged the ushers to tell everybody to move down but they all "dutifully stayed in their assigned seats" and the entire front of the theatre was empty! (I once did *The Fantasticks* at the Sullivan Street Playhouse and we had more people in the cast than in the audience! And we didn't have a hurricane to blame it on.)

Julia Murney (who went with Hunter and Jen on one of their many Staten Island Superstorm Sandy clean-ups) came on *Seth Speaks* and told me that it's especially hard for Off-Broadway post-hurricane. Right now Julia is starring in *Falling* at the Minetta Lane Theatre and she got amazing reviews but it's not selling as well as it should because people aren't coming to NYC.

After my depressing JFK laptop loss, I flew to L.A. to do my show and spent the weekend with my friend Jack Plotnick. My show was sponsored by a group called Broadway Knights and they hooked me and Jack up with a day at Disneyland! I get nauseous/scared from basically all rides so I only deigned to go on two: It's a Small World and The Little Mermaid. I am essentially a four-year-old girl. On Sunday, Broadway Knights got us two second-row seats to *The Book of Mormon* and it was great! I know so many people in the cast and was super excited to see Gavin Creel! He was fabulous as Elder Price and so was Jared Gertner who plays Elder Cunningham.

However, I was most impressed with Jared's Broadway Cares/Equity Fights AIDS speech at the end. He was so funny: "I'm told that these *Book of Mormon* tote bags can be used as a stocking stuffer but I'm Jewish so I don't know what that means." And so sassy: "This is a fundraising competition. All the touring shows are trying to raise the most money, and if those bitches from *Wicked* win over us...it will not be cool. I'm just kidding. I know those ladies from *Wicked* and only one is a bitch." Pause. "The other is a slut." Yes, it's borscht belt but it's funny!

This weekend I'm heading to Las Vegas for the ALAN conference. "ALAN" stands for Assembly on Literature for Adolescents, and I was invited because one of the ALAN bigwigs liked my young adult book "My Awesome/Awful Popularity Plan"! The conference has educators from all over the country and I'm excited to enjoy the Vegas heat while talking about my book and then possibly seeing a strip show/doing a slow striptease. Or both?

Peter Gallagher Makes Music; Lonny Price Talks *Company*
November 19, 2012

Hello. Yes, I am writing this on a computer. Sadly, it is a new computer. That's right, I still have not found my backpack (containing my laptop) that I left in a cab last week at JFK so I went out and bought a new computer. The "fun" part is that the computer I left in the cab is only a year old *and* just two months ago I spent $250 replacing the broken screen. To add to the "fun," my backpack also had my checkbook. Yay! However, I still have a small shred of hope that I'll get everything back because the computer has iCloud which tells you if it's gone online and so far it's been offline so I think it's sitting in some random lost and found. The question is, "Where?" The answer is I may never know. The subtext is constant anxiety. *P.S. I never found it. ARGH!*

What else? Oh, right! I had Peter Gallagher as a guest on my SiriusXM show. I've known Peter ever since I left him a note at the stage door of *Noises Off* asking him to do my Chatterbox 11 years ago. He had never met me, but he called me, said yes and I found out what a nice guy he is! A year later, I asked him to be Nicky Arnstein in my Actors Fund *Funny Girl* concert, and he was truly fantastic. Not only is he such a great actor and singer (and *so* good looking), but because my concept for the concert was having a different Fanny Brice for each scene/song, he had to rehearse and perform opposite a multitude of women. He was so gracious and supportive with every single one. All of those ladies felt the pressure of having just one scene/song to bring down the house, and he was their rock. The weirdest part for him was Julia Murney, with whom he did the scene that led into "People." In the show, it's Fanny Brice's first kiss and they both acted the moment so beautifully. But Peter Flynn (the director) and I had made sure we cast the show with the Fannys getting progressively older. Since "People" is fairly early in the show, we use Julia who's much younger than Peter. And Peter remembered that back in the 1970s he used to hang out with her father when Julia was just a little kid! And now he was smooching with her on Broadway. Not since Frederick Egerman (see plot of *A Little Night Music*).

I told Peter that when he was cast in Jerry Zaks' *Guys and Dolls* I had only known him from "sex, lies and videotapes," and judged him as a Hollywood actor trying to infiltrate Broadway. I didn't know he was a Broadway baby back in the 1970s. He told me that his first open call was for the revival of *Hair*, and he wound up being cast as the understudy for Claude as well as the soloist in "Electric Blues" (he sang "An old fashioned me-e-e-elody...."). Well, when he was in previews for *Hair* he was also in callbacks for *Grease*. He didn't have an agent at that point and no one had told him you probably shouldn't be auditioning for other shows when the current show you're in hasn't even opened yet. He wound up being cast as Danny Zuko in the bus and truck tour. He went up to the director and creators of *Hair* and told them that he had this great opportunity to play the lead in the tour of *Grease* and asked if they would mind if he quit. He added that not only had he never seen the country before, he had never even been on an airplane. They thought about it and, two days later, released him from his contract. But before he left, the director asked him if he wanted to go on as Claude! I thought that was such an amazing offer to get, but Peter told him that he had never had a rehearsal and he would be way too terrified to do it. Peter was replaced and went on to do the *Grease* tour *and* the Broadway company!

Speaking of replacements, I remember that Donna Murphy once told me that when she was at NYU, she auditioned to be a replacement in the *Hair* revival and her audition went *really* well. She pretty much knew she was cast, and just had to wait for the official phone call. Well, she went back to her dorm and obsessively kept asking the dorm monitor if she had gotten any phone calls. No. This went on for days. She was devastated! She was so certain she was cast and then had no contact from them. It was like an amazing first date followed by complete silence (AKA me in my 20s). Finally, Donna found out the reason why her phone was silent; right after her audition, the show had closed.

I told Peter how great he was in the film "American Beauty," and also how much older he looked! Turns out, he felt his real estate king character should have grey in his hair, but his hair is so black that when you strip it to dye it, it turns yellow. So, they decided to wig him. He was nervous they wouldn't find a wig for him because he said he has a really big head. Well, they tried one wig on him and it was *way* too big for his head! He asked why there was a wig for someone who obviously had a non-human sized head. The wig designer sheepishly told him that it had been a wig for Charlton Heston. That still didn't make sense until she explained further: Turns out, Charlton Heston wore a toupee but didn't want people to know. Therefore, all of his wigs had to be big enough to fit over his head *and* the wig he was wearing. I guess whenever Charlton was in a film, his toupée became a *two*-pée! Yeah! Now we're having *pun*!

Peter did musicals in college, too, and his college was the first to get the rights to *Follies* right after it closed! They invited Stephen Sondheim to see it. Though he didn't come, he wrote them back a great letter saying, "We lost $800,000 on our production. I hope yours does better!" When Peter got to meet Hal Prince a few years later, he told him the story. Peter decidedly did *not* get the big laugh he thought he'd get from Hal. Instead he got a glare while Hal walked away muttering, "We did *not* lose $800,000!" Yowza. Don't make "investors-lose-massive-amounts-of-money" jokes with a producer.

I also interviewed Lonny Price who was promoting the DVD of the *Company* concert, which was just released. This is the all-star version (with the New York Philharmonic) that he directed, with Neil Patrick Harris as Bobby. Lonny also said he would *never* do something like that again! I thought he meant a one-night concert, but he more specifically meant a one-night concert where everyone had tons of other commitments. Everyone had to be rehearsed completely separately. It was essentially a rehearsal period for people with intimacy issues (just like Bobby!) P.S. Just last week was the 32nd anniversary (!) of *Merrily We Roll Along* opening on Broadway. Sadly, a few days later was the anniversary of the closing. How crazy that a show with such a brilliant score would close after just a few performances. Can't people just ignore whatever didn't work and revel in what did? I did a deconstruction of "Opening Doors," and I sent it to Lonny. He gave me some inside scoop on one of the things I pointed out: For some reason, in one section, Lonny says, "Yeah!" two octaves above his speaking voice. I thought it was simply an odd, random choice with no subtext. He informed me that, in actuality, it was his private homage to...Angela Lansbury! He loved her in *Sweeney Todd* and, in his mind, that was his way of paying tribute to her. He told me that he tried to make the "yeah" sound like the way she would do it (a la "Worst Pies in London") and he kept waiting for it to get cut. It stayed and became immortalized on the record! *P.S. You must see the documentary he did on MERRILY. It's called "The Best Worst Thing That Ever Could Have Happened" and you will flip out from the found footage of auditions and the Broadway show!*

OK. I'm on a flight to New York from Las Vegas, where I was just part of a fancy *and* shmancy conference about young adult books! It was very cool to walk around with my nametag that also said "Random House." I kept the whole "Almost kicked out of AP English in high school" thing under wraps. Happy Thanksgiving!

My So-Called Stand-Up Career
November 26, 2012

One more week until the Broadway Cares/Equity Fights AIDS *Gypsy of the Year* performances at the New Amsterdam Theatre! I'm hosting for the fifth year in a row (!) and I'm very excited. The excitement is tempered with nervousness that all of my comedy bits will get crickets.

Speaking of comedy, I thought I would share the story of how I got into stand-up as an inspirational tale to struggling actors. Back in the '90s I was subbing in the orchestra for a lot of Broadway shows (*Grease*, *Les Miz*, *Phantom*, *How to Succeed...* etc...) and also doing sketch comedy with my friend, Jack Plotnick. Jack wound up moving to L.A. because he got a pilot with Bob Odenkirk (who later went on to co-create "Mr. Show") and Janeane Garofalo. Suddenly, I didn't have a comedy partner. While Jack was in L.A. he did some stand-up and he kept telling me I should try it. I saw a listing in Backstage about an event called "The Stars of Tomorrow," and I decided to give it a try. It was at 11 PM at the Duplex on Christopher Street, which was perfect because I had started playing *Grease* full time at that point and it ended at 10:30. I asked my friend Kali Rocha to come with me for moral support and when I got there, I got the spiel from Amanda David, who ran it: Each comic was given three minutes to perform. At two minutes, a red light would shine near the back of the house indicating there was one minute left.

It's a fake waterbug...but just as scary.

She had a list of names and I was scheduled to go on around halfway through. Kali and I watched a string of comics, some funny and some quite the opposite, and I was finally called to the stage. I decided that my act was not going to be joke-oriented, but I would base it on how I made my friends laugh, AKA I was going to tell a story. I hauled out one of my classics that happened to me when I was 22 years old and living in Brooklyn. It was 2 AM in the morning and I decided to take a shower because I didn't have air conditioning. As I was toweling off, I heard loud clicking and clacking right next to me. I thought someone was typing in my bathroom or doing a solo version of the opening number from *42nd Street*. Turns out, it was neither; the clicking/clacking was coming from a giant *water bug* walking across the bathroom tiles! It was so large that I literally heard its footsteps! I quickly put on my underwear (in case it was one of those waterbugs that could fly) and I started chasing it through my apartment. I picked up one of my sneakers so I could smash it but it had the nerve to sneak underneath my front door and into the hallway of the building. I followed it outside my apartment, feeling triumphant that I was about to corner it, but soon my triumph turned into devastation. Why? Because I heard my apartment door close behind me. And I had one of the doorknobs that automatically locks from the outside. Yes, I was locked outside of my apartment. In Brooklyn. At 2 AM. Wearing only underwear and *a* sneaker. And, if I recall correctly, a gold necklace because it was 1989.

Anyhoo, there's more to the story, but suffice it to say I got laughs and at the end of it, Amanda told me that I made the semi-finals! I didn't even know that "Stars of Tomorrow" was a contest, so I was extra excited. Well, I came back for the semi-finals and this time I was extremely nervous. I knew what it felt like to do well and I desperately wanted to recreate my first time. And I made the bold choice of not practicing because I thought that would ruin my spontaneity. Suffice it to say, the only thing that was ruined was the audience's expectation of seeing someone funny. I clanked. And I mean, *clanked*. Nary a laugh in the house. Mortifying. Amanda read the list of the finalists and my name was decidedly *not* said. I went home (and herein lies the first lesson) and I thought, "You know, I definitely didn't do well tonight. But I saw the comics who did do well and I know that they're not funnier than I am in real life. I just have to figure out how to be funny in performance."

I knew I had to keep practicing to perfect my act. But the only place I could go to do my newly formed act was The Duplex, and I was way too mortified to have to face Amanda again — as well as all those comics who saw me bomb. However, I didn't know where else to go, so I *forced* myself to show up the following week. As soon as I walked in, I ran into to another comic who saw me bomb. I thought to myself, "It's all in my head. I'm sure he didn't even notice how horrible I was." Instead he looked at me and said, "I thought you quit the business." Anyhoo, I was apparently now known as a terrible comic, so Amanda put me on *way* late in the show, probably hoping that most of the audience would be gone by the time I soured the room. Since it began at 11 PM, I wound up going on after 12:30 AM. This happened week after week, but I began to get better. Each week helped me understand how to make my set work. Suddenly, after a few months, Amanda came up to me after a set and asked me back to the semi-finals! Another chance! At the end of the semis, Amanda read the list of the finalists and this time, I was on it! I came back to do the finals and at the end, there was a 3rd prize winner, a 2nd prize winner...and I wound up winning the Grand Prize!

What is the point of that story? Besides bragging? It's that if you fail, you have to try again! I could have completely given up, but I knew that if I kept practicing, I would get better. Another message is, don't take in the comments from the negative mother-effers around you. I could have listened to the other comics — whose message was a clear and concise "You are not funny" — but I ignored them because I knew I was. Another message is: Don't be afraid to fail. I compare it to babies; when a baby is crawling and decides it wants to walk, it doesn't think, "Hmm... I want to walk, but when I fall down it's going to be so embarrassing. I totally don't want people to see that. I think I'll keep crawling." No. A baby doesn't care how stupid it looks because it knows it will eventually walk! On a side note, just in case you're wondering, the Grand prize was my own show at the Duplex (which I never wound up doing...I wonder if the expiration date lasts past 16 years) and $50, which I spent on a pair of jeans from the Gap. And just in case you wonder if I think of myself as the so-called success story from the Duplex, let me say that one of my fellow comics who did the weekly 3-minute set (with the red light at 2 minutes) was a young and really funny Zach Galifianakis. His story ends with a bigger finish than mine. And a bigger bank account. And actual success.

Broadway-wise, I interviewed cast members from *Chaplin* at *Seth's Broadway Chatterbox* and it was super fun. Michael McCormick (who plays a variety of roles in the show including Mack Sennett) told me that he did the tour *and* Broadway companies of *Oliver!* when he was a kid. I asked for a stage mishap and he gave an amazing domino-effect story. In the show, Bill Sikes (the villain) climbs up a ladder and gets shot. When he's shot, he's so high up that the audience can't see him and a fake body falls to the ground. Michael said that during one show, Bill got to the top of the ladder and the shot rang out as usual. But the actor playing Bill had been drinking between shows and he wound up being so unsteady that before the fake body fell, the actor himself let go of the ladder and plunged to the ground! Thankfully, he wasn't hurt but right after that, Bill's dog is supposed to come out and look for him. Well, that night the dog came out all right, but decided to use his foray onstage as a substitute walk. That's right, he literally pooped in the middle of the stage! There wasn't enough time to clean it up or to warn the cast, so as the kids came on for the next scene they were all stepping in it. *And*, the dog had done it while standing on the part of the stage that was a turntable so when it started spinning, the dog's

237

"present" got into the grooves and the stagehands couldn't remove it for days. Please sir, I *don't* want some more.

And now, peace out and go work out that Thanksgiving bloat!

Backstage With Patti LuPone at *The Anarchist*; Bill Berloni Talks to the Animals
December 3, 2012

Hello from United 3533 from Chicago to New York. I saw that my ticket had me in seat 3F. Yay! First class! I then found out the plane is so small that only the first two rows are first class and Row 3 is actually coach. Hmph. That's like when my mom got tickets for me and my sisters to *The Fantasticks* when I was in 6th grade and I was prepared for horrible balcony seats like we always got. Well, I was pleasantly surprised when she told me she got us 3rd Row Center! Yay! Now imagine the look on my face when I arrived and found out the theatre only had three rows. It's not called "third row center" it's called "back row center."

James and I saw David Mamet's *The Anarchist* last week, and on the way out someone called my name. Turns out, it was Adam Guettel whom I haven't seen in years! I begged him to come back to Broadway with a show. He said he's working on a few new shows (!) *and* he's planning on doing a whole week at 54 Below! I've been an obsessed fan of his ever since I played auditions for *Floyd Collins* many years ago and then became the assistant music director for the reading of *Myths and Hymns* (but had to leave in the middle when I started writing for "The Rosie O'Donnell Show"). I told him I had just been watching the terrifying *Light in the Piazza* Tony Awards performance, and loving it/sweating. If you don't know, they decided to give Vicki Clark a monologue before the song that introduced her character and told what the show was about. She was nervous about remembering the lines but knew if she concentrated, she could do it. Then, 30 seconds before she went on, her body mic stopped working! They quickly handed her an enormous handheld mic and suddenly she was on! She was in front of tons of viewers, trying to remember her lines, holding the mic as well as holding all of her props (a bag and a pair of gloves). All the while, a camera was in front of her and a soundman was next to the camera talking to her! As she was doing her speech he was saying, "Your mic is almost on...keep using the handheld...now get ready to hand it to me...and it's working! Hand me the mic!" *Right* at the moment she started to sing. I love to watch it for fun and to give myself an anxiety attack.

On *Seth Speaks* I interviewed Jackie Hoffman who's starring again in her Jewish version of *A Christmas Carol* called *A Chanukkah Charol*. Yes, "Charol" has the Jewish phlegmy pronunciation. This is the second year she's done it at New World Stages and I noticed she brought cards to my radio show to promote the show. When I asked her to hand them out, she refused. Why? "Because," she glared, "last year I put them on the chairs, your audience sat on them and then left them." Hmm... she takes the Jewish expression "Never Forget" to new levels. Speaking of Jewish, we were comparing neurotic Jewish upbringings and she told me that whenever the phone rings, her family picks up and immediately asks *"Who died????"*

I also had Bill Berloni as a guest on *Seth Speaks*. What a story! Bill started out as an apprentice at Goodspeed Opera House back in the '70s. During his second summer, *Annie* was scheduled to open and the theatre realized they needed a dog but couldn't afford a dog trainer. The head of Goodspeed called Bill into his office and asked him if he wanted his Equity card. Bill told me that he was so proud his acting talent was finally recognized...even though he couldn't quite figure out how anyone saw it since he spent all of his time lifting and building things. Turns out, the head of the theatre said he could get his Equity card not from acting, *but* if he could train a dog to play Sandy. Bill grew up on a farm with dogs, so he said yes. He went to a shelter and saw a very sweet but very abused dog. The people who ran the shelter told him that if he wanted that dog, he had to take him right away because the next morning he was being "put to sleep." Bill didn't know what that meant. He was then told it meant that the dog's time had run out at the shelter and they were going to end its life. Bill never realized that animals had limited time at shelters and were killed every day. He told them that he wanted the dog and they told him the cost was $7. He only had $3 and they told him to forget it. He went home despondent but couldn't ask for help from Martin Charnin (the director) or the head of Goodspeed because they were out of town. Finally, his roommate gave him $4 and told him to get there as early in the morning as possible. Bill got there right when it opened and, thankfully, got the dog. Of course, now the problem was the training. He had never done it before *and* the dog was not particularly outgoing because it had been abused. Bill decided that if he played with the dog around the theatre, the dog would consider the theatre its home and not be nervous on stage. The dog got more and more outgoing and then Bill was told to rehearse with the girl playing Annie (Kristen Vigard). He didn't know how to rehearse them so he just told her to play with the dog. Soon, the dog (Sandy!) became attached to her so when Bill would stand in the wings and let him go, he would run right to Kristin! That was the only scene in the show with Sandy, and it always worked. Then, on a Sunday night, Martin Charnin told him that Kristin was going to be replaced with Andrea McArdle! Bill had two days to get Sandy to become attached to Andrea…and he did!

The show closed (with not very good reviews) and Bill went back to NYC (with Sandy) to pursue his acting career. A year later, he got a call from Mike Nichols (!) with the shocking news that *Annie* was coming to Broadway and asking if he could train the Sandy (and the understudy). Bill, who was still thinking of it as a sideline, said yes…but soon realized that it was his true career. And the amazing part is, he *always* uses animals that are rescued.

Which brings me to my gym. A woman there showed me a picture of the little dog she just got that cost her a ton of money. I told her that dogs are killed every single day and need to be rescued. She told me that she would love to rescue a dog but "a dog from a shelter can't be trained." Really? *Every* single animal Bill has used for the last 30 years has been a rescue! He trained all the little "Bruisers" for *Legally Blonde*, the cats at the beginning of the Rum Tum Tugger *Cats* video on MTV and a rat for *The Woman in White*. The British director told him that if he wasn't able to train it, "his career would be over." His career as a rat trainer? Who cares? Bill was able to do it, but not the way he trains dogs. Sandy always gets a little food reward onstage when he comes over. However, during *The Woman in White*, Michael Ball would have to use hand sanitizer to get rid of all food smells and then pull the rat out of his pocket. Why? Because if it smelled any food on the hand of the actor, it would bite. Instead, the rat would be pulled from his pocket, do it's little trick (run across his shoulders) and when it went backstage, it would then get food. This is why I can never work with a rat. There isn't a minute of the day when my hands aren't in, just coming from, or going towards food.

Bill was very complimentary of my SiriusXM radio show and said that he currently has more than 20 dogs at home, many of whom have done Broadway shows. When he leaves his house, he keeps his radio tuned to the Broadway station because he thinks they'll feel comfortable if they hear songs from shows they starred in! I love it!

And now begins an exciting week! Monday and Tuesday, I'll be hosting Gypsy of the Year competition performances, and then on Wednesday night I leave on the Playbill Broadway On the High Seas cruise for Buenos Aires. Peace out!

Gypsy of the Year, Maltby & Shire, and the Launch of Playbill's Broadway On the High Seas Cruise
December 10, 2012

Greetings from the high seas! I'm on the Playbill cruise along the eastern edge of South America and today is a "sea day." That means that we're traveling a long distance to the next port, so we don't stop 'til we get there. I haven't been able to get off the boat since we got on because I've been so busy. So, I was super-excited that yesterday I had some hours off to get on dry land and do some shopping. The boat docked in Rio Grande, Brazil. We got a list of destinations from the ship; there were three shopping areas mentioned, and my Mom and I decided to take a cab to the largest. Well, what we didn't know is that, because it's a Sunday, every single store is closed. So basically, we took a cab to see a commercial neighborhood...literally to *see* the neighborhood, and then took a cab back.

Today, however, is going to be fun because I have an onboard *Chatterbox* with Christine Ebersole, and then I'm doing a show where I deconstruct my favorite video clips! But before I write more about the cruise, let me give an update from pre-Brazil.

At the *Chatterbox* in Manhattan, I interviewed the composing team of Richard Maltby, Jr. and David Shire and found out they met at Yale. Even though they're not a couple, they met romantic comedy-style — meaning they both took an instant dislike to each other. David thought Richard was a big snob and Richard thought David was a hick. Of course, they then wound up loving each other and they've been great friends for the last 40 years. They started writing songs at Yale and when they graduated they heard about a young singer from Broadway who was taking the nightclub scene by storm. They had a meeting with her and pitched some songs.... and that's how Barbra Streisand came to record "Autumn"! They had written that song at Yale for their musical version of *Cyrano*.

I was surprised that Barbra took songs from such young songwriters because I remember John Kander telling me what he had to do to Barbra to record one of the songs that he and Fred Ebb wrote. John was working as a rehearsal pianist on *Funny Girl* and, trickster style, casually left handwritten sheet music on top of the piano. Barbra picked it up asked what it was and he told her that it was a song he wrote with Fred but it was *completely* not right for her. Of course, she then insisted on hearing it.... and that's how she came to record "My Coloring Book." David and Richard nodded and then told me a similar story. They had written a song for Robert Goulet that Barbra heard about. She asked to hear it and they told her that it wasn't right for her because it was written for a man. Of course, she then insisted upon doing it — and that's how she came to record "Starting Here, Starting Now." As she said as Fanny Brice, "Don't tell me don't!"

Speaking of Fanny, David mentioned that he was a pianist in the pit of *Funny Girl* and then took over as conductor. When I asked him how he got the gig, he told me that the conductor was also dating Lainie Kazan (Barbra's understudy) and playing for her act. When Lainie needed a few extra songs, he "lent" her some of Barbra's arrangements. Uh-oh. That's all David had to tell me. I immediately knew why there was suddenly a vacancy on the conductor's podium.

I mentioned the song "It Goes Like It Goes," which David Shire wrote as the theme to the film "Norma Rae." He said that it was nominated for an Oscar along with *another* song he had written that same year. He assumed that he wouldn't win for either because they'd probably cancel each other out, but he wound up winning for "It Goes Like It Goes"! Before the Oscar ceremony, Richard told him if he won for either of the songs, he wanted him to receive the award with the ultimate Jewish response: He said David should go onstage, walk to the microphone and ask, "So, what was wrong with the other one?"

David opted out.

I saw their recent York Theatre Company production of *Closer Than Ever* twice and I'm very excited to say that there'll be a new cast recording coming soon! I also told them how obsessed I am with *Baby*. If you've never heard that score, go buy the original cast recording ASAP! I'll wait.

Gypsy of the Year!

You're back! So, the week began with Gypsy of the Year, which I hosted for the fifth time. As usual, it was so much fun! And, also as usual, I made my signature wrong entrance. I did my opening which went great and then ran out after the first act to do my whole bit about the song "Tomorrow." I gave the set-up and turned back to the piano to play a little and was surprised to see that the piano wasn't there. I was confused for a moment 'til I heard the announcer's voice tell me (and the entire audience) I wasn't supposed to be onstage. I promptly ran offstage. I was mortified, but not as much as last year when I made my wrong entrance right before the Moment of Silence! That's right, in 2011 the most solemn moment of the show (which featured Judith Light making an incredibly moving speech) began with me bounding out, landing a few zingers, looking offstage and seeing Judith Light prepared to make her entrance and then slinking offstage. The good news is, the "Tomorrow" section (which I then did at the correct time) wound up being amazing!

I came out and described my childhood obsession with Dynamite magazine. If you're not familiar, it was sort of People magazine for 'tweens. I got a pen pal through Dynamite. Her name was Debbie. After she wrote me, I thought, "Why should I write her back a plain ol' letter when instead I can make her a 45-minute tape of myself playing the piano and singing." I started by recording the Haydn e minor sonata (I had just won a talent contest with that song) and then I counteracted my classical chops by funking out and playing and singing Stevie Wonder's "Don't You Worry 'Bout a Thing." I followed it with the hit love song of the day ("Nobody Does It Better") and then closed with my audition song from that year which was, 'natch, "Tomorrow." After I recorded everything I had a listen and decided that the tape was "too good to send." I held onto it. I then listened to it again 20 years later. Turns out, it wasn't so good. I told the audience I had the tape digitally transferred and brought to Gypsy of the Year. I informed them I was going to play eight measures from "Tomorrow" and within them there would be many lessons to be gleaned...on how not to sing a song.

Suffice it to say, one of the horrific things I added to the song to "make it my own" was a blue note. That's right, I fancied myself a young Ella Fitzgerald so I added a jazzy blue note to "Tomorrow"...the whitest song in the world. I played the recording for everyone and the audience was duly horrified and then, from stage right, Lilla Crawford (the current *Annie*) came onstage with her hands over her ears. Of course, the audience loved it. And when her hands were removed, I asked her to "cleanse the palate." Lilla sang the refrain and I then asked her to "jazz it up." Lilla sang it again but this time, she added my signature blue note. Hilarious/devastating. Then, Lilla turned to me and said, "Seth, let's kick it old school!" I asked her what she meant and she said, "I think you know what I mean!" She pointed stage right and out came Andrea McArdle! The audience again went crazy and Andrea started the song from the bridge (sounding amazing). When she got to the last refrain, she and Lilla sang it together and on the last note, Andrea reached around and guided Lilla's left arm up in the classic Annie slow-arm raise. It was so fantastic. Of course, afterwards I had tears in my eyes because I would have passed out as a kid if I knew that one day I'd be playing piano on Broadway for two different Annies...especially Andrea, whom I never got to see. You can see the Lilla/Andrea video on Youtube!

And now, the cruise. Well, the good news is, I didn't leave my laptop in the cab on the way to the airport. Instead, I got into the cab in front of my apartment and right before I pulled out, as I was saying goodbye to James and Juli on the street, I yelled, "I left my laptop on the kitchen table!" James ran back and got it. The only thing I forgot was my sweatshirt somewhere at JFK. I remember wearing it through security. I realized it was missing once I boarded the plane. At least I'm consistent(ly annoying). My mom and I had fancy/shmancy business-class tickets to Buenos Aires. It was a 10-hour plane ride to South America. We embarked on the cruise in Buenos Aires and it's been great. The first show was Sherie Rene Scott followed by Marin Mazzie and Jason Danieley doing a duo act. Then I led a trivia game with the passengers, who were super smart.

ME: When Liza Minnelli checked herself into the Betty Ford Clinic after a matinee of The Rink, who took over for —

PASSENGER: (Interrupting) Mary Testa!

I was incredibly impressed! First I thought he knew the answer because he had seen this Playbill "Obsessed!" video. But then he told us that he happened to see *The Rink* during the two weeks Mary was on for Liza (while Stockard Channing was preparing to take over the role...before the show closed two weeks later!).

Writing about *The Rink* reminds me of something that happened at *Gypsy of the Year* that also would have made me pass out as a child. Every year in school I would become obsessed with a show, and in 5th grade it was *Chicago*. I listened to it all the time, hoping one day I would meet Chita Rivera. Cut to: After Gypsy of the Year, Chita came up to me said, "You've really got it, don't you? Every f***ing word you say is funny!" AH! So amazing! And on that note, peace out!

Cruising With Lewis Black, Jason Danieley, Christine Ebersole, Marin Mazzie and Sherie Rene Scott
December 17, 2012

And now, farewell, Playbill Broadway on the High Seas cruise! I'm writing this on the balcony of cabin 890 and looking at the water off of Rio De Janeiro. All in all, the cruise was a big, fat success!

We were on the Regent Mariner and it consisted of 800 people taking a Brazilian-coast cruise and around 300 people taking the same cruise — but also part of the Playbill group, which meant special onboard events and performances throughout the 10-day experience. On the first night, Phil Birsh (the President and Publisher of Playbill) introduced me and all of the Broadway performers (Christine Ebersole, Marin Mazzie, Jason Danieley and Sherie Rene Scott) and I soon noticed that everyone standing next to me was blonde. As a matter of fact, Marin took the mic and told the room that when she was doing *Next to Normal* a man sent her a letter telling her that he was a major fan and had seen her in *everything*. He asked her if she would kindly sign the enclosed photo. Marin took out the picture... and it was a headshot of Sherie! I wasn't surprised because they really do look alike. I actually wound up calling Marin "Sherie" at one point, and briefly considered a revival of *Side Show*.

Speaking of Sherie, she was the first Playbill entertainer to perform and her show was a brava. She wrote it specifically for the cruise and it had her signature humor. She began by greeting the audience with: "Hi, I'm Sherie Rene Scott and I'm not ashamed to say I'm a proud, 39-year-old woman. I'm not ashamed to say it because it's not true." The whole show had lots of standards like "Old Black Magic" and "Since I Fell For You," but she ended with a four-song Brazilian medley including "How Insensitive" (one of my faves) and "I Go To Rio" ('natch). She started off by telling everyone that she's a fun-loving, single woman. She followed it with "I can't wait to tell my husband I'm single. I became single as soon as I set foot on the boat." She then explained that she brought along her mom (Esther) or as she called her, "Eagle-eyed Esther." Esther supposedly was there to keep Sherie out of trouble. Sherie claimed that as soon as she walked into the plane's luxurious business class she wanted to start partying "but Ol' Eagle Eye was glaring at me from coach."

Sherie was also my first guest in an onboard *Chatterbox* event. When I mentioned her Broadway debut in *Tommy*, she remembered that she had 11 auditions for the show! By the end, Pete Townshend told his driver he was considering a couple of girls to play Sally Simpson and the driver mentioned Sherie, shrugged, and said, "I'd do her." So, Sherie said her Broadway debut was not because a rock legend chose her, but because the rock legend's *driver* thought she was attractive.

Then I did a *Chatterbox* with Christine Ebersole. Or, as she is now always introduced, "two-time Tony Award winner Christine Ebersole." She said that once you win a Tony, it's always part of your intro...like "Dr." She recently finished filming "The Wolf of Wall Street," in which she plays Leonardo DiCaprio's mother. She got the script and told her agent, "I have no lines." He told her not to worry and, sure enough, every time she went to film a scene, Martin Scorsese (the director) would tell her to make something up like "Tell the bride you're happy for her wedding," etc. It was the same way "Tootsie" was filmed: Years ago, she auditioned for the film by meeting Dustin Hoffman at a hotel and hanging out with him. He then invited her to a screening of himself in drag. He wanted to see what he'd look like as a woman so he hired the make-up artist from "Little Big Man" (who eventually wound up *not* doing "Tootsie") and asked him to make him into a believable-looking lady. Well, on the day that Christine met Dustin he had just been nominated for an Oscar for "Kramer Vs. Kramer," and he was on his way to England to meet the Queen. As he and Christine were watching the filmed footage of him in drag, he began to moan and say, "Who am I kidding? I can't do this! Forget it!" and Christine felt compelled to encourage him. Or as she says, "There I was, a young girl from the Midwest sitting next to Dustin Hoffman… who had just been nominated for an Oscar *and* was on his way to meet the Queen… and I'm grabbing his hand and saying 'Stop it, Dustin! You've *got* to do this!'"

A year or so later, she was offered a scene in "Tootsie." Her agent told her it was too small to take but she told him it was her first film and she was taking it! For the scene, the director simply told Dustin and Christine what the plot moment was, and then they improvised the entire scene! P.S. Don't people write scripts in Hollywood anymore?

In Christine's solo show she started with "Welcome to the Theater," which I saw her sing when she played Margo Channing in *Applause* for Encores! at City Center. She then did standards like "Right as the Rain" and an amazing coloratura version of "Beyond the Blue Horizon." She did a thrilling version of "Around the World" that made the *Grey Gardens* fans in the audience go crazy. Before her encore, she played a recording of herself at three-years-old singing "Jingle Bells." Totally on pitch! She then made a joke by saying, "And that was recorded 75 years ago!" After her performance, an older woman walked up to her and said, "Wow. You look great for 78." That's right. *And*, I one point during the show, Christine mentioned that her mom is 95 years old. Everyone applauded and she added, "But the real miracle is that she gave birth to me at 60!" I told Christine that she had made two jokes about her age, but the age the woman chose to believe was 78. Christine shrugged and said, "Well, whichever one's more realistic."

Lewis Black was also onboard and did a great evening of comedy. One of my favorite lines happened when he was raging about all the television options we now have but how every show still sucks. He talked about a fishing show featuring bass, and said, with an amazing line reading, "If *you*…are watching a show about bass fishing…then *you*….have had a stroke." I thought it was hilarious!

Marin Mazzie and her husband Jason Danieley did an act together and sang up a storm. The theme was how they first met and how they've now been together for 14 years. It was especially moving to couples on the boat, and one woman came up to them afterwards and said, "After the show, I kept kissing my husband." Sweet! Speaking of husbands, Jason told us a hilarious Marin story that happened the day we got to Buenos Aires. They stayed in a hotel the night before they got on the ship and in the morning they passed a maid in the hallway. The maid walked by, nodded and said, "Buenos dias." Marin nodded back and replied, "Buenos Aires." Huh? I guess Marin had been saying the name of the city a lot and that's why it came out so easily but Jason's obsessed with responding to a greeting by naming the city you're in. He said it's like being at the Plaza and after someone says "Hi" and you say, "New York."

A few nights after Marin and Jason's show, we had a little get-together for all the Playbill passengers and I asked them to call out names of their fave Broadway stars and I'd tell stories I've learned about them from years of interviews. When someone yelled out "Idina Menzel!" I told them what she told me about being a Long Island girl surrounded by Long Island accents: it wasn't until she was an adult that she realized heavy traffic wasn't called "Bumpita Bumpa" traffic. She thought it was some sassy percussive name…and after many years realized it was actually "Bumper to bumper traffic."

Marin ended the week with the act she recently did at 54 Below and it was so fun. It featured great pop songs from the '60s and '70s like "That's the Way I've Always Heard it Should Be," "Weekend in New England" and "Evergreen." Then, she came out for the encore, which she admitted had nothing to do with the show. She said that she had had many requests for "Back to Before" so she would sing it *but* she had to take off her high heels. "This is not because my feet are ki-i-i-i-illing me right now. It is because I'm a method actress and in *Ragtime* I sang this song barefoot." (Hmm… she also played Mother while dressed in a full 1918 bustle but I didn't notice her haul that out!) Speaking of bustles, Lewis Black said that he's going to start marketing male spanx because his goal on the cruise was to eat 100,000 calories.

All right, I'm getting ready to catch my flight from Rio to NYC. Hopefully, after I land in JFK, the drive back to Manhattan won't be "bumpita-bumpa." Peace out!

Twas the Shopping Day Before Christmas
December 24, 2012

It's Christmas Eve, and I j-u-s-t bought the last present I needed to get. I pretty much started shopping two days ago. I'd love to blame it on the fact that I was away on the Playbill on the High Seas cruise, but the reality is that last year I had plenty of time in NYC yet I was still frantically shopping on Christmas Day itself. And, P.S., *nothing* was open. I literally had to go to one of those stores on 8th Avenue that only caters to tourists, and essentially all of my presents featured some aspect of "I Heart New York." Anyhoo, this year I was able to find everything I wanted to buy, and I'm on my way to my mother-in-law's house for severe acting out with food. Delish!

This week I had a little Playbill cruise reunion on my SiriusXM talk show.. Jason Danieley and Christine Ebersole came by, and we told stories about what it was like spending ten days in South America. Jason and I wound up leaving a day before Christine, and she told us what she did on her last day below the Equator. She and a group from the cruise spent the day in a *favela*, which is the extremely poor section of Rio de Janiero. It's also where Michael Jackson shot the "They Don't Care About Us" video. Christine said it was really wonderful. First there was a drumming circle, which she joined in, and then one of the men in the circle invited her into his house. She described it as incredibly tiny and yet his whole family lived there. She also noticed that, despite the poverty, everybody in the *favela* seemed extremely happy. Speaking of poverty, she was mortified when, after an hour passed, her husband Bill whispered, "I'm surprised no one's recognized you." What? She was about to glare and tell him that his comment made no sense when a young woman approached her. The woman pointed at Christine and asked, "Actress?" Christine slowly nodded and then the woman said, in perfect English, "I saw you this morning in 'Confessions of a Shopaholic'!" Brava Bill for being psychic!

Marin Mazzie couldn't be at the SiriusXM show because she had a gig in Texas, but I remembered a story Marin told on the ship that I love. Back in the '90's, she went on the national tour of *The World Goes 'Round with Kander and Ebb*. They were playing in a city where her understudy grew up so Marin (graciously) planned on letting her go on for a performance. Her understudy invited everyone she knew from her hometown, and Marin made plans for a delicious dinner. Cut to, an hour into her dinner, Marin got a phone call at the restaurant (this was before cell phones). The *other* actress in the show had sprained her ankle and couldn't continue with the show. That meant that Marin's understudy had to take over the other role and Marin had to come back and finish out the show. Unfortunately, Marin was enjoying her night off from the show, and her way of enjoying was drinking a glass of wine. Or more. Before you judge, there was no reason she shouldn't drink because she didn't have a show! Cut to, not only did she have to rush back to the theatre and go on while slightly (or more) tipsy, she had to start from the part of the show where she was on roller skates! *And*, she had to do a cartwheel! I'm obsessed with the announcement that was made when the show started up again. Because Marin was returning after her understudy was on for her, the announcement was "Ladies and Gentleman, the role usually played by Marin Mazzie will be played by... Marin Mazzie." What? The sweet and mystical part of the story is that after it ended she was approached by someone at the stage door. He was very sickly looking, but she soon recognized him as one of her old college friends. He had advanced AIDS and had planned on coming to the show just to see Marin. Naturally, he was very upset when she was out but then elated when she came back! He was so sick that, sadly, he died shortly afterwards, but it was as if he was meant to see Marin perform no matter what, and the universe conspired to make it happen.

Speaking of a mystical universe, I saw Jackie Hoffman's *A Chanukah Charol*, and it was great. It's a one-woman show where she plays a variety of roles; most notably the narrator (as Patrick Stewart) and the

Ghost of Christmas Present (as Shelley Winters a la *The Posiedon Adventure*). There were so many hilarious lines, but one of my favorites is when she talks about performing for Jewish groups or non-Jewish groups. Jackie said she always knows when she's not performing in a synagogue because she's able to go an entire show without someone yelling "*LOUDER*!!!!" I was also obsessed with her imitation of her mother serving a holiday meal: "There's veal, steak, chicken, brisket, white rice, yellow rice, potatoes, kugel, latkes and tsimis. I spent all day making *food*. Please take *food*. I hope there's enough *food*." Pause. "*Food*."

L'chaim!

Andrea Martin in *Pippin*
December 31, 2012

Here's my last diary entry of 2012!

Jack Plotnick, my great friend and co-writer of *Disaster!*, stayed with me last week after his first directing gig. He co-wrote *and* directed the film "Space Station '76" and it's chock-full of stars: Liv Tyler, Jerry O'Connell, Matt Bohmer and Patrick Wilson. Such a brava! I saw it and it's fantastic!

I'm writing this from the Hyatt Regency in Boston where my family and I have been on a mini-vacation. We came up here to see Andrea Martin in *Pippin*, which is playing at American Repertory Theater (the same place where *Once* and *Porgy and Bess* began). Diane Paulus (*Hair*) is the director, and the concept for the show is really cool. Normally, all the players (except Pippin) are part of a traveling troupe of performers. This time, they're a traveling troupe of circus acrobats. And they're brilliant acrobats. *Yet* they all sing, dance and act. Brava on being quadruple threats! And quadruple-jointed. Andrea plays the grandmother (originally played by Irene Ryan) who sings "No Time At All." When she was offered the part she told the director she would love to do it *if* she could also do something acrobatic. Well, Andrea was right to ask because the song has always been a crowd-pleaser but now it's a show-stopper. Andrea plays her scene with Pippin and, of course, gets tons of laughs. (Spoilers coming!) Then she starts the song in her old-lady granny outfit and asks the audience to sing along (just like it's usually done). Suddenly, she rips off her old-lady dress and she's standing in a sexy leotard and tights, showing off her crazily fit body. The next thing you know, she's high above the stage on a trapeze. A trapeze! And it's not just generic hanging and swinging. She does an incredible (and terrifying) long routine. So thrilling! As soon as the song ended, James leaned over and said "If this comes to Broadway, she's going to win her second Tony Award." Brava! *Wow! I forgot James said that and he was right! She won and so did the show.*

It was such a pleasure hearing the *Pippin* score, which I think is one of the best written for Broadway. And it's mind-boggling to know that Stephen Schwartz was in his early 20s when he wrote both the music and the lyrics. When you hear it you realize that he was a pioneer in a new Broadway sound that would be echoed by Jason Robert Brown, William Finn, Andrew Lippa, Tom Kitt and so many more who have roots in the singer-songwriter style.

Well, at least one person is famous...

After *Pippin* in Boston, we all went out to eat something and Andrea brought out her iPhone so we could all open an app she's obsessed with called Akinator, the Genie. It works by guessing a person you're thinking of — and it's *completely* mind-blowing. I thought of a person and the app asked me around 14 questions. Basic ones (like, "Is it a woman?" and "Is she alive?") to specific ones (like, "Is she on a Disney show" and "Was she married to someone famous?"). Suddenly, it asked if I was thinking of Carly Simon! The answer was *YES*! So freaky! We kept doing random people and having the best time and when we decided to ask about Andrea, she told us that she's not one of the celebrities the Akinator knows. We thought that was crazy but she assured us that she's tried numerous times, and so had her brother, Debra Monk, Victor Garber and others, and it never, ever guessed her. How could she be not famous enough? It was depressing to think that a computerized app was a starf*cker. Then Juli decided to have the Akinator guess a celebrity and she wouldn't tell us who it was. It asked her a round of questions and suddenly the Akinator asked her if it was *Seth Rudetsky*! We all literally screamed in the restaurant. So hilarious that I was on it and not Andrea!

Well, after I found out it was able to guess *me* I knew Andrea *must* be in there. I took the iPhone and answered all the Akinator questions but this time instead of telling it that Andrea is American, I said no. It kept mentioning different countries and finally when it got to Canadian, I said yes. Andrea is from Maine but SCTV fans all think she's Canadian. It asked if she's been on Broadway and in hit movies and suddenly it asked if I was thinking of Andrea Martin! Phew! She's still got it!

Speaking of that, she's in such incredible shape because of her eight-show-a-week acrobatics, but the two of us are always complaining about how fat we are. I wanted her to know that I dropped off a little gift for her before the show, so I texted "I left something for you at the stage door." She wrote back, "Please let it be a girdle."

Right now I'm in the pool area in the Hyatt and there are three 'tween girls in the water who are performing in *The Nutcracker* next door. How do I know they're dancers? Well, the fun game they're doing right now is extending their right leg completely up to their ear and then seeing if they can walk that way across the length of the pool. I love "games" that are actually excuses to show off amazing flexibility.

I had John Bolton from *A Christmas Story, The Musical* as a guest at my recent *Chatterbox* and we discovered that we shared a very similar childhood. First of all, we were both obsessed with Dynamite magazine. John and I also shared an obsession with *Annie* — and a devastation that boys weren't in the show. He went a little further than me, though. He read a book about Broadway shows and in the *Annie* section it said that every night, at 8:07, the overture began to play. Therefore, from that day on, he would go into his room, put the album on at exactly 8:07 (he lived in Rochester and was therefore in the same time zone as Broadway) and he'd go under the covers of his bed just like he was at "places," along with all the orphans on Broadway. He would then do the show along with the record. Brava on the commitment! (As well as the blurred line between reality and fantasy.)

John and I also share a worship of the stars from yesteryear. He was on a soap opera for a few episodes and he noticed than an extra looked familiar. He stared and stared and finally asked her if they knew each other. She shrugged and said that she was originally from Boston. Suddenly, he thought "Boston. Hmm...all those kids were from Boston..." He then freaked out when he realized it was Donna from "Zoom"! Anybody?

The very first Broadway show John and I did together was *How To Succeed...* where I was a rehearsal pianist/pit sub and he was the cover for Finch (Matthew Broderick) and Frump (Jeff Blumenkrantz). Of course, it's always a nightmare going on for a role when the audience is there to see a certain celeb. If an announcement is made before the show, there's always an audible audience reaction. Usually, one can avoid it by turning down the squawk box (intercom) in one's dressing room. But poor John had to make his first entrance for Matthew as a window washer high above the stage. In other words, he had to get to his perch before places which was when they announced, "The role of Finch usually played by Matthew Broderick will be played by John Bolton," and John would be all set to go on, only to be be affronted by devastated and angry groans. Since there was no squawk box to turn down he said he literally had to put his hands over his ears in advance to block it out.Happy New Year!

And thanks for reading this edition of my diary. Stay tuned for Volume Four!

Acknowledgements

Thank you to …

All the theater people who told me amazing stories at my Chatterbox, on SiriusXM or on the subway, at brunch or literally anywhere. Everything is material!

My Mom, Dad and sisters for bringing me to Broadway when I was a kid.

Tiffany Grant for the amazing transcriptions/editing of each column.

Dress Circle Publishing for giving me the chance to create these books and for being so nice!

Joey Monda for contacting Dress Circle Publishing in the first place.

My myriad of interns who all deal so well with my A.D.D.

And, of course, James and Juli and our two doggies, Mandy and Bagel, and our kitty cat Romeo!

Also From Dress Circle Publishing

By Seth Rudetsky
Seth's Broadway Diary, Volume 1
Seth's Broadway Diary, Volume 2
Seth's Broadway Diary, Volume 3

By Jennifer Ashley Tepper
Untold Stories of Broadway Volume 1
Untold Stories of Broadway Volume 2
Untold Stories of Broadway Volume 3

By Ruby Preston:
Showbiz
Staged
Starstruck

By Jeremy Scott Blaustein
The Home For Wayward Ladies

Founded in 2011 by Brisa Trinchero and Roberta Pereira, Dress Circle Publishing is committed to taking readers "behind the curtain" through our catalogue of books about Broadway written by members of the Broadway community.

Dress Circle Publishing
www.dresscirclepublishing.com

Made in the USA
Las Vegas, NV
20 December 2020